Complete
Indian
Cooking

Complete
Indian
Cooking

325 deliciously authentic recipes for the adventurous cook

Mridula Baljekar, Rafi Fernandez,
Shehzad Husain and Manisha Kanani

southwater

Contents

Introduction to
Indian Cooking

INDIAN COOKING displays a remarkable range of influences, as befits a subcontinent that has been subject to British, Italian, Dutch, Portuguese and French colonial rule, and which remains home to a vast number of religious practices. As new migrants of all nationalities flock into the streets of Mumbai, Delhi and Kolkata, and neighbours such as China and Myanmar exert their influence on ingredients and cooking techniques, the evolution and diversification of this popular cuisine may never be complete.

Within these pages you'll find classics with which you are already familiar, simple country dishes little known outside their area of origin, contemporary recipes that utilize convenience ingredients, and even fusion foods. Indian cooking also boasts the world's greatest array of vegetarian dishes, with flavoursome dishes based on pulses, dried beans and vegetables. All are delicious, and equally suited to entertaining friends, or cooking for the family.

Principles of Indian Cooking

Until recently, no written record of Indian recipes has existed in India itself. Recipes have traditionally been handed down from one generation to another. Far from being a disadvantage, this has actually helped to fire the imagination of the creative cook, and many dishes that first started out as experiments in spice blends and flavour combinations have now become world classics.

Spices and aromatics

The key to successful Indian cooking lies in the art of blending spices and herbs, rather than sophisticated cooking techniques. The traditional Indian cook relies on instinct rather than written recipes when measuring and combining spices, and in this way unique and very personal tastes can be created. This is one reason why the same dish from one region can look and taste quite different, depending on who has cooked it.

Herbs are added to a dish during the cooking time to add flavour and aroma,

but spices, including those used mainly for taste or for aroma, perform a more complex role.

Spices can be divided into two main groups: those that are integrated into a dish by the end of the cooking process, and those that are later removed. Those in the first group add taste, texture and colour. Different combinations are used, and no single spice is allowed to dominate the final flavour. Useful spices in this group include coriander, cumin, turmeric and garam masala, all in ground form.

Spices from the second group add aroma to a dish. They remain identifiable at the end of cooking, as most of them are used whole. Once these spices have released their aroma, their function is complete and they are not eaten, but removed from the dish before serving or simply left on one side of the plate. Examples of this type of spice are whole cloves, cardamom pods, cinnamon sticks and bay leaves. These spices can also be ground, in which case they will

blend into the sauce during cooking, and will be eaten in the dish in the same way as any other ground spice.

Adding flavour

Having chosen which spices to use, you can then decide what kind of flavours you would like to create. For instance, dry-roasting and grinding flavouring ingredients before adding them to a dish creates a completely different taste and aroma from frying the raw ground spices in hot fat before adding the main ingredients. The flavour of a dish will also vary according to the sequence in which the spices are added, and the length of time each spice is fried and allowed to release its flavour.

Indian cooking lends itself to being personalized by different cooks, and with even just two or three spices, you can create distinctly varied dishes.

Below: Spices and seasonings are what gives Indian food its unique character.

What is a curry?

In India, the word curry refers to a sauce or gravy which is used as an accompaniment to moisten grains of *chawal* (rice) or to make *rotis* (bread) more enjoyable. The rice or bread is considered the main dish of the meal.

The word curry is generally believed to be an anglicized version of the south Indian word *kaari*. It belongs to the Tamil language, which is spoken in the state of Tamil Nadu, of which Madras is the capital. In Tamil, the word means sauce and it is thought that when the British were active in this area, the spelling was somehow changed to curry. Other theories suggest that the word *cury* has existed in English in the context of cooking since the 14th century, and that it was originally derived from the French verb *cuire* (to cook).

The main ingredients of a curry can vary enormously, and two highly dissimilar dishes can be equally deserving of the name. Even the lentil dish known as *dhal*, which bears no resemblance to a sauce, falls under the definition of a curry; in India, *dhal-chawal* and *dhal-roti* are eaten on a daily basis.

A vegetable curry usually consists of a selection of fresh vegetables cooked in a sauce, which can have a thick or a thin consistency, depending on the style of cooking in the region. The sauces for meat, poultry and fish curries also vary in consistency, and are all designed to be served with rice or bread. Gujarat in the west and Punjab in the north also make spiced curries using just yogurt mixed with a little *besan* (gram flour). Made without meat, poultry or vegetables, these dishes are known as *khadis*.

Above: Most of the key ingredients needed for Indian dishes are now available from large supermarkets, but Indian food stores will usually stock a wider selection.

What to eat with a curry

In south and eastern India, curries are always served with rice, which, as the region's main crop, is the staple food of the area, and is eaten daily. Wheat grows abundantly in north India, and in most northern regions, breads such as naan, chapatis and parathas are eaten with curries and with dry, spiced vegetable and lentil dishes. In the Punjab region, however, breads made from *besan* and *makki* (cornmeal) are more usually served. In western India, curries are eaten with breads made with flour from *jowar* (millet) and *bajra* (milo), a form of sorghum.

Preparing an Indian Curry

While there may be no such thing as a definitive curry recipe, there certainly is an established procedure to follow when preparing a curry. Deciding what type of curry you are going to make is the first step. Choose your main ingredient, and select your cooking pan accordingly, as this will affect the ultimate success of the dish. A deep-sided pan will be necessary if the curry is to contain lots of liquid, while for fish, a wide, flat pan is needed to allow the pieces of fish to be laid flat, side by side, in a single layer.

Cooking fats
You need to decide whether you want to use ghee, which is clarified butter, or oil as your cooking medium. Traditionally, the Indian housewife would use ghee, not just for its rich flavour, but also because dairy products are believed to be more nutritious. Modern Indian families are now deviating from this practice, however, because of a growing awareness of the dangers of eating too much saturated fat. Sunflower, vegetable and corn oils will all make suitable alternatives. Olive oil is not normally used, although a basic cooking version (not virgin or extra virgin) will work perfectly well. Ghee can be reserved for special occasion dishes, if you like.

Cooking liquids
Most curries are water-based. Stock is sometimes used in Indian cooking, but it is not a common practice as meat is always cooked on the bone, and this creates a sufficiently robust flavour. Whether you use stock or water as your cooking liquid, it is important to make sure the liquid is at least lukewarm. Adding cold liquid to carefully blended spices will impair the flavours.

Adding salt
Pay careful attention when using salt in an Indian dish. Do not be afraid to use the amount specified in a recipe; even if it seems a lot, it will have been worked out to achieve an overall balance of flavours. There are now

Above: Fresh and dried herbs provide colour, flavour, aroma and texture to Indian food.

several brands of low-sodium salt on the market, which can be substituted, if you prefer.

Thickening agents
Indian cooking does not rely on flour to thicken sauces. Instead, the correct consistency is more usually achieved by adding ingredients such as dairy cream or coconut cream, nut pastes, onion purée, tomatoes, or ground seeds such as poppy, sesame and sunflower.

Adding colour
Some of the ingredients added to curries not only determine their texture and consistency, but also their colour. In Mughlai sauces and curries, the onions are softened but not browned, which gives the dishes their distinctive pale colour. Bhoona (stir-fried) curries, on the other hand, use browned onions, making the final dishes reddish-brown in colour.

Souring agents
Some of the souring agents used in curries also affect their colour and consistency. Tamarind, for instance, darkens and thickens a sauce at the same time. Lime, lemon and white vinegar, however, will neither alter the colour of a curry nor thicken it, and a thickening agent such as coconut milk or a nut or seed paste will need to be used too. Ingredients such as dry mango

---

COLOURING INGREDIENTS
The depth of the curry's colour will depend on the amount of colorant used in relation to other ingredients.
turmeric: bright yellow
saffron: pale apricot
red chillies: reddish brown
fresh coriander (cilantro) leaves: green
tomatoes: reddish, if used alone; pinkish if combined with yogurt
onions: brown
ground coriander: deep brown if fried for 5–6 minutes
garam masala: deep brown if fried for 1 minute

powder (*amchur*), dried pomegranate seeds (known as *anardana*), as well as tomatoes and yogurts are all used to lend a distinctive tangy flavour to a curry, and they will also affect the colour to varying degrees.

Adding heat

The most important ingredient for achieving a fiery flavour and appearance is chilli. Although chillies were unknown in India before the Portuguese settlers introduced them in the 15th century, it is difficult to imagine Indian food without them today. It is chilli in its powdered form that contributes to the colour of a curry, and chilli powder is readily available in a range of heat levels. Always be sure to check the label carefully. If you want the curry to be appealing to the eye without scorching the taste buds, choose a chilli powder made from either Kashmiri or Byadigi chillies. This will lend a rich colour to the dish, but the flavour will be fairly mild. You can always use a mild powder with a hot chilli powder if you prefer to give the curry some kick. Another way to achieve both colour and heat in the same dish is to combine chilli powder with fresh chillies: fresh chillies are always hotter than dried.

When buying fresh chillies, try to find the ones used in Indian cooking, rather than Mexican varieties. Those used in Indian cooking are long and slim, and are sometimes labelled "finger chillies". Thai chillies make a good substitute, and are available from Asian food stores.

Paste made from dried red chillies also gives a very good colour and quite a different flavour from chilli powder. To make it, all you need to do is to soak the chillies for 15–20 minutes in hot water and then purée them. The paste will keep well in an airtight jar in the refrigerator for 4–5 days.

Cooking a curry

Several factors will influence the making of a good curry, and one of the most important of these is the cooking temperature. The fat should be heated to the right temperature and maintained at a steady heat until the spices have released their flavour. A heavy pan, such as a karahi, wok or large pan, will help to maintain the temperature, so that the spices can cook without burning. While recipes may vary, the usual procedure is to start by cooking the onions over a medium heat. Once the onions have softened, the ground spices are added and the temperature is lowered.

Another important factor is how the onions are chopped. The finer an onion is chopped, the better it will blend

Below: The secret of Indian cooking lies in the use of spices, and blending spices at home will give more flavoursome curries.

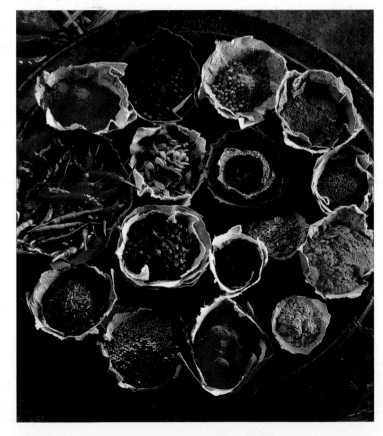

into the sauce. In many recipes, onion, ginger and garlic are puréed to make a wet spice paste, which is fried until all the moisture has evaporated, before the ground spices are added. It is crucial to follow the timings specified in a recipe for each of these cooking stages.

Adding spices in the correct sequence is also vital. While some spices take only a few seconds to release their flavour, others need a few minutes, and if you add spices that require less cooking time together with those that need more, some will burn and others will remain raw. The simplest way to avoid this is to keep to the order in which the spices are listed in the recipe, and to be very exact about following the specified cooking time for each ingredient.

Planning an Indian Meal

When planning your menu, always bear in mind that an everyday Indian meal features only three items: the main dish, a side dish and a staple, which would be rice or bread. Chutneys, salads and raitas can also be served to add a tangy taste.

Planning the menu

When deciding which foods to serve, consider the main dish. Is it going to be highly spiced, such as a vindaloo or a bhoona? Or will it have subtle flavours, such as a korma or a pasanda? A little careful planning will ensure that the flavours of the dishes complement, rather than compete with, each other. Choose the side dish according to the strength of the main one. A lightly spiced side dish is more enjoyable when the main dish is spicier. This does not

Below: There is no rigid structure to an Indian meal, but there should always be a good balance of dry and moist dishes.

apply in reverse, however, and a side dish with complex spicing is not the ideal accompaniment to a mild main dish.

Dishes with a drier consistency are generally accompanied by a vegetable curry or a lentil dish. Biryanis and pilaus are traditionally served with a simple raita, although they are more usually served with a vegetable curry in Indian restaurants in the West.

How to serve

An Indian meal is not served as separate courses, with an appetizer, followed by a main dish and one or two side dishes. Although the meal will usually consist of several dishes, all complement each other and are brought to the table at the same time, with diners helping themselves to each dish in any order.

For entertaining and more lavish occasions, you can add other dishes to the standard three-dish Indian menu. One or two dry meat dishes, such as a kebab or tandoori chicken, in addition

USEFUL STANDBYS
• Use bottled ginger and garlic purée (paste) rather than peeling and chopping the fresh aromatics.
• Canned chopped tomatoes can be used instead of fresh tomatoes, although you may need to increase the quantities of souring agent, salt and chilli to compensate for the depleted flavour.
• Canned or packet creamed coconut (coconut cream) is a convenient replacement for fresh coconut. Follow the manufacturer's instructions.

to some chutneys, pickles, raitas and poppadums, with a dessert to follow, can turn an ordinary family meal into dinner-party fare.

Indian desserts
In India, a meal will usually end with fresh fruit, rather than elaborate fresh or

cooked desserts. Fruits are served with real flair, however, and are often combined with other ingredients to create imaginative and exciting flavours. Choose one or two exotic fruits, such as papaya, pomegranate or star fruit, and combine them with everyday fruits in a fruit salad. Serve with Greek (US strained plain) yogurt flavoured with rose water and a little ground cardamom.

Indian sweets (candies) are quite heavy and are served as a snack with tea and coffee, in the same way as cakes and biscuits (cookies) are eaten in the West.

Freezing curries

In today's busy world, it is not always possible to serve a meal while it is still sizzling in the pan. If you are cooking for guests, you may prefer to cook the curry in advance to save yourself time

COOKING FOR A PARTY

It is a good idea to cook the curry dishes a day ahead of the party, storing them in the refrigerator until you are ready to reheat them. Accompanying dhal dishes can also be prepared 24 hours in advance, although the seasonings should not be added until just before serving. You can prepare vegetables in advance, but do not cook them more than a few hours ahead. Likewise, you can prepare ingredients for raitas a day ahead, but do not assemble them until a few hours before they are needed; the yogurt for raitas should always be fresh. Pickles and chutneys will benefit from advance preparation, but follow individual recipes for timing guides, as some will deteriorate more quickly than others. The bread dough for rotis can be made the day before. The rotis can be made 2 hours before you plan to serve them. Spread them with butter and wrap in foil to keep warm, then set them aside; reheat in the oven before serving.

on the day, or you may like to cook a larger quantity than you will need and freeze some for another meal; you may even have leftovers.

Spicy food is ideal for freezing as the flavours seem to improve when the food is thawed and reheated. Most of the spices used in Indian cooking have natural preservative qualities, as does the acid in souring agents. However, you should bear in mind the following factors if cooking specifically for the freezer:
• Leave the food slightly underdone.
• Cool the food rapidly. The best way to do this is to tip it into a large tray (a large roasting pan is ideal) and leave it in a cool place.
• Once the food has cooled completely, spoon it into plastic containers, cover, label and chill it in the refrigerator for a couple of hours, then transfer it to the freezer. The food will keep in the freezer for 6–8 months, depending on the star rating of your freezer.

Food that you did not plan to freeze, such as leftovers, should not be kept in the freezer for longer than 2–3 months, again, depending on the efficiency of your freezer. Meat and poultry curries freeze very successfully, as do curries made from vegetables, lentils and pulses. Fish curries can be frozen, but they are generally less successful as changes in the water balance may damage the more delicate texture of cooked fish.

Thawing and reheating

It is important to thaw frozen food thoroughly and slowly. Leave it in the refrigerator for 18–24 hours before reheating. After reheating, always make sure the food is piping hot before serving. These steps are crucial in order to ensure that any potentially harmful bacteria are destroyed. If you have a temperature probe, check that the reheated food is at least 85°C/185°F right the way through before serving.

A certain amount of water separation is to be expected as a frozen dish thaws out. The dish will return to its normal

REHEATING LEFTOVERS

This method will make leftover food that has been frozen taste really fresh. The method can also be used to reheat food that has been stored for a day or two in the refrigerator.

Heat about 10ml/2 tsp vegetable oil in a karahi, wok or large pan over a medium heat. Add up to 1.5ml/¼ tsp garam masala (depending on the quantity of food), and allow to bubble gently for 10–15 seconds. Add the thawed food to the pan and increase the heat to high. Let the food bubble or sizzle in the pan until it is heated through, stirring from time to time to make sure the heat is well distributed. Add a little water if the food looks particularly dry. Stir in 15ml/1 tbsp chopped fresh coriander (cilantro). Remove from the heat, transfer to a warmed platter and serve immediately.

consistency when it is reheated, as the water will be reabsorbed by the meat or vegetables.

Thawed food can be reheated in the microwave or in a covered casserole on the stove top. If using a microwave, cover the food with microwave clear film (plastic wrap). Stir the food from time to time as it is heated, to ensure the heat passes right the way through. You may need to add a small amount of water when reheating, to ensure that the dish does not dry out.

Aromatics, Spices and Herbs

Spices are integral to both the flavour and aroma of a dish. Some spices are used principally for the taste they impart, while ingredients known as aromatics are used mainly for their aroma. One individual spice can completely alter the taste of a dish and a combination of several spices will also affect its colour and texture.

The quantities of spices and salt specified in recipes are measured to achieve a balance of flavours, although you may prefer to increase or decrease the quantities according to taste. This is particularly true of fresh chillies and chilli powder: experiment with quantities, adding less or more than specified.

Fresh and dried herbs also play an important part in the combinations of colour, flavour, aroma and texture that make up a curry. Because herbs require only a minimal amount of cooking, they retain a marvellous intensity of flavour and fragrance.

Garlic
Widely available fresh and dried, garlic is used for its strong, aromatic flavour, and is a standard ingredient, along with ginger, in most curries. Fresh garlic can be pulped, crushed or chopped, or the cloves can be used whole. Garlic powder is mainly used in spice mixtures.

Ginger
One of the most popular spices in India and also one of the oldest, fresh root ginger is an important ingredient in many Indian curries. Its refreshing scent is reminiscent of citrus and it has a pleasant, sharp flavour. The root should be plump with a fairly smooth skin, which is peeled off before use. Young root ginger is tender and mild, whereas older roots are quite fibrous, with a more pungent flavour. Dried powdered ginger is a useful standby, but the flavour is not identical. Ginger is often blended with other spices to make curry powder.

Below: *Fresh root ginger*

Below: *Ground ginger*

PULPING GARLIC
Fresh garlic is used so regularly in Indian cooking that you may find it more practical to prepare garlic in bulk and store it in the refrigerator or freezer until needed.

Separate the garlic bulb into cloves and peel off the papery skin. Process the whole cloves in a food processor until smooth. Freeze the garlic pulp in ice-cube trays used especially for the purpose. Put 5ml/1 tsp in each compartment, freeze, remove from the tray and store in the freezer in a sealed plastic bag. Alternatively, store the pulp in an airtight container in the refrigerator for 3–4 weeks.

PREPARING FRESH ROOT GINGER
Fresh root ginger has a delightfully clean and pungent taste, and is easy to prepare. It is widely available from supermarkets and markets.

To grate ginger, carefully remove the skin using a sharp knife or vegetable peeler. Grate the peeled ginger using the fine side of a metal cheese grater. To chop, slice the ginger into fine strips, then chop as required.

PULPING FRESH ROOT GINGER
Pulped fresh root ginger is time-consuming to prepare for each individual recipe. Instead, prepare a large quantity and store in the freezer until needed.

Peel off the tough outer skin using a sharp knife or a vegetable peeler. Roughly chop, then process in a food processor, adding a little water to get a smooth consistency. Store the pulp in the refrigerator for 3–4 weeks or freeze in ice-cube trays used for the purpose.

Left: Green and red bird's eye chillies.

Chillies

These hot peppers belong to the genus capsicum, along with sweet (bell) peppers. Some varieties are extremely fiery and all chillies should be used with caution. Much of the severe heat of fresh chillies is contained in the seeds, and the heat can be toned down by removing these before use. Like other spicy foods, chillies are perfect for hot climates as they cause blood to rush to the surface of the skin, promoting instant cooling.

Chillies vary in size and colour, but as a rule, dark green chillies tend to be hotter than light green ones. Red chillies are usually hotter still, and some will darken to brown or black when fully ripe. Shape and colour give no sure indication of the hotness, and it is wise to be wary of any unfamiliar variety. Dried chillies can be used whole or coarsely crushed. Chilli powder is a fiery ground spice that should be used with great caution. The heat varies from brand to brand, so adjust quantities to suit your taste buds. Some brands include other spices and herbs, as well as ground chillies, and these may not be appropriate to the dish you are cooking. Always check the label carefully.

PREPARING DRIED CHILLIES

Dried chillies are available from good supermarkets and Indian food stores.

To prepare the chillies, remove the stems and seeds, then break each chilli into two or three pieces. Put the pieces in a small bowl and cover with hot water. Leave to stand for 30 minutes, then drain (using the soaking water in the recipe, if appropriate). Use the chilli pieces as they are, or chop them finely.

WATCHPOINT

All chillies contain capsaicin, an oily substance, that can cause intense irritation to sensitive skin. If you get capsaicin on your hands and transfer it to your eyes by rubbing, you will experience considerable pain. Wash hands with soapy water after handling. Dry your hands and rub a little oil into the skin to remove any stinging juices. Many cooks prefer to wear rubber gloves.

Above: The colour of chillies gives no sure indication of heat, although red chillies are usually hotter.

PREPARING FRESH CHILLIES

Using two or more fresh chillies will make a dish quite hot. If you prefer a milder flavour, reduce the amount of chilli used, and remove the seeds and pithy membrane. If you have sensitive skin, you may prefer to wear rubber gloves to protect your hands when preparing chillies.

1 Cut the chillies in half lengthways. Remove the membranes and seeds.

2 Cut the chilli flesh lengthways into long, thin strips.

3 If required, cut the strips of chilli crossways into tiny dice.

Below: *From left, cloves, ground cinnamon, and cinnamon sticks*

Aniseed

These liquorice-flavoured seeds are used in many fried and deep-fried Indian dishes as an aid to digestion.

Cinnamon

One of the earliest known spices, cinnamon has a highly aromatic, sweet, warm flavour. It is sold ready-ground and as sticks, which are quill-like shapes rolled from the bark of the cinnamon tree. Use cinnamon sticks whole or broken, and remove them from the food before serving. Finely ground cinnamon is a useful pantry staple, but for a finer flavour grind stick cinnamon in a mill or coffee grinder, kept exclusively for spices.

Cloves

The unopened flower buds of a tree that belongs to the myrtle family, cloves have an aromatic and sometimes fiery flavour and an intense fragrance, and are used to flavour many sweet and savoury dishes. Cloves are usually added whole to recipes. Their warm flavour complements all rich meats, and they need no preparation. Ground cloves are one of the ingredients added to spice mixtures.

Above: *From left, cumin seeds, fenugreek and ground cumin*

Cumin

White cumin seeds are oval, ridged and greenish brown in colour. They have a strong aroma and flavour and can be used whole or ground. Ready-ground cumin powder is widely available, but it should be bought in small quantities as it loses its flavour rapidly. Black cumin seeds are dark and aromatic. This is one of the ingredients used in garam masala.

Left: *Ground and fresh turmeric*

Turmeric

A member of the ginger family but without ginger's characteristic heat, turmeric is a rhizome that is indigenous to Asia. Turmeric is sometimes referred to as Indian saffron, as it shares saffron's ability to colour food yellow, although it lacks that spice's subtlety. Fresh turmeric adds a warm and slightly musky flavour to food, but it has a strong, bitter flavour and should be used sparingly. Turmeric has a natural affinity with fish, and is also used in rice, dhal and vegetable dishes.

Dhania jeera powder

This spice mixture is made from ground roasted coriander and cumin seeds. The proportions are generally two parts coriander to one part cumin.

Fennel seeds

Similar in appearance to cumin, fennel seeds have a sweet taste and are used to flavour curries. They can be chewed as a mouth-freshener after a spicy meal.

Mustard seeds

Whole black and brown mustard seeds are indigenous to India and appear often in Indian cooking. The seeds have no aroma in their raw state, but when roasted or fried in *ghee* or hot oil they release a rich, nutty flavour and aroma. Mustard seeds are commonly used with vegetables and dhal dishes.

Nigella seeds

Also known as kalonji or wild onion seeds, this aromatic spice has a sharp and tingling taste, and is frequently used in Indian vegetarian dishes.

Onion seeds

Black, triangular shaped and aromatic, onion seeds are used in pickles and to flavour vegetable curries and lentil dishes.

Garam masala

This is a mixture of spices that can be made at home from freshly ground spices, or purchased ready-made. There is no set recipe, but a typical mixture might include black cumin seeds, peppercorns, cloves, cinnamon and black cardamom pods. Many variations on garam masala are sold commercially, as pastes ready-made in jars. These can be subtituted for homemade garam masala.

Below: *From left, paprika, whole nutmeg and grated nutmeg*

Left: Small green cardamom pods and the larger brown variety

Asafoetida

This seasoning is a resin with an acrid and very bitter taste and a strong odour. It is used primarily as an anti-flatulent, and only minute quantities are used in recipes. Store in a glass jar with a strong airtight seal to prevent the smell contaminating into other ingredients in the pantry.

Cardamom pods

This spice is native to India, where it is considered the most prized spice after saffron. The pods can be used whole or the husks can be removed to release the seeds; whole pods should be always removed from the dish before serving. They have a slightly pungent, but very aromatic taste. They come in three colours: green, white and black or brown. The green and white pods can be used for both sweet and savoury dishes or to flavour rice. Black or brown pods are used only for savoury dishes.

Nutmeg

Whole nutmeg should be grated to release its sweet, nutty flavour. Ground nutmeg imparts a similar, though less intense, flavour, and makes a very useful pantry standby.

DRY-FRYING MUSTARD SEEDS

Mustard seeds release their aroma when heated so should be dry-fried before being added to a dish.

Heat a little *ghee* or vegetable oil in a karahi, wok or large pan, and add the mustard seeds. Shake the pan over the heat until the seeds start to change colour. Stir the seeds from time to time. Use the pan lid to stop the seeds jumping out of the pan when they start to splutter and pop.

Peppercorns

Black peppercorns are native to India, and are an essential ingredient in garam masala. White peppercorns are less aromatic. Use peppercorns whole or ground. Pink peppercorns are an unrelated spice used in some contemporary Indian dishes. Treat with caution as they are mildly toxic.

Paprika

A mild, sweet red powder, paprika is often used in place of or alongside chillies in westernized Indian cooking to add colour to a dish.

Saffron

The dried stigmas of the saffron crocus, which is native to Asia Minor, is the world's most expensive spice. To produce 450g/1lb of saffron requires 60,000 stigmas. Fortunately, only a small quantity of saffron is needed to flavour and colour a dish. Saffron is sold as threads and as a powder. It has a beautiful flavour and aroma.

Above: *From left, white, black and pink peppercorns*

Below: *From left, saffron powder and threads*

Curry leaves

Bright green and shiny, curry leaves are similar in appearance to bay leaves, but they have a different flavour. The leaves of a hardwood tree that is indigenous to India, they are widely used in Indian cooking, particularly in southern and western India (although not in Goa) and in Sri Lanka. Curry leaves have a warm fragrance with a subtle hint of sweet, green pepper or tangerine. They release their full flavour when bruised, and impart a highly distinctive flavour to curries. Curry leaves are sold dried and occasionally fresh in Indian food stores. Fresh leaves freeze well, but the dried leaves make a poor substitute, as they rapidly lose their fragrance.

Bay leaves

Indian bay leaves come from the cassia tree, which is similar to the tree from which cinnamon is taken. Bay leaves sold in the West are taken from the laurel tree. When used fresh, bay leaves have a deliciously sweet flavour, but they keep well in dried form, if stored in a cool, dark place in an airtight jar. Bay leaves are used in meat and rice dishes.

Left: *Dried curry leaves*

Below: *Bay leaves*

Below: Fresh coriander

FREEZING FRESH CORIANDER

Fresh coriander (cilantro) is widely used in Indian cooking. Its flavour and aroma make it an important ingredient, and the fresh leaves make a attractive garnish. Buy bunches of coriander and freeze what is not required immediately.

1 Cut off the roots and any thick stalks, retaining the fine stalks.

2 Wash the leaves in cold water and leave in a strainer to drain.

3 When the leaves are dry, chop them finely and store them in small quantities in plastic bags or airtight containers in the freezer.

Coriander

There is no substitute for fresh coriander (cilantro), and the more that is used in Indian cooking the better. Coriander imparts a wonderful aroma and flavour, and is used both as an ingredient in cooking, and sprinkled over dishes as a garnish. Chopped coriander can be frozen successfully; the frozen herb does not need to be thawed before use. Coriander seeds and ground coriander powder are used for flavouring. The seeds have a pungent, slightly lemony flavour, and are used coarsely ground in meat, fish and poultry dishes. Ground coriander, a brownish powder, is an important constituent of any curry spice mixture.

Mint

There are many varieties of mint available, and the stronger-flavoured types tend to be used in Indian cooking. These taste slightly sweet and have a cool aftertaste. Mint has a fresh, stimulating aroma and is traditionally used with lamb, as well as for flavouring some vegetables, and for making chutneys and refreshing raitas. Mint is added at the end of cooking time, in order to retain the flavour.

Fenugreek

Fresh fenugreek is generally sold in bunches. It has very small leaves and is used to flavour meat and vegetarian dishes. Always discard the stalks, which will impart an unpleasant bitterness to a dish if used. The seeds are hard, pungent and slightly bitter. They can be used whole, often in rice, pulse and vegetable dishes, or ground to a yellow powder. They have a tangy flavour and powerful scent, and for this reason should be used moderately. Dried fenugreek leaves are sold in Indian food stores. Store them in an airtight jar, in a cool, dark place; they will keep for about 12 months.

Below: Aromatic fresh fenugreek leaves are widely used in savoury Indian dishes.

Curry Powders and Pastes

Powders and pastes are blends of spices, chillies and herbs that are used as the basis of a curry. Traditional Indian households would blend individual spices as needed, but for convenience you may prefer to prepare a quantity in advance.

Curry powder

This is a basic recipe for a dry spice blend. It is a mild recipe, but you could increase the quantity of dried chilli.

INGREDIENTS

Makes 115g/4oz/½ cup
50g/2oz/½ cup coriander seeds
60ml/4 tbsp cumin seeds
30ml/2 tbsp fennel seeds
30ml/2 tbsp fenugreek seeds
4 dried red chillies
5 curry leaves
15ml/1 tbsp chilli powder
15ml/1 tbsp ground turmeric
2.5ml/½ tsp salt

1 Dry-roast the whole spices in a karahi, wok or large pan for 8–10 minutes, shaking the pan until the spices darken and release a rich aroma. Leave to cool.

2 Put the dry-roasted whole spices in a spice mill and grind to a fine powder.

3 Add the ground, roasted spices to the chilli powder, turmeric and salt in a large glass bowl and mix well. Store the curry powder in an airtight container.

Garam masala

Garam means hot and masala means spices, and this mixture uses spices that are known to heat the body, such as black peppercorns and cloves. Garam masala is used mainly for meat, although it can be used in poultry and rice dishes. It is generally too strong for fish or vegetables.

INGREDIENTS

Makes 50g/2oz/¼ cup
10 dried red chillies
3 × 2.5cm/1in pieces cinnamon stick
2 curry leaves
30ml/2 tbsp coriander seeds
30ml/2 tbsp cumin seeds
5ml/1 tsp black peppercorns
5ml/1 tsp cloves
5ml/1 tsp fenugreek seeds
5ml/1 tsp black mustard seeds
1.5ml/¼ tsp chilli powder

1 Dry-roast the whole dried red chillies, cinnamon sticks and curry leaves in a karahi, wok or large pan over a low heat for about 2 minutes.

2 Add the coriander and cumin seeds, black peppercorns, cloves, fenugreek and mustard seeds, and dry-roast for 8–10 minutes, shaking the pan from side to side until the spices begin to darken in colour and release a rich aroma. Leave the mixture to cool.

3 Using either a spice mill or a stainless steel mortar and pestle, grind the roasted spices to a fine powder.

4 Transfer the powder to a glass bowl and mix in the chilli powder. Store in an airtight container.

COOK'S TIP

Both the curry powder and the garam masala will keep for 2–4 months in an airtight container in a cool, dark place. Once opened, store in the refrigerator.

VARIATIONS

For convenience, you can buy garam masala ready-made, or try any of the following pastes in alternative flavours:
• Tandoori masala   • Kashmiri masala
• Madras masala   • Sambhar masala
• Dhansak masala   • Green masala

Curry paste

A curry paste is a wet blend of spices, herbs and chillies cooked with oil and vinegar, which help to preserve the spices during storage. It is a quick and convenient way of adding a spice mixture to a curry, and different blends will produce different flavours. As only a small amount of paste is added at a time, a little will last a long time. Store in the refrigerator and use as required.

INGREDIENTS

Makes 600ml/1 pint/2½ cups
50g/2oz/½ cup coriander seeds
60ml/4 tbsp cumin seeds
30ml/2 tbsp fennel seeds
30ml/2 tbsp fenugreek seeds
4 dried red chillies
5 curry leaves
15ml/1 tbsp chilli powder
15ml/1 tbsp ground turmeric
150ml/¼ pint/⅔ cup wine vinegar
250ml/8fl oz/1 cup vegetable oil

1 Grind the whole spices to a powder in a spice mill. Transfer to a bowl and add the remaining ground spices.

2 Mix the spices until well blended. Add the wine vinegar and stir. Add 75ml/5 tbsp water and stir to form a paste.

3 Heat the oil in a karahi, wok or large pan and stir-fry the spice paste for about 10 minutes, or until all the water has been absorbed. When the oil rises to the surface the paste is cooked. Allow to cool slightly in the pan before spooning the paste into airtight jars.

— COOK'S TIP —

Curry pastes will keep for 3–4 weeks after opening, if stored in the refrigerator.

Tikka paste

This is a delicious, versatile paste. It has a slightly sour flavour, and can be used in a variety of Indian dishes, including chicken tikka, tandoori chicken and tikka masala. Use sparingly as a little bit goes a long way. Store the paste in airtight glass jars in the refrigerator until required.

INGREDIENTS

Makes 475ml/16fl oz/2 cups
30ml/2 tbsp coriander seeds
30ml/2 tbsp cumin seeds
25ml/1½ tbsp garlic powder
30ml/2 tbsp paprika
15ml/1 tbsp garam masala
15ml/1 tbsp ground ginger
10ml/2 tsp chilli powder
2.5ml/½ tsp ground turmeric
15ml/1 tbsp dried mint
1.5ml/¼ tsp salt
5ml/1 tsp lemon juice
few drops of red food colouring
few drops of yellow food colouring
150ml/¼ pint/⅔ cup wine vinegar
150ml/¼ pint/⅔ cup vegetable oil

1 Grind the coriander and cumin seeds to a fine powder using a spice mill or mortar and pestle. Spoon the mixture into a bowl and add the remaining spices, the mint and salt, stirring well.

2 Mix the spice powder with the lemon juice, food colourings and wine vinegar and add 30ml/2 tbsp water to form a thin paste.

3 Heat the oil in a large pan, karahi or wok, and stir-fry the paste for 10 minutes, until all the water has been absorbed. When the oil rises to the surface, the paste is cooked. Leave to cool before spooning into airtight jars.

Additional Ingredients

Besides the essential spices, aromatics and herbs, there are several other ingredients that are central to Indian cooking. Among the additional ingredients listed here are popular thickening and souring agents, flavourings and Indian cheese.

Almonds
In the West, almonds are readily available whole, sliced, ground, and as thin slivers. The whole kernels should be soaked in boiling water before use to remove the thin red skin; once blanched, they can be eaten raw. Almonds have a uniqe aroma and they impart a sumptuous richness to curries. They make an effective thickener for sauces, and are also used for garnishing. Almonds are considered a delicacy in India and, because they are not indigenous, they are very expensive to buy.

Cashew nuts
These full-flavoured nuts can be used raw and roasted in Indian cooking. Cashews are ground and used in korma dishes to enrich and thicken the sauce,

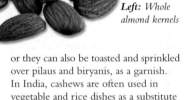

Above: Cashew nuts

Left: Whole almond kernels

or they can also be toasted and sprinkled over pilaus and biryanis, as a garnish. In India, cashews are often used in vegetable and rice dishes as a substitute for the more expensive almonds.

Pistachio nuts
These small, greenish purple nuts are not indigenous to India, but they are frequently used as a thickening agent and to add their characteristic rich and creamy flavour. Raw or toasted pistachio nuts also make an attractive garnish.

Poppy seeds
These seeds are usually toasted to bring out their full, nutty flavour. They can be sprinkled over dry meat and vegetable dishes, or ground and added to curries to thicken sauces.

Sesame seeds
These small, flat, pear-shaped seeds probably originated in Africa but have been cultivated in India since ancient times. They are usually white but can be cream to brown, red or black. Raw sesame seeds have very little aroma and taste until they have been roasted or dry-fried, when they take on a slightly nutty taste. They can be ground with a mortar and pestle, or in a spice mill, and used to enrich curries. They are also added to chutneys. The high fat content of sesame seeds means that they do not keep well: buy them in small quantities and store in a cool, dark place.

Pomegranate seeds
These can be extracted from fresh pomegranates or, for convenience, they can be bought in jars from Asian food stores. Pomegranate seeds impart a delicious tangy flavour.

Dry mango powder
Mangoes are indigenous to India, and they have many uses in Indian cooking. The fruit is used in curries at different stages of ripeness, but the unripe fruit is also sun-dried and ground into a dry powder called amchur. The powder has a sour taste, and is sprinkled over dishes as a garnish; it is seldom used in cooking.

Above: White and black poppy seeds

Right: Black sesame seeds and white sesame seeds

Above: Fresh coconut

Coconut

Used in both sweet and savoury Indian dishes, fresh coconut is available from Indian food stores and supermarkets. Desiccated (dry unsweetened shredded) coconut, and coconut cream and creamed coconut, which are made from grated coconut, will all make acceptable substitutes in most recipes if fresh coconut is out of season. Coconut milk is used in Indian curries to thicken and enrich sauces. In Western supermarkets, it is sold in cans and in powdered form, as a convenient alternative to the fresh fruit; the powdered milk has to be blended with hot water before use. Coconut milk can be made at home from desiccated coconut. Coconut cream is used to add fragrance and aroma to dishes, while creamed coconut adds richness.

Below: Clockwise from left, coconut cream, coconut milk and desiccated coconut

MAKING COCONUT MILK

You can make as much of the milk as you like from this recipe by adapting the quantities accordingly, although the method is more practical for larger quantities.

Tip 225g/8oz/2⅔ cups desiccated (dry unsweetened shredded) coconut into a food processor and pour over 450ml/¾ pint/scant 2 cups boiling water. Process for 20–30 seconds, then cool. Place a sieve lined with muslin (cheesecloth) over a bowl in the sink. Ladle some of the softened coconut into the muslin. Bring up the ends of the cloth and twist it over the sieve to extract the liquid. Use the milk as directed in recipes. Coconut milk will keep for 1–2 days in the refrigerator, or it can be frozen for use on a later occasion.

Yogurt

In India, yogurt is known as curd. It can be added to sauces to give a thick and creamy texture, although it is most often used as a souring agent, particularly in the dairy-dominated north. Yogurt will curdle quickly when heated, and it should be used with care in recipes: add only a spoonful at a time, stir well and allow the sauce to simmer for 5 minutes before adding the next spoonful. In India, yogurt would be made at home on a daily basis, although ready-made natural (plain) yogurt is an acceptable substitute. Always choose live yogurt because of its beneficial effect on the digestive system.

Below: Fresh paneer

Paneer

This traditional North Indian cheese is made from rich dairy milk. Paneer is white in colour and smooth-textured. It is usually available from Indian food stores and supermarkets, but beancurd (tofu) is an adequate substitute.

MAKING PANEER

Paneer is very easy to make, and adventurous cooks may prefer to make their own at home.

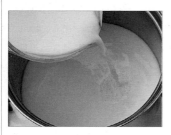

Bring 1 litre/1¾ pints/4 cups milk to the boil over a low heat. Add 30ml/ 2 tbsp lemon juice, and stir gently until the milk thickens and begins to curdle. Strain the curdled milk through a sieve lined with muslin (cheesecloth). Set the curd aside for 1½–2 hours, under a heavy weight to press it into a flat shape, about 1cm/½in thick. Cut into wedges and use as required. Paneer will keep for up to 1 week in the refrigerator.

Tamarind

The brown fruit pods of the tamarind tree are 15–20cm/6–8in long. Inside, the seeds are surrounded by a sticky brown pulp. Tamarind is cultivated in India, as well as in other parts of South-east Asia, East Africa and the West Indies, and it is undoubtably one of the natural treasures of the East. The high tartaric acid content makes tamarind an excellent souring agent, and for this purpose it has no substitute. It doesn't have a strong aroma but the flavour is wonderful: tart without being bitter, fruity and refreshing. Tamarind is sold compressed in blocks, and dried in slices. Fresh tamarind and concentrate and paste are also available.

PREPARING COMPRESSED TAMARIND

Asian food stores and supermarkets sell compressed tamarind in a solid block, and in this form it looks rather like a packet of dried dates.

To prepare compressed tamarind, tear off a piece that is roughly equivalent to 15ml/1 tbsp. Put the tamarind in a jug (pitcher) and add 150ml/¼ pint/⅔ cup warm water. Leave to soak for 10 minutes. Swirl the tamarind around with your fingers so that the pulp is released from the seeds. Using a nylon sieve, strain the juice into a bowl. Discard the contents of the sieve, and use the liquid as required. Store any leftover liquid in the refrigerator for use in another recipe.

Below: Tamarind, compressed into a block

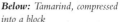

Fruits

Indians love fruit and, as well as eating fresh fruits raw as a dessert at the end of a meal, they will also cook them with spices, chilli and coconut milk in savoury dishes. The exotic fruits listed here are all native to India, and they are as diverse in colour and shape as they are in flavour.

Mangoes

Ripe, fresh mangoes grow in India throughout the summer months, and are used in sweet dishes. Unripe green mangoes, sold in the springtime, are used to make tangy pickles and chutneys, and are added to curries as a souring agent for seasoning.

Papayas

Also known as pawpaws, these pear-shaped fruits are native to tropical America, and were not introduced to Asia until the 17th century. When ripe, the green skin turns a speckled yellow and the pulp is a vibrant orange-pink. The edible small black seeds taste peppery when dried. Peel off the skin using a sharp knife and eat the creamy flesh of the ripe fruit raw. The unripe green fruit is used in cooking: one of the unique properties of papaya is that it will help to tenderize meat.

Pineapples

These distinctive-looking fruits have a sweet, golden and exceedingly juicy flesh. Unlike most other fruits, pineapples do not ripen after picking, although leaving a slightly unripe fruit at room temperature will help to reduce its acidity. Pineapples are cultivated in India, mainly in the South, and are gently cooked with spices to make palate-cleansing side dishes.

Bananas

The soft and creamy flesh of bananas is high in starch, and is an excellent source of energy. Indians use several varieties of banana in vegetarian curries, including plantains, green bananas, and the sweet red-skinned variety.

Lemons and limes

These citrus fruits are indigenous to India, although limes, which in India are confusingly called lemons, are the most commonly available of the two. Both fruits are used as souring agents and are added to curries at the end of the cooking process; adding them any sooner would prevent any meat in the dish from becoming tender while it cooks.

Above: *Lemons (top) and limes are used as souring agents in Indian curries.*

Above: *A whole papaya, with the cut fruit showing the small black, edible seeds.*

Right: *Sweet, red-skinned bananas and the more familiar large and small yellow-skinned varieties.*

Vegetables

Indian cooking specializes in a huge range of excellent vegetable dishes, using everything from cauliflower, potatoes and peas to the more exotic and unusual varieties, such as okra, bottle gourds and aubergines (eggplant). When it comes to Indian cooking, vegetables are simply indispensable.

Right: Small and large onions

Left: Various sizes of purple aubergines

Aubergines
Available in different varieties, the shiny deep purple aubergine is the most common and widely used variety in Indian cooking. Aubergines have a strong flavour and some have a slightly bitter taste. The cut flesh can be sprinkled with salt to extract these bitter juices.

Bottle gourds
One of the many bitter vegetables used in Indian cooking, this long, knobbly green vegetable comes from Kenya and has a strong, bitter taste. It is known to have properties that purify the blood. To prepare a gourd, peel the ridged skin with a sharp knife, scrape away and discard the seeds and chop the flesh.

Okra
Also known as ladies' fingers, okra are among the most popular vegetables in Indian cooking. These small green five-sided pods are indigenous to India. They have a very distinctive flavour and a sticky, pulpy texture when they are cooked.

Onions
A versatile vegetable belonging to the allium family, onions have a strong pungent flavour and aroma. Globe onions are the most commonly used variety for Indian cooking. Spring onions (scallions) are also used in some dishes to add colour and for their mild taste.

Peppers
Large, hollow pods belonging to the capsicum family, (bell) peppers are available in a variety of colours. Red peppers are sweeter than green peppers. They are used in a wide variety of dishes, adding both colour and flavour.

Left: Peppers

Spinach
Available all year round, this leafy green vegetable has a mild, delicate flavour. The leaves vary in size and only the large thick leaves need to be trimmed of their stalks. Spinach is a favourite vegetable in Indian cooking, and it is cooked in many ways, with meat, other vegetables, and with beans, peas and lentils.

Corn
Although it originated in South America, corn is now grown worldwide, and is widely cultivated in North India. It has a delicious sweet, juicy flavour, which is at its best just after picking.

Tomatoes
These are an essential ingredient, and are used to make sauces for curries, chutneys and relishes. Salad tomatoes are quite adequate but are usually peeled. Use canned tomatoes in sauces and curries for their rich colour.

Beans, Peas and Lentils

These play an important role in Indian cooking and are an excellent source of protein and fibre. Some are cooked whole, some are puréed and made into soups or dhals, and some are combined with vegetables or meat. Beans and chickpeas should be soaked before cooking. Lentils do not need to be soaked. Red and green split lentils cook to a soft purée when left to simmer, and whole lentils hold their shape when cooked.

Black-eyed beans
These are small and cream-coloured, with a black spot or "eye". When cooked, black-eyed beans (peas) have a tender, creamy texture and a mild, smoky flavour. They are used widely in Indian cooking.

PREPARING AND COOKING BEANS AND PEAS
Beans and chickpeas should be boiled for at least 10 minutes at the start of cooking to destroy harmful toxins that may be present.

Wash the beans or chickpeas under cold running water, then place in a large bowl of fresh cold water and leave to soak overnight. Discard any pulses that float to the surface, drain and rinse again. Put in a large pan and cover with plenty of fresh cold water. Bring to the boil and boil rapidly for 10–15 minutes. Reduce the heat and simmer until tender. Drain and use as required.

Above: Chickpeas

Chana dhal
This round, yellow split lentil is similar in appearance to the yellow split pea, which will make a good substitute. It is cooked in a variety of vegetable dishes and can be deep-fried and mixed with spices for the Indian snack Bombay mix. Chana dhal is often used as a binding agent in Indian curries.

Chickpeas
These round, beige-coloured pulses have a strong, nutty flavour when cooked. As well as being used for curries, they are also ground into gram flour which is used in many Indian dishes, such as pakoras and bhajiyas, and are also added to Indian snacks.

Left: From left, haricot (navy) beans, red kidney beans and pinto beans

Flageolet beans
These white or pale green oval beans have a very mild, refreshing flavour.

Green lentils
Also known as continental lentils, these have a strong flavour and they retain their shape during cooking.

Haricot beans
These small, white oval beans come in different varieties. Known as navy beans in the United States, these are ideal for Indian cooking because they retain their shape and absorb flavours.

Kidney beans
These red-brown kidney-shaped beans have a distinctive flavour. They belong to the same family as the pinto bean.

Mung beans
These small, round green beans have a sweet flavour and creamy texture. They are the most commonly used bean for sprouting. Split mung beans are also used, often with rice.

Red split lentils
Another lentil that can be used for making dhal. Use instead of tuvar dhal.

Tuvar dhal
A dull orange-coloured split pea with a distinctive earthy flavour. Tuvar dhal is available plain and in an oily variety.

Urid dhal
This lentil is available split, either with the blackish hull retained or removed. It has quite a dry texture when cooked.

Above: Red lentils

Rice

This staple grain is served with almost every meal in some parts of India, so it is no surprise that the Indians have created a variety of ways of cooking it, each quite distinctive. Plain boiled rice is an everyday accompaniment; for special occasions and entertaining, it is often combined with other ingredients.

There is no definitive way to cook plain rice, but whatever the recipe, the aim is to produce dry, separate-grained rice that is cooked through yet still retains some bite. The secret is the amount of water added: the rice must be able to absorb it all.

Basmati rice

Known as the prince of rices, basmati is the recommended rice for Indian curries, not only because it is easy to cook and produces an excellent finished result, but because it has a cooling effect on hot and spicy curries. Basmati is a slender, long grain, milled rice grown in northern India, the Punjab, parts of Pakistan and in the foothills of the Himalayas. Its name means fragrant, and it has a distinctive and appealing aroma. After harvesting it is aged for a year, which gives it the characteristic flavour and a light, fluffy texture. Basmati can be used in almost any savoury dish, particularly curries or pilaus, and is the essential ingredient in biryanis. White and brown basmati rice are widely available from supermarkets and Indian food stores.

Above: White basmati, probably the most commonly eaten rice in India.

COOKING PLAIN BOILED RICE

Always make sure you use a tight-fitting lid for your rice pan. If you do not have a lid that fits tightly, you can either wrap a dishtowel around the lid or put some foil between the lid and the pan to make a snug fit. Try not to remove the lid until the rice is cooked. (The advantage of using just a lid is that you can tell when the rice is ready because steam begins to escape, visibly and rapidly.)

As a rough guide, allow 75g/3oz/ scant ½ cup rice per person.

1 Put the dry rice in a colander and rinse it under cold running water until the water runs clear.

2 Place the rice in a large, deep pan and pour in enough cold water to come 2cm/¾in above the surface of the rice. Add a pinch of salt and, if you like, 5ml/1 tsp vegetable oil, stir once and bring to the boil.

3 Stir once more, reduce the heat to the lowest possible setting and cover the pan with a tight-fitting lid.

4 Cook the rice for 12–15 minutes, then turn off the heat and leave the rice to stand, still tightly covered, for about 10 minutes.

5 Before serving, gently fluff up the rice with a fork or slotted rice spoon – the slotted spoon will help you to avoid breaking up the grains, which would make the rice mushy.

Below: Patna rice, a long grain rice native to eastern India.

Patna rice

This rice takes its name from Patna in eastern India. At one time, most of the long grain rice sold in Europe came from Patna, and the term was used loosely to mean any long grain rice, whatever its origin. The custom still persists in parts of the United States, but elsewhere Patna is used to describe the specific variety of rice grown in the eastern state of Bihar. Patna rice is used in the same way as other long grain rices, and is suitable for use wherever plain boiled rice is called for.

Breads

Breads are an integral part of any Indian meal. Most traditional Indian breads are unleavened, that is, made without any raising agent, and are made with whole-meal (whole-wheat) flour, known as chapati flour or atta.

Throughout India, breads vary from region to region, depending on local ingredients. Some breads are cooked dry on a hot griddle, while some are fried with a little oil, and others are deep-fried to make small savoury puffs. To enjoy Indian breads at their best they should be made just before you are ready to serve the meal, so that they can be eaten hot.

Naan
Probably the most well-known Indian bread outside India is naan, from the north of the country. Naan is made with plain (all-purpose) flour, yogurt and yeast; some contemporary recipes favour the use of a chemical raising agent such as bicarbonate of soda (baking soda) or self-raising (self-rising) flour as a leaven in place of yeast. The yogurt is important for the fermentation of the dough, and some naan are made entirely using a yogurt fermentation. Fermentation gives the bread its characteristic light, puffy texture and soft crust. The flavour comes partly from the soured yogurt and partly from the *tandoor*, which is the the clay oven, sunk into the ground, in which the bread is traditionally cooked. The bread is flattened against the blisteringly hot walls of the oven and the pull of gravity produces the characteristic teardrop shape. As the dough scorches and puffs up, it produces a bread that is soft and crisp. Naan can be eaten with almost any meat or vegetable dish. There are many types of flavoured naan sold commercially, including plain, coriander (cilantro) and garlic, and masala naan.

Chapatis
The favourite bread of central and southern India is the chapati, a thin, flat,

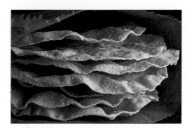

Above: Chapatis and parathas

Below: Poppadums

unleavened bread made from ground wholemeal flour. Chapatis are cooked on a hot *tava*, a concave-shaped Indian griddle. Chapatis have a light texture and fairly bland flavour, which makes them an ideal accompaniment for highly spiced curry dishes. Spices can be added to the flour to give more flavour.

Rotis
There are many variations of chapatis, including *rotis* and *dana rotis*. These are unleavened breads, made using chapati flour to which ghee, oil, celery seeds and/or fresh coriander are added. They are rolled out thinly and cooked like chapatis.

Parathas
A paratha is similar to a chapati except that it contains ghee, which gives the bread a richer flavour and flakier texture. Parathas are much thicker than chapatis and are shallow-fried.

Plain parathas are often eaten for lunch, and they go well with most vegetable dishes. They can be stuffed with various fillings, the most popular being spiced potato. Stuffed parathas are served as a snack.

Pooris
Another popular variation on the chapati is the poori, which is a small, deep-fried puffy bread made from chapati flour. Pooris are best eaten hot and are traditionally served for breakfast. They can be plain or flavoured with spices, such as cumin, turmeric and chilli powder, which are mixed into the dough. Pooris are often served with fish or vegetable curries.

Poppadums
These are now widely available outside of India. These are large, thin crisp discs, which can be bought ready-cooked or ready-to-cook. In India they are served with vegetarian meals. They are sold in markets and by street vendors, and are available plain, flavoured with spices or seasoned with ground red or black pepper. The dough is generally made from dried beans, but can also be made from potatoes or sago. It is thinly rolled and left to dry in the sun. Poppadums are cooked either by deep-frying or placing under a hot grill (broiler).

Above: Naan

Equipment and Utensils

While a reasonably stocked kitchen will provide most of the equipment needed for cooking Indian curries, it may still be necessary to invest in one or two more specialist items to ensure perfect results.

Chapati griddle
Known in India as a *tava*, the chapati griddle allows chapatis and other breads to be cooked without burning. The heavy wrought-iron pan can also be used to dry-roast spices. Traditionally, the griddle would be set over an open fire but it will work equally well on a gas flame or electric hob.

Chapati rolling board
This round wooden board on short stubby legs is used to mould breads into shape; the extra height provided by the legs helps to disperse excess dry flour. A wooden pastry board makes an appropriate substitute.

Chapati rolling pin
The traditional chapati rolling pin is thinner in shape than Western rolling pins, and comes in many different sizes. Use whichever size feels the most comfortable in your hands.

Chapati spoon
The square, flat-headed chapati spoon is used for turning roasting breads on the hot chapati griddle. A fish slice or spatula can also be used.

Grinding stone and roller
The traditional oblong grinding stone is the Indian equivalent of the Western food processor. Fresh and dry ingredients are placed on the heavy slate stone, which is marked with notches to hold ingredients in place. The heavy roller is then used to pulverize the ingredients against the stone.

Table sizzler
This heated appliance allows food that is still cooking to be brought to the dinner table ready for serving. It is very useful for entertaining.

Slotted spoon
Stirring cooked, drained rice with a slotted spoon will make the rice soft and fluffy by introducing air between the grains; slots in the spoon prevent the grains from breaking as the rice is moved around the pan. The spoon is also used to remove foods from hot oil or other cooking liquids.

Above: Chapati griddle and chapati rolling pin

Left: Grinding stone and roller, tongs and stainless steel mortar and pestle

Below right: Heat diffuser

Heat diffuser
Many curries are left to simmer slowly over a low heat, and a heat diffuser will help to prevent burning on the base of the karahi or wok. Check that the diffuser can be used on your type of hob (stovetop).

Below:
A traditional
cast-iron karahi

Karahi
Basically an Indian frying pan, the karahi is similar to a wok but is more rounded in shape and is made of heavier metal: originally, the karahi would be cast iron, although a variety of metals are now used. Karahis are available in various sizes, including small ones for single portions. Serving food from a karahi at the table adds an authentic touch to the meal.

Wok
This is a good substitute for a karahi for cooking most types of Indian food. Buy the appropriate wok for your cooker. Round-bottomed woks can be used on gas hobs only; flat-bottomed woks are for use on electric hobs.

Spice mill
An electric spice mill is useful for grinding small quantities of ingredients such as spices. A coffee grinder – used solely for spices – makes a good substitute.

Stainless steel mortar and pestle
These are ideal for grinding small amounts of wet ingredients, such as fresh root ginger, chillies and garlic. Stainless steel is very durable and will not retain the strong flavours of the spices.

Stone mortar and pestle
A heavy granite mortar and pestle is used to grind small amounts of ingredients, both wet and dry.

Pastry brush
Use for brushing and basting meats and vegetables lightly with oil before and during grilling (broiling).

Balloon whisk
A metal whisk is useful for beating yogurt and dairy or coconut cream before adding to recipes.

Knives
Kitchen knives in a range of sizes are essential. Keep knives sharp to make it easier to chop ingredients and to ensure neat edges when cutting.

Stainless steel pans
Quality kitchen pans in various sizes are essential for cooking rice, vegetables, meats and other ingredients. A heavy non-stick frying pan can be used in place of a karahi or wok.

Above: *Stainless steel pans*

Colander and sieve
Use for draining boiled rice and vegetables, and for straining ingredients. Choose long-handled, sturdy utensils made from stainless steel – the handles allow you to stand back to pour steaming rice out of a pan, and the utensils will not discolour like plastic ones.

Food processor
This is essential for blending the ingredients. Smaller quantities can be ground in a mortar and pestle.

Right:
From left,
stainless steel
colander and
sieve

Soups
and Appetizers

THE CONCEPT of starting a meal with a tempting morsel to whet the appetite is not widely adopted in India, where it is usual for most of the dishes to be brought to the table at the same time. Snacks, on the other hand, are hugely popular, and a samosa or spiced potato cake goes down well at any time of day.

India has only a few soups, but those that exist are famous the world over. South Indian Pepper Water and Chicken Mulligatawny are substantial enough to be served solo, or with deliciously warmed naan as an accompaniment. Both of these soups are highly spiced, whereas Tomato and Coriander

Soup is simply soothing, and a perfect antidote to summer heat. Also included in this chapter are delicious fish, chicken and meaty appetizers, from koftas to kebabs, bhajias to Indian-style pancakes, tikka to tandoori. All are ideal for serving either as Western-style first courses, as snacks or light suppers.

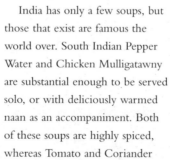

Tomato and Coriander Soup

Although soups are not often eaten in India or Pakistan, tomato soup bucks the trend and is very popular. This is excellent on a cold winter's day.

INGREDIENTS

Serves 4

675g/1½lb tomatoes, peeled
  and chopped
15ml/1 tbsp oil
1 bay leaf
4 spring onions (scallions), chopped
5ml/1 tsp salt
2.5ml/½ tsp crushed garlic
5ml/1 tsp crushed black peppercorns
30ml/2 tbsp chopped fresh
  coriander (cilantro)
750ml/1¼ pints/generous 3 cups water
15ml/1 tbsp cornflour (cornstarch)
30ml/2 tbsp single (light) cream,
  to garnish (optional)

NUTRITIONAL NOTES	
Per Portion	
Energy	76Kcals/315KJ
Fat	3.40g
Saturated Fat	0.43g
Carbohydrate	10.10g
Fibre	1.90g

COOK'S TIP

If the only fresh tomatoes available are rather pale and under-ripe, add 15ml/1 tbsp tomato purée to the pan with the chopped tomatoes to enhance the colour and flavour of the soup.

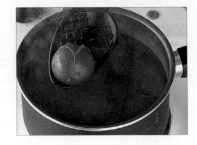

1 To peel the tomatoes, plunge them in very hot water, leave for 30 seconds, then take them out. The skin should now peel off easily. If not, put the tomatoes back in the water for a little longer. Once they have been peeled, roughly chop the tomatoes.

2 In a medium heavy pan, heat the oil and fry the tomatoes, bay leaf and spring onions for a few minutes until soft.

3 Gradually add the salt, garlic, peppercorns and coriander. Pour in the water. Stir, then simmer gently over a low heat for 15–20 minutes.

4 Meanwhile, dissolve the cornflour in a little cold water to form a thick creamy paste.

5 Remove the soup from the heat and leave to cool slightly for a few minutes. Press through a sieve, or purée in a blender or food processor.

6 Return the puréed soup to the pan, add the cornflour mixture and stir over a gentle heat for about 3 minutes until thickened.

7 Pour the soup into individual serving dishes and garnish with a swirl of cream, if using. Serve hot.

Spiced Cauliflower Soup

Light and tasty, this creamy, mildly spicy vegetable soup is multi-purpose. It makes a wonderful warming first course, an appetizing quick meal and is delicious chilled.

INGREDIENTS

Serves 4–6

1 large potato, diced
1 small cauliflower, chopped
1 onion, chopped
15ml/1 tbsp oil
1 garlic clove, crushed
15ml/1 tbsp grated fresh root ginger
10ml/2 tsp ground turmeric
5ml/1 tsp cumin seeds
5ml/1 tsp black mustard seeds
10ml/2 tsp ground coriander
1 litre/1¾ pints/4 cups vegetable stock
300ml/½ pint/1¼ cups natural (plain)
   low fat yogurt
salt and black pepper
fresh coriander (cilantro),
   to garnish

NUTRITIONAL NOTES	
Per Portion (4)	
Energy	188Kcals/789KJ
Fat	5.40g
Saturated Fat	0.77g
Carbohydrate	24.60g
Fibre	3.00g

──────── COOK'S TIP ────────

To make home-made vegetable stock, add to 3.5 litres/6 pints/15 cups of water, 2 sliced leeks, 3 chopped celery sticks, 1 chopped onion, 1 chopped parsnip, 1 seeded and chopped yellow (bell) pepper, 3 crushed garlic cloves, fresh herbs and 45ml/3 tbsp light soy sauce. Season, then slowly bring to the boil. Lower the heat and simmer for 30 minutes, stirring from time to time. Leave to cool. Strain, discard the vegetables, and use the stock as indicated in the recipe.

1 Put the potato, cauliflower and onion into a large heavy pan with the oil and 45ml/3 tbsp water. Heat until hot and bubbling, then stir well, cover the pan and turn the heat down. Continue cooking the mixture for about 10 minutes.

2 Add the garlic, ginger and spices. Stir well, and cook for another 2 minutes, stirring occasionally. Pour in the stock and season well. Bring to the boil, then cover and simmer for about 20 minutes. Purée in a food processor and return to the pan. Stir in the yogurt, adjust the seasoning, and serve garnished with coriander or parsley.

Yogurt and Chilli Soup

Hot chillies, cool yogurt – this is an unusual and tasty soup.

INGREDIENTS

Serves 2–3
450ml/³/₄ pint/scant 2 cups natural
   (plain) low fat yogurt, beaten
60ml/4 tbsp gram flour
2.5ml/½ tsp chilli powder
2.5ml/½ tsp ground turmeric
salt, to taste
2 fresh green chillies, finely chopped
30ml/2 tbsp vegetable oil
4 whole dried red chillies
5ml/1 tsp cumin seeds
3–4 curry leaves
3 garlic cloves, crushed
5cm/2in piece of fresh root
   ginger, crushed
fresh coriander (cilantro) leaves,
   chopped, to garnish

NUTRITIONAL NOTES	
Per Portion (4)	
Energy	321Kcals/1344KJ
Fat	13.7g
Saturated Fat	2.5g
Carbohydrate	33.8g
Fibre	1.5g

1 Mix the yogurt, gram flour, chilli powder, turmeric and salt in a bowl. Press the mixture through a strainer into a pan. Add the green chillies and simmer for 10 minutes, without boiling, stirring occasionally.

2 Heat the oil in a heavy pan and fry the remaining spices, crushed garlic and fresh ginger until the dried chillies turn black.

_____ COOK'S TIP _____

For a lower fat version drain off some of the oil before adding it to the yogurt. Adjust the amount of chillies according to how hot you want the soup to be.

3 Pour the oil and the spices over the yogurt soup, cover the pan and leave to rest for 5 minutes off the heat. Mix well and gently reheat for a further 5 minutes. Ladle into warmed soup bowls and serve hot, garnished with the coriander leaves.

Spicy Chicken and Mushroom Soup

This creamy chicken soup has just enough spice to make it a great winter warmer, but not so much that it overwhelms the flavour of the mushrooms.

INGREDIENTS

Serves 4

225g/8oz boneless chicken, skinned
75g/3oz/6 tbsp ghee or unsalted (sweet) butter
2.5ml/½ tsp crushed garlic
5ml/1 tsp garam masala
5ml/1 tsp crushed black peppercorns
5ml/1 tsp salt
1.5ml/¼ tsp grated nutmeg
1 medium leek, sliced
75g/3oz/1 cup mushrooms, sliced
50g/2oz/⅓ cup corn
300ml/½ pint/1¼ cups water
250ml/8fl oz/1 cup single (light) cream
15ml/1 tbsp chopped fresh coriander (cilantro)
5ml/1 tsp crushed dried red chillies (optional)

1 Cut the chicken pieces into very fine strips.

2 Melt the ghee or butter in a medium pan. Lower the heat slightly and add the garlic and garam masala. Lower the heat even further and add the black peppercorns, salt and nutmeg. Finally, add the chicken pieces, sliced leek, mushrooms and corn, and cook, stirring constantly, for 5–7 minutes, or until the chicken is cooked through.

────── VARIATION ──────

For a vegetarian version of this soup, omit the chicken and use 350g/12oz/4½ cups mushrooms instead.

3 Remove from the heat and leave to cool slightly. Transfer three-quarters of the mixture into a food processor or blender. Add the water and process for about 1 minute.

4 Pour the resulting purée back into the pan and stir with the rest of the mixture. Bring to the boil over a medium heat. Lower the heat and stir in the cream.

5 Add the fresh coriander (cilantro) and taste for seasoning. Serve hot, garnished with the crushed red chillies, if you like.

NUTRITIONAL NOTES	
Per Portion	
Energy	342Kcals/1417KJ
Fat	28.5g
Saturated Fat	17.6g
Carbohydrate	4.8g
Fibre	1g

Chicken and Almond Soup

This soup makes an excellent appetizer and served with naan bread will also make a satisfying lunch or supper dish.

INGREDIENTS

Serves 4

75g/3 oz/6 tbsp ghee or unsalted (sweet) butter
1 medium leek, chopped
2.5ml/½ tsp shredded fresh root ginger
75g/3oz/1 cup ground almonds
5ml/1 tsp salt
2.5ml/½ tsp crushed black peppercorns
1 fresh green chilli, chopped
1 medium carrot, sliced
50g/2oz/½ cup frozen peas
115g/4oz/¾ cup cubed skinned chicken breast fillet
15ml/1 tbsp chopped fresh coriander (cilantro), plus extra to garnish
450ml/¾ pint/scant 2 cups water
250ml/8fl oz/1 cup single (light) cream

1 Melt the ghee or butter in a large karahi, wok or deep pan, and sauté the leek with the ginger until softened.

2 Lower the heat and tip in the ground almonds, salt, peppercorns, chilli, carrot, peas and chicken. Fry for about 10 minutes or until the chicken is completely cooked, stirring constantly. Add the chopped fresh coriander.

3 Remove from the heat and leave to cool slightly. Transfer the mixture to a food processor or blender and process for about 1½ minutes. Pour in the water and blend for a further 30 seconds.

NUTRITIONAL NOTES	
Per Portion	
Energy	429Kcals/1777KJ
Fat	39.2g
Saturated Fat	18.4g
Carbohydrate	5.5g
Fibre	2.7g

4 Pour back into the pan and bring to the boil, stirring. Lower the heat and gradually stir in the cream. Cook gently for a further 2 minutes, stirring occasionally. Serve garnished with more coriander.

South Indian Pepper Water

This soothing broth is perfect for winter evenings. The quantity of lemon juice can be adjusted to taste, but this dish should be distinctly sour.

INGREDIENTS

Serves 4–6
30ml/2 tbsp vegetable oil
2.5ml/½ tsp black pepper
5ml/1 tsp cumin seeds
2.5ml/½ tsp mustard seeds
1.5ml/¼ tsp asafoetida
2.5ml/½ tsp ground turmeric
2 dried red chillies
4–6 curry leaves
2 garlic cloves, crushed
300ml/½ pint/1¼ cups tomato juice
juice of 2 lemons
120ml/4fl oz/½ cup water
salt, to taste
fresh coriander (cilantro), to garnish

1 Heat the oil in a large pan and fry the next 8 ingredients until the chillies are nearly black and the garlic is golden brown.

2 Lower the heat and pour in the tomato juice, lemon juice and water. Bring to the boil then simmer for 10 minutes. Season to taste with salt. Pour into heated bowls, garnish with the chopped coriander if you like, and serve.

NUTRITIONAL NOTES	
Per Portion	
Energy	60Kcals/250KJ
Fat	5.5g
Saturated Fat	0.7g
Carbohydrate	2.3g
Fibre	0.5g

Chicken Mulligatawny

This world famous broth hails from the days of the British Raj.

INGREDIENTS

Serves 4–6
900g/2lb boneless chicken portions, skinned
600ml/1 pint/2½ cups water
6 green cardamom pods
5cm/2in piece cinnamon stick
4–6 curry leaves
15ml/1 tbsp ground coriander
5ml/1 tsp ground cumin
2.5ml/½ tsp ground turmeric
3 garlic cloves, crushed
1 onion, finely chopped
115g/4oz creamed coconut (coconut cream)
juice of 2 lemons
deep-fried onions, to garnish

1 Place the chicken in a large pan with the water. Bring to the boil, then simmer for about 1 hour or until the chicken is tender.

2 Skim the surface, then remove the chicken pieces with a slotted spoon and keep warm.

3 Reheat the stock in the pan. Add all the remaining ingredients, except the chicken and deep-fried onions. Simmer for 10–15 minutes, then strain and return the chicken to the soup. Reheat the soup and serve garnished with the deep-fried onions.

NUTRITIONAL NOTES	
Per Portion	
Energy	444Kcals/1860KJ
Fat	22.3g
Saturated Fat	17.7g
Carbohydrate	5g
Fibre	0.5g

Onion Bhajias

A favourite snack in India, Bhajias consist of a savoury vegetable mixture in a spicy batter. They can be served as an appetizer or as a side dish with curries.

INGREDIENTS

Makes 20–25

225g/8oz/2 cups gram flour
2.5ml/½ tsp chilli powder
5ml/1 tsp ground turmeric
5ml/1 tsp baking powder
1.5ml/¼ tsp asafoetida
salt, to taste
2.5ml/½ tsp each, nigella, fennel, cumin and onion seeds, coarsely crushed
2 large onions, finely sliced
2 fresh green chillies, finely chopped
50g/2oz/2 cups fresh coriander (cilantro), chopped
water, to mix
vegetable oil, for deep-frying

2 In a bowl mix together the flour, chilli powder, ground turmeric, baking powder and asafoetida. Add salt to taste. Sift the mixture into a large mixing bowl.

3 Add the coarsely crushed seeds, onion slices, green chillies and fresh coriander and toss together well.

4 Add enough cold water to make a paste, then stir in more water to make a thick batter that coats the onions and spices.

5 Heat enough oil in a karahi or wok for deep-frying. Drop spoonfuls of the mixture into the hot oil and fry the bhajias until they are golden brown. Leave enough space to turn the bhajias. Drain well and serve hot.

VARIATION

This versatile batter can be used with other vegetables, including okra, cauliflower and broccoli.

1 Using a sharp knife, slice the onions into thin rounds. Separate the slices and set them aside on a plate.

NUTRITIONAL NOTES	
Per Portion	
Energy	157Kcals/650KJ
Fat	12.7g
Saturated Fat	1.5g
Carbohydrate	8.2g
Fibre	0.9g

Vegetable Samosas

A selection of highly spiced vegetables in a pastry casing makes these samosas a delicious snack at any time of the day.

INGREDIENTS

Makes 28
14 sheets of filo pastry, thawed and
    wrapped in a damp dishtowel
oil for brushing the pastries

For the filling
3 large potatoes, boiled and
    roughly mashed
75g/3oz/¾ cup frozen peas, thawed
50g/2oz/⅓ cup canned
    sweetcorn, drained
5ml/1 tsp ground coriander
5ml/1 tsp ground cumin
5ml/1 tsp dry mango powder (*amchur*)
1 small onion, finely chopped
2 fresh green chillies, finely chopped
30ml/2 tbsp coriander (cilantro)
    leaves, chopped
30ml/2 tbsp fresh mint
    leaves, chopped
juice of 1 lemon
salt, to taste

NUTRITIONAL NOTES	
Per Samosa	
Energy	50Kcals/205KJ
Fat	0.78g
Saturated Fat	0.10g
Carbohydrate	9.40g
Fibre	0.50g

1 Preheat the oven to 200°C/400°F/ Gas 6. Cut each sheet of filo pastry in half lengthways and fold each piece in half lengthways to give 28 thin strips. Lightly brush with oil.

___ COOK'S TIP ___

Work with one or two sheets of filo pastry at a time and keep the rest covered with a damp dishtowel to prevent it drying out.

2 Toss all the filling ingredients together in a large mixing bowl until they are well blended. Adjust the seasoning with salt and lemon juice if necessary.

3 Using one strip of the pastry at a time, place 15ml/1 tbsp of the filling mixture at one end and fold the pastry diagonally over. Continue folding to form a triangle shape. Brush the samosas with oil. Bake for 10–15 minutes, until golden brown.

Curried Lamb Samosas

Filo pastry is perfect for making samosas. Once you've mastered folding them, you'll be amazed how quick they are to make.

INGREDIENTS

Makes 12

25g/1oz/2 tbsp butter
225g/8oz/1 cup minced (ground) lamb
30ml/2 tbsp mild curry paste
12 sheets of filo pastry, thawed and
   wrapped in a damp dishtowel
salt and black pepper

1 Heat a little of the butter in a large pan and add the lamb. Fry for 5–6 minutes, stirring occasionally until browned. Stir in the curry paste and cook for 1–2 minutes. Season and set aside. Preheat the oven to 200°C/400°F/Gas 6.

2 Melt the remaining butter in a pan. Cut the pastry sheets in half lengthways. Brush one strip of pastry with butter, then lay another strip on top and brush with more butter.

3 Place a spoonful of lamb in the corner of the strip and fold over to form a triangle at one end. Keep folding over in the same way to form a triangular package.

4 Brush with butter and place on a baking sheet. Repeat using the remaining pastry and filling. Bake for 10–15 minutes until golden. Serve hot.

NUTRITIONAL NOTES	
Per Portion	
Energy	81Kcals/341KJ
Fat	5.2g
Saturated Fat	2.4g
Carbohydrate	4.9g
Fibre	0.2g

Spiced Potato Cakes with Chickpeas

This is a typical Mumbai street snack; the kind that locals would happily eat while walking along the beach or watching a cricket match. It is the kind of food that unites different communities.

INGREDIENTS

Makes 10–12
30ml/2 tbsp vegetable oil
30ml/2 tbsp ground coriander
30ml/2 tbsp ground cumin
2.5ml/½ tsp ground turmeric
2.5ml/½ tsp salt
2.5ml/½ tsp granulated sugar
30ml/2 tbsp gram flour, mixed with
    a little water to make a paste
450g/1lb/3 cups cooked
    chickpeas, drained
2 fresh green chillies, chopped
5cm/2in piece fresh root
    ginger, crushed
75g/3oz/1 cup fresh coriander
    (cilantro), chopped
2 firm tomatoes, chopped
fresh mint sprigs, to garnish

For the potato cakes
450g/1lb potatoes, boiled and mashed
4 fresh green chillies, finely chopped
50g/2oz fresh coriander (cilantro),
    finely chopped
7.5ml/1½ tsp ground cumin
5ml/1 tsp dry mango powder (amchur)
vegetable oil, for shallow frying
salt

1 To prepare the chickpeas, heat the oil in a karahi, wok or large pan. Add the coriander, cumin, turmeric, salt, sugar and gram flour paste and cook until the water has evaporated and the oil has separated.

2 Add the chickpeas to the spices in the pan, and stir in the chopped chillies, ginger, fresh coriander and tomatoes. Toss the ingredients well and simmer gently for about 5 minutes. Transfer to a serving dish and keep warm.

3 To make the potato cakes, place the mashed potato in a large bowl and add the green chillies, chopped fresh coriander, cumin, dry mango powder and salt. Mix together until all the ingredients are well blended.

4 Using your hands, shape the potato mixture into little cakes. Heat the oil in a shallow frying pan and fry the cakes on both sides until golden brown. Transfer to a serving dish, garnish with mint sprigs and serve with the spicy chickpeas.

NUTRITIONAL NOTES	
Per Portion	
Energy	91Kcals/383KJ
Fat	3.3g
Saturated Fat	0.4g
Carbohydrate	11.9g
Fibre	2.2g

Crisp Fried Aubergine

The spicy gram flour coating on these slices is deliciously crisp, providing the perfect contrast to the succulent aubergine. Choose a large aubergine with an unblemished, glossy skin.

INGREDIENTS

Serves 4

50g/2oz/½ cup gram flour
15ml/1 tbsp semolina or ground rice
2.5ml/½ tsp onion seeds
5ml/1 tsp cumin seeds
2.5ml/½ tsp fennel seeds or aniseeds
2.5–5ml/½–1 tsp hot chilli powder
2.5ml/½ tsp salt, or to taste
1 large aubergine (eggplant)
vegetable oil, for deep-frying

NUTRITIONAL NOTES	
Per Portion	
Energy	288Kcals/1192KJ
Fat	25.4g
Saturated Fat	3.1g
Carbohydrate	13.7g
Fibre	1.4g

1 Sift the gram flour into a large mixing bowl and add all the remaining ingredients except the aubergine and the vegetable oil.

COOK'S TIP

Fennel and aniseeds aid digestion, and most deep-fried Indian recipes use them.

2 Halve the aubergine lengthways and cut each half into 5mm/¼in thick slices. Rinse them and shake off the excess water, but do not pat dry. With some of the water still clinging to the slices, add them to the spiced gram flour mixture. Toss them around until they are evenly coated with the flour. Use a spoon if necessary to ensure that all the flour is used.

3 Heat the oil in a deep-fat fryer or other suitable pan over a medium-high heat. If you have a thermometer, check that the oil has reached 190°C/375°F. Alternatively, drop a small piece of day-old bread into the oil. If it floats immediately, the oil has reached the right temperature.

4 Fry the spice-coated aubergine slices in a single layer. Avoid overcrowding the pan as this will lower the oil temperature, resulting in a soggy texture. Fry until the aubergines are crisp and well browned. Drain on kitchen paper and serve with a chutney.

Glazed Garlic Prawns

It is best to peel the prawns for this dish as it helps them to absorb maximum flavour. Serve with salad as a first course or with rice and accompaniments for a more substantial meal.

INGREDIENTS

Serves 4

15ml/1 tbsp oil
3 garlic cloves, roughly chopped
15–20 cooked king prawns (jumbo shrimp)
3 tomatoes, chopped
2.5ml/½ tsp salt
5ml/1 tsp crushed red chillies
5ml/1 tsp lemon juice
15ml/1 tbsp mango chutney
1 fresh green chilli, chopped
fresh coriander (cilantro) sprigs, to garnish

NUTRITIONAL NOTES	
Per Portion	
Energy	73Kcals/302KJ
Fat	3.30g
Saturated Fat	0.38g
Carbohydrate	4.90g
Fibre	0.80g

1 Heat the oil in a medium heavy pan. Add the garlic and cook gently for a few minutes.

COOK'S TIP

Use a skewer or the point of a knife to remove the black intestinal vein running down the back of the prawns (shrimp).

2 Set aside 4 whole prawns for the garnish. Peel the remainder. Lower the heat and add the chopped tomatoes to the pan with the salt, crushed red chillies, lemon juice, mango chutney and fresh green chilli. Stir gently to mix and cook for 2–3 minutes.

3 Add the peeled prawns, increase the heat and stir-fry until heated through. Transfer the prawns to a serving dish. Serve garnished with fresh coriander sprigs. Add a whole cooked prawn, in the shell, to each portion.

Prawn and Vegetable Kebabs

This light and refreshing first course, with its delicate tang of coriander and lemon juice, looks great on a bed of lettuce leaves, and makes a perfect summer starter at a barbecue. To upgrade the recipe to a light lunch dish, simply add some Peshwari naan and follow with a mango sorbet.

INGREDIENTS

Serves 4

30ml/2 tbsp chopped fresh
coriander (cilantro)
5ml/1 tsp salt
2 fresh green chillies
45ml/3 tbsp lemon juice
30ml/2 tbsp oil
20 cooked king prawns
(jumbo shrimp), peeled
1 medium courgette (zucchini),
thickly sliced
1 medium onion, cut into 8 chunks
8 cherry tomatoes
8 baby corn cobs
mixed salad leaves, to serve

NUTRITIONAL NOTES	
Per Portion	
Energy	183Kcals/767KJ
Fat	7.70g
Saturated Fat	1.04g
Carbohydrate	4.50g
Fibre	1.30g

1 Place the chopped coriander, salt, chillies, lemon juice and oil in a food processor and process for a few seconds to form a paste.

2 Scrape the spice paste from the food processor and transfer it to a medium mixing bowl.

3 Add the peeled prawns to the spices and stir to coat well. Cover the bowl and set aside to marinate for about 30 minutes.

4 Preheat the grill (broiler) to very hot. Arrange the vegetables and prawns alternately on 4 skewers.

5 Reduce the temperature of the grill to medium and grill (broil) the prawn kebabs for 5–7 minutes until cooked and browned, turning once.

6 Serve immediately on a bed of mixed salad leaves.

--- COOK'S TIP ---

King prawns (jumbo shrimp) are a luxury, but well worth buying for a special dinner. Their size means that they remain succulent when grilled (broiled). The spice marinade gives extra protection.

Prawn and Spinach Pancakes

Serve these delicious filled pancakes hot. They can be eaten in the hand, but are rather messy, so do provide plenty of paper napkins if you choose the casual approach. Try to use red onions for this recipe, although they are not essential.

INGREDIENTS

Makes 4–6 pancakes
For the pancakes
175g/6oz/1½ cups plain (all-purpose) flour
2.5ml/½ tsp salt
3 eggs
350ml/12fl oz/1½ cups semi-skimmed (low-fat) milk
15g/½oz/1 tbsp low-fat spread
1 tomato, quartered, fresh coriander (cilantro) sprigs and lemon wedges, to garnish

For the filling
30ml/2 tbsp oil
2 medium red onions, sliced
2.5ml/½ tsp crushed garlic
2.5cm/1in piece fresh root ginger, shredded
5ml/1 tsp chilli powder
5ml/1 tsp garam masala
5ml/1 tsp salt
2 tomatoes, sliced
225g/8oz frozen leaf spinach, thawed and drained
115g/4oz/1 cup frozen cooked peeled prawns (shelled shrimp), thawed
30ml/2 tbsp chopped fresh coriander (cilantro)

NUTRITIONAL NOTES	
Per Portion (6)	
Energy	389Kcals/1633KJ
Fat	14.70g
Saturated Fat	2.83g
Carbohydrate	48.80g
Fibre	4.00g

1 To make the pancakes, sift the flour and salt together. Beat the eggs and add to the flour, beating continuously. Gradually stir in the milk. Leave the batter to stand for 1 hour.

2 Make the filling. Heat the oil in a deep frying pan and fry the sliced onions until golden.

3 Gradually add the garlic, ginger, chilli powder, garam masala and salt, followed by the tomatoes and spinach, stirring constantly.

4 Add the prawns and chopped coriander. Cook for a further 5–7 minutes or until any excess liquid has been absorbed. Keep warm.

5 Heat about 2.5ml/½ tsp of the low fat margarine in a 25cm/10in non-stick frying pan or pancake pan. Pour in about one-quarter of the pancake batter, tilting the pan so that the batter spreads well, coats the bottom of the pan and is evenly distributed.

6 When fine bubbles begin to appear on the surface, flip the pancake over using a spatula and cook for a further minute or so. Transfer to a plate and keep warm. Cook the remaining pancakes in the same way.

7 Fill the pancakes with the spinach and prawns. Serve warm, garnished with the tomato, coriander sprigs and lemon wedges.

COOK'S TIP

To keep the pancakes warm while cooking the remainder, pile them on top of each other on a plate with a sheet of greaseproof paper between each one to prevent them sticking. Place in a low oven.

Prawns with Pomegranate Seeds

This pretty dish makes an impressive appetizer, and is delicious served with a mixed salad.

INGREDIENTS

Serves 4
5ml/1 tsp crushed garlic
5ml/1 tsp grated fresh root ginger
5ml/1 tsp coarsely ground
   pomegranate seeds
5ml/1 tsp ground coriander
5ml/1 tsp salt
5ml/1 tsp chilli powder
30ml/2 tbsp tomato purée (paste)
60ml/4 tbsp water
45ml/3 tbsp chopped fresh
   coriander (cilantro)
30ml/2 tbsp corn oil
12 large cooked prawns (shrimp)
1 medium onion, sliced into rings

1 Put the garlic, ginger, pomegranate seeds, ground coriander, salt, chilli powder, tomato purée and water into a bowl. Stir in 30ml/2 tbsp of the chopped coriander. Add the oil and mix well.

2 Peel the prawns, rinse them gently and pat them dry on kitchen paper. Using a sharp knife, make a small slit at the back of each prawn and remove the black vein. Open out each prawn to make a butterfly shape.

NUTRITIONAL NOTES	
Per Portion	
Energy	88Kcals/364KJ
Fat	5.8g
Saturated Fat	0.8g
Carbohydrate	4g
Fibre	0.7g

3 Add the prawns to the spice mixture, making sure they are all well coated. Leave to marinate for about 2 hours.

4 Meanwhile, cut four squares of foil, about 20 × 20cm/8 × 8in. Preheat the oven to 230°C/450°F/Gas 8. When the prawns are ready, place 3 prawns and a few onion rings on each square of foil, garnishing each with a little fresh coriander, and fold up into little packages. Bake for about 12–15 minutes and open up the foil to serve.

Grilled Prawns

Prawns taste delicious when grilled, especially if they are first flavoured with spices.

INGREDIENTS

Serves 4–6
18 large cooked prawns (shrimp)
60ml/4 tbsp lemon juice
5ml/1 tsp salt
5ml/1 tsp chilli powder
5ml/1 tsp crushed garlic
7.5ml/1½ tsp soft light brown sugar
45ml/3 tbsp corn oil, plus extra
   for basting
30ml/2 tbsp chopped fresh coriander
   (cilantro)
1 fresh green chilli, sliced
1 tomato, sliced
1 small onion, cut into rings
lemon wedges

1 Peel the prawns and rinse them gently under cold water. Pat dry. Make a slit at the back of each prawn and remove the black vein. Open each prawn out into a butterfly shape.

2 Mix the remaining ingredients, except for the chilli, tomato, onion and lemon wedges, in a bowl. Stir in the prawns and marinate for 1 hour.

3 Preheat the grill (broiler) to the maximum setting. Place the green chilli, tomato slices and onion rings in a flameproof dish. Add the prawn mixture.

4 Grill (broil) for 10–15 minutes, basting several times with a brush dipped in oil. Serve immediately, garnished with the lemon wedges.

NUTRITIONAL NOTES	
Per Portion	
Energy	122Kcals/504KJ
Fat	8.7g
Saturated Fat	1.3g
Carbohydrate	1.9g
Fibre	0.4g

Quick-fried Prawns with Spices

These spicy prawns are stir-fried in moments to make a wonderful appetizer. This is fabulous finger food, so be sure to provide your guests with finger bowls.

INGREDIENTS

Serves 4

450g/1lb large raw prawns (shrimp)
2.5cm/1in fresh root ginger, grated
2 garlic cloves, crushed
5ml/1 tsp hot chilli powder
5ml/1 tsp ground turmeric
10ml/2 tsp black mustard seeds
seeds from 4 green cardamom
  pods, crushed
50g/2oz/4 tbsp ghee or butter
120ml/4fl oz/½ cup coconut milk
salt and black pepper
30–45ml/2–3 tbsp chopped fresh
  coriander, to garnish
naan bread, to serve

1 Peel the prawns carefully, leaving the tails attached.

2 Using a small sharp knife, make a slit along the back of each prawn and remove the dark vein. Rinse under cold running water, drain and pat dry.

3 Put the ginger, garlic, chilli powder, turmeric, mustard seeds and cardamom seeds in a bowl. Add the prawns and toss to coat completely in the spice mixture.

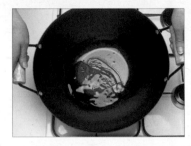

4 Heat a karahi or wok until hot. Add the ghee or butter and swirl it around until foaming.

5 Add the marinated prawns and stir-fry for 1–1½ minutes until they are just turning pink.

6 Stir in the coconut milk and simmer for 3–4 minutes until the prawns are just cooked through. Season to taste with salt and pepper. Sprinkle with the coriander and serve at once with naan bread.

NUTRITIONAL NOTES	
Per Portion	
Energy	196Kcals/817KJ
Fat	11.5g
Saturated Fat	7g
Carbohydrate	2.1g
Fibre	0g

Spicy Fried Fish Cubes

Firm white fish cubes, coated in a spicy tomato mixture and deep-fried, make an excellent appetizer. They are slightly messy for eating with the fingers, but taste so good that guests will waste no time in popping them into their mouths. Have plenty of paper napkins handy.

INGREDIENTS

Serves 4-6

675g/1½ lb cod fillet, or any other firm, white fish
1 medium onion
15ml/1 tbsp lemon juice
5ml/1 tsp salt
5ml/1 tsp grated garlic
5ml/1 tsp crushed dried red chillies
7.5ml/1½ tsp garam masala
30ml/2 tbsp chopped fresh coriander (cilantro)
2 medium tomatoes
30ml/2 tbsp cornflour (cornstarch)
150ml/¼ pint/⅔ cup corn oil

1 Skin the fish and remove any remaining bones. Cut it into small cubes. Place in a bowl, cover and put into the refrigerator to chill.

2 Using a sharp knife, cut the onion into thin slices. Put into a bowl and add the lemon juice and salt.

3 Add the garlic, crushed red chillies, garam masala and fresh coriander. Mix well.

4 Peel the tomatoes by dropping them into boiling water for a few seconds. Remove with a slotted spoon and gently peel off the skins. Chop the tomatoes roughly and add to the onion mixture in the bowl.

5 Tip the contents of the bowl into a food processor or blender and process for about 30 seconds. Remove the fish from the refrigerator. Pour the contents of the food processor or blender over the fish and mix well.

6 Add the cornflour and mix again until the fish pieces are well coated.

7 Heat the oil in a wok, karahi or deep pan. Lower the heat slightly and add the fish pieces, a few at a time. Turn them gently with a slotted spoon as they are liable to break easily. Cook for about 5 minutes until the fish is lightly browned.

8 Remove the fish pieces from the pan and drain on kitchen paper. Keep warm and continue frying the remaining fish. This dish is delicious served with apricot chutney and parathas.

NUTRITIONAL NOTES	
Per Portion	
Energy	434Kcals/1809KJ
Fat	26.5g
Saturated Fat	3.2g
Carbohydrate	18.2g
Fibre	1g

Goan-style Mussels

Mussels make a marvellous appetizer. Serve them Goan-style, in a fragrant coconut sauce. They take only minutes to cook, and the wonderful aroma will stimulate the most jaded appetite.

INGREDIENTS

Serves 4

900g/2lb live mussels
115g/4oz creamed coconut
   (coconut cream)
450ml/¾ pint/1¾ cups boiling water
45ml/3 tbsp oil
1 onion, finely chopped
3 garlic cloves, crushed
2.5cm/1in piece fresh root ginger,
   peeled and finely chopped
2.5ml/½ tsp ground turmeric
5ml/1 tsp ground cumin
5ml/1 tsp ground coriander
1.5ml/¼ tsp salt
chopped fresh coriander (cilantro),
   to garnish

1 Scrub the mussels under cold water and pull off any beards that remain attached to the shells. Discard any mussels that are open, or which fail to snap shut when tapped.

NUTRITIONAL NOTES	
Per Portion	
Energy	339Kcals/1405KJ
Fat	29.5g
Saturated Fat	18.3g
Carbohydrate	5g
Fibre	0.5g

2 Put the creamed coconut in a measuring jug or cup and pour in the boiling water. Stir with a wooden spoon until all the coconut has dissolved, then set aside until required. Heat the oil in a karahi, wok or heavy pan. Add the onion and fry for 5 minutes, stirring frequently.

3 Add the garlic and ginger and fry for 2 minutes. Stir in the turmeric, cumin, coriander and salt and fry for 2 minutes. Pour in the coconut liquid, stir well and bring to the boil. Reduce the heat and simmer for 5 minutes.

4 Add the mussels, cover the pan and cook over medium heat for 6–8 minutes, by which time all the mussels should have opened. Spoon the mussels on to a serving platter. If any of the mussels have failed to open, discard them immediately.

5 Pour the sauce over the mussels, garnish with the chopped fresh coriander, and serve.

Chilli Crabs

The ingredients of this delicious dish owe more to South-east Asia than India, and it is not surprising to discover that it comes from the eastern part of the country, close to the border with Myanmar.

INGREDIENTS

Serves 4

2 cooked crabs, about 675g/1½lb
1cm/½in cube shrimp paste
2 garlic cloves
2 fresh red chillies, seeded, or 5ml/ 1 tsp chopped chilli from a jar
1cm/½in fresh root ginger, peeled and sliced
60ml/4 tbsp sunflower oil
300ml/½ pint/1¼ cups tomato ketchup
15ml/1 tbsp dark brown sugar
150ml/¼ pint/⅔ cup warm water
4 spring onions (scallions), chopped
cucumber chunks and hot toast, to serve (optional)

1 Remove the large claws of one crab and turn on to its back, with the head facing away from you. Use your thumbs to push the body up from the main shell. Discard the stomach sac and "dead men's fingers", i.e. lungs and any green matter. Leave the creamy brown meat in the shell and cut the shell in half, with a cleaver or strong knife. Cut the body section in half and crack the claws with a sharp blow from a hammer or cleaver. Avoid splintering the claws. Repeat with the other crab.

2 Grind the shrimp paste, garlic, chillies and ginger to a paste in a food processor or with a pestle and mortar.

3 Heat a Kerahi or wok and add the oil. Fry the spice paste, stirring constantly, without browning.

4 Stir in the tomato ketchup, sugar and water and mix the sauce well. When just boiling, add all the crab pieces and toss in the sauce until well-coated and hot. Serve in a large bowl, sprinkled with the spring onions. Place in the centre of the table for everyone to help themselves. Accompany this dish with cool cucumber chunks and hot toast for mopping up the sauce, if you like.

NUTRITIONAL NOTES	
Per Portion	
Energy	276Kcals/1152KJ
Fat	14.3g
Saturated Fat	1.7g
Carbohydrate	25.4g
Fibre	0.7g

Spicy Crab with Coconut

This simple appetizer looks pretty and tastes delicious. Have all the ingredients ready and cook it just before calling your guests to the table. It needs no accompaniment other than some plain warm naan bread.

INGREDIENTS

Serves 4

40g/1½oz/½ cup desiccated (dry unsweetened shredded) coconut
2 garlic cloves
5cm/2in piece fresh root ginger, peeled and grated
2.5ml/½ tsp cumin seeds
1 small cinnamon stick
2.5ml/½ tsp ground turmeric
2 dried red chillies
15ml/1 tbsp coriander seeds
2.5ml/½ tsp poppy seeds
15ml/1 tbsp vegetable oil
1 medium onion, sliced
1 small green (bell) pepper, seeded and cut into strips
16 crab claws
fresh coriander (cilantro) sprigs, to garnish
150ml/¼ pint/⅔ cup natural (plain) low fat yogurt, to serve

2 Heat the oil in a karahi, wok or heavy pan. Add the onion slices and fry over a medium heat for 2–3 minutes, until softened but not coloured.

3 Stir in the green pepper strips and toss over the heat for 1 minute. Using a slotted spoon, remove the vegetables from the pan and place them in a bowl.

4 Place the pan over a high heat. When it is hot, add the crab claws and stir-fry for 2 minutes. Return the vegetables to the pan with the coconut mixture. Toss over the heat until the mixture is fragrant and the crab claws and vegetables are coated in the spices. Serve on individual plates, garnished with the coriander. Offer the cooling yogurt separately.

NUTRITIONAL NOTES	
Per Portion	
Energy	186Kcals/777KJ
Fat	10.1g
Saturated Fat	5.8g
Carbohydrate	4.8g
Fibre	2.6g

—————— COOK'S TIP ——————

The heat of this dish will depend upon the type of dried chillies you use. To make them somewhat less fiery, remove the seeds before processing the chillies with the coconut and other spices.

1 Put the shredded coconut in a food processor and add the garlic, ginger, cumin seeds, cinnamon stick, turmeric, red chillies, coriander and poppy seeds. Process until well blended.

Fish Cakes

Goan fish and shellfish are skilfully prepared with spices to make cakes of all shapes and sizes, while the rest of India makes fish kababs. Although haddock is used in this recipe, you can use other less expensive white fish, such as coley or whiting.

INGREDIENTS

Makes 20
450g/1lb skinned haddock or cod
2 potatoes, peeled, boiled and
    coarsely mashed
4 spring onions (scallions),
    finely chopped
4 fresh green chillies, finely chopped
5cm/2in piece fresh root
    ginger, crushed
a few fresh coriander (cilantro) and
    mint sprigs, chopped
2 eggs
breadcrumbs, for coating
vegetable oil, for shallow frying
salt and black pepper
lemon wedges and chilli sauce,
    to serve

_____ COOK'S TIP _____

For a quick version, used canned tuna in brine and omit step 1. Make sure the tuna is thoroughly drained before use.

NUTRITIONAL NOTES
Per Portion

Energy	56Kcals/234KJ
Fat	3.3g
Saturated Fat	0.5g
Carbohydrate	1.5g
Fibre	0.1g

1 Place the skinned fish in a lightly greased steamer and steam gently until cooked. Remove the steamer from the hob (stovetop) but leave the fish on the steaming tray until cool.

2 When the fish is cool, crumble it coarsely into a large bowl, using a fork. Mix in the mashed potatoes.

3 Add the spring onions, chillies, crushed ginger, chopped coriander and mint, and one of the eggs. Mix well and season to taste with salt and pepper.

4 Shape into cakes. Beat the remaining egg and dip the cakes in it, then coat with the breadcrumbs. Heat the oil and fry the cakes until brown on all sides. Serve as an appetizer or as a side dish, with the lemon wedges and chilli sauce.

Ginger Chicken Wings

Many people regard chicken wings as the best part of the bird. Served this way, they are certainly delicious.

INGREDIENTS

Serves 4

10–12 chicken wings, skinned
175ml/6fl oz/³/₄ cup natural (plain) low fat yogurt
7.5ml/1½ tsp crushed fresh root ginger
5ml/1 tsp salt
5ml/1 tsp Tabasco sauce
15ml/1 tbsp tomato ketchup
5ml/1 tsp crushed garlic
15ml/1 tbsp lemon juice
15ml/1 tbsp fresh coriander (cilantro) leaves
15ml/1 tbsp oil
2 medium onions, sliced
15ml/1 tbsp shredded root ginger

1 Place the chicken wings in a glass or china bowl. Pour the yogurt into a separate bowl along with the ginger pulp, salt, Tabasco sauce, tomato ketchup, garlic pulp, lemon juice and half the fresh coriander leaves. Whisk everything together, then pour the mixture over the chicken wings and stir gently to coat the chicken.

2 Heat the oil in a wok or heavy-based frying pan and fry the onions until soft.

3 Pour in the chicken wings and cook over a medium heat, stirring occasionally, for 10–15 minutes.

4 Add the remaining coriander and the shredded ginger and serve hot.

COOK'S TIP

You can substitute drumsticks or other chicken portions for the wings in this recipe, but remember to increase the cooking time.

NUTRITIONAL NOTES	
Per Portion	
Energy	224Kcals/936KJ
Fat	9.00g
Saturated Fat	2.23g
Carbohydrate	12.64g
Fibre	1.24g

Chicken Tikka

This extremely popular Indian first course is quick and easy to cook. The dish can also be served as a main course for four.

INGREDIENTS

Serves 6 as an appetizer

450g/1lb boneless chicken, skinned and cubed
5ml/1 tsp crushed fresh root ginger
5ml/1 tsp crushed garlic
5ml/1 tsp chilli powder
1.5ml/¼ tsp ground turmeric
5ml/1 tsp salt
150ml/¼ pint/⅔ cup natural (plain) low fat yogurt
60ml/4 tbsp lemon juice
15ml/1 tbsp chopped fresh coriander (cilantro)
15ml/1 tbsp oil

For the garnish
mixed salad leaves
1 small onion, cut into rings
lime wedges
fresh coriander (cilantro)

NUTRITIONAL NOTES	
Per Portion	
Energy	134Kcals/561KJ
Fat	5.50g
Saturated Fat	1.49g
Carbohydrate	3.90g
Fibre	0.30g

—— COOK'S TIP ——

To make the turning and basting of the chicken easier, thread the chicken pieces on to six wooden skewers before placing under the grill.

1 In a medium bowl, mix together the chicken pieces, ginger, garlic, chilli powder, turmeric and salt.

2 Stir in the yogurt, lemon juice and fresh coriander and leave to marinate for at least 2 hours.

3 Place in a grill (broiler) pan or in a flameproof dish lined with foil and baste with the oil.

4 Preheat the grill (broiler) to medium. Grill (broil) the chicken for 15–20 minutes until cooked, turning and basting several times. Serve on a bed of mixed salad leaves, garnished with onion rings, lime wedges and coriander.

Chicken Kofta Balti with Paneer

This rather unusual appetizer looks most elegant when served in small individual karahis.

INGREDIENTS

Serves 6
For the koftas
450g/1lb boneless chicken, skinned
and cubed
5ml/1 tsp crushed garlic
5ml/1 tsp shredded fresh root ginger
7.5ml/1½ tsp ground coriander
7.5ml/1½ tsp chilli powder
7.5ml/1½ tsp ground fenugreek
1.5ml/¼ tsp turmeric
5ml/1 tsp salt
30ml/2 tbsp chopped fresh
coriander (cilantro)
2 fresh green chillies, chopped
600ml/1 pint/2½ cups water
corn oil, for frying

For the paneer mixture
1 medium onion, sliced
1 red (bell) pepper, seeded and cut
into strips
1 green (bell) pepper, seeded and cut
into strips
175g/6oz paneer, cubed
175g/6oz/1 cup corn
fresh mint sprigs
1 dried red chilli, crushed (optional)

1 Put all the kofta ingredients, apart from the oil, into a medium pan. Bring to the boil slowly, over a medium heat, and cook until all the liquid has evaporated.

2 Remove from the heat and leave to cool slightly. Put the mixture into a food processor or blender and process for 2 minutes, stopping once or twice to loosen the mixture with a spoon.

3 Scrape the mixture into a large mixing bowl, using a wooden spoon. Taking a little of the mixture at a time, shape it into small balls, using your hands. You should be able to make about 12 koftas.

4 Heat the oil in a karahi, wok or deep pan over a high heat. Reduce the heat slightly and drop the koftas carefully into the oil. Move them around gently to ensure that they cook evenly.

5 When the koftas are lightly browned, remove them from the oil with a slotted spoon and drain on kitchen paper. Set aside.

6 Heat the oil still remaining in the karahi, and flash fry all the ingredients for the paneer mixture. This should take about 3 minutes over a high heat.

7 Divide the paneer mixture evenly between six individual karahis. Add two koftas to each serving, and garnish with mint sprigs. Add the crushed red chilli, if you like.

NUTRITIONAL NOTES	
Per Portion	
Energy	235Kcals/984KJ
Fat	10.3g
Saturated Fat	2.1g
Carbohydrate	12.3g
Fibre	1.9g

Pineapple Chicken Kebabs

This chicken dish has a delicate tang and the meat is very tender. The pineapple not only tenderizes the chicken but also gives it a slight sweetness.

INGREDIENTS

Serves 6
227g/8oz can canned pineapple chunks
5ml/1 tsp ground cumin
5ml/1 tsp ground coriander
5ml/1 tsp chilli powder
2.5ml/½ tsp crushed garlic
5ml/1 tsp salt
30ml/2 tbsp natural (plain)
   low fat yogurt
15ml/1 tbsp chopped fresh
   coriander (cilantro)
few drops of orange food
   colouring, optional
275g/10oz boneless chicken, skinned
½ red (bell) pepper, seeded
½ yellow or green (bell) pepper, seeded
1 large onion
6 cherry tomatoes
15ml/1 tbsp oil
salad leaves, to serve

NUTRITIONAL NOTES	
Per Portion	
Energy	183Kcals/768KJ
Fat	6.60g
Saturated Fat	1.47g
Carbohydrate	15.40g
Fibre	1.80g

1 Drain the pineapple juice into a bowl. Reserve 8 large chunks of pineapple and squeeze the juice from the remaining chunks into the bowl and set aside. You should have about 120ml/4fl oz/½ cup pineapple juice.

2 In a large bowl, mix together the spices, garlic, salt, yogurt, fresh coriander and food colouring, if using. Mix in the reserved pineapple juice.

3 Cut the chicken into bite-size cubes, add to the yogurt and spice mixture, cover and leave to marinate in a cool place for about 1–1½ hours.

4 Cut the peppers and onion into bite-sized chunks.

5 Preheat the grill (broiler) to medium. Arrange the chicken pieces, vegetables and reserved pineapple chunks alternately on 6 metal skewers.

6 Brush the kebabs lightly with the oil, then place the skewers on a flameproof dish or in a grill (broiler) pan, turning the chicken pieces and basting with the marinade regularly, for about 15 minutes until cooked through. Serve with salad leaves.

COOK'S TIPS

• If possible, use a mixture of chicken breast and thigh meat for this recipe.
• Use wooden skewers, if you prefer, but soak them in water for at least 30 minutes first, to prevent them from scorching under the grill (broiler).

Mini Mince Koftas in a Spicy Sauce

This kofta curry is very popular in most Indian homes. It is also extremely easy to make.

INGREDIENTS

Serves 4

225g/8oz lean minced (ground) lamb
10ml/2 tsp poppy seeds
1 medium onion, chopped
5ml/1 tsp crushed fresh root ginger
5ml/1 tsp crushed garlic
5ml/1 tsp salt
5ml/1 tsp chilli powder
7.5ml/1½ tsp ground coriander
30ml/2 tbsp fresh coriander
   (cilantro) leaves
1 small egg

For the sauce

75ml/3fl oz/⅓ cup natural (plain)
   low fat yogurt
30ml/2 tbsp tomato purée (paste)
5ml/1 tsp chilli powder
5ml/1 tsp salt
5ml/1 tsp crushed garlic
5ml/1 tsp crushed fresh root ginger
5ml/1 tsp garam masala
10ml/2 tsp oil
1 cinnamon stick
400ml/14fl oz/1⅔ cups water

1 Place the lamb in a food processor and grind it further for about 1 minute. Remove from the processor, scrape into a bowl, tip the poppy seeds on top and set aside.

2 Place the onion in the food processor, with the crushed ginger, garlic, salt, chilli powder, ground coriander and half the fresh coriander. Grind this spice mixture for about 30 seconds, then add it to the lamb. Mix well.

3 Whisk the egg and thoroughly mix it into the spiced lamb. Leave to stand for about 1 hour.

4 For the sauce, whisk together the yogurt, tomato purée, chilli powder, salt, crushed garlic, ginger and garam masala.

5 Heat the oil with the cinnamon stick in a karahi or wok for about 1 minute, then pour in the prepared sauce. Lower the heat and cook for about 1 minute. Remove the karahi or wok from the heat and set aside.

6 Break off small balls of the meat mixture and make the koftas using your hands. When all the koftas are ready, return the sauce to the heat and stir in the water. Drop in the koftas one by one. Place the remaining fresh coriander on top, cover with a lid and cook for 7–10 minutes, stirring gently several times to turn the koftas around. Serve hot.

NUTRITIONAL NOTES	
Per Portion	
Energy	155Kcals/647KJ
Fat	9.24g
Saturated Fat	2.79g
Carbohydrate	7.56g
Fibre	1.16g

Stuffed Aubergines with Lamb

Lamb and aubergines go really well together. This dish uses different coloured peppers in the lightly spiced filling mixture.

INGREDIENTS

Serves 4

2 medium aubergines (eggplant)
15ml/1 tbsp oil, plus extra for brushing
1 medium onion, sliced
5ml/1 tsp crushed fresh root ginger
5ml/1 tsp chilli powder
5ml/1 tsp crushed garlic
1.5ml/¼ tsp ground turmeric
5ml/1 tsp salt
5ml/1 tsp ground coriander
1 medium tomato, chopped
350g/12oz lean leg of lamb,
    minced (ground)
1 medium green (bell) pepper, seeded
    and roughly chopped
1 medium orange (bell) pepper, seeded
    and roughly chopped
30ml/2 tbsp chopped fresh
    coriander (cilantro)
plain rice, to serve

For the garnish

½ onion, sliced
2 cherry tomatoes, quartered
fresh coriander

1 Cut the aubergines in half lengthways and scoop out most of the flesh and discard.

2 Preheat the oven to 180°C/350°F/ Gas 4. Place the aubergine shells cut side up in a lightly greased ovenproof dish.

3 In a medium heavy pan, heat the oil and fry the onion until golden brown.

4 Gradually stir in the ginger, chilli powder, garlic, turmeric, salt and ground coriander. Add the chopped tomato, lower the heat and cook for about 5 minutes, stirring frequently.

5 Add the minced lamb and cook for 7–10 minutes more.

NUTRITIONAL NOTES	
Per Portion	
Energy	238Kcals/997KJ
Fat	11.70g
Saturated Fat	4.08g
Carbohydrate	12.60g
Fibre	5.90g

6 Add the chopped peppers and chopped fresh coriander to the lamb mixture and stir well.

7 Spoon the lamb mixture into the aubergine shells and brush the edge of the shells with a little oil. Bake in the oven for 1 hour or until cooked through and browned on top.

8 Serve with the garnish ingredients on a bed of plain rice.

COOK'S TIP

For a special occasion, stuffed baby aubergines (eggplant) look particularly attractive. Use 4 small aubergines, leaving the stalks intact, and prepare and cook as described above, reducing the baking time slightly. Large tomatoes or courgettes (zucchini) make an excellent alternative to aubergines.

Tandoori Masala Spring Lamb Chops

These spicy, lean and trimmed lamb chops are marinated for three hours and then cooked in the oven using very little oil. They make a tasty appetizer, served with a salad garnish, and would also serve three as a main course if served with rice.

INGREDIENTS

Serves 6 as an appetizer
6 small lean spring lamb chops
30ml/2 tbsp natural (plain)
   low fat yogurt
15ml/1 tbsp tomato purée (paste)
10ml/2 tsp ground coriander
5ml/1 tsp crushed fresh root ginger
5ml/1 tsp crushed garlic
5ml/1 tsp chilli powder
few drops of red food
   colouring (optional)
5ml/1 tsp salt
15ml/1 tbsp oil, plus extra
   for basting
45ml/3 tbsp lemon juice

For the salad garnish
lettuce leaves (optional)
lime wedges
1 small onion, sliced
fresh coriander (cilantro)

NUTRITIONAL NOTES	
Per Portion	
Energy	117Kcals/488KJ
Fat	6.60g
Saturated Fat	2.42g
Carbohydrate	3.10g
Fibre	0.30g

1 Rinse the chops and pat dry. Trim off all excess fat.

2 In a medium bowl, mix together the yogurt, tomato purée, ground coriander, ginger and garlic, chilli powder, food colouring (if using), salt, oil and lemon juice.

3 Rub this spice mixture over the lamb chops, using your hands, and leave the chops to marinate in a cool place for at least 3 hours.

4 Preheat the oven to 240°C/475°F/ Gas 9. Place the marinated chops in an ovenproof dish.

5 Using a brush, baste the chops with about 5ml/1 tsp oil and cook in the oven for 15 minutes. Lower the heat to 180°C/350°F/Gas 4 and cook for a further 10–15 minutes.

6 Check that the chops are cooked and serve immediately on a bed of lettuce leaves, if wished, and garnish with lime wedges, sliced onion and fresh coriander.

COOK'S TIP

This bright red tandoori masala mixture is used to colour and spice both meat and chicken and give the effect of a tandoori-style dish without the need to cook it in a traditional clay oven (*tandoor*).

Lamb Kebabs

First introduced by the Muslims, kebabs have now become a favourite Indian dish.

INGREDIENTS

Serves 8

For the kebabs
900g/2lb lean minced (ground) lamb
1 large onion, roughly chopped
5cm/2in piece fresh root
  ginger, chopped
2 garlic cloves, crushed
1 fresh green chilli, finely chopped
5ml/1 tsp chilli powder
30ml/2 tbsp chopped fresh
  coriander (cilantro)
5ml/1 tsp garam masala
10ml/2 tsp ground coriander
5ml/1 tsp ground cumin
5ml/1 tsp salt
1 egg
15ml/1 tbsp natural (plain)
  low fat yogurt
15ml/1 tbsp oil
mixed salad, to serve

For the raita
250ml/8fl oz/1 cup natural (plain)
  low fat yogurt
½ cucumber, finely chopped
30ml/2 tbsp chopped fresh mint
1.5ml/¼ tsp salt

1 Put all the ingredients for the kebabs, except the yogurt and oil, into a food processor or blender and process until the mixture binds together. Spoon into a bowl, cover and leave to marinate for 1 hour.

2 For the raita, mix together all the ingredients and chill for at least 15 minutes in a refrigerator.

3 Preheat the grill (broiler). Divide the lamb mixture into eight equal portions with lightly floured hands and mould into long sausage shapes. Thread on to skewers and chill.

4 Brush the kebabs lightly with the yogurt and oil and cook under a hot grill for 8–10 minutes, turning occasionally, until brown all over. Serve the kebabs on a bed of mixed salad accompanied by the raita.

NUTRITIONAL NOTES	
Per Portion	
Energy	249Kcals/1045KJ
Fat	12.75g
Saturated Fat	5.30g
Carbohydrate	7.00g
Fibre	0.60g

Shammi Kabab

These Indian treats are derived from the kebabs of the Middle East, but Indian cooks changed the spelling, dispensed with the skewers and formed the mixture into large patties, which they deep-fried. Kababs can be served either as appetizers or side dishes with an accompanying raita or chutney.

INGREDIENTS

Serves 5–6

2 onions, finely chopped
250g/9oz lean lamb, boned and cubed
50g/2oz/⅓ cup chana dhal or yellow
   split peas
5ml/1 tsp cumin seeds
5ml/1 tsp garam masala
4–6 fresh green chillies
5cm/2in piece fresh root ginger, grated
175ml/6fl oz/¾ cup water
a few fresh coriander (cilantro) and
   mint leaves, chopped, plus extra
   coriander (cilantro) sprigs to garnish
juice of 1 lemon
15ml/1 tbsp gram flour (besan)
2 eggs, beaten
vegetable oil, for shallow frying
salt

1 Put the first seven ingredients and the water into a large pan with salt, and bring to the boil. Simmer, covered, until the meat and dhal are cooked. Remove the lid and continue to cook for a few more minutes, to reduce the excess liquid. Set aside to cool.

2 Transfer the cooled meat and dhal mixture to a food processor or blender and process well until the mixture becomes a rough, gritty paste.

3 Put the paste into a large mixing bowl and add the chopped coriander and mint leaves, lemon juice and gram flour. Knead well with your fingers for a good couple of minutes, to ensure that all ingredients are evenly distributed through the mixture, and any excess liquid has been thoroughly absorbed. When the colour appears even throughout, and the mixture has taken on a semi-solid, sticky rather than powdery consistency, the kababs are ready for shaping into portions.

4 Divide the mixture into 10–12 even-size portions and use your hands to roll each into a ball, then flatten slightly. Chill for 1 hour. Dip the kababs in the beaten egg and shallow fry each side until golden brown. Pat dry on kitchen paper.

NUTRITIONAL NOTES	
Per Portion	
Energy	179Kcals/750KJ
Fat	8.5g
Saturated Fat	3.4g
Carbohydrate	10.4g
Fibre	1.3g

Fish
and Seafood

SURROUNDED ON three sides by sea, India has a vast coastline. The waters of the Arabian Sea, the Indian Ocean and the Bay of Bengal lap its shores, so it is not at all surprising that some of the most delectable Indian dishes are based on fish and shellfish.

Freshwater rivers and lakes contribute their own bounty, and the resulting catch is cooked in a variety of ways, some of which are unique to this land. This chapter invites you to try a vast range of specialities, such as Kerala's famous Marinated Fried Fish, a delightfully unusual Monkfish and Okra Curry, and a hearty Fish Stew which hails from Eastern India.

Also on the menu are shellfish dishes like Curried Prawns in Coconut Milk and King Prawn Bhoona. Fish has the advantage of being quick and easy to cook – many of the following dishes can be prepared in no time at all. For the most part, spicing is subtle, to allow the full flavour to shine.

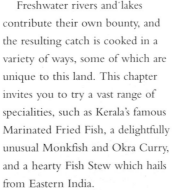

Marinated Fried Fish

Fish and shellfish are a strong feature of the cuisine in the coastal region of southern India. Kerala, in the southernmost part of the country, produces some of the finest fish and shellfish dishes. These are flavoured with local spices, grown in the fabulous spice plantation that is the pride and joy of the state.

INGREDIENTS

Serves 4–6

1 small onion, coarsely chopped
4 garlic cloves, crushed
5cm/2in piece fresh root
   ginger, chopped
5ml/1 tsp ground turmeric
10ml/2 tsp chilli powder
4 red mullets or snappers
vegetable oil, for shallow frying
5ml/1 tsp cumin seeds
3 fresh green chillies, finely sliced
salt
lemon or lime wedges, to serve

COOK'S TIP

To enhance the flavour, add 15ml/1 tbsp chopped fresh coriander (cilantro) leaves to the spice paste in step 1.

NUTRITIONAL NOTES
Per Portion

Energy	336Kcals/1403KJ
Fat	20.1g
Saturated Fat	1.5g
Carbohydrate	1.2g
Fibre	0.2g

1 In a food processor, grind the first five ingredients with salt to a smooth paste. Make several slashes on both sides of the fish and rub them with the paste. Leave to rest for 1 hour. Excess fluid will be released as the salt dissolves, so lightly pat the fish dry with kitchen paper without removing the paste.

2 Heat the oil and fry the cumin seeds and sliced chillies for 1 minute. Add the fish, in batches if necessary, and fry on one side. When the first side is sealed, turn them over very gently to ensure they do not break. Fry until golden brown on both sides and fully cooked. Drain and serve hot, with lemon or lime wedges.

Fish with Mango Sauce

This salad is best served during the summer months, preferably out of doors. The dressing combines the flavour of rich mango with hot chilli, ginger and lime.

INGREDIENTS

Serves 4

1 French loaf
4 redfish, black bream or porgy, each about 275g/10oz
15ml/1 tbsp vegetable oil
1 mango
1cm/½in fresh root ginger
1 fresh red chilli, seeded and finely chopped
30ml/2 tbsp lime juice
30ml/2 tbsp chopped fresh coriander (cilantro)
175g/6oz young spinach
150g/5oz pak choi (bok choy)
175g/6oz cherry tomatoes, halved

1 Preheat the oven to 180°C/350°F/ Gas 4. Cut the French loaf into 20cm/8in lengths. Slice lengthways, then cut into thick fingers. Place the bread on a baking sheet and leave to dry in the oven for 15 minutes.

2 Preheat the grill (broiler) or light the barbecue and allow the embers to settle. Slash the fish deeply on both sides and moisten with oil. Grill (broil) or cook the fish on the barbecue for 6 minutes, turning once.

3 Peel the mango and cut in half, discarding the stone. Thinly slice one half and set aside. Place the other half in a food processor. Peel the ginger, grate finely, then add to the mango with the chilli, lime juice and coriander. Process until smooth. Adjust to a pouring consistency with 30–45ml/2–3 tbsp water.

4 Wash the spinach and pak choi leaves and spin dry, then distribute them among four serving plates. Place the fish on the leaves. Spoon on the mango dressing and finish with the reserved slices of mango and the tomato halves. Serve with the fingers of crisp French bread.

NUTRITIONAL NOTES	
Per Portion	
Energy	512Kcals/2164KJ
Fat	12.3g
Saturated Fat	0.8g
Carbohydrate	50g
Fibre	4.9g

Braised Whole Fish in Chilli and Garlic Sauce

Although every region of India has its own cuisine, and traditional dishes are what Western visitors expect to find, there is in India, as elsewhere in the world, an increasing number of dishes that borrow from other cultures. The vinegar in the sauce for this fish dish is typical of Goa, but the rice wine and bean sauce reveal a distinct Szechuan influence.

INGREDIENTS

Serves 4–6

1 carp, bream, sea bass, trout, grouper or grey mullet, about 675g/1½lb, gutted
15ml/1 tbsp light soy sauce
15ml/1 tbsp rice wine or dry sherry
vegetable oil, for deep frying

For the sauce
2 garlic cloves, finely chopped
2–3 spring onions (scallions), finely chopped, the white and green parts separated
5ml/1 tsp finely chopped fresh root ginger
30ml/2 tbsp chilli bean sauce
15ml/1 tbsp tomato purée (paste)
10ml/2 tsp light brown sugar
15ml/1 tbsp rice vinegar
120ml/4fl oz/½ cup chicken stock
15ml/1 tbsp cornflour (cornstarch), mixed to a paste with 10ml/2 tsp water
few drops of sesame oil

NUTRITIONAL NOTES	
Per Portion	
Energy	292Kcals/1222KJ
Fat	16.1g
Saturated Fat	2.5g
Carbohydrate	10.7g
Fibre	0.4g

1 Rinse and dry the fish well. Using a sharp knife, score both sides of the fish down to the bone with diagonal cuts about 2.5cm/1in apart. Rub both sides of the fish with the soy sauce and rice wine or sherry. Set aside for 10–15 minutes to marinate.

2 Heat sufficient oil for deep frying in a wok. When it is hot, add the fish and fry for 3–4 minutes on both sides, until golden brown.

3 To make the sauce pour away all but about 15ml/1 tbsp of the oil. Push the fish to one side of the wok and add the garlic, the white part of the spring onions, the ginger, chilli bean sauce, tomato purée, sugar, vinegar and stock. Bring to the boil and braise the fish in the sauce for 4–5 minutes, turning it over once. Add the green of the spring onions. Stir in the cornflour paste to thicken the sauce. Sprinkle over a little sesame oil and serve.

Spicy Grilled Fish Fillets

The good thing about fish is that it can be grilled beautifully without sacrificing any flavour.

INGREDIENTS

Serves 4

4 medium flatfish fillets, such as plaice, sole or flounder, about 115g/4oz each
5ml/1 tsp crushed garlic
5ml/1 tsp garam masala
5ml/1 tsp chilli powder
1.5ml/¼ tsp ground turmeric
2.5ml/½ tsp salt
15ml/1 tbsp finely chopped fresh coriander (cilantro)
15ml/1 tbsp oil
30ml/2 tbsp lemon juice
tomato wedges, lime slices and grated carrot, to garnish

1 Line a flameproof dish or grill (broiler) pan with foil. Rinse the fish fillets, pat dry and put them in the foil-lined dish or pan.

2 In a bowl, mix the garlic, garam masala, chilli powder, turmeric, salt, coriander, oil and lemon juice.

3 Brush the fish fillets evenly all over with the spice mixture.

4 Preheat the grill (broiler) to very hot, then lower the heat. Grill (broil) the fish for 10 minutes, basting with the spice mixture, until it is cooked.

5 Serve immediately with a garnish of tomato wedges, lime slices and grated carrot.

NUTRITIONAL NOTES
Per Portion

Energy	152Kcals/641KJ
Fat	5.90g
Saturated Fat	0.88g
Carbohydrate	3.70g
Fibre	0.70g

COOK'S TIP

Use lime juice instead of lemon to give the dish a slightly more sour flavour.

Sweet and Sour Fish

When fish is cooked in this way the skin becomes crispy on the outside, while the flesh remains moist and juicy inside. The sweet and sour sauce, with its colourful cherry tomatoes, complements the fish beautifully.

Ingredients

Serves 4–6

1 large or 2 medium-size fish such as
   snapper or mullet, heads removed
20ml/4 tsp cornflour (cornstarch)
120ml/4fl oz/½ cup vegetable oil
15ml/1 tbsp chopped garlic
15ml/1 tbsp chopped root ginger
30ml/2 tbsp chopped shallots
225g/8oz cherry tomatoes
30ml/2 tbsp red wine vinegar
30ml/2 tbsp granulated sugar
30ml/2 tbsp tomato ketchup
45ml/3 tbsp water
salt and black pepper
coriander (cilantro) leaves, to garnish
shredded spring onions (scallions),
   to garnish

1 Thoroughly rinse and clean the fish. Score the skin diagonally on both sides of the fish.

2 Coat the fish lightly on both sides with 15ml/3 tsp of the cornflour. Shake off any excess.

3 Heat the oil in a kerahi or wok and slide the fish into the pan. Reduce the heat to medium and fry the fish until crisp and brown, about 6–7 minutes on both sides.

4 Remove the fish with a spatula and place on a large platter.

5 Pour off all but 30ml/2 tbsp of the oil and add the garlic, ginger and shallots. Fry until golden.

6 Add the cherry tomatoes and cook until they burst open. Stir in the vinegar, sugar and tomato ketchup. Simmer gently for 1–2 minutes and adjust the seasoning.

7 Mix the remaining 5ml/1 tsp cornflour with the water. Stir into the sauce and heat until it thickens. Pour the sauce over the fish and garnish with coriander leaves and shredded spring onions.

Nutritional Notes	
Per Portion	
Energy	297Kcals/1236KJ
Fat	21.5g
Saturated Fat	2.8g
Carbohydrate	6g
Fibre	0.7g

Vinegar Fish

Fish cooked in a spicy mixture that includes chillies, ginger and vinegar is delicious. The method lends itself particularly well to strong-flavoured, oily fish, such as the mackerel that are regularly caught off the coast of Goa.

INGREDIENTS

Serves 2–3

2–3 mackerel, filleted
2-3 fresh red chillies, seeded
4 macadamia nuts or 8 almonds
1 red onion, quartered
2 garlic cloves, crushed
1cm/½in piece fresh root ginger, peeled
   and sliced
5ml/1 tsp ground turmeric
45ml/3 tbsp coconut oil or
   vegetable oil
45ml/3 tbsp wine vinegar
150ml/¼ pint/⅔ cup water
salt
deep-fried onions and finely chopped
   fresh chilli, to garnish
boiled rice or coconut rice,
   to serve, optional

1 Rinse the mackerel fillets in cold water and dry well on kitchen paper. Set aside.

COOK'S TIP

To make coconut rice, put 400g/14oz/ 2 cups washed long grain rice in a heavy pan with 2.5ml/½ tsp salt, a 5cm/2in piece of lemon grass and 25g/1oz creamed coconut (coconut cream). Add 750ml/ 1¼ pints/3 cups boiling water and stir once to prevent the grains sticking together. Simmer over a medium heat for 10–12 minutes. Remove the pan from the heat, cover and set aside for 5 minutes. Fluff the rice with a fork or chopsticks before serving.

2 Put the chillies, macadamia nuts or almonds, onion, garlic, ginger, turmeric and 15ml/1 tbsp of the oil in a food processor and process to form a paste. Alternatively, pound them together in a mortar with a pestle to form a paste. Heat the remaining oil in a karahi or wok. Add the paste and cook for 1–2 minutes without browning. Stir in the vinegar and water and season with salt to taste. Bring to the boil, then lower the heat.

NUTRITIONAL NOTES	
Per Portion	
Energy	659Kcals/2727KJ
Fat	54.8g
Saturated Fat	8.1g
Carbohydrate	7.7g
Fibre	2.9g

3 Add the mackerel fillets to the sauce and simmer for 6–8 minutes or until the fish is tender and cooked.

4 Transfer the fish to a warm serving dish. Bring the sauce to a boil and cook for 1 minute or until it has reduced slightly. Pour the sauce over the fish, garnish with the deep-fried onions and chopped chilli and serve with rice, if you like.

Stuffed Fish

Every community in India prepares stuffed fish but the Parsi version must rank top of the list. The most popular fish in India is the pomfret. These are available from Indian and Chinese grocers or large supermarkets.

INGREDIENTS

Serves 4
2 large pomfrets, or Dover or lemon sole
10ml/2 tsp salt
juice of 1 lemon

For the masala
115g/4oz/1⅓ cups desiccated (dry unsweetened shredded) coconut
115g/4oz/4 cups fresh coriander (cilantro), including the tender stalks
8 fresh green chillies (or to taste)
5ml/1 tsp cumin seeds
6 garlic cloves
10ml/2 tsp granulated sugar
10ml/2 tsp lemon juice

1 Scale the fish and cut off the fins. Gut the fish and remove the heads, if desired. Using a sharp knife, make 2 diagonal gashes on each side, then pat dry with kitchen paper.

2 Rub the fish inside and out with salt and lemon juice. Cover and leave to stand in a cool place for about 1 hour. Pat dry thoroughly.

3 For the masala, grind all the ingredients together using a pestle and mortar or food processor. Stuff the fish with most of the masala mixture. Rub the rest into the gashes and all over the fish on both sides.

4 Place each fish on a separate piece of greased foil. Tightly wrap the foil over each fish. Place in a steamer and steam for 20 minutes, or bake in a preheated oven for 30 minutes at 200°C/400°F/Gas 6 or until cooked. Remove the fish from the foil and serve hot.

COOK'S TIP

In India, this fish dish is always steamed wrapped in banana leaves. Banana leaves are generally available from Indian or Chinese grocers.

NUTRITIONAL NOTES
Per Portion

Energy	247Kcals/1028KJ
Fat	14.3g
Saturated Fat	10g
Carbohydrate	1.2g
Fibre	2.6g

Pickled Fish Steaks

This dish is served cold, often as an appetizer. It also makes an ideal lunch when served with salad on a hot summer's day. Prepare it a day or two in advance, to allow the flavours to blend.

INGREDIENTS

Serves 4-6

juice of 4 lemons
2.5cm/1in piece fresh root ginger, finely sliced
2 garlic cloves, crushed
2 fresh red chillies, finely chopped
3 fresh green chillies, finely chopped
4 thick firm fish steaks
60ml/4 tbsp vegetable oil
4–6 curry leaves
1 onion, finely chopped
2.5ml/½ tsp ground turmeric
15ml/1 tbsp ground coriander
150ml/¼ pint/⅔ cup pickling vinegar
15ml/1 tbsp granulated sugar
salt, to taste
salad leaves and ½ tomato, to garnish

1 In a bowl, mix the lemon juice with the ginger, garlic and chillies. Pat the fish dry and rub the mixture on all sides of the fish. Cover and marinate for 3–4 hours in the refrigerator.

2 Heat the oil in a frying pan and fry the curry leaves, onion, turmeric and coriander until the onion is translucent.

3 Place the fish steaks and their marinade in the frying pan and spoon the onion mixture over them. Cook for 5 minutes, then turn the fish over gently to prevent damaging the steaks.

4 Pour in the vinegar and add the sugar and salt. Bring to the boil, then lower the heat and simmer until the fish is cooked. Carefully transfer the steaks to a large platter or individual serving dishes and pour over the vinegar mixture. Cool, then chill for 24 hours before serving, garnished with the salad leaves and tomato.

NUTRITIONAL NOTES	
Per Portion	
Energy	233Kcals/968KJ
Fat	12.1g
Saturated Fat	1.5g
Carbohydrate	3g
Fibre	0.5g

Fish and Vegetable Skewers

Threading firm fish cubes and colourful vegetables on skewers scores on several fronts. Not only does the food look good, but it is also easy to cook and serve.

Ingredients

Serves 4

275g/10oz firm white fish fillets, such as cod
45ml/3 tbsp lemon juice
5ml/1 tsp grated fresh root ginger
2 fresh green chillies, very finely chopped
15ml/1 tbsp very finely chopped fresh coriander (cilantro)
15ml/1 tbsp very finely chopped fresh mint
5ml/1 tsp ground coriander
5ml/1 tsp salt
1 red (bell) pepper
1 green (bell) pepper
½ medium cauliflower
8–10 button (white) mushrooms
8 cherry tomatoes
15ml/1 tbsp oil
1 lime, quartered, to garnish (optional)
yellow rice, to serve

Nutritional Notes	
Per Portion	
Energy	131Kcals/551KJ
Fat	4.40g
Saturated Fat	0.51g
Carbohydrate	7.20g
Fibre	3.00g

1 Cut the fish fillets into large and even-size chunks.

2 In a large mixing bowl, stir together the lemon juice, ginger, chopped green chillies, fresh coriander, mint, ground coriander and salt. Add the fish chunks, cover and leave to marinate for about 30 minutes.

3 Cut the red and green peppers into large squares and divide the cauliflower into individual florets.

4 Preheat the grill (broiler) to hot. Arrange the peppers, cauliflower florets, button mushrooms and cherry tomatoes alternately with the fish pieces on four skewers.

5 Brush the kebabs with the oil and any remaining marinade. Transfer to a flameproof dish and grill (broil) for 7–10 minutes, turning occasionally, or until the fish is cooked right through.

6 Garnish with lime quarters, if wished, and serve the kebabs on a bed of yellow rice.

Cook's Tip

Try baby corn cobs instead of mushrooms and broccoli or one of the new cultivated brassicas in place of the cauliflower.

Cod in a Tomato Sauce

Dusting cod with spices before cooking it gives it a delectable coating. The spices are echoed in the tomato sauce. Creamy mashed potatoes are the perfect accompaniment, although pilau rice is the traditional choice.

INGREDIENTS

Serves 4

30ml/2 tbsp cornflour (cornstarch)
5ml/1 tsp salt
5ml/1 tsp garlic powder
5ml/1 tsp chilli powder
5ml/1 tsp ground ginger
5ml/1 tsp ground fennel seeds
5ml/1 tsp ground coriander
2 medium cod fillets, each cut
   into 2 pieces
15ml/1 tbsp oil
mashed potatoes, to serve

For the sauce

30ml/2 tbsp tomato purée (paste)
5ml/1 tsp garam masala
5ml/1 tsp chilli powder
5ml/1 tsp crushed garlic
5ml/1 tsp grated fresh root ginger
2.5ml/½ tsp salt
175ml/6fl oz/¾ cup water
15ml/1 tbsp oil
1 bay leaf
3–4 black peppercorns
1 cm/½in piece cinnamon stick
15ml/1 tbsp chopped fresh
   coriander (cilantro)
15ml/1 tbsp chopped fresh mint

NUTRITIONAL NOTES	
Per Portion	
Energy	122Kcals/509KJ
Fat	6.65g
Saturated Fat	0.89g
Carbohydrate	4.73g
Fibre	0.48g

1 Mix together the cornflour, salt, garlic powder, chilli powder, ground ginger, ground fennel seeds and ground coriander.

2 Spoon the mixture over the 4 cod pieces and make sure that they are well coated in the spices.

3 Preheat the grill (broiler) to very hot, then reduce the heat slightly and place the fish fillets under the heat. After about 5 minutes spoon the oil over the cod. Turn the cod over and repeat the process. Cook for a further 5 minutes, check that the fish is cooked through and set aside.

4 Make the sauce by mixing together the tomato purée, garam masala, chilli powder, garlic, ginger, salt and water. Set aside.

5 Heat the oil in a karahi or wok and add the bay leaf, peppercorns and cinnamon. Pour the sauce into the pan and reduce the heat to low. Bring slowly to the boil, stirring occasionally, then simmer for about 5 minutes. Gently slide the pieces of fish into this mixture and cook for a further 2 minutes.

6 Finally, add the chopped fresh coriander and mint and serve the dish with mashed potatoes.

Green Fish Curry

This dish combines all the
flavours of the East.

INGREDIENTS

Serves 4

1.5ml/¼ tsp ground turmeric
30ml/2 tbsp lime juice
pinch of salt
4 cod fillets, skinned and cut into
    5cm/2in chunks
1 onion, chopped
1 fresh green chilli, sliced
1 garlic clove, crushed
25g/1oz/¼ cup cashew nuts
2.5ml/½ tsp fennel seeds
30ml/2 tbsp desiccated (dry
    unsweetened shredded) coconut
30ml/2 tbsp oil
1.5ml/¼ tsp cumin seeds
1.5ml/¼ tsp ground coriander
1.5ml/¼ tsp ground cumin
1.5ml/¼ tsp salt
150ml/¼ pint/⅔ cup water
175ml/6fl oz/¾ cup natural (plain)
    low fat yogurt
45ml/3 tbsp finely chopped fresh
    coriander (cilantro), plus extra
    to garnish

1 Mix together the turmeric, lime
juice and salt and rub over the fish.
Cover and marinate for 15 minutes.

2 Meanwhile, grind the onion,
chilli, garlic, cashew nuts, fennel
seeds and coconut to a paste. Spoon
the paste into a bowl and set aside.

3 Heat the oil in a large heavy pan
and fry the cumin seeds for
2 minutes or until they begin to
splutter. Add the paste and fry for
5 minutes, then stir in the ground
coriander, cumin, salt and water and
cook for about 2–3 minutes.

4 Stir in the yogurt and chopped
fresh coriander. Simmer gently for
5 minutes. Add the fish pieces and
gently stir in. Cover and cook gently
for 10 minutes until the fish is tender.
Garnish with more coriander. This is
good served with a vegetable pulao.

NUTRITIONAL NOTES	
Per Portion	
Energy	244Kcals/1016KJ
Fat	14.30g
Saturated Fat	5.21g
Carbohydrate	5.40g
Fibre	1.70g

Cod with a Spicy Mushroom Sauce

Grilling fish before adding it
to a sauce helps to prevent it
from breaking up during the
cooking process.

INGREDIENTS

Serves 4
4 cod fillets
15ml/1 tbsp lemon juice
15ml/1 tbsp oil
1 medium onion, chopped
1 bay leaf
4 black peppercorns, crushed
115g/4oz/1 cup mushrooms
175ml/6fl oz/³⁄₄ cup natural (plain)
   low fat yogurt
5ml/1 tsp grated fresh root ginger
5ml/1 tsp crushed garlic
2.5ml/¹⁄₂ tsp garam masala
2.5ml/¹⁄₂ tsp chilli powder
5ml/1 tsp salt
15ml/1 tbsp fresh coriander (cilantro)
   leaves, to garnish
lightly cooked green beans, to serve

COOK'S TIP

If you can find tiny button (white) mushrooms they look very attractive in this fish
dish. Alternatively, choose from the many
other pretty coloured varieties, such as ceps
and oyster mushrooms.

2 Heat the oil in a karahi or wok
and fry the onion with the bay leaf
and peppercorns for 2–3 minutes.
Lower the heat, then add the whole
mushrooms and stir-fry for a further
4–5 minutes.

3 In a bowl mix together the yogurt,
ginger and garlic, garam masala,
chilli and salt. Pour this over the onions
and stir-fry for 3 minutes.

1 Remove the skin and any bones
from the cod fillets. Sprinkle with
lemon juice, then par-cook under a
preheated grill (broiler) for 5 minutes
on each side. Remove the fillets from
the heat and set aside.

NUTRITIONAL NOTES	
Per Portion	
Energy	170Kcals/715KJ
Fat	4.32g
Saturated Fat	0.79g
Carbohydrate	7.67g
Fibre	1.00g

4 Add the cod fillets to the sauce
and cook for a further 2 minutes.
Serve garnished with the fresh
coriander and accompanied by lightly
cooked green beans.

Fish Fillets with a Chilli Sauce

For this recipe, the fish fillets are first marinated with fresh coriander and lemon juice, then cooked quickly before being served with a chilli sauce.

INGREDIENTS

Serves 4

4 flatfish fillets, such as plaice, sole
  or flounder, about 115g/4oz each
30ml/2 tbsp lemon juice
15ml/1 tbsp finely chopped fresh
  coriander (cilantro)
15ml/1 tbsp oil
lime wedges and a fresh coriander
  (cilantro) sprig, to garnish
yellow rice, to serve

For the sauce

5ml/1 tsp grated fresh root ginger
30ml/2 tbsp tomato purée (paste)
5ml/1 tsp granulated sugar
5ml/1 tsp salt
15ml/1 tbsp chilli sauce
15ml/1 tbsp malt vinegar
300ml/½ pint/1¼ cups water

NUTRITIONAL NOTES	
Per Portion	
Energy	149Kcals/627KJ
Fat	5.40g
Saturated Fat	0.81g
Carbohydrate	3.90g
Fibre	0.20g

————— COOK'S TIP —————

Fresh coriander (cilantro) and lemon juice are popular marinade ingredients for Indian fish dishes. For a subtle change in flavour, you can substitute an equal quantity of lime juice for the lemon juice in the marinade, and then garnish the dish with lemon wedges rather than lime.

1 Rinse and pat dry the fish fillets and place in a medium bowl. Add the lemon juice, coriander and oil and rub into the fish. Leave to marinate for at least 1 hour.

2 Make the sauce. Mix the grated ginger, tomato purée, sugar, salt and chilli sauce in a bowl. Stir in the vinegar and water.

3 Pour into a small pan and simmer gently over a low heat for about 6 minutes, stirring occasionally.

4 Meanwhile, preheat the grill (broiler) to medium. Lift the fish fillets out of the marinade and place them in a grill (broiler) pan. Grill (broil) for about 5–7 minutes.

5 When the fish is cooked, arrange it on a warmed serving dish.

6 The chilli sauce should now be fairly thick – about the consistency of a thick chicken soup.

7 Spoon the sauce over the fish fillets, garnish with the lime wedges and coriander sprig and serve immediately with yellow rice.

Fish Stew

Cooking fish with vegetables is a tradition in eastern regions of India. This hearty dish with potatoes, peppers and tomatoes is perfect served with breads such as chapatis or parathas. You can try other combinations, such as green beans and spinach, but you do need a starchy vegetable in order to thicken the sauce.

INGREDIENTS

Serves 4
30ml/2 tbsp vegetable oil
5ml/1 tsp cumin seeds
1 onion, chopped
1 red (bell) pepper, thinly sliced
1 garlic clove, crushed
2 fresh red chillies, finely chopped
2 bay leaves
2.5ml/½ tsp salt
5ml/1 tsp ground cumin
5ml/1 tsp ground coriander
5ml/1 tsp chilli powder
400g/14oz can chopped tomatoes
2 large potatoes, cut into
   2.5cm/1in chunks
300ml/½ pint/1¼ cups fish stock
4 cod fillets
chapatis, to serve

2 Add the salt, ground cumin, ground coriander and chilli powder to the onion and red pepper mixture. Cook for 1–2 minutes, stirring occasionally.

1 Heat the oil in a karahi, wok or large pan over a medium heat and fry the cumin seeds for 30–40 seconds until they begin to splutter. Add the onion, red pepper, garlic, chillies and bay leaves and fry for 5–7 minutes more until the onions have browned.

3 Stir in the tomatoes, potatoes and fish stock. Bring to the boil, then lower the heat and simmer for a further 10 minutes, or until the potatoes are almost tender.

4 Add the fish fillets, then cover the pan and leave to simmer for 5–6 minutes until the fish is just cooked. Serve hot with chapatis, if you like.

NUTRITIONAL NOTES	
Per Portion	
Energy	251Kcals/1053KJ
Fat	7.2g
Saturated Fat	0.9g
Carbohydrate	8.4g
Fibre	1.8g

Fish in a Rich Tomato and Onion Sauce

It is difficult to imagine the cuisine of eastern India without fish. Bengal is as well known for its fish and shellfish dishes as Goa on the west coast. In both regions, coconut is used extensively, and the difference in the taste, as always, lies in the spicing. This onion-rich dish is known as *kalia* in Bengal, and a firm-fleshed fish is essential.

INGREDIENTS

Serves 4

675g/1½lb steaks of firm-textured fish such as tuna or monkfish, skinned
30ml/2 tbsp lemon juice
5ml/1 tsp salt
5ml/1 tsp ground turmeric
vegetable oil, for shallow frying
40g/1½oz/⅓ cup plain (all-purpose) flour
2.5ml/¼ tsp ground black pepper
60ml/4 tbsp vegetable oil
10ml/2 tsp granulated sugar
1 large onion, finely chopped
15ml/1 tbsp grated fresh root ginger
15ml/1 tbsp crushed garlic
5ml/1 tsp ground coriander
2.5–5ml/½–1 tsp hot chilli powder
175g/6oz canned chopped tomatoes, including the juice
300ml/½ pint/1¼ cups warm water
30ml/2 tbsp chopped fresh coriander (cilantro) leaves, to garnish
plain boiled rice, to serve

1 Cut the fish into 7.5cm/3in pieces and put into a large bowl. Add the lemon juice and sprinkle with half the salt and half the turmeric. Mix gently with your fingertips, then cover and set aside for 15 minutes.

2 Pour enough oil into a 23cm/9in frying pan to cover the base to a depth of 1cm/½in and heat over a medium setting. Mix the flour and pepper and dust the fish in the seasoned flour. Add to the oil in a single layer and fry until browned on both sides and a light crust has formed. Drain on kitchen paper.

3 In a karahi, wok or large pan, heat 60ml/4 tbsp oil. When the oil is hot, but not smoking, add the sugar and let it caramelize. As soon as the sugar is brown, add the onion, ginger and garlic and fry for 7–8 minutes, until just beginning to colour. Stir regularly.

4 Add the ground coriander, chilli powder and the remaining turmeric. Stir-fry for about 30 seconds and add the tomatoes. Cook until the tomatoes are mushy and the oil separates from the spice paste, stirring regularly.

5 Pour the warm water and remaining salt into the pan, and bring to the boil. Carefully add the fried fish, reduce the heat to low and simmer, uncovered, for 5–6 minutes.

6 Transfer to a serving dish and garnish with the coriander leaves. Serve with plain boiled rice.

NUTRITIONAL NOTES	
Per Portion	
Energy	435Kcals/1811KJ
Fat	30.7g
Saturated Fat	3.8g
Carbohydrate	12.5g
Fibre	1.2g

Tuna Fish Curry

This not-very-authentic fish curry can be made in minutes. It's the ideal dish for a wannabe Bollywood star on a tight schedule.

INGREDIENTS

Serves 4
1 onion
1 red (bell) pepper
1 green (bell) pepper
30ml/2 tbsp oil
1.5ml/¼ tsp cumin seeds
2.5ml/½ tsp ground cumin
2.5ml/½ tsp ground coriander
2.5ml/½ tsp chilli powder
1.5ml/¼ tsp salt
2 garlic cloves, crushed
400g/14oz can tuna in brine, drained
1 fresh green chilli, finely chopped
2.5cm/1in piece fresh root
    ginger, grated
1.5ml/¼ tsp garam masala
5ml/1 tsp lemon juice
30ml/2 tbsp chopped fresh
    coriander (cilantro)
fresh coriander (cilantro) sprig,
    to garnish
pitta bread and cucumber raita,
    to serve

COOK'S TIP

Place the pitta bread on a grill (broiler) rack and grill (broil) until it just puffs up. It will be easy to split with a sharp knife.

NUTRITIONAL NOTES
Per Portion

Energy	165Kcals/690KJ
Fat	6.80g
Saturated Fat	0.97g
Carbohydrate	8.70g
Fibre	1.80g

1 Thinly slice the onion and the red and green peppers, discarding the seeds from the peppers.

2 Heat the oil in a karahi, wok or heavy pan and stir-fry the cumin seeds for 2–3 minutes until they begin to spit and splutter.

3 Add the ground cumin, coriander, chilli powder and salt and cook for 2–3 minutes. Then add the garlic, onion and peppers.

4 Fry the vegetables, stirring from time to time, for 5–7 minutes until the onion has browned.

5 Stir in the tuna, green chilli and ginger and cook for 5 minutes.

6 Add the garam masala, lemon juice and chopped fresh coriander and continue to cook the curry for a further 3–4 minutes. Serve in warmed, split pitta bread with the cucumber raita, garnished with a coriander sprig.

Monkfish and Okra Curry

An interesting combination of flavours and textures is used in this delicious fish dish.

Ingredients

Serves 4

450g/1lb monkfish
5ml/1 tsp ground turmeric
2.5ml/½ tsp chilli powder
2.5ml/½ tsp salt
5ml/1 tsp cumin seeds
2.5ml/½ tsp fennel seeds
2 dried red chillies
30ml/2 tbsp oil
1 onion, finely chopped
2 garlic cloves, crushed
4 tomatoes, peeled and finely chopped
150ml/¼ pint/⅔ cup water
225g/8oz okra, trimmed and cut into
   2.5cm/1in lengths
5ml/1 tsp garam masala
plain rice, to serve

1 Remove the membrane and bones from the monkfish, cut into 2.5cm/1in cubes and place in a dish. Mix together the turmeric, chilli powder and 1.5ml/¼ tsp of the salt and rub the mixture all over the fish. Cover and marinate for 15 minutes.

COOK'S TIP

Coconut rice would also go very well with this fish curry, making a very attractive presentation. Or serve it with plain rice, if you prefer.

2 Put the cumin seeds, fennel seeds and chillies in a large heavy pan and dry-roast the spice mixture for 3–4 minutes. Put the spices into a blender or use a pestle and mortar to grind to a coarse powder.

3 Heat 15ml/1 tbsp of the oil in the frying pan and fry the monkfish cubes for about 4–5 minutes. Remove with a slotted spoon and drain on kitchen paper.

4 Add the remaining oil to the pan and fry the onion and garlic for about 5 minutes. Add the roasted spice powder and remaining salt and fry for 2–3 minutes. Stir in the tomatoes and water and simmer for 5 minutes.

5 Add the prepared okra and cook for about 5–7 minutes.

6 Return the fish to the pan together with the garam masala. Cover and simmer for 5–6 minutes or until the fish is tender. Serve at once with plain rice.

NUTRITIONAL NOTES	
Per Portion	
Energy	193Kcals/805KJ
Fat	8.80g
Saturated Fat	1.31g
Carbohydrate	9.40g
Fibre	3.60g

Goan Fish Casserole

The cooking of Goa is a mixture of Portuguese and Indian; the addition of tamarind gives a slightly sour note to the spicy coconut sauce.

INGREDIENTS

Serves 4

7.5ml/1½ tsp ground turmeric
5ml/1 tsp salt
450g/1lb monkfish fillet, cut into
  eight pieces
15ml/1 tbsp lemon juice
5ml/1 tsp cumin seeds
5ml/1 tsp coriander seeds
5ml/1 tsp black peppercorns
1 garlic clove, chopped
5cm/2in piece fresh root ginger,
  finely chopped
25g/1oz tamarind paste
150ml/¼ pint/⅔ cup hot water
30ml/2 tbsp vegetable oil
2 onions, halved and sliced lengthways
400ml/14fl oz/1⅔ cups coconut milk
4 mild fresh green chillies, seeded and
  cut into thin strips
16 large raw prawns (shrimp), peeled
30ml/2 tbsp chopped fresh coriander
  (cilantro) leaves, to garnish

1 Mix together the ground turmeric and salt in a small bowl. Place the monkfish in a shallow dish and sprinkle over the lemon juice, then rub the turmeric and salt mixture over the fish fillets to coat them completely. Cover and chill until ready to cook.

2 Put the cumin seeds, coriander seeds and black peppercorns in a blender or small food processor and grind to a powder. Add the garlic and ginger and process for a few seconds more.

3 Preheat the oven to 200°C/400°F/ Gas 6. Mix the tamarind paste with the hot water and set aside.

4 Heat the oil in a frying pan, add the onions and cook for 5–6 minutes, until softened and golden. Transfer the onions to a shallow earthenware dish.

5 Add the fish fillets to the oil remaining in the frying pan, and fry briefly over a high heat, turning them to seal on all sides. Remove the fish from the pan and place on top of the onions.

6 Add the ground spice mixture to the frying pan and cook over a medium heat, stirring constantly, for 1–2 minutes. Stir in the tamarind liquid, coconut milk and chilli strips and bring to the boil. Pour the sauce into the earthenware dish to coat the fish completely.

7 Cover the earthenware dish and cook the fish casserole in the oven for about 10 minutes.

8 Add the prawns, pushing them into the liquid, then cover the dish again and return it to the oven for 5 minutes, or until the prawns turn pink. Do not overcook them or they will toughen. Check the seasoning, sprinkle with coriander leaves and serve.

NUTRITIONAL NOTES	
Per Portion	
Energy	211Kcals/889KJ
Fat	6.7g
Saturated Fat	1g
Carbohydrate	10.8g
Fibre	1.1g

Stir-fried Monkfish with Vegetables

Monkfish is a rather expensive fish, but ideal to use in stir-fry recipes as it is robust and will hold its shape when cooked.

INGREDIENTS

Serves 4
30ml/2 tbsp oil
2 medium onions, sliced
5ml/1 tsp crushed garlic
5ml/1 tsp ground cumin
5ml/1 tsp ground coriander
5ml/1 tsp chilli powder
175g/6oz monkfish, cut into cubes
30ml/2 tbsp fresh fenugreek leaves
2 tomatoes, seeded and sliced
1 courgette (zucchini), sliced
salt
15ml/1 tbsp lime juice

1 Heat the oil in a karahi, wok or heavy pan and fry the onions over a low heat until soft.

2 Meanwhile mix together the garlic, cumin, coriander and chilli powder. Add this spice mixture to the onions and stir-fry for about 1 minute.

3 Add the fish and continue to stir-fry for 3–5 minutes until the fish is well cooked through.

4 Add the fenugreek, tomatoes and courgette, followed by salt to taste, and stir-fry for a further 2 minutes. Sprinkle with lime juice before serving.

NUTRITIONAL NOTES	
Per Portion	
Energy	86Kcals/360KJ
Fat	2.38g
Saturated Fat	0.35g
Carbohydrate	8.32g
Fibre	1.87g

—— COOK'S TIP ——

Try to use monkfish for this recipe, but if it is not available, either cod or prawns (shrimp) make a suitable substitute.

Fish and Prawns in Herb Sauce

Bengalis are famous for their seafood dishes and like to use mustard oil in recipes because it imparts a unique taste, flavour and aroma. No feast in Bengal is complete without one of these celebrated fish dishes.

INGREDIENTS

Serves 4-6
3 garlic cloves
5cm/2in piece fresh root ginger
1 large leek, roughly chopped
4 fresh green chillies
60ml/4 tbsp mustard oil, or
   vegetable oil
15ml/1 tbsp ground coriander
2.5ml/½ tsp fennel seeds
15ml/1 tbsp crushed yellow mustard
   seeds, or 5ml/1 tsp mustard powder
175ml/6fl oz/¾ cup thick coconut milk
225g/8oz huss or monkfish fillets, cut
   into thick chunks
225g/8oz king prawns (jumbo shrimp),
   peeled and deveined, with tails intact
salt, to taste
115g/4oz/4 cups fresh coriander
   (cilantro), chopped
2 fresh green chillies, to garnish

1 In a food processor, grind the garlic, ginger, leek and chillies to a coarse paste. Add a little vegetable oil if the mixture is too dry and process the mixture again.

2 In a large frying pan, heat the mustard or vegetable oil with the paste until it is well blended. Keep the window open and take care not to overheat the mixture as any smoke from the mustard oil will sting the eyes.

3 Stir in the ground coriander, fennel seeds, mustard and coconut milk. Gently bring the mixture to the boil and then lower the heat and simmer, uncovered, for about 5 minutes.

4 Add the fish chunks. Simmer for 2 minutes, then fold in the prawns and cook until the prawns turn a bright orange/pink colour. Season with salt, fold in the fresh coriander and serve hot. Garnish with the fresh green chillies, if you like.

NUTRITIONAL NOTES	
Per Portion	
Energy	204Kcals/852KJ
Fat	12.1g
Saturated Fat	1.6g
Carbohydrate	3.7g
Fibre	1.4g

Prawns with Chayote in Turmeric Sauce

This delicious, attractively coloured dish reveals the influence of Malaysian immigrants.

INGREDIENTS

Serves 4

1–2 chayotes or 2–3 courgettes
  (zucchini)
2 fresh red chillies, seeded
1 onion, quartered
5ml/1 tsp grated fresh root ginger
1 lemon grass stem, lower 5cm/2in
  sliced, top bruised
2.5cm/1in fresh turmeric, peeled
200ml/7fl oz/scant 1 cup water
lemon juice
400ml/14fl oz can coconut milk
450g/1lb cooked, peeled prawns (shrimp)
salt
fresh red chilli shreds, to garnish
boiled rice, to serve

1 Peel the chayotes, remove the seeds and cut into strips. If using courgettes, cut into 5cm/2in strips.

2 Grind the fresh red chillies, onion, ginger, sliced lemon grass and the fresh turmeric to a paste in a food processor or with a pestle and mortar. Add the water to the paste mixture, with a squeeze of lemon juice and salt to taste.

3 Pour into a pan. Add the top of the lemon grass stem. Bring to the boil and cook for 1–2 minutes. Add the chayote or courgette pieces and cook for 2 minutes. Stir in the coconut milk. Taste and adjust the seasoning.

4 Stir in the prawns and cook gently for 2–3 minutes. Remove the lemon grass stem. Garnish with shreds of chilli and serve with rice.

NUTRITIONAL NOTES	
Per Portion	
Energy	132Kcals/559KJ
Fat	1.3g
Saturated Fat	0.4g
Carbohydrate	9g
Fibre	1.1g

Mackerel in Tamarind

A delicious dish originating from Western India.

INGREDIENTS

Serves 6–8

1kg/2¼lb fresh mackerel fillets, skinned
30ml/2 tbsp tamarind pulp, soaked in
  200ml/7fl oz/scant 1 cup water
1 onion
1cm/½in piece fresh root ginger
2 garlic cloves
1–2 fresh red chillies, seeded, or 5ml/
  1 tsp chilli powder
5ml/1 tsp ground coriander
5ml/1 tsp ground turmeric
2.5ml/½ tsp ground fennel seeds
15ml/1 tbsp dark brown sugar
90–105ml/6–7 tbsp oil
200ml/7fl oz/scant 1 cup
  coconut cream
fresh chilli shreds, to garnish

1 Rinse the fish fillets in cold water and dry them well on kitchen paper. Put into a shallow dish and sprinkle with a little salt. Strain the tamarind and pour the juice over the fish fillets. Leave for 30 minutes.

2 Quarter the onion, peel and slice the ginger and peel the garlic. Grind the onion, ginger, garlic and chillies or chilli powder to a paste in a food processor or with a pestle and mortar. Add the ground coriander, turmeric, fennel seeds and sugar.

3 Heat half of the oil in a frying pan. Drain the fish fillets and fry for 5 minutes, or until cooked. Set aside.

4 Wipe out the pan and heat the remaining oil. Fry the spice paste, stirring all the time, until it gives off a spicy aroma. Do not let it brown. Add the coconut cream and simmer gently for a few minutes. Add the fish fillets and gently heat through.

5 Taste for seasoning and serve scattered with shredded chilli.

NUTRITIONAL NOTES	
Per Portion	
Energy	482Kcals/1999KJ
Fat	38g
Saturated Fat	6.9g
Carbohydrate	3.6g
Fibre	0.4g

Pineapple Curry with Prawns and Mussels

The delicate sweet and sour flavour of this curry comes from the pineapple and although it seems an odd combination, it is rather delicious. Use the freshest shellfish that you can find.

INGREDIENTS

Serves 4–6

600ml/1 pint/2½ cups coconut milk
30ml/2 tbsp curry paste
15ml/1 tbsp granulated sugar
225g/8oz king prawns (jumbo shrimp), shelled and deveined
450g/1lb mussels, cleaned and beards removed
175g/6oz fresh pineapple, finely crushed or chopped
2 bay leaves
2 fresh red chillies, chopped, to garnish
coriander (cilantro) leaves, to garnish

1 In a large pan, bring half the coconut milk to the boil and heat, stirring, until it separates.

2 Add the curry paste and cook until fragrant. Add the sugar and continue to cook for 1 minute.

3 Stir in the rest of the coconut milk and bring back to the boil. Add the king prawns, mussels, pineapple and bay leaves.

4 Reheat until boiling and then simmer for 3–5 minutes, until the prawns are cooked and the mussels have opened. Remove any mussels that have not opened and throw them away. Discard the bay leaves if you like. Serve the curry garnished with chopped red chillies and coriander leaves.

NUTRITIONAL NOTES	
Per Portion	
Energy	125Kcals/534KJ
Fat	1.7g
Saturated Fat	0.5g
Carbohydrate	12.8g
Fibre	0.5g

Curried Prawns in Coconut Milk

A curry-like dish where the prawns are cooked in a spicy coconut gravy.

INGREDIENTS

Serves 4–6

600ml/1 pint/2½ cups coconut milk
30ml/2 tbsp yellow curry paste
2.5ml/½ tsp salt
5ml/1 tsp granulated sugar
450g/1lb king prawns (jumbo shrimp), shelled, tails left intact, deveined
225g/8oz cherry tomatoes
juice of ½ lime, to serve
red chilli strips, to garnish
coriander (cilantro) leaves, to garnish

1 Put half the coconut milk into a pan or wok and bring to the boil.

2 Add the curry paste to the coconut milk, stir until it disperses, then simmer for about 10 minutes.

3 Add the salt, sugar and remaining coconut milk. Simmer for another 5 minutes.

4 Add the prawns and cherry tomatoes. Simmer very gently for about 5 minutes until the prawns are pink and tender.

5 Serve sprinkled with lime juice and garnish with chillies and coriander.

NUTRITIONAL NOTES	
Per Portion	
Energy	129Kcals/547KJ
Fat	1.4g
Saturated Fat	0.5g
Carbohydrate	9g
Fibre	0.6g

Red and White Prawns with Green Vegetables

Reflecting the influence of neighbouring mainland China, this colourful dish has a fresh and pleasing flavour.

INGREDIENTS

Serves 4–6

450g/1lb raw prawns (shrimp)
½ egg white
15ml/1 tbsp cornflour (cornstarch), mixed to a paste with 10ml/2 tsp water
175g/6oz mangetouts (snow peas)
about 600ml/1 pint/2½ cups vegetable oil
5ml/1 tsp light brown sugar
15ml/1 tbsp finely chopped spring onion (scallion)
5ml/1 tsp finely chopped fresh root ginger
15ml/1 tbsp light soy sauce
15ml/1 tbsp Chinese rice wine or dry sherry
5ml/1 tsp chilli bean sauce
15ml/1 tbsp tomato purée (paste)
salt

1 Peel the prawns and remove the black intestinal vein that runs down the back of each one. Place in a bowl and mix with the egg white, cornflour paste and a pinch of salt.

2 Trim the mangetouts. If necessary, string them, but keep the pods whole.

3 Heat 30–45ml/2–3 tbsp of the oil in a preheated wok and stir-fry the mangetouts for about 1 minute.

4 Add the sugar and a little salt and continue stirring for 1 more minute. Remove and place in the centre of a warmed serving platter.

5 Add the remaining oil to the wok and cook the prawns for 1 minute. Remove and drain.

6 Pour off all but about 15ml/1 tbsp of the oil. Add the spring onion and ginger to the wok.

NUTRITIONAL NOTES	
Per Portion	
Energy	551Kcals/2275KJ
Fat	50.7g
Saturated Fat	6.1g
Carbohydrate	1.8g
Fibre	1g

7 Return the prawns to the wok and stir-fry for 1 minute, then add the soy sauce and rice wine or dry sherry. Blend the mixture thoroughly. Transfer half the prawns to one end of the serving platter.

8 Add the chilli bean sauce and tomato purée to the remaining prawns in the wok, blend well and place the "red" prawns at the other end of the platter. Serve.

_____ COOK'S TIP _____

All raw prawns (shrimp) have an intestinal tract that runs just beneath the outside curve of the tail. The tract is not poisonous, but it can taste unpleasant. It is, therefore, best to remove it – devein. To do this, peel the prawns, leaving the tail intact. Score each prawn lightly along its length to expose the tract. Remove the tract by lifting it out with the tip of a small knife.

King Prawns with Onions and Curry Leaves

An excellent partner for this mildly spiced prawn dish would be a basmati rice with vegetables.

INGREDIENTS

Serves 4

3 medium onions
15ml/1 tbsp oil
6–8 curry leaves
1.5ml/¼ tsp onion seeds
1 fresh green chilli, seeded and diced
1 fresh red chilli, seeded and diced
12–16 frozen cooked king prawns
 (jumbo shrimp), thawed and peeled
5ml/1 tsp shredded fresh root ginger
5ml/1 tsp salt
15ml/1 tbsp fresh fenugreek leaves

1 Cut the onions into thin slices, using a sharp knife.

2 Heat the oil in a karahi, wok or heavy pan and fry the onions with the curry leaves and onion seeds for about 3 minutes.

3 Add the diced green and red chillies, followed by the prawns. Cook for about 5–7 minutes before adding the ginger and salt.

4 Finally, add the fenugreek leaves, cover and cook for a further 2–3 minutes before serving.

COOK'S TIP

For a quicker and less expensive meal, use ready-peeled small prawns (shrimp) sold in most supermarkets. Allow 115g/4oz prawns per person, and cook the prawns for slightly less time than the larger ones.

NUTRITIONAL NOTES
Per Portion

Energy	97Kcals/403KJ
Fat	3.29g
Saturated Fat	0.45g
Carbohydrate	9.39g
Fibre	1.58g

Prawn and Mangetout Stir-fry

Keep some prawns in the freezer, as they are handy for a quick stir-fry like this one. Serve with rice or chapatis.

INGREDIENTS

Serves 4

15ml/1 tbsp oil
2 medium onions, diced
15ml/1 tbsp tomato purée (paste)
5ml/1 tsp Tabasco sauce
5ml/1 tsp lemon juice
5ml/1 tsp grated fresh root ginger
5ml/1 tsp crushed garlic
5ml/1 tsp chilli powder
5ml/1 tsp salt
15ml/1 tbsp chopped fresh
  coriander (cilantro)
175g/6oz/1½ cups frozen cooked
  peeled prawns (shrimp), thawed
12 mangetouts (snow peas), halved

1 Heat the oil in a karahi, wok or heavy pan and fry the onions until golden brown.

2 Mix the tomato purée with 30ml/ 2 tbsp water in a bowl. Stir in the Tabasco sauce, lemon juice, ginger and garlic, chilli powder and salt.

4 Add the coriander, prawns and mangetouts to the pan and stir-fry for 5–7 minutes, or until the sauce is thick. Serve immediately.

3 Lower the heat, pour the sauce over the onions and stir-fry for a few seconds until well mixed in.

NUTRITIONAL NOTES	
Per Portion	
Energy	108Kcals/451KJ
Fat	3.48g
Saturated Fat	0.49g
Carbohydrate	7.96g
Fibre	1.60g

_____ COOK'S TIP _____

Mangetouts, being small and almost flat, are perfect for stir-frying and are a popular ingredient in Indian cooking. They are particularly good stir-fried with prawns which need only minutes to heat through.

King Prawn Bhoona

The unusual and delicious flavour of this dish is achieved by grilling the marinated prawns to give them a chargrilled taste and then adding them to stir-fried onions and peppers.

Ingredients

Serves 4

45ml/3 tbsp natural (plain) low fat yogurt
5ml/1 tsp paprika
5ml/1 tsp grated fresh root ginger
salt
12–16 frozen cooked king prawns (jumbo shrimp), thawed and peeled
15ml/1 tbsp oil
3 medium onions, sliced
2.5ml/½ tsp fennel seeds, crushed
1 piece cinnamon stick
5ml/1 tsp crushed garlic
5ml/1 tsp chilli powder
1 medium yellow (bell) pepper, seeded and roughly chopped
1 medium red (bell) pepper, seeded and roughly chopped
15ml/1 tbsp fresh coriander (cilantro) leaves, to garnish

COOK'S TIP

Although frozen coriander (cilantro) is convenient and good to use in cooking, the fresh herb is more suitable for garnishes.

NUTRITIONAL NOTES
Per Portion

Energy	132Kcals/552KJ
Fat	3.94g
Saturated Fat	0.58g
Carbohydrate	15.95g
Fibre	3.11g

1 In a bowl, mix the yogurt, paprika, ginger and salt to taste. Pour this mixture over the prawns and leave to marinate for 30–45 minutes.

2 Heat the oil in a karahi, wok or heavy pan and fry the onions with the fennel seeds and the piece of cinnamon stick.

3 Lower the heat and add the garlic and chilli powder. Stir over the heat until well mixed.

4 Add the peppers and stir-fry gently for 3–5 minutes.

5 Remove from the heat and transfer to a warm serving dish, discarding the cinnamon.

6 Preheat the grill (broiler) to medium. Put the prawns in a grill (broiler) pan or flame-proof dish and place under the heat to darken their tops and get a chargrilled effect. Add to the onion mixture, garnish with the coriander and serve.

Prawns with Fenugreek and Seeds

Tender seafood, crunchy vegetables and a thick curry sauce combine to produce a dish rich in flavour and texture.

INGREDIENTS

Serves 4
30ml/2 tbsp oil
1 tsp mixed fenugreek, mustard and
    onion seeds
2 curry leaves
½ medium cauliflower, cut into
    small florets
8 baby carrots, halved lengthways
6 new potatoes, thickly sliced
50g/2 oz/½ cup frozen peas
2 medium onions, sliced
30ml/2 tbsp tomato purée (paste)
2.5ml/1½ tsp chilli powder
5ml/1 tsp ground coriander
5ml/1 tsp grated fresh root ginger
5ml/1 tsp crushed garlic
5ml/1 tsp salt
30ml/2 tbsp lemon juice
450g/1lb frozen cooked peeled prawns
    (shrimp), thawed
30ml/2 tbsp chopped fresh
    coriander (cilantro)
1 fresh red chilli, seeded and sliced
120ml/4fl oz/½ cup natural (plain)
    low fat yogurt

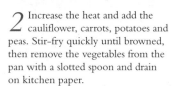

1 Heat the oil in a karahi, wok or heavy pan. Lower the heat slightly and add the fenugreek, mustard and onion seeds and the curry leaves.

2 Increase the heat and add the cauliflower, carrots, potatoes and peas. Stir-fry quickly until browned, then remove the vegetables from the pan with a slotted spoon and drain on kitchen paper.

3 Add the onions to the oil left in the pan and fry over a medium heat until golden brown.

4 While the onions are cooking, mix together the tomato purée, chilli powder, ground coriander, ginger, garlic, salt and lemon juice and pour the paste on to the onions.

5 Add the prawns and stir fry over a low heat for about 5 minutes or until they are heated through.

6 Add the fried vegetables to the pan and mix together well. Add the fresh coriander and red chilli and pour in the yogurt. Warm through and serve.

NUTRITIONAL NOTES	
Per Portion	
Energy	288Kcals/1208KJ
Fat	9.20g
Saturated Fat	1.34g
Carbohydrate	20.10g
Fibre	3.10g

Parsi Prawn Curry

This dish comes from the west coast of India, where fresh seafood is eaten in abundance. Fresh king prawns (jumbo shrimp) or 'tiger' prawns are ideal.

INGREDIENTS

Serves 4-6

4 tbsp vegetable oil
1 medium onion, finely sliced
6 cloves garlic, finely crushed
1 tsp chilli powder
1½ tsp turmeric
2 medium onions, finely chopped
4 tbsp tamarind juice
1 tsp mint sauce
1 tbsp demerara (raw) sugar
salt, to taste
450g/1lb fresh king prawns (jumbo shrimp), peeled and deveined
75g/3oz/3 cups fresh coriander (cilantro), chopped

2 Add the chopped onions to the pan and fry until they become translucent, stirring frequently. Stir in the tamarind juice, mint sauce, sugar and salt and gently simmer for a further 3 minutes.

3 Pat the prawns dry with kitchen paper (paper towel). Add to the spice mixture with a small amount of water and stir-fry until the prawns turn a bright orange/pink colour.

4 When the prawns are cooked, add the fresh coriander and stir-fry over a high heat for a few minutes to thicken the sauce. Serve hot.

NUTRITIONAL NOTES	
Per Portion	
Energy	244Kcals/1015KJ
Fat	12g
Saturated Fat	1.4g
Carbohydrate	13.2g
Fibre	1.6g

1 Heat the oil in a frying pan (skillet) and fry the sliced onion until golden brown. In a bowl, mix the garlic, chilli powder and turmeric with a little water to form a paste. Add to the browned onion and simmer for 3 minutes.

Cod and Prawn Green Coconut Curry

This quick curry involves very little preparation, and takes just minutes to cook, so it's ideal if friends spring a surprise visit. If you can't find green masala curry paste at your local grocer or supermarket, simply substitute another variety – the curry will taste just as good.

INGREDIENTS

Serves 4

675g/1½lb cod fillets, skinned
90ml/6 tbsp green masala curry paste
175ml/6fl oz/¾ cup canned coconut
  milk or 200ml/7fl oz/scant 1 cup
  creamed coconut (coconut cream)
175g/6oz raw or cooked, peeled
  prawns (shrimp)
fresh coriander (cilantro), to garnish
basmati rice, to serve

VARIATION

Any firm fish, such as monkfish, can be used instead of cod. Whole fish steaks can be cooked in the sauce, but allow an extra 5 minutes' cooking time and baste them with the sauce from time to time.

1 Using a sharp knife, cut the skinned cod fillets into 4cm/1½in pieces.

2 Put the green masala curry paste and the coconut milk or cream into a frying pan. Heat to simmering and simmer gently for 5 minutes, stirring occasionally.

3 Add the cod pieces and prawns (if raw) to the cream mixture and cook gently for 5 minutes. If using ready cooked prawns rather than raw shellfish, add them to the pan after this time has elapsed, and heat through.

4 Spoon into a serving dish, garnish the curry with fresh coriander and serve immediately with basmati rice.

NUTRITIONAL NOTES	
Per Portion	
Energy	227Kcals/954KJ
Fat	7.1g
Saturated Fat	1g
Carbohydrate	2.2g
Fibre	0g

Goan Prawn Curry

The cuisine of Goa is well known for its excellent range of fish and shellfish-based recipes, such as this one for prawns. Numerous varieties of fish and shellfish are found along the extended coastline and the network of inland waterways.

INGREDIENTS

Serves 4

15g/½oz/1 tbsp ghee or butter
2 garlic cloves, crushed
450g/1lb small raw prawns (shrimp), peeled and deveined
15ml/1 tbsp groundnut (peanut) oil
4 cardamom pods
4 cloves
5cm/2in piece cinnamon stick
15ml/1 tbsp mustard seeds
1 large onion, finely chopped
½–1 fresh red chilli, seeded and sliced
4 tomatoes, peeled, seeded and chopped
175ml/6fl oz/¾ cup fish stock or water
350ml/12fl oz/1½ cups coconut milk
45ml/3 tbsp Fragrant Spice Mix (see Cook's Tip)
10–20ml/2–4 tsp chilli powder
salt
turmeric-coloured basmati rice, to serve

1 Melt the ghee or butter in a wok, karahi or large pan, add the garlic and stir over a low heat for a few seconds. Add the prawns and stir-fry briskly to coat. Transfer to a plate and set aside.

2 In the same pan, heat the oil and fry the cardamom, cloves and cinnamon for 2 minutes. Add the mustard seeds and fry for 1 minute.

3 Add the onion and chilli and fry for 7–8 minutes or until softened and lightly browned.

4 Add the remaining ingredients and bring to a slow simmer. Cook gently for 6–8 minutes and add the prawns. Simmer for 5–8 minutes until the prawns are cooked through. Serve the curry with basmati rice cooked with turmeric so that it is tinted a pale yellow colour, and lightly flavoured with the spice.

NUTRITIONAL NOTES	
Per Portion	
Energy	187Kcals/784KJ
Fat	7g
Saturated Fat	2.8g
Carbohydrate	10.5g
Fibre	1.3g

COOK'S TIP

To make a Fragrant Spice Mix, dry-fry 25ml/1½ tbsp coriander seeds, 15ml/1 tbsp mixed peppercorns, 5ml/1 tsp cumin seeds, 1.5ml/¼ tsp fenugreek seeds and 1.5ml/ ¼ tsp fennel seeds until aromatic, then grind finely in a spice mill.

King Prawn Korma

This korma has a light, mild, creamy texture, and makes a good introduction to Indian cuisine for people who claim not to like spicy food.

INGREDIENTS

Serves 4

12–16 frozen cooked king prawns
    (jumbo shrimp), thawed and peeled
45ml/3 tbsp natural (plain)
    low fat yogurt
45ml/3 tbsp low fat fromage frais or
    ricotta cheese
5ml/1 tsp ground paprika
5ml/1 tsp garam masala
15ml/1 tbsp tomato purée (paste)
45ml/3 tbsp coconut milk
5ml/1 tsp chilli powder
150ml/¼ pint/⅔ cup water
15ml/1 tbsp oil
5ml/1 tsp crushed garlic
5ml/1 tsp grated fresh root ginger
½ piece cinnamon stick
2 green cardamom pods
salt
15ml/1 tbsp chopped fresh coriander
    (cilantro), to garnish

NUTRITIONAL NOTES	
Per Portion	
Energy	93Kcals/391KJ
Fat	4.10g
Saturated Fat	0.57g
Carbohydrate	7.20g
Fibre	0.40g

_____ COOK'S TIPS _____

• Paprika gives a good rich colour to the curry without adding extra heat.
• Do not let the prawns overcook in the sauce or they will toughen.

1 Drain the prawns to ensure that all excess liquid is removed.

2 Place the yogurt, fromage frais or ricotta, paprika, garam masala, tomato purée, coconut milk, chilli powder and water in a bowl.

3 Blend all the ingredients together well and set aside.

4 Heat the oil in a karahi, wok or heavy pan, add the garlic, ginger, cinnamon, cardamoms and salt to taste and fry over a low heat.

5 Increase the heat and pour in the spice mixture. Bring to the boil, stirring occasionally.

6 Add the prawns to the spices and continue to stir-fry until the prawns have heated through and the sauce is quite thick. Serve garnished with the chopped fresh coriander.

Rich Prawn Curry

A rich, flavoursome curry made with prawns and a delicious blend of aromatic spices.

INGREDIENTS

Serves 4

675g/1½lb uncooked tiger
  prawns (shrimp)
4 dried red chillies
25g/1oz/½ cup desiccated (dry
  unsweetened shredded) coconut
5ml/1 tsp black mustard seeds
1 large onion, chopped
30ml/2 tbsp oil
4 bay leaves
2.5cm/1in piece fresh root ginger,
  finely chopped
2 garlic cloves, crushed
15ml/1 tbsp ground coriander
5ml/1 tsp chilli powder
5ml/1 tsp salt
4 tomatoes, finely chopped
plain rice, to serve

1 Peel the prawns and discard the shells. Run a sharp knife along the centre back of each prawn to make a shallow cut and carefully remove the thin black intestinal vein.

COOK'S TIP

Serve extra tiger prawns (shrimp) unpeeled, on the edge of each plate, for an attractive garnish. Cook them with the peeled prawns until they turn pink.

2 Put the dried red chillies, coconut, mustard seeds and onion in a large heavy frying pan and dry-fry for 8–10 minutes or until the spices begin to brown. The onion should turn a deep golden brown but do not let it burn or it will taste bitter.

3 Tip the mixture into a food processor or blender and process to a coarse paste.

4 Heat the oil in the frying pan and fry the bay leaves for 1 minute. Add the chopped ginger and the garlic and fry for 2–3 minutes.

NUTRITIONAL NOTES
Per Portion

Energy	289Kcals/1212KJ
Fat	12.13g
Saturated Fat	4.18g
Carbohydrate	12.77g
Fibre	2.65g

5 Add the coriander, chilli powder, salt and the coconut paste and fry gently for 5 minutes.

6 Stir in the chopped tomatoes and about 175ml/6fl oz/¾ cup water and simmer gently for 5–6 minutes or until the sauce has thickened.

7 Add the prawns and cook for about 4–5 minutes or until they turn pink and the edges are curling slightly. Serve with plain boiled rice.

Basmati Mushroom Rice with Prawns

Although mushrooms are not a particularly popular vegetable in India, they go well with the prawns in this dish.

INGREDIENTS

Serves 4

150g/5oz/⅔ cup basmati rice
15ml/1 tbsp oil
1 medium onion, chopped
4 black peppercorns
2.5cm/1in cinnamon stick
1 bay leaf
1.5ml/¼ tsp cumin seeds
2 cardamom pods
5ml/1 tsp crushed garlic
5ml/1 tsp grated fresh root ginger
5ml/1 tsp garam masala
5ml/1 tsp chilli powder
7.5ml/1½ tsp salt
115g/4oz/1 cup frozen cooked peeled
   prawns (shrimp), thawed
115g/4oz/1½ cups mushrooms, cut
   into large pieces
30ml/2 tbsp chopped fresh
   coriander (cilantro)
120ml/4fl oz/½ cup natural (plain) low
   fat yogurt
15ml/1 tbsp lemon juice
50g/2oz/½ cup frozen peas
250ml/8fl oz/1 cup water
1 fresh red chilli, seeded and sliced,
   to garnish

1 Wash the rice well and leave to soak in water for 30 minutes.

2 Heat the oil in a heavy pan and add the chopped onion, peppercorns, cinnamon, bay leaf, cumin seeds, cardamom pods, garlic, ginger, garam masala, chilli powder and salt. Lower the heat and stir-fry the mixture for 2–3 minutes.

3 Add the prawns to the spice mixture and cook for 2 minutes, then add the mushrooms.

-------- COOK'S TIP --------

Basmati rice grows in the foothills of the Himalayas. The delicate, slender grains have a unique aroma and flavour. The rice cooks to light, separate, fluffy grains, making it perfect for a dish like this.

NUTRITIONAL NOTES
Per Portion

Energy	248Kcals/1050KJ
Fat	5.20g
Saturated Fat	0.99g
Carbohydrate	40.04g
Fibre	1.85g

4 Stir in the coriander and yogurt, followed by the lemon juice and peas and cook for 2 more minutes.

5 Drain the rice and add it to the prawn mixture. Pour in the water, cover the pan and cook over a medium heat for about 15 minutes, checking once to make sure that the rice has not stuck to the base of the pan.

6 Remove the pan from the heat and leave to stand, still covered, for about 5 minutes. Transfer to a serving dish and serve garnished with the sliced red chilli.

Ragout of Shellfish with Coconut Milk

Green curry paste, made with green chillies and plenty of fresh coriander, is what gives this seafood dish its unique flavour. This recipe recalls the days when the French were influential in India, first through their trading interests, and later, when they ruled Pondicherry.

INGREDIENTS

Serves 4–6

450g/1lb mussels in their shells
60ml/4 tbsp water
225g/8oz medium cuttlefish or squid
400ml/14fl oz/1⅔ cups coconut milk
300ml/½ pint/1¼ cups chicken or
  vegetable stock
350g/12oz monkfish, hoki or red
  snapper, skinned
150g/5oz raw or cooked prawn tails,
  peeled and deveined
75g/3oz green beans, trimmed
  and cooked
1 tomato, peeled, seeded and
  roughly chopped
torn basil leaves, to garnish
boiled rice, to serve

For the green curry paste

10ml/2 tsp coriander seeds
2.5ml/½ tsp cumin seeds
3–4 medium fresh green chillies,
  finely chopped
20ml/4 tsp granulated sugar
10ml/2 tsp salt
2cm/¾in fresh root ginger, peeled and
  finely chopped
3 garlic cloves, crushed
1 medium onion, finely chopped
50g/2oz/2 cups fresh coriander leaves,
  finely chopped
2.5ml/½ tsp grated nutmeg
30ml/2 tbsp vegetable oil

1 Scrub the mussels in cold running water and pull off the "beards". Discard any that do not shut when sharply tapped. Put them in a pan with the water, cover and cook for 6–8 minutes. Discard any mussels that remain closed and remove three-quarters of the mussels from their shells. Set aside. Strain the cooking liquid and set aside.

2 To prepare the cuttlefish or squid, trim off the tentacles and discard the gut. Remove the cuttle shell from inside the body and rub off the skin. Cut the body open and score in a criss-cross pattern with a sharp knife. Cut into strips and set aside.

3 To make the green curry paste, dry-fry the coriander and cumin seeds in a karahi or wok. Grind the chillies with the sugar and salt in a pestle with a mortar or in a food processor. Add the coriander and cumin seeds, ginger, garlic and onion and grind to a paste. Add the fresh coriander, nutmeg and oil and combine thoroughly.

4 Strain the coconut milk and pour the thin liquid into a karahi or wok with the stock and reserved cooking liquid from the mussels. Reserve the thick part of the coconut milk. Add 60–75ml/4–5 tbsp of the green curry paste to the wok and bring the mixture to the boil. Boil rapidly for a few minutes, until the liquid has reduced completely.

5 Add the thick part of the coconut milk. Stir well, then add the cuttlefish or squid and monkfish, hoki or red snapper. Simmer for 15–20 minutes. Then add the prawns, mussels, beans and tomato. Simmer for 2–3 minutes until heated through. Transfer to a warmed serving dish, garnish with torn basil leaves and serve immediately with boiled rice.

NUTRITIONAL NOTES	
Per Portion	
Energy	270Kcals/1142KJ
Fat	8.6g
Saturated Fat	1.5g
Carbohydrate	9g
Fibre	0.9g

Prawn Salad with Curry Dressing

Curry spices add an unexpected twist to this salad. The warm flavours combine especially well with the sweet shellfish and grated apple. Curry paste is needed here rather than curry powder as there is no cooking, which is necessary for bringing out the flavours of powdered spices.

INGREDIENTS

Serves 4
1 ripe tomato
½ iceberg lettuce
1 small onion
1 small bunch fresh coriander (cilantro)
15ml/1 tbsp lemon juice
450g/1lb shelled cooked prawns (shrimp)
1 apple
8 whole cooked prawns (shrimp), 8 lemon wedges and 4 fresh coriander sprigs, to garnish
salt

For the curry dressing
75ml/5 tbsp mayonnaise
5ml/1 tsp mild curry paste
15ml/1 tbsp tomato ketchup

1 To peel the tomato, cut a cross in the skin with a knife and immerse in boiling water for 30 seconds. Drain and cool under cold water. Peel off the skin. Cut the tomato in half and squeeze each half gently to remove the seeds. Discard them, then cut each tomato half into large dice.

2 Wash the lettuce leaves, place them in a soft dishtowel and gently pat them dry. Shred the leaves finely and put in a large bowl.

3 Finely chop the onion and coriander. Add to the bowl together with the tomato, moisten with lemon juice and season with salt.

4 To make the dressing, combine the mayonnaise, curry paste and tomato ketchup in a small bowl. Add 30 ml/2 tbsp water to thin the dressing and season to taste with salt.

5 Combine the prawns with the dressing and stir gently so that all the prawns are evenly coated with the dressing.

6 Quarter and core the apple and grate into the prawn and dressing mixture.

7 Distribute the shredded lettuce mixture among four serving plates or bowls. Pile the prawn mixture in the centre of each and decorate each with two whole prawns, two lemon wedges and a sprig of coriander.

NUTRITIONAL NOTES	
Per Portion	
Energy	73Kcals/311KJ
Fat	0.6g
Saturated Fat	0.1g
Carbohydrate	6.8g
Fibre	1.3g

——— COOK'S TIP ———

Fresh coriander (cilantro) is inclined to wilt if it is kept out of water. Put it in a jar of water, cover with a plastic bag and place in the refrigerator and it will stay fresh for several days.

Poultry Dishes

SOME OF the most deliciously spiced Indian dishes are based on chicken. Perhaps because this bird is such a familiar – and inexpensive – ingredient, chicken curries have become the mainstay of menus at Indian restaurants the world over.

Curiously, some of the most popular poultry dishes in the West, like Chicken Tikka Masala, are little known in what many assume to be their country of origin, but are now being introduced to India by travellers from the UK. More authentic Indian dishes include Chicken Dopiaza, Chicken Jalfrezi and the milder kormas, whose rich content can be adapted by using low-fat yogurt instead of cream.

All of these, plus some less well known – but equally sumptuous – dishes, are to be found in the pages that follow. Whether you favour a Red Hot Chicken Curry or a quick and easy one-pot Chicken Pulao, these flavoursome dishes are equally suited to family meals or more formal occasions.

Tandoori Chicken

A delicious popular Indian/ Pakistani chicken dish which is cooked in a clay oven called a *tandoor*, this is extremely popular in the West and appears on the majority of restaurant menus. Although the authentic tandoori flavour is very difficult to achieve in a conventional oven, this version still makes a very tasty dish.

INGREDIENTS

Serves 4
4 chicken quarters, skinned
175ml/6fl oz/¾ cup natural (plain) low fat yogurt
5ml/1 tsp garam masala
5ml/1 tsp grated fresh root ginger
5ml/1 tsp crushed garlic
7.5ml/1½ tsp chilli powder
1.5ml/¼ tsp ground turmeric
5ml/1 tsp ground coriander
15ml/1 tbsp lemon juice
5ml/1 tsp salt
few drops of red food colouring
15ml/1 tbsp oil
mixed salad leaves and lime wedges, to garnish

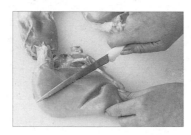

1 Rinse and pat dry the chicken quarters. Make two deep slits in the flesh of each piece, place in a dish and set aside.

COOK'S TIP

The traditional bright red colour is derived from food colouring. This is only optional and may be omitted if you prefer.

2 Mix together the yogurt, garam masala, ginger, garlic, chilli powder, turmeric, coriander, lemon juice, salt, red food colouring and oil, and beat so that all the ingredients are well combined.

NUTRITIONAL NOTES	
Per Portion	
Energy	300Kcals/1256KJ
Fat	12.00g
Saturated Fat	3.39g
Carbohydrate	5.90g
Fibre	0.20g

3 Cover the chicken quarters with the spice mixture, cover and leave to marinate for about 3 hours.

4 Preheat the oven to 240°C/475°F/ Gas 9. Transfer the chicken pieces to an ovenproof dish.

5 Bake the chicken in the oven for 20–25 minutes or until the chicken is cooked right through and evenly browned on top.

6 Remove from the oven, transfer to a serving dish and garnish with the salad leaves and lime wedges.

Chicken Naan Pockets

This quick-and-easy dish is ideal for a light snack lunch or supper. For speed, use the ready-to-bake naans available in most of today's supermarkets and Asian stores, but beware that as they are larger than typical home-cooked naan they will contain more fat.

INGREDIENTS

Serves 4

4 small naan, about 90g/3½oz each
45ml/3 tbsp natural (plain)
    low fat yogurt
7.5ml/1½ tsp garam masala
5ml/1 tsp chilli powder
5ml/1 tsp salt
45ml/3 tbsp lemon juice
15ml/1 tbsp chopped fresh
    coriander (cilantro)
1 fresh green chilli, chopped
450g/1lb boneless chicken, skinned
    and cubed
8 onion rings
2 tomatoes, quartered
½ white cabbage, shredded

For the garnish
mixed salad leaves
2 small tomatoes, halved
lemon wedges
fresh coriander (cilantro)

NUTRITIONAL NOTES	
Per Portion	
Energy	472Kcals/1986KJ
Fat	15.30g
Saturated Fat	6.46g
Carbohydrate	53.40g
Fibre	4.20g

_____ COOK'S TIP _____

For a version that is even lower in fat, substitute wholemeal or plain pitta bread for the naan. Warm the pitta in the oven, split to form a pocket and then follow the recipe from step 2.

1 Cut into the middle of each naan to make a pocket, then set aside.

2 Mix together the yogurt, garam masala, chilli powder, salt, lemon juice, fresh coriander and chopped green chilli. Pour the marinade over the chicken, cover and leave to marinate for about 1 hour.

3 Preheat the grill (broiler) to very hot, then lower to medium. Put the chicken in a pan or flameproof dish lined with foil. Grill (broil) for 15–20 minutes until tender and fully cooked, turning the chicken twice.

4 Remove from the heat and fill each naan with the chicken and then with the onion rings, tomatoes and cabbage. Serve garnished with mixed salad leaves, tomato halves, lemon wedges and coriander.

Goan Chicken Curry

Lines of swaying palm trees and the raised borders of a vast patchwork of paddy fields are just two of the features typical of the superb landscape of Goa. Not surprisingly, coconut, in all of its forms, is widely used to enrich Goan cuisine.

INGREDIENTS

Serves 4

75g/3oz/1½ cups desiccated (dry unsweetened shredded) coconut
30ml/2 tbsp vegetable oil
2.5ml/½ tsp cumin seeds
4 black peppercorns
15ml/1 tbsp fennel seeds
15ml/1 tbsp coriander seeds
2 onions, finely chopped
2.5ml/½ tsp salt
8 small chicken pieces, such as thighs and drumsticks, skinned
fresh coriander (cilantro) sprigs and lemon wedges, to garnish

1 Put the desiccated coconut in a bowl with 45ml/3 tbsp water. Leave to soak for 15 minutes.

2 Heat 15ml/1 tbsp of the oil in a karahi, wok or large pan and fry the cumin seeds, peppercorns, fennel and coriander seeds over a low heat for 3–4 minutes until they begin to splutter.

3 Add the finely chopped onions and fry for about 5 minutes, stirring occasionally, until the onion has softened and turned opaque.

4 Stir in the coconut, along with the soaking water and salt, and continue to fry for a further 5 minutes, stirring occasionally to prevent the mixture from sticking to the pan.

5 Put the coconut mixture into a food processor or blender and process to form a coarse paste. Spoon into a bowl and set aside until required.

6 Heat the remaining oil and fry the chicken for 10 minutes. Add the coconut paste and cook over a low heat for 15–20 minutes, or until the coconut mixture is golden brown and the chicken is tender.

7 Transfer the curry to a warmed serving plate, and garnish with sprigs of fresh coriander and lemon wedges. Mint and coconut chutney, plain boiled rice or a lentil dish would all make good accompaniments.

COOK'S TIP

If you prefer, make the spiced coconut mixture the day before and chill it in the refrigerator, then continue from step 6.

NUTRITIONAL NOTES	
Per Portion	
Energy	305Kcals/1271KJ
Fat	21.4g
Saturated Fat	12.1g
Carbohydrate	1.2g
Fibre	2.6g

Chicken Dopiaza

Dopiaza translates literally as "two onions" and describes this chicken dish in which two types of onion – large and small – are used at different stages during the cooking process.

INGREDIENTS

Serves 4

30ml/2 tbsp oil
8 small onions, halved
2 bay leaves
8 green cardamom pods
4 cloves
3 dried red chillies
8 black peppercorns
2 onions, finely chopped
2 garlic cloves, crushed
2.5cm/1in piece fresh root ginger,
  finely chopped
5ml/1 tsp ground coriander
5ml/1 tsp ground cumin
2.5ml/½ tsp ground turmeric
5ml/1 tsp chilli powder
2.5ml/½ tsp salt
4 tomatoes, peeled and finely chopped
120ml/4fl oz/½ cup water
8 chicken pieces, such as thighs and
  drumsticks, skinned
plain rice, to serve

COOK'S TIP

Soak the small onions in boiling water for 2–3 minutes to make them easier to peel.

NUTRITIONAL NOTES
Per Portion

Energy	352Kcals/1469KJ
Fat	15.10g
Saturated Fat	3.67g
Carbohydrate	22.60g
Fibre	3.90g

1 Heat half the oil in a large heavy pan or wok and fry the small onions for 10 minutes, or until golden brown. Remove and set aside.

2 Add the remaining oil and fry the bay leaves, cardamoms, cloves, chillies and peppercorns for 2 minutes. Add the onions, garlic and ginger and fry for 5 minutes. Stir in the ground spices and salt and cook for 2 minutes.

3 Add the tomatoes and water and simmer for 5 minutes until the sauce thickens. Add the chicken and cook for about 15 minutes.

4 Add the reserved small onions, then cover and cook for a further 10 minutes, or until the chicken is cooked through. Spoon the mixture onto a serving dish or individual plates. Serve with plain boiled rice.

Chicken Dhansak

Dhansak curries originate from the Parsee community and traditionally include lentils.

INGREDIENTS

Serves 4

75g/3oz/½ cup green lentils
475ml/16fl oz/2 cups chicken stock
15ml/1 tbsp oil
5ml/1 tsp cumin seeds
2 curry leaves
1 onion, finely chopped
2.5cm/1in piece fresh root
    ginger, chopped
1 fresh green chilli, finely chopped
5ml/1 tsp ground cumin
5ml/1 tsp ground coriander
1.5ml/¼ tsp salt
1.5ml/¼ tsp chilli powder
400g/14oz can chopped tomatoes
8 chicken pieces, skinned
90ml/6 tbsp chopped fresh
    coriander (cilantro)
5ml/1 tsp garam masala
plain and yellow rice, to serve

1 Rinse the lentils under cold running water. Put into a pan with the stock. Bring to the boil, cover and simmer for about 15–20 minutes. Put the lentils and stock to one side.

2 Heat the oil in a large heavy pan and fry the cumin seeds and curry leaves for 2 minutes. Add the onion, ginger and chilli and fry for about 5 minutes. Stir in the cumin, ground coriander, salt and chilli powder with 30ml/2 tbsp water.

NUTRITIONAL NOTES	
Per Portion	
Energy	328Kcals/1376KJ
Fat	10.80g
Saturated Fat	2.54g
Carbohydrate	19.70g
Fibre	3.50g

3 Add the tomatoes and the chicken pieces to the spices. Cover and cook for 10–15 minutes.

4 Add the lentils and stock, half the chopped fresh coriander and the garam masala. Cook for a further 10 minutes or until the chicken is tender. Garnish with the remaining fresh coriander and serve with spiced plain and yellow rice.

Hot Chilli Chicken

Not for the faint-hearted, this fiery, hot curry is made with a spicy chilli masala paste.

INGREDIENTS

Serves 4
30ml/2 tbsp tomato purée (paste)
2 garlic cloves, roughly chopped
2 fresh green chillies, roughly chopped
5 dried red chillies
2.5ml/½ tsp salt
1.5ml/¼ tsp granulated sugar
5ml/1 tsp chilli powder
2.5ml/½ tsp paprika
15ml/1 tbsp curry paste
15ml/1 tbsp oil
2.5ml/½ tsp cumin seeds
1 onion, finely chopped
2 bay leaves
5ml/1 tsp ground coriander
5ml/1 tsp ground cumin
1.5ml/¼ tsp ground turmeric
400g/14oz can chopped tomatoes
150ml/¼ pint/⅔ cup water
8 chicken thighs, skinned
5ml/1 tsp garam masala
sliced fresh green chillies, to garnish
chapatis and natural (plain) low fat
    yogurt, to serve

1 Put the tomato purée, chopped garlic cloves, fresh green chillies and the dried red chillies into a food processor or blender.

2 Add the salt, sugar, chilli powder, paprika and curry paste. Process all the ingredients to a smooth paste, stopping once or twice to scrape down any of the mixture that has stuck to the sides of the bowl.

3 Heat the oil in a large heavy pan and fry the cumin seeds for 2 minutes. Add the onion and bay leaves and fry for about 5 minutes.

4 Add the chilli paste and fry for 2–3 minutes. Add the ground coriander, cumin and turmeric and cook for 2 minutes. Tip in the tomatoes.

5 Pour in the water and stir to mix. Bring to the boil and simmer for 5 minutes until the sauce thickens.

6 Add the chicken and garam masala. Cover and simmer for 25–30 minutes until the chicken is tender. Garnish with sliced green chillies and serve with chappatis and natural low fat yogurt.

NUTRITIONAL NOTES	
Per Portion	
Energy	290Kcals/1212KJ
Fat	13.00g
Saturated Fat	3.50g
Carbohydrate	11.60g
Fibre	1.40g

Chicken Saag

A mildly spiced dish using a popular combination of spinach and chicken. This recipe is best made using fresh spinach.

INGREDIENTS

Serves 4

225g/8oz fresh spinach leaves, washed but not dried
2.5cm/1in piece fresh root ginger, grated
2 garlic cloves, crushed
1 fresh green chilli, roughly chopped
200ml/7fl oz/scant 1 cup water
15ml/1 tbsp oil
2 bay leaves
1.5ml/¼ tsp black peppercorns
1 onion, finely chopped
4 tomatoes, peeled and finely chopped
10ml/2 tsp curry powder
5ml/1 tsp salt
5ml/1 tsp chilli powder
45ml/3 tbsp natural (plain) low fat yogurt
8 chicken thighs, skinned
naan bread, to serve
natural (plain) low fat yogurt and chilli powder, to garnish

1 Cook the spinach leaves, without extra water, in a tightly covered pan for 5 minutes. Put the cooked spinach, ginger, garlic and chilli with 50ml/2fl oz/¼ cup of the measured water into a food processor or blender and process to a thick purée. Set aside.

2 Heat the oil in a large heavy pan, add the bay leaves and black peppercorns and fry for 2 minutes. Stir in the onion and fry for a further 6–8 minutes or until the onion has browned.

3 Add the tomatoes and simmer for about 5 minutes.

4 Stir in the curry powder, salt and chilli powder. Cook for 2 minutes over a medium heat, stirring once or twice.

NUTRITIONAL NOTES	
Per Portion	
Energy	283Kcals/1182KJ
Fat	12.70g
Saturated Fat	3.48g
Carbohydrate	9.70g
Fibre	3.10g

5 Stir in the spinach purée and the remaining measured water, then simmer for 5 minutes.

6 Add the yogurt, 15ml/1 tbsp at a time, and simmer for 5 minutes.

7 Add the chicken thighs and stir to coat them in the sauce. Cover and cook for 25–30 minutes until the chicken is tender. Serve on naan bread, drizzle over some yogurt and dust with chilli powder.

Jeera Chicken

An aromatic dish with a
delicious, distinctive taste of
cumin. Serve simply with a
cooling cucumber raita.

INGREDIENTS

Serves 4

45ml/3 tbsp cumin seeds
15ml/1 tbsp oil
2.5ml/½ tsp black peppercorns
4 green cardamom pods
2 fresh green chillies, finely chopped
2 garlic cloves, crushed
2.5cm/1in piece fresh root
   ginger, grated
5ml/1 tsp ground coriander
10ml/2 tsp ground cumin
2.5ml/½ tsp salt
8 chicken pieces, skinned
5ml/1 tsp garam masala
fresh coriander (cilantro) and chilli
   powder, to garnish
cucumber raita, to serve

1 Dry-roast 15ml/1 tbsp of the
cumin seeds for 5 minutes and
then set aside.

COOK'S TIP

Dry-roast the cumin seeds in a small, heavy
frying pan over a medium heat, stirring
them until they turn a few shades darker
and give off a wonderful roasted aroma.

2 Heat the oil in a large heavy pan
or wok and fry the remaining
cumin seeds, black peppercorns and
cardamoms for about 2–3 minutes.

3 Add the chillies, garlic and ginger
and fry for about 2 minutes.

4 Add the ground coriander, ground
cumin and salt. Stir well, then
cook for a further 2–3 minutes.

5 Add the chicken and stir to coat
the pieces in the sauce. Cover and
simmer for 20–25 minutes.

6 Add the garam masala and reserved
toasted cumin seeds and cook for
a further 5 minutes. Garnish with fresh
coriander and chilli powder and serve
with cucumber raita.

NUTRITIONAL NOTES	
Per Portion	
Energy	286Kcals/1198KJ
Fat	14.10g
Saturated Fat	3.19g
Carbohydrate	7.60g
Fibre	0.10g

Chicken in Cashew Nut Sauce

This strongly flavoured chicken dish has a deliciously thick and nutty sauce, and is best served with plain boiled rice.

INGREDIENTS

Serves 4

2 medium onions
30ml/2 tbsp tomato purée (paste)
50g/2oz/½ cup cashew nuts
7.5ml/1½ tsp garam masala
5ml/1 tsp crushed garlic
5ml/1 tsp chilli powder
15ml/1 tbsp lemon juice
1.5ml/¼ tsp ground turmeric
5ml/1 tsp salt
15ml/1 tbsp natural (plain)
   low fat yogurt
30ml/2 tbsp oil
30ml/2 tbsp chopped fresh
   coriander (cilantro)
15ml/1 tbsp sultanas (golden raisins)
450g/1lb boneless chicken, skinned
   and cubed
175g/6oz/2½ cups button
   (white) mushrooms
300ml/½ pint/1¼ cups water

1 Cut the onions into quarters, place in a food processor or blender and process for about 1 minute.

_____ COOK'S TIP _____

Cut the chicken into small, equal-size cubes for quick and even cooking.

2 Add the tomato purée, cashew nuts, garam masala, garlic, chilli powder, lemon juice, turmeric, salt and yogurt to the processed onions.

3 Process the spiced onion mixture in the food processor for a further 1–1½ minutes.

4 In a heavy pan or karahi, heat the oil, lower the heat to medium and pour in the spice mixture from the food processor. Fry for 2 minutes, lowering the heat more if necessary.

5 When the spice mixture is lightly cooked, add half the chopped fresh coriander, the sultanas and the chicken cubes and continue to stir-fry for a further 1 minute.

6 Add the mushrooms, pour in the water and bring to a simmer. Cover the pan and cook over a low heat for about 10 minutes.

7 After this time, check that the chicken is cooked through and the sauce is thick. Cook for a little longer if necessary, then spoon into a serving bowl. Garnish with the remaining fresh coriander and serve.

NUTRITIONAL NOTES	
Per Portion	
Energy	286Kcals/1199KJ
Fat	13.30g
Saturated Fat	2.39g
Carbohydrate	12.90g
Fibre	2.10g

Chicken with Green Mango

Green, unripe mango is used for making various dishes on the Indian subcontinent, including pickles, chutneys and some meat, chicken and vegetable dishes. This is a fairly simple chicken dish to prepare and is good served with rice and dhal.

INGREDIENTS

Serves 4

1 medium green mango
450g/1lb boneless chicken, skinned
    and cubed
1.5ml/¼ tsp onion seeds
5ml/1 tsp grated fresh root ginger
2.5ml/½ tsp crushed garlic
5ml/1 tsp chilli powder
1.5ml/¼ tsp ground turmeric
5ml/1 tsp salt
5ml/1 tsp ground coriander
30ml/2 tbsp oil
2 medium onions, sliced
4 curry leaves
300ml/½ pint/1¼ cups water
2 medium tomatoes, quartered
2 fresh green chillies, chopped
30ml/2 tbsp chopped fresh
    coriander (cilantro)

1 To prepare the mango, peel the skin and slice the flesh thickly. Discard the stone from the middle. Place the mango slices in a small bowl, cover and set aside.

2 Place the chicken cubes in a bowl and add the onion seeds, ginger, garlic, chilli powder, turmeric, salt and ground coriander. Mix to coat the chicken with the spices, then add half the mango slices.

3 In a medium heavy pan, heat the oil and fry the sliced onions until golden brown. Add the curry leaves and stir lightly.

4 Gradually add the chicken pieces and mango, stirring all the time.

5 Pour in the water, lower the heat and cook for about 12–15 minutes, stirring occasionally, until the chicken is cooked through and the water has been absorbed.

6 Add the remaining mango slices, the tomatoes, green chillies and fresh coriander and serve hot.

VARIATION

A good, firm cooking apple can be used instead of unripe green mango, if you like. Prepare and cook in the same way.

NUTRITIONAL NOTES
Per Portion

Energy	281Kcals/1172KJ
Fat	11.20g
Saturated Fat	2.44g
Carbohydrate	20.60g
Fibre	3.60g

Chicken Tikka Masala

This is another of those dishes that is celebrated in the West but less well known in India. It is said to be Britain's favourite chicken dish. In this version, tender chicken pieces are cooked in a creamy, spicy tomato sauce and served on naan bread.

INGREDIENTS

Serves 4

675g/1½lb chicken breast
  portions, skinned
90ml/6 tbsp tikka paste
120ml/4fl oz/½ cup natural (plain)
  low fat yogurt
15ml/1 tbsp oil
1 onion, chopped
1 garlic clove, crushed
1 fresh green chilli, seeded and chopped
2.5cm/1in piece fresh root
  ginger, grated
15ml/1 tbsp tomato purée (paste)
250ml/8fl oz/1 cup water
a little melted ghee or butter
15ml/1 tbsp lemon juice
fresh coriander (cilantro) sprigs, natural
  (plain) low fat yogurt and toasted
  cumin seeds, to garnish
naan bread, to serve

NUTRITIONAL NOTES	
Per Portion	
Energy	315Kcals/1321KJ
Fat	12.50g
Saturated Fat	4.00g
Carbohydrate	7.50g
Fibre	0.60g

COOK'S TIPS

• Make your own paste, using the basic recipe in the introduction to this book, or use a good-quality bought paste.
• Soak the wooden skewers in cold water before using, to prevent them from burning while under the grill.

1 Remove any visible fat from the chicken and cut the meat into 2.5cm/1in cubes. Mix 45ml/3 tbsp of the tikka paste and 60ml/4 tbsp of the yogurt into a bowl. Add the chicken and leave to marinate for 20 minutes.

2 Heat the oil in a heavy pan and fry the onion, garlic, chilli and ginger for 5 minutes. Add the remaining tikka paste and fry for 2 minutes. Stir in the tomato purée and water, bring to the boil and simmer for 15 minutes.

3 Meanwhile, thread the chicken pieces on to wooden kebab skewers. Preheat the grill (broiler).

4 Brush the chicken pieces lightly with melted ghee or butter and cook under a medium heat for 15 minutes, turning the skewers occasionally.

5 Put the tikka sauce into a food processor or blender and process until smooth. Return to the pan.

6 Add the remaining yogurt and the lemon juice, remove the grilled (broiled) chicken from the skewers and add to the pan, then simmer for 5 minutes. Garnish with the fresh coriander, yogurt and toasted cumin seeds and serve on naan bread.

Spicy Masala Chicken

These tender chicken pieces have a sweet-and-sour taste. Serve cold with a salad and rice or hot with potatoes.

INGREDIENTS

Serves 6

12 chicken thighs, skinned
90ml/6 tbsp lemon juice
5ml/1 tsp grated fresh root ginger
5ml/1 tsp crushed garlic
5ml/1 tsp crushed dried red chillies
5ml/1 tsp salt
5ml/1 tsp soft brown sugar
30ml/2 tbsp clear honey
30ml/2 tbsp chopped fresh
    coriander (cilantro)
1 fresh green chilli, finely chopped
30ml/2 tbsp vegetable oil
fresh coriander (cilantro), to garnish
yellow rice and salad, to serve

1 Prick the chicken thighs with a fork, rinse them, pat dry with kitchen paper and set aside in a bowl.

2 In a large mixing bowl, mix together the lemon juice, ginger, garlic, crushed dried red chillies, salt, sugar and honey.

3 Transfer the chicken thighs to the spice mixture and coat well. Cover and set aside for about 45 minutes.

4 Preheat the grill (broiler) to medium. Add the fresh coriander and chopped chilli to the chicken and place them in a flameproof dish.

5 Pour any remaining marinade over the chicken and brush with the oil.

6 Grill (broil) the chicken thighs for 15–20 minutes, turning and basting with the marinade occasionally, until cooked through and browned.

7 Serve cold, garnished with fresh coriander and accompanied by yellow rice and salad.

NUTRITIONAL NOTES	
Per Portion	
Energy	243Kcals/1017KJ
Fat	12.00g
Saturated Fat	3.18g
Carbohydrate	5.30g
Fibre	0.00g

Chicken in Orange and Black Pepper Sauce

A low-fat version of a favourite
Indian dish, this is very creamy.

INGREDIENTS

Serves 4

225g/8oz low fat fromage frais or
  ricotta cheese
50ml/2fl oz/¼ cup natural (plain)
  low fat yogurt
120ml/4fl oz/½ cup orange juice
7.5ml/1½ tsp grated fresh root ginger
5ml/1 tsp crushed garlic
5ml/1 tsp ground black pepper
5ml/1 tsp salt
5ml/1 tsp ground coriander
1 small chicken, about 675g/1½lb,
  skinned and cut into 8 pieces
15ml/1 tbsp oil
1 bay leaf
1 large onion, chopped
15ml/1 tbsp fresh mint leaves
1 fresh green chilli, seeded and chopped

1 In a small mixing bowl whisk the
fromage frais or ricotta with the
yogurt, orange juice, ginger, garlic,
pepper, salt and coriander.

3 Heat the oil with the bay leaf in a
wok or heavy frying pan and fry
the chopped onion until soft.

4 Pour in the chicken mixture and
stir-fry for 3–5 minutes over a
medium heat. Lower the heat, cover
and cook for 7–10 minutes, adding a
little water if the sauce is too thick.
Add the fresh mint and chilli and serve.

2 Pour this over the chicken, cover,
and set aside for 3–4 hours.

NUTRITIONAL NOTES	
Per Portion	
Energy	199Kcals/836KJ
Fat	5.11g
Saturated Fat	1.06g
Carbohydrate	14.40g
Fibre	1.02g

—————— COOK'S TIP ——————

If you prefer the taste of curry leaves, you
can use them instead of the bay leaf, but
you will need to double the quantity.

Chicken Korma

Although kormas are traditionally rich and high in fat, this recipe uses low fat yogurt instead of cream, which gives the sauce a delicious flavour while keeping down the fat content. To prevent the yogurt from curdling, add it very slowly to the sauce and keep stirring until it is incorporated.

INGREDIENTS

Serves 4
675g/1½lb chicken breast
   portions, skinned
2 garlic cloves, crushed
2.5cm/1in piece fresh root ginger,
   roughly chopped
15ml/1 tbsp oil
3 green cardamom pods
1 onion, finely chopped
10ml/2 tsp ground cumin
1.5ml/¼ tsp salt
300ml/½ pint/1¼ cups natural (plain)
   low fat yogurt
toasted flaked or sliced almonds
   (optional) and a fresh coriander
   (cilantro) sprig, to garnish
plain rice, to serve

1 Using a sharp knife, remove any visible fat from the chicken breast portions and cut the meat into 2.5cm/1in cubes.

2 Put the garlic and ginger into a food processor or blender with 30ml/2 tbsp water and process to a smooth, creamy paste.

3 Heat the oil in a large heavy pan and cook the chicken cubes for 8–10 minutes until browned on all sides. Remove the chicken cubes with a slotted spoon and set aside.

4 Add the cardamom pods and fry for 2 minutes. Add the onion and fry for a further 5 minutes.

NUTRITIONAL NOTES
Per Portion

Energy	288Kcals/1211KJ
Fat	9.30g
Saturated Fat	2.54g
Carbohydrate	9.80g
Fibre	0.50g

5 Stir in the garlic and ginger paste, cumin and salt and cook, stirring, for a further 5 minutes.

6 Add half the yogurt, stirring in a tablespoonful at a time, and cook over a low heat, until it has all been absorbed.

7 Return the chicken to the pan. Cover and simmer over a low heat for 5–6 minutes or until the chicken is tender.

8 Add the remaining yogurt and simmer for a further 5 minutes. Garnish with toasted almonds and coriander and serve with rice.

COOK'S TIP

Traditionally, kormas are spicy dishes with a rich, creamy texture. They are not meant to be very hot curries.

Mild Chicken Curry with Lentils

In this dish, the mildly spiced sauce is thickened using low fat lentils rather than the traditional onions fried in ghee.

INGREDIENTS

Serves 4–6

75g/3oz/½ cup red lentils
30ml/2 tbsp mild curry powder
10ml/2 tsp ground coriander
5ml/1 tsp cumin seeds
475ml/16fl oz/2 cups vegetable stock
8 chicken thighs, skinned
225g/8oz fresh spinach, shredded, or frozen spinach, thawed and well drained
15ml/1 tbsp chopped fresh coriander (cilantro), plus extra to garnish
salt and black pepper
white or brown basmati rice and grilled poppadums, to serve

1 Put the lentils in a large heavy pan and add the curry powder, ground coriander, cumin seeds and vegetable stock.

2 Bring the mixture to the boil, then lower the heat. Cover and simmer for 10 minutes, stirring often.

3 Add the chicken and spinach. Replace the cover and simmer gently for a further 40 minutes, or until the chicken is cooked through.

4 Stir in the chopped coriander and season to taste. Serve garnished with fresh coriander sprigs and accompanied by white or brown basmati rice and poppadums.

NUTRITIONAL NOTES	
Per Portion (4)	
Energy	296Kcals/1244KJ
Fat	10.20g
Saturated Fat	2.83g
Carbohydrate	15.10g
Fibre	3.80g

_____ COOK'S TIP _____

Lentils are an excellent low fat source of vitamins and fibre, as well as adding subtle colour and texture to dishes. Yellow and red lentils, in particular, are very popular in Indian cooking.

Chicken Jalfrezi

A Jalfrezi is a stir-fried curry which features onions, ginger and garlic in a rich pepper sauce.

INGREDIENTS

Serves 4

675g/1½lb chicken breast portions
15ml/1 tbsp oil
5ml/1 tsp cumin seeds
1 onion, finely chopped
1 green (bell) pepper, seeded and
  finely chopped
1 red (bell) pepper, seeded and
  finely chopped
1 garlic clove, crushed
2cm/¾in piece fresh root ginger,
  finely chopped
15ml/1 tbsp curry paste
1.5ml/¼ tsp chilli powder
5ml/1 tsp ground coriander
5ml/1 tsp ground cumin
2.5ml/½ tsp salt
400g/14oz can chopped tomatoes
30ml/2 tbsp chopped fresh coriander
  (cilantro), plus extra to garnish
plain rice, to serve

1 Skin the chicken breast portions and remove any visible fat. Cut the meat into 2.5cm/1in cubes.

2 Heat the oil in a karahi, wok or heavy pan and fry the cumin seeds for 2 minutes until they splutter. Add the onion, peppers, garlic and ginger and fry for 6–8 minutes.

NUTRITIONAL NOTES	
Per Portion	
Energy	291Kcals/1224KJ
Fat	9.80g
Saturated Fat	2.24g
Carbohydrate	11.70g
Fibre	3.50g

3 Add the curry paste and fry for about 2 minutes. Stir in the chilli powder, ground coriander, cumin and salt and add 15ml/1 tbsp water; fry for a further 2 minutes.

4 Add the chicken cubes and fry for about 5 minutes. Add the canned tomatoes and chopped fresh coriander. Cover the pan tightly with a lid and cook for about 15 minutes or until the chicken cubes are tender. Garnish with sprigs of fresh coriander and serve with rice.

Karahi Chicken with Fresh Fenugreek

Fresh fenugreek is a flavour that not many people are familiar with and this recipe is a good introduction to this delicious herb. Once again, the chicken is boiled before it is quickly stir-fried, to make sure it is cooked through.

INGREDIENTS

Serves 4

115g/4oz boneless chicken thigh meat, skinned and cut into strips
115g/4oz chicken breast fillet, skinned and cut into strips
2.5ml/½ tsp crushed garlic
5ml/1 tsp chilli powder
2.5ml/½ tsp salt
10ml/2 tsp tomato purée (paste)
30ml/2 tbsp oil
1 bunch fresh fenugreek leaves
15ml/1 tbsp chopped fresh coriander (cilantro)
300ml/½ pint/1¼ cups water
pilau rice and wholemeal chapatis, to serve (optional)

1 Bring a pan of water to the boil, add the chicken strips and cook for about 5–7 minutes. Drain the chicken and set aside.

2 In a mixing bowl, combine the garlic, chilli powder and salt with the tomato purée.

3 Heat the oil in a large heavy pan. Lower the heat and stir in the tomato purée and spice mixture.

4 Add the chicken pieces to the spices and stir-fry for 5–7 minutes, then lower the heat further.

5 Add the fenugreek leaves and fresh coriander. Continue to stir-fry for 5–7 minutes until all the ingredients are mixed well together.

6 Pour in the water, cover and cook for about 5 minutes, stirring several times, until the dish is simmering. Serve hot with some pulao rice and some warm wholemeal chapatis, if you like.

NUTRITIONAL NOTES	
Per Portion	
Energy	127Kcals/528KJ
Fat	7.90g
Saturated Fat	1.51g
Carbohydrate	1.20g
Fibre	0.10g

Karahi Chicken with Mint

Another herb that goes well with spicy chicken is mint, which has cooling qualities to counter the heat of ginger and chillies.

INGREDIENTS

Serves 4

275g/10oz chicken breast fillets, skinned and cut into strips
300ml/½ pint/1¼ cups water
30ml/2 tbsp oil
2 small bunches spring onions (scallions), roughly chopped
5ml/1 tsp shredded fresh root ginger
5ml/1 tsp crushed dried red chillies
30ml/2 tbsp lemon juice
15ml/1 tbsp chopped fresh coriander (cilantro)
15ml/1 tbsp chopped fresh mint
3 tomatoes, peeled, seeded and roughly chopped
5ml/1 tsp salt
mint and coriander (cilantro) sprigs, to garnish

1 Put the chicken and water into a saucepan, bring to the boil and lower the heat to medium. Cook for about 10 minutes or until the water has evaporated and the chicken is cooked. Remove from the heat and set aside.

2 Heat the oil in a heavy pan and stir-fry the spring onions for 2 minutes until soft but not browned.

3 Add the cooked chicken strips and stir-fry for about 3 minutes over a medium heat.

NUTRITIONAL NOTES	
Per Portion	
Energy	157Kcals/655KJ
Fat	8.20g
Saturated Fat	1.50g
Carbohydrate	4.20g
Fibre	1.40g

4 Gradually add the shredded ginger, dried red chillies, lemon juice, chopped coriander and mint, tomatoes and salt and gently stir to blend all the flavours together.

5 Transfer the spicy chicken mixture to a serving dish and garnish with a few sprigs of fresh mint and coriander before serving.

Aromatic Chicken Curry

Tender pieces of chicken are lightly cooked with fresh vegetables and aromatic spices.

INGREDIENTS

Serves 4

675g/1½lb chicken breast
    portions, skinned
15ml/1 tbsp oil
2.5ml/½ tsp cumin seeds
2.5ml/½ tsp fennel seeds
1 onion, thickly sliced
2 garlic cloves, crushed
2.5cm/1in piece fresh root ginger,
    finely chopped
15ml/1 tbsp curry paste
225g/8oz broccoli, broken into florets
4 tomatoes, cut into thick wedges
5ml/1 tsp garam masala
30ml/2 tbsp chopped fresh
    coriander (cilantro)
naan bread, to serve

1 Remove any visible fat from the chicken and cut the meat into 2.5cm/1in cubes.

NUTRITIONAL NOTES	
Per Portion	
Energy	286Kcals/1201KJ
Fat	9.80g
Saturated Fat	2.19g
Carbohydrate	8.50g
Fibre	3.70g

2 Heat the oil in a karahi, wok or heavy pan and fry the cumin and fennel seeds for 2 minutes until the seeds begin to splutter. Add the onion, garlic and ginger and cook for 5–7 minutes. Stir in the curry paste and cook for a further 2–3 minutes.

3 Add the broccoli florets and fry for about 5 minutes. Add the chicken cubes and fry for 5–8 minutes.

4 Add the tomato wedges to the pan with the garam masala and the chopped fresh coriander. Cook the curry for a further 5–10 minutes or until the chicken cubes are tender. Serve with the naan bread.

Traditional Chicken Curry

Chicken curry is always popular whether served at a family dinner or a banquet. This version is cooked with a lid on, giving a thin consistency. If you would prefer a thick curry, cook uncovered for the last 15 minutes.

INGREDIENTS

Serves 4-6

60ml/4 tbsp vegetable oil
4 cloves
4–6 green cardamom pods
5cm/2in piece cinnamon stick
3 whole star anise
6–8 curry leaves
1 large onion, finely chopped
5cm/2in piece fresh root ginger, crushed
4 garlic cloves, crushed
60ml/4 tbsp mild curry paste
5ml/1 tsp ground turmeric
1.6kg/3½lb chicken, skinned
   and jointed
400g/14oz can chopped tomatoes
115g/4oz creamed coconut, broken
   into small pieces, or 120ml/4fl oz/
   ½ cup coconut cream
2.5ml/½ tsp granulated sugar
salt, to taste
50g/2oz/2 cups fresh coriander
   (cilantro), chopped

1 Heat the oil in a pan and fry the cloves, cardamoms, cinnamon stick, star anise and curry leaves over a medium heat for about 5 minutes until the cloves swell and the curry leaves are slightly burnt.

2 Add the onion, ginger and garlic and fry until the onion turns brown. Add the curry paste and turmeric and fry until the oil separates.

3 Add the chicken pieces and mix well. When all the pieces are evenly sealed, cover the pan and cook until the meat is nearly cooked.

4 Add the canned chopped tomatoes and the creamed coconut. Simmer gently until the coconut dissolves. Mix well and add the sugar and salt. Fold in the chopped fresh coriander, then reheat briefly. Spoon into a dish and serve hot.

NUTRITIONAL NOTES	
Per Portion	
Energy	647Kcals/2683KJ
Fat	49.3g
Saturated Fat	17g
Carbohydrate	8.7g
Fibre	1.9g

Red Hot Chicken Curry

This curry has a satisfyingly thick sauce, and uses red and green peppers for extra colour.

INGREDIENTS

Serves 4
2 medium onions
½ red (bell) pepper
½ green (bell) pepper
30ml/2 tbsp oil
1.5ml/¼ tsp fenugreek seeds
1.5ml/¼ tsp onion seeds
2.5ml/½ tsp crushed garlic
2.5ml/½ tsp grated fresh root ginger
5ml/1 tsp ground coriander
5ml/1 tsp chilli powder
5ml/1 tsp salt
400g/14oz can tomatoes
30ml/2 tbsp lemon juice
350g/12oz chicken, skinned and cubed
30ml/2 tbsp chopped fresh
   coriander (cilantro)
3 fresh green chillies, chopped
fresh coriander (cilantro), to garnish

NUTRITIONAL NOTES	
Per Portion	
Energy	214Kcals/895KJ
Fat	10.00g
Saturated Fat	2.08g
Carbohydrate	11.00g
Fibre	2.20g

1 Using a sharp knife, dice the onions. Seed the peppers and cut them into chunks.

2 In a medium heavy pan, heat the oil and fry the fenugreek and onion seeds until they turn a shade darker. Add the chopped onions, garlic and ginger. Fry for about 5 minutes until the onions turn golden brown. Reduce the heat to very low.

3 In a bowl, mix together the ground coriander, chilli powder, salt, canned tomatoes and lemon juice. Stir well.

4 Pour this mixture into the pan and increase the heat to medium. Stir-fry for about 3 minutes.

5 Add the chicken cubes and stir-fry for 5–7 minutes.

6 Add the chopped fresh coriander and green chillies and the red and green pepper chunks.

7 Lower the heat, cover the saucepan and allow to simmer for about 10 minutes until the chicken cubes are cooked.

8 Serve the curry hot, garnished with fresh coriander.

VARIATION
For a milder version of this delicious curry, simply omit some, or even all, of the green chillies.

Mughlai-style Chicken

The cuisine of Andhra Pradesh is renowned for its pungency because the hottest variety of chilli is grown there. In sharp contrast, however, the region is also home to the subtle flavours of a style of cooking known as *nizami*, which has a distinct Mogul influence. This recipe, with the heady aroma of saffron and the captivating flavour of a silky almond and cream sauce, is a typical example.

INGREDIENTS

Serves 4–6

1 large onion
2 eggs
4 chicken breast fillets
15–30ml/1–2 tbsp garam masala
90ml/6 tbsp ghee or vegetable oil
5cm/2in piece fresh root ginger, finely crushed
4 garlic cloves, finely crushed
4 cloves
4 green cardamom pods
5cm/2in piece cinnamon stick
2 bay leaves
15–20 saffron threads
150ml/¼ pint/⅔ cup natural (plain) yogurt, beaten with 5ml/1 tsp cornflour (cornstarch)
75ml/5 tbsp/⅓ cup double (heavy) cream
50g/2oz/½ cup ground almonds
salt and pepper

1 Chop the onion finely. Break the eggs into a bowl and season with salt and pepper.

2 Rub the chicken fillets with the garam masala, then brush with the beaten egg. In a karahi, wok, or large pan, heat the ghee or vegetable oil and fry the chicken until cooked through and browned on both sides. Remove from the pan and keep warm.

3 In the same pan, fry the chopped onion, ginger, garlic, cloves, cardamom pods, cinnamon and bay leaves. When the onion turns golden, remove the pan from the heat, allow the contents to cool a little and add the saffron and yogurt mixture. Stir well to prevent the yogurt from curdling.

4 Return the chicken to the pan, along with any juices, and gently cook until the chicken is tender. Adjust the seasoning if necessary.

5 Just before serving, pour in the cream. Fold it in then repeat the process with the ground almonds. Make sure the curry is piping hot before serving.

NUTRITIONAL NOTES	
Per Portion	
Energy	514Kcals/2141KJ
Fat	32.3g
Saturated Fat	9.9g
Carbohydrate	7.9g
Fibre	0.9g

___ COOK'S TIP ___

The whole spices used in this curry look attractive and are usually left in for serving, but you can remove the cloves, cinnamon stick and bay leaves if you like.

Kashmiri Chicken Curry

Surrounded by the snow-capped Himalayas, Kashmir is popularly known as the "Switzerland of the East". The state is also renowned for its rich culinary heritage, and this aromatic dish is one of the simplest among the region's repertoire.

INGREDIENTS

Serves 4–6
20ml/4 tsp Kashmiri masala paste
60ml/4 tbsp tomato ketchup
5ml/1 tsp Worcestershire sauce
5ml/1 tsp five-spice powder
5ml/1 tsp granulated sugar
8 chicken joints, skinned
5cm/2in piece fresh root ginger
45ml/3 tbsp vegetable oil
4 garlic cloves, crushed
juice of 1 lemon
15ml/1 tbsp coriander (cilantro) leaves, finely chopped
salt

1 To make the marinade, mix the masala paste, tomato ketchup, Worcestershire sauce, and five-spice powder, with the sugar and a little salt. Leave the mixture to rest in a warm place until the sugar has dissolved.

COOK'S TIP

You can buy specialist masala pastes, including Kashmiri paste, from some Indian grocers. Alternatively, make your own paste or use an all-purpose curry paste.

2 Rub the chicken pieces with the marinade and set aside in a cool place for a further 2 hours, or in the refrigerator overnight. Bring to room temperature before cooking.

3 Thinly peel the ginger, using a sharp knife or vegetable peeler. Grate the peeled root finely.

4 Heat the oil in a karahi, wok or large pan and fry half the ginger and all the garlic until golden.

5 Add the chicken and fry until both sides are sealed. Cover and cook until the chicken is tender, and the oil has separated from the sauce.

6 Sprinkle the chicken with the lemon juice, remaining ginger and chopped coriander leaves, and mix in well. Serve hot. Plain boiled rice would make a good accompaniment.

NUTRITIONAL NOTES	
Per Portion	
Energy	483Kcals/2009KJ
Fat	34.9g
Saturated Fat	8.2g
Carbohydrate	5.7g
Fibre	0.2g

Chicken Curry with Sliced Apples

This mild yet flavoursome dish is given a special lift by the addition of sliced apples.

INGREDIENTS

Serves 4

10ml/2 tsp oil
2 medium onions, diced
1 bay leaf
2 cloves
2.5cm/1in cinnamon stick
4 black peppercorns
1 baby chicken, about 675g/1½lb, skinned and cut into 8 pieces
5ml/1 tsp garam masala
5ml/1 tsp grated fresh root ginger
5ml/1 tsp crushed garlic
5ml/1 tsp salt
5ml/1 tsp chilli powder
15ml/1 tbsp ground almonds
150ml/¼ pint/⅔ cup natural (plain) low fat yogurt
2 green eating apples, peeled, cored and roughly sliced
15ml/1 tbsp chopped fresh coriander (cilantro)
15g/½oz flaked (sliced) almonds, lightly toasted, and fresh coriander (cilantro) leaves, to garnish

2 Add the chicken pieces to the onions and continue to stir-fry for at least another 3 minutes.

3 Lower the heat and add the garam masala, ginger, garlic, salt, chilli powder and ground almonds and cook, stirring constantly, for 2–3 minutes.

4 Pour in the yogurt and stir for a couple more minutes.

5 Add the apples and chopped coriander, cover and cook for about 10–15 minutes.

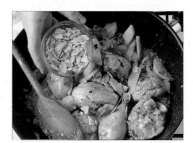

6 Check that the chicken is cooked through and serve immediately, garnished with the flaked almonds and whole coriander leaves.

1 Heat the oil in a karahi, wok or heavy pan and fry the onions with the bay leaf, cloves, cinnamon and peppercorns for about 3–5 minutes until the onions are beginning to soften but have not yet begun to brown.

NUTRITIONAL NOTES

Per Portion

Energy	237Kcals/994KJ
Fat	8.25g
Saturated Fat	1.31g
Carbohydrate	17.21g
Fibre	2.88g

———— COOK'S TIP ————

To keep the fat content of this dish at a minimum, you could omit the ground and flaked (sliced) almonds. Serve the dish with plain rice and it will be delicious.

Rice Layered with Chicken and Potatoes

This dish, *Murgh Biryani*, is mainly prepared for important occasions, and is truly fit for royalty. Every cook in India has a subtle variation which is kept a closely guarded secret.

INGREDIENTS

Serves 4-6

1.3kg/3lb chicken breast portions, skinned and cut into large pieces
60ml/4 tbsp biryani masala paste
2 fresh green chillies, chopped
15ml/1 tbsp grated fresh root ginger
15ml/1 tbsp crushed garlic
50g/2oz/2 cups fresh coriander (cilantro), chopped
6–8 fresh mint leaves, chopped
150ml/¼ pint/⅔ cup natural (plain) yogurt, beaten
2 tbsp tomato purée (paste)
4 onions, finely sliced, deep-fried and crushed
salt, to taste
450g/1lb/2¼ cups basmati rice, washed and drained
5ml/1 tsp black cumin seeds
5cm/2in piece cinnamon stick
4 green cardamom pods
2 black cardamom pods
vegetable oil, for shallow-frying
4 large potatoes, peeled and quartered
175ml/6fl oz/¾ cup milk, mixed with 90ml/6 tbsp water
1 sachet saffron powder, mixed with 90ml/6 tbsp milk
25g/1oz/2 tbsp ghee or unsalted (sweet) butter
1 tomato, sliced

For the garnish

ghee or unsalted (sweet) butter, for shallow-frying
50g/2oz/½ cup cashew nuts
50g/2oz/⅓ cup sultanas (golden raisins)

1 Mix the chicken pieces with the next 10 ingredients in a large bowl and marinate, covered, in a cool place for about 2 hours. Place in a large heavy pan and cook over a low heat for about 10 minutes. Set aside.

4 Place half the rice on top of the chicken in the pan in an even layer. Then make an even layer with the potatoes. Put the remaining rice on top of the potatoes and spread to make an even layer.

2 Boil a large pan of water and soak the rice with the cumin seeds, cinnamon stick and green and black cardamom pods for about 5 minutes. Drain well. If you prefer, some of the whole spices may be removed at this stage and discarded.

5 Sprinkle the water mixed with milk all over the rice. Make random holes through the rice with the handle of a spoon and pour into each a little saffron milk. Place a few knobs of ghee or butter on the surface, cover the pan and cook over a low heat for 35–45 minutes.

3 Heat the oil for shallow-frying and fry the potatoes until they are evenly browned on all sides. Drain the potatoes and set aside.

6 While the biryani is cooking, make the garnish. Heat a little ghee or butter and fry the cashew nuts and sultanas until they swell. Drain and set aside. When the biryani is ready, gently toss the rice, chicken and potatoes together, garnish with the nut mixture and serve hot.

NUTRITIONAL NOTES	
Per Portion	
Energy	1032Kcals/4349KJ
Fat	9.8g
Saturated Fat	2.4g
Carbohydrate	131.1g
Fibre	2.9g

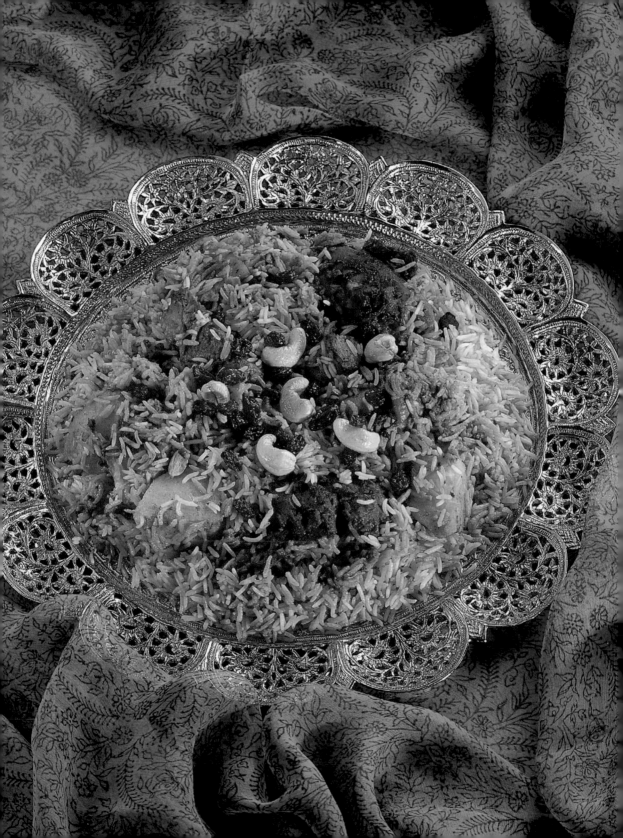

Chicken Pulao

Like biryanis, pulaos that include cooked meat and poultry make a convenient one-pot meal. A vegetable curry makes a good accompaniment, although for a simpler meal, such as supper, you could serve the pulao with a simple raita, combining natural yogurt with any raw vegetable, such as white cabbage, grated carrots, or cauliflower florets.

INGREDIENTS

Serves 4

400g/14oz/2 cups basmati rice
75g/3oz/6 tbsp ghee or unsalted (sweet) butter
1 onion, sliced
1.5ml/¼ tsp mixed onion and mustard seeds
3 curry leaves
5ml/1 tsp grated fresh root ginger
5ml/1 tsp crushed garlic
5ml/1 tsp ground coriander
5ml/1 tsp chilli powder
7.5ml/1½ tsp salt
2 tomatoes, sliced
1 potato, cubed
50g/2oz/½ cup frozen peas, thawed
175g/6oz chicken breast fillets, skinned and cubed
60ml/4 tbsp chopped fresh coriander (cilantro)
2 fresh green chillies, chopped
750ml/1¼ pints/3 cups water

NUTRITIONAL NOTES	
Per Portion	
Energy	603Kcals/2515KJ
Fat	16.8g
Saturated Fat	10g
Carbohydrate	91.9g
Fibre	2.1g

1 Wash the rice thoroughly under running water, then leave to soak for 30 minutes. Drain in a strainer or colander and set aside.

2 In a pan, melt the ghee or butter and fry the sliced onion until golden.

3 Add the onion and mustard seeds, the curry leaves, ginger, garlic, ground coriander, chilli powder and salt. Stir-fry for about 2 minutes over a low heat.

4 Add the sliced tomatoes, cubed potato, peas and chicken cubes and mix everything together well.

_____ COOK'S TIP _____

There's no need to have the heat high when stir-frying the spices. When ground, spices require only gentle warmth to release their flavours.

5 Add the rice and stir gently to combine with the other ingredients.

6 Add the coriander and chillies. Mix and stir-fry for 1 minute. Pour in the water, bring to the boil and then lower the heat. Cover tightly and cook for 20 minutes. Remove from the heat, leaving the lid in place, and leave the pulao to stand for 6–8 minutes. Serve.

Chicken Biryani

Biryani is a meal in itself and needs no accompaniment, except for a raita and some poppadums. It is a dish that is equally at home on the family dining table or as a dinner-party centrepiece.

INGREDIENTS

Serves 4

275g/10oz/1½ cups basmati rice
10 whole green cardamom pods
2.5ml/½ tsp salt
2–3 whole cloves
5cm/2in piece cinnamon stick
45ml/3 tbsp vegetable oil
3 onions, sliced
4 chicken breast fillets, each about
    175g/6oz, skinned and cubed
1.5ml/¼ tsp ground cloves
1.5ml/¼ tsp hot chilli powder
5ml/1 tsp ground cumin
5ml/1 tsp ground coriander
2.5ml/½ tsp ground black pepper
3 garlic cloves, chopped
5ml/1 tsp finely chopped fresh
    root ginger
juice of 1 lemon
4 tomatoes, sliced
30ml/2 tbsp chopped fresh coriander
    (cilantro)
150ml/¼ pint/⅔ cup natural (plain)
    yogurt, plus extra to serve
4–5 saffron threads, soaked in
    10ml/2 tsp warm milk
150ml/¼ pint/⅔ cup water
toasted flaked (sliced) almonds and fresh
    coriander (cilantro) sprigs, to garnish

NUTRITIONAL NOTES	
Per Portion	
Energy	548Kcals/2298KJ
Fat	11.1g
Saturated Fat	1.7g
Carbohydrate	67.5g
Fibre	2.2g

1 Wash the rice well and leave to soak in water for 30 minutes.

2 Preheat the oven to 190°C/375°F/Gas 5. Remove the seeds from half the cardamom pods and grind them finely, using a pestle and mortar. Set aside the ground seeds.

3 Bring a pan of water to the boil. Drain the rice and add it with the salt, whole cardamom pods, cloves and cinnamon stick. Boil for 2 minutes, then drain, leaving the whole spices in the rice. Keep the rice hot in a covered pan.

4 Heat the oil in a karahi, wok or large pan, and fry the onions for 8 minutes, until softened and browned.

5 Add the chicken and the ground spices, including the ground cardamom seeds. Mix well, then add the garlic, ginger and lemon juice. Stir-fry for about 5 minutes.

6 Transfer the chicken mixture to a casserole and arrange the tomatoes on top. Sprinkle on the fresh coriander, spoon the yogurt evenly on top and cover with the drained rice.

7 Drizzle the saffron milk over the rice and pour over the water. Cover, then bake in the oven for 1 hour. Transfer to a serving platter and discard the whole spices. Garnish with the toasted flaked almonds and coriander sprigs and serve immediately.

Chicken with Spicy Onions

Chunky onion slices infused with toasted cumin seeds and shredded ginger add a delicious contrast to the flavour of the chicken.

INGREDIENTS

Serves 4–6

1.5kg/3lb chicken, jointed and skinned
½ tsp turmeric
½ tsp chilli powder
salt, to taste
4 tbsp oil
4 small onions, finely chopped
175g/6oz/6 cups fresh coriander
   (cilantro), coarsely chopped
5cm/2in piece fresh ginger,
   finely shredded
2 fresh green chillies, finely chopped
10ml/2 tsp cumin seeds, dry-roasted
75ml/5 tbsp natural (plain) yogurt
75ml/5 tbsp double (heavy) cream
½ tsp cornflour (cornstarch)

1 Rub the chicken joints with the turmeric, chilli powder and salt. Heat the oil in a large frying pan and fry the chicken pieces in batches until both sides are sealed. Remove to a plate and keep hot.

COOK'S TIP

Make a few slashes in the chicken joints before rubbing them with the spice mixture, to encourage the flavours to penetrate the meat.

2 Reheat the oil remaining in the pan and add 3 of the chopped onions, most of the fresh coriander, half the ginger, the green chillies and the cumin seeds and fry until the onions are translucent.

3 Return the chicken to the pan with any juices and mix well. Cover and cook gently for 15 minutes.

NUTRITIONAL NOTES	
Per Portion	
Energy	819Kcals/3391KJ
Fat	65.4g
Saturated Fat	23.4g
Carbohydrate	8.2g
Fibre	0.9g

4 Remove the pan from the heat and leave to cool a little. Mix the yogurt, cream and cornflour in a bowl and gradually fold into the chicken, mixing well.

5 Return the pan to the heat and cook gently until the chicken is tender. Just before serving, stir in the reserved onion, coriander and ginger. Spoon into a bowl and serve hot.

Hot Sweet and Sour Duck Casserole

This recipe can be made with any game bird, or even rabbit. It is a distinctively sweet, sour and hot dish best eaten with rice as an accompaniment.

INGREDIENTS

Serves 4–6

1.3kg/3lb duck, jointed and skinned
4 bay leaves
10ml/2 tsp salt
75ml/5 tbsp vegetable oil
juice of 5 lemons
8 medium onions, finely chopped
4–5 garlic cloves, crushed
15ml/1 tbsp chilli powder
300ml/½ pint/1¼ cups pickling vinegar
5cm/2in piece fresh root ginger, peeled and shredded
115g/4oz/½ cup granulated sugar
15ml/1 tbsp garam masala

1 Place the duck, bay leaves and salt in a large pan and cover with cold water. Bring to the boil then simmer for 30–45 minutes, or until the duck is fully cooked. Remove the pieces of duck and keep warm. Reserve the liquid as a base for stock or soup.

NUTRITIONAL NOTES	
Per Portion	
Energy	444Kcals/1860KJ
Fat	17.5g
Saturated Fat	3.3g
Carbohydrate	53.8g
Fibre	4.2g

2 In a large pan, heat the oil and lemon juice until it reaches smoking point. Add the onions, garlic and chilli powder and fry the onions until they are golden brown.

3 Add the vinegar, ginger and sugar and simmer until the sugar dissolves and the oil has separated from the mixture.

4 Return the duck to the pan and add the garam masala. Mix well, then reheat until the masala clings to the pieces of duck and the sauce is thick. Adjust the seasoning if necessary. If you prefer a thinner sauce, add a little of the reserved stock.

--- COOK'S TIP ---

Be very careful when adding the onions and garlic to the oil and lemon juice mixture. Stand well back and use a spoon to scrape the onions into the pan, a few at a time. The hot mixture is likely to spit or splutter.

Meat Dishes

INDIAN COOKS have perfected the art of tenderizing meat, thanks to their use of marinades and slow, careful cooking. Lamb is a popular choice for dishes, since it can be enjoyed by all those whose religion permits them to eat meat. Many Hindus avoid pork, and this meat is forbidden to those of the Muslim faith. Only in Goa, and other parts of India with significant Christian populations, can pork be found on the menu. Beef is forbidden to Hindus, although Muslims enjoy it.

Vegetables and pulses are used to great effect in meat dishes. Lamb with Spinach, Hot and Sour Lamb and Lentil Curry, and Beef with Green Beans are typical examples of these hearty combinations, rich in flavour and texture. The most important addition to any meat dish, however, is the spices. The types and quantities used, and the time at which they are added, are two of the variables that contribute to making Indian meat dishes among the very best in the world.

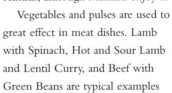

Spicy Lamb Tikka

One of the best ways of tenderizing meat is to marinate it in papaya, which must be unripe or it will lend its sweetness to what should be a savoury dish. Papaya, or paw-paw, is readily available from most large supermarkets.

INGREDIENTS

Serves 4

675g/1½lb lean lamb, cubed
1 unripe papaya
45ml/3 tbsp natural (plain) yogurt
5ml/1 tsp grated fresh root ginger
5ml/1 tsp chilli powder
5ml/1 tsp crushed garlic
1.5ml/¼ tsp turmeric
10ml/2 tsp ground coriander
5ml/1 tsp ground cumin
5ml/1 tsp salt
30ml/2 tbsp lemon juice
15ml/1 tbsp chopped fresh coriander
   (cilantro), plus extra to garnish
1.5ml/¼ tsp red food colouring
300ml/½ pint/1¼ cups corn oil
lemon wedges
onion rings

1 Place the lamb in a large mixing bowl. Peel the papaya, cut it in half and scoop out the seeds. Cut the flesh into cubes and place in a food processor or blender. Process in bursts until the papaya forms a purée, adding about 15ml/1 tbsp water if necessary.

2 Pour 30ml/2 tbsp of the papaya pulp over the lamb cubes and rub it in well with your fingers. Cover and set aside for at least 3 hours.

3 Meanwhile, mix the yogurt, ginger, chilli powder, garlic, turmeric, ground coriander, ground cumin, salt and lemon juice in a bowl. Add the fresh coriander, red food colouring and 30ml/2 tbsp of the oil and mix well.

4 Pour the spicy yogurt mixture over the lamb and mix well.

5 Heat the remaining oil in a karahi, wok or deep pan. Lower the heat slightly and add the lamb cubes, a few at a time.

6 Deep-fry each batch for 5–7 minutes or until the lamb is thoroughly cooked and tender. Keep the cooked pieces warm while frying the remainder.

7 Transfer to a serving dish and garnish with lemon wedges, onion rings and fresh coriander. Serve with raita and freshly baked naan bread.

COOK'S TIP

A good-quality meat tenderizer, available from supermarkets, can be used in place of the papaya. However, the meat will need a longer marinating time and should ideally be left to tenderize overnight.

NUTRITIONAL NOTES	
Per Portion	
Energy	438Kcals/1820KJ
Fat	32.7g
Saturated Fat	10.4g
Carbohydrate	2.4g
Fibre	0.7g

Indian Lamb Burgers

Serve this Indian hamburger in a bun with chilli sauce and salad or unaccompanied as an appetizer.

INGREDIENTS

Serves 4-6

50g/2oz/¼ cup chickpeas, soaked
 overnight in water
2 onions, finely chopped
250g/9oz lean lamb, cut into small cubes
5ml/1 tsp cumin seeds
5ml/1 tsp garam masala
4–6 fresh green chillies,
 roughly chopped
5cm/2in piece fresh ginger, crushed
salt, to taste
175ml/6fl oz/¾ cup water
few fresh coriander (cilantro) and mint
 leaves, chopped
juice of 1 lemon
15ml/1 tbsp gram flour
2 eggs, beaten
vegetable oil, for shallow-frying
half a lime

1 Drain the chickpeas and cook them in a pan of boiling water for 1 hour. Drain again, return to the pan and add the next 8 ingredients. Bring to the boil. Simmer, covered, until the meat and chickpeas are cooked.

2 Remove the lid and cook uncovered to reduce the excess liquid. Cool, and grind to a paste in a food processor.

NUTRITIONAL NOTES	
Per Portion	
Energy	357Kcals/1485KJ
Fat	25.1g
Saturated Fat	6g
Carbohydrate	15.6g
Fibre	1.5g

3 Scrape the mixture into a mixing bowl and add the fresh coriander and mint, lemon juice and flour. Knead well. Divide into 10–12 portions and roll each into a ball, then flatten slightly. Chill for 1 hour. Dip the burgers in the beaten egg and shallow-fry each side until golden brown. Serve hot with the lime.

Lamb Meatballs

The word "meatballs" conjures up something quite humdrum, but these spicy little patties, with their delectable sauce, are exciting and full of flavour.

INGREDIENTS

Serves 6
For the meatballs
675g/1½lb lean minced (ground) lamb
1 fresh green chilli, roughly chopped
1 garlic clove, chopped
2.5cm/1in piece fresh root
   ginger, chopped
1.5ml/¼ tsp garam masala
1.5ml/¼ tsp salt
45ml/3 tbsp chopped fresh coriander
   (cilantro), plus extra to garnish
pilau rice, to serve

FOR THE SAUCE
15ml/1 tbsp oil
1.5ml/¼ tsp mustard seeds
2.5ml/½ tsp cumin seeds
1 onion, chopped
1 garlic clove, chopped
2.5cm/1in piece fresh root ginger,
   finely chopped
5ml/1 tsp ground cumin
5ml/1 tsp ground coriander
2.5ml/½ tsp salt
2.5ml/½ tsp chilli powder
15ml/1 tbsp tomato purée (paste)
400g/14oz can chopped tomatoes

3 Add the onion, garlic and ginger and fry for 5 minutes. Stir in the remaining sauce ingredients and simmer for 5 minutes.

2 To make the sauce, heat the oil in a heavy pan and fry the mustard and cumin seeds until they splutter.

NUTRITIONAL NOTES	
Per Portion	
Energy	231Kcals/968KJ
Fat	12.30g
Saturated Fat	5.00g
Carbohydrate	5.40g
Fibre	0.90g

4 Add the meatballs to the sauce. Bring to the boil, cover and simmer for 25–30 minutes or until the meatballs are cooked through. Serve on a bed of pilau rice and garnish with fresh coriander.

1 To make the meatballs, put all the ingredients into a food processor or blender and process until the mixture binds together. Shape the mixture into 18 balls. Cover and chill for 10 minutes.

Lamb Chops Kashmiri-style

These chops are cooked in a unique way, being first boiled in milk, and then fried. Despite the large number of spices used in this recipe, the actual dish has a mild flavour, and is delicious served with fried rice and a lentil dish.

INGREDIENTS

Serves 4

8-12 lamb chops, about 50–75g/
   2–3oz each
1 piece cinnamon bark
1 bay leaf
2.5ml/½ tsp fennel seeds
2.5ml/½ tsp black peppercorns
3 green cardamom pods
5ml/1 tsp salt
600ml/1 pint/2½ cups milk
150ml/¼ pint/⅔ cup evaporated milk
150ml/¼ pint/⅔ cup natural
   (plain) yogurt
30ml/2 tbsp plain (all-purpose) flour
5ml/1 tsp chilli powder
5ml/1 tsp grated fresh root ginger
2.5ml/½ tsp garam masala
2.5ml/½ tsp crushed garlic
pinch of salt
300ml/½ pint/1¼ cups corn oil
fresh mint sprigs
lime quarters

1 Trim the lamb chops to remove any excess fat, and place them in a large pan.

2 Add the cinnamon bark, bay leaf, fennel seeds, peppercorns, cardamoms and salt. Pour in the milk. Bring to the boil over a high heat.

3 Lower the heat and cook for 12–15 minutes, or until the milk has reduced to about half its original volume. At this stage, pour in the evaporated milk and lower the heat further. Simmer until the chops are cooked through and all the milk has evaporated.

4 While the chops are cooking, blend together the yogurt, flour, chilli powder, ginger, garam masala, crushed garlic and a pinch of salt in a mixing bowl.

5 Remove the chops from the pan and discard the whole spices. Add the chops to the spicy yogurt mixture.

6 Heat the oil in a deep pan, wok or medium karahi. Lower the heat slightly and add the chops. Fry until they are golden brown, turning them once or twice as they cook.

7 Transfer the chops to a serving dish, and garnish with mint sprigs and lime quarters. Serve immediately.

NUTRITIONAL NOTES	
Per Portion	
Energy	484Kcals/2022KJ
Fat	29g
Saturated Fat	9.3g
Carbohydrate	17.6g
Fibre	0.2g

Spring Lamb Chops

Tender spring lamb is perfect for this quick and easy dish.

INGREDIENTS

Serves 4

8 small lean spring lamb chops
1 large fresh red chilli, seeded
30ml/2 tbsp chopped fresh
   coriander (cilantro)
15ml/1 tbsp chopped fresh mint
5ml/1 tsp salt
5ml/1 tsp soft brown sugar
5ml/1 tsp garam masala
5ml/1 tsp crushed garlic
5ml/1 tsp grated fresh root ginger
175ml/6fl oz/³⁄₄ cup low fat natural
   (plain) yogurt
10ml/2 tsp oil
mixed salad, to serve

NUTRITIONAL NOTES	
Per Portion	
Energy	207Kcals/864KJ
Fat	10.29g
Saturated Fat	4.26g
Carbohydrate	6.63g
Fibre	0.27g

1 Trim the lamb chops of any excess fat. Place them in a large bowl.

2 Finely chop the chilli, then place in a bowl and mix with the coriander, mint, salt, brown sugar, garam masala, garlic and ginger.

3 Pour the yogurt into the chilli mixture and, using a small whisk or a fork, mix together thoroughly. Pour this mixture over the top of the chops and turn them with your fingers to make sure that they are completely covered. Cover and marinate overnight in the refrigerator.

4 Heat the oil in a karahi, wok or heavy pan and add the chops. Cook over a medium heat for about 20 minutes or until cooked right through, turning the chops from time to time. Alternatively, grill (broil) the chops, basting often with oil. Serve with the mixed salad.

Lamb Korma with Mint

Cutting the lamb into strips for this lovely dish makes it easier and quicker to cook.

INGREDIENTS

Serves 4

2 fresh green chillies
120ml/4fl oz/½ cup natural (plain) low fat yogurt
50ml/2fl oz/¼ cup coconut milk
15ml/1 tbsp ground almonds
5ml/1 tsp salt
5ml/1 tsp crushed garlic
5ml/1 tsp grated fresh root ginger
5ml/1 tsp garam masala
1.5ml/¼ tsp ground cardamom
large pinch of ground cinnamon
15ml/1 tbsp chopped fresh mint
15ml/1 tbsp oil
2 medium onions, diced
1 bay leaf
4 black peppercorns
225g/8oz lean lamb, cut into strips
150ml/¼ pint/⅔ cup water
fresh mint leaves, to garnish

1 Finely chop the chillies. Whisk the yogurt with the chillies, coconut milk, ground almonds, salt, garlic, ginger, garam masala, cardamom, cinnamon and mint.

2 Heat the oil in a karahi, wok or heavy pan and fry the onions with the bay leaf and peppercorns for about 5 minutes.

3 When the onions are soft and golden brown, add the lamb and stir-fry for about 2 minutes.

4 Pour in the yogurt mixture and water, lower the heat, cover and cook for about 15 minutes or until the lamb is cooked through, stirring occasionally. Using two spoons, toss over the heat for a further 2 minutes. Serve garnished with fresh mint leaves.

NUTRITIONAL NOTES	
Per Portion	
Energy	193Kcals/803KJ
Fat	10.14g
Saturated Fat	2.91g
Carbohydrate	11.50g
Fibre	1.60g

COOK'S TIP

Rice with peas and curry leaves goes very well with this korma.

Stir-fried Lamb with Baby Onions

The baby onions are stir-fried whole before being added to the lamb and pepper mixture in this recipe. Serve this dish with rice, lentils or naan bread.

INGREDIENTS

Serves 4

15ml/1 tbsp oil
8 baby onions
225g/8oz boned lean lamb, cut into strips
5ml/1 tsp ground cumin
5ml/1 tsp ground coriander
15ml/1 tbsp tomato purée (paste)
5ml/1 tsp chilli powder
5ml/1 tsp salt
15ml/1 tbsp lemon juice
2.5ml/½ tsp onion seeds
4 curry leaves
300ml/½ pint/1¼ cups water
1 small red (bell) pepper, seeded and roughly sliced
1 small green (bell) pepper, seeded and roughly sliced
15ml/1 tbsp chopped fresh coriander (cilantro)
15ml/1 tbsp chopped fresh mint

1 Heat the oil in a karahi, wok or heavy pan and stir-fry the whole baby onions for about 3 minutes. Using a slotted spoon, remove the onions from the pan and set aside to drain. Set the pan aside, with the oil remaining in it.

2 Mix together the lamb, cumin, ground coriander, tomato purée, chilli powder, salt and lemon juice in a bowl and set aside.

3 Reheat the oil and briskly stir-fry the onion seeds and curry leaves for 2–3 minutes.

COOK'S TIP

This dish benefits from being cooked a day in advance and kept in the refrigerator overnight, making it a very good choice to serve for a relaxed dinner party.

NUTRITIONAL NOTES
Per Portion

Energy	155Kcals/644KJ
Fat	9.48g
Saturated Fat	2.82g
Carbohydrate	5.74g
Fibre	1.49g

4 Add the lamb and spice mixture and stir-fry for about 5 minutes, then pour in the water, lower the heat and cook gently for about 10 minutes, until the lamb is cooked through.

5 Add the peppers and half the fresh coriander and mint. Stir-fry for a further 2 minutes.

6 Finally, add the baby onions and the remaining chopped fresh coriander and mint and serve.

Lamb with Spinach

Lamb with Spinach, or *Saag Gosht*, is a well-known recipe from the Punjab. It is important to use red peppers as they add such a distinctive flavour to the dish. Serve with plain boiled rice, naan bread or parathas.

INGREDIENTS

Serves 4–6

5ml/1 tsp grated fresh root ginger
5ml/1 tsp crushed garlic
7.5ml/1½ tsp chilli powder
5ml/1 tsp salt
5ml/1 tsp garam masala
90ml/6 tbsp corn oil
2 medium onions, sliced
675g/1½lb lean lamb, cut into
    5cm/2in cubes
600–900ml/1–1½ pints/2½–3¾ cups
    water
400g/14oz fresh spinach
1 large red (bell) pepper, seeded
    and chopped
3 fresh green chillies, chopped
45ml/3 tbsp chopped fresh
    coriander (cilantro)
15ml/1 tbsp lemon juice (optional)

1 Mix together the ginger, garlic, chilli powder, salt and garam masala in a bowl. Set to one side.

2 Heat the oil in a medium pan. Add the onions and fry for 10–12 minutes or until well browned.

3 Add the cubed lamb to the sizzling onion slices and fry for about 2 minutes, stirring frequently.

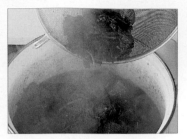

4 Tip in the spice mixture and stir thoroughly until the meat pieces are well coated.

5 Pour in the water and bring to the boil. As soon as it is boiling, cover the pan and lower the heat. Cook gently for 25–35 minutes without letting the contents of the pan burn.

6 If there is still a lot of water in the pan when the meat has become tender, remove the lid and boil briskly to evaporate any excess.

7 Meanwhile, wash and chop the spinach roughly, then blanch it for about 1 minute in a pan of boiling water. Drain well.

8 Add the spinach to the lamb as soon as the water has evaporated. Fry over a medium heat for 7–10 minutes, using a wooden spoon in a semi-circular motion, scraping the bottom of the pan as you stir.

9 Add the red pepper, green chillies and fresh coriander to the pan and stir over a medium heat for 2 minutes. Sprinkle on the lemon juice (if using) and serve immediately.

COOK'S TIP

Frozen spinach can also be used for the dish, but try to find whole leaf spinach rather than the chopped kind. Allow the frozen spinach to thaw, then drain well; there is no need to blanch it.

NUTRITIONAL NOTES
Per Portion

Energy	500Kcals/2079KJ
Fat	36.4g
Saturated Fat	11.3g
Carbohydrate	6.8g
Fibre	3.2g

Courgettes with Lamb

For this simple supper dish, lamb is cooked first with yogurt and then the sliced courgettes, which have already been browned, are added to the mixture.

INGREDIENTS

Serves 4

15ml/1 tbsp oil
2 medium onions, chopped
225g/8oz lean lamb steaks, cut
 into strips
120ml/4fl oz/½ cup natural (plain)
 low fat yogurt
5ml/1 tsp garam masala
5ml/1 tsp chilli powder
5ml/1 tsp crushed garlic
5ml/1 tsp grated fresh root ginger
2.5ml/½ tsp ground coriander
2 medium courgettes (zucchini), sliced
15ml/1 tbsp chopped fresh coriander
 (cilantro), to garnish

NUTRITIONAL NOTES	
Per Portion	
Energy	178Kcals/742KJ
Fat	8.36g
Saturated Fat	2.78g
Carbohydrate	10.83g
Fibre	1.99g

COOK'S TIP

Frying onions in very little oil needs to be done over a low heat and requires some patience. They will take a little longer to brown and should be gently stirred only occasionally. Excessive stirring will draw the moisture out of the onions and make them even more difficult to fry.

1 Heat the oil in a karahi, wok or heavy pan and fry the onions until golden brown.

2 Add the lamb strips and stir-fry for 1 minute to seal the meat.

3 Put the yogurt, garam masala, chilli powder, garlic, ginger and ground coriander into a bowl. Whisk the mixture together.

4 Pour the yogurt mixture over the lamb and stir-fry for 2 minutes. Cover and cook over a medium to low heat for 12–15 minutes.

5 Preheat the grill (broiler). Put the courgettes in a flameproof dish and brown lightly under the heat for about 3 minutes, turning once.

6 Check that the lamb is cooked through and the sauce is quite thick, then add the courgettes and serve garnished with the fresh coriander.

Spiced Lamb with Tomatoes and Peppers

Select lean tender lamb from the leg for this lightly spiced curry with juicy peppers and wedges of onion. Serve warm naan bread to mop up the tomato-rich juices.

INGREDIENTS

Serves 6

2.5cm/1in piece fresh root ginger
1.5kg/3¼lb lean boneless lamb, cubed
250ml/8fl oz/1 cup natural
   (plain) yogurt
30ml/2 tbsp sunflower oil
3 onions
2 red (bell) peppers, seeded and cut
   into chunks
3 garlic cloves, finely chopped
1 fresh red chilli, seeded and chopped
30ml/2 tbsp mild curry paste
2 x 400g/14oz cans chopped tomatoes
large pinch of saffron threads
800g/1¾lb plum tomatoes, halved,
   seeded and cut into chunks
salt and black pepper
chopped fresh coriander (cilantro),
   to garnish

1 Thinly peel the ginger, using a sharp knife or a vegetable peeler, then grate the peeled root finely. Set the grated ginger aside.

VARIATION

Although pork would be unlikely to be used in India, it would work well for this dish. Use pork fillet (tenderloin) instead of the lamb.

2 Mix the lamb with the yogurt in a bowl. Cover and chill for about 1 hour.

3 Heat the oil in a large pan. Drain the lamb and reserve the yogurt, then cook the lamb in batches until it is golden on all sides – this will take about 15 minutes in total. Remove the lamb from the pan using a slotted spoon and set aside.

4 Cut two of the onions into wedges (six from each onion) and add to the oil remaining in the pan. Fry the onions over a medium heat for 10 minutes, or until they are beginning to colour.

5 Add the peppers and cook for 5 minutes. Use a slotted spoon to remove the vegetables from the pan and set aside.

6 Meanwhile, chop the remaining onion. Add it to the rest of the oil in the pan with the chopped garlic, chilli and grated ginger, and cook for 4–5 minutes, stirring frequently, until the onion has softened.

7 Stir in the curry paste and canned tomatoes with the reserved yogurt. Return the lamb to the pan, season and stir well. Bring to the boil, then reduce the heat and simmer for 30 minutes.

8 Pound the saffron to a powder in a mortar, then stir in a little boiling water to dissolve the saffron. Add this liquid to the curry and stir well.

9 Return the onion and pepper mixture to the pan, then stir in the fresh tomatoes. Bring the curry back to simmering point and cook for 15 minutes. Garnish with chopped fresh coriander to serve.

NUTRITIONAL NOTES	
Per Portion	
Energy	594Kcals/2445KJ
Fat	32.8g
Saturated Fat	13.8g
Carbohydrate	19.7g
Fibre	4.3g

Khara Masala Lamb

This is a dish which involves a technique called *bhooning* – stirring with a semi-circular motion. Whole spices are used, so warn the diners of their presence in advance! This curry is delicious served with freshly baked naan bread or plain rice.

INGREDIENTS

Serves 4
3 small onions, chopped
15ml/1 tbsp oil
5ml/1 tsp shredded fresh root ginger
5ml/1 tsp sliced garlic
6 dried red chillies
3 cardamom pods
2 cinnamon sticks
6 black peppercorns
3 cloves
2.5ml/½ tsp salt
450g/1lb boned lean leg of
  lamb, cubed
600ml/1 pint/2½ cups water
2 fresh green chillies, sliced
30ml/2 tbsp chopped fresh
  coriander (cilantro)

_____ VARIATION _____

For a tasty alternative, instead of the boned leg of lamb used here, use the equivalent weight of either lean skinned chicken or beef cut into cubes.

1 Using a sharp knife, chop the onions finely. Heat the oil in a large pan.

2 Add the onions to the oil. Lower the heat and fry the onions until they are lightly browned, stirring occasionally.

3 Add half the ginger and half the garlic and stir well.

4 Drop in half the red chillies, the cardamom pods, cinnamon, peppercorns, cloves and salt.

5 Add the lamb and fry over a medium heat. Stir continuously with a semi-circular movement, using a wooden spoon to scrape the bottom of the pan and prevent the meat from burning. Cook for about 5 minutes.

6 Stir in the water, cover with a lid and cook slowly over a medium-low heat for 35–40 minutes, or until the water has evaporated and the meat is tender, stirring from time to time to prevent the mixture from burning on the bottom of the pan.

7 Add the rest of the shredded ginger and sliced garlic and the remaining dried red chillies, along with the sliced fresh green chillies and the chopped coriander.

8 Continue to stir the mixture over the heat until some free oil is visible on the sides of the pan. Remove the pan from the heat. Transfer the curry to a serving dish and serve immediately.

NUTRITIONAL NOTES	
Per Portion	
Energy	242Kcals/1012KJ
Fat	13.20g
Saturated Fat	5.19g
Carbohydrate	6.70g
Fibre	0.90g

Spiced Lamb with Chillies

This is a fairly hot stir-fry dish, although you can, of course, make it less so by either discarding the seeds from the chillies, or using just one of each colour.

INGREDIENTS

Serves 4

225g/8oz lean lamb fillet (tenderloin)
120ml/4fl oz/½ cup natural (plain) low fat yogurt
1.5ml/¼ tsp ground cardamom
5ml/1 tsp grated fresh root ginger
5ml/1 tsp crushed garlic
5ml/1 tsp chilli powder
5ml/1 tsp garam masala
5ml/1 tsp salt
15ml/1 tbsp oil
2 medium onions, chopped
1 bay leaf
300ml/½ pint/1¼ cups water
2 fresh green chillies, sliced lengthways
2 fresh red chillies, sliced lengthways
30ml/2 tbsp fresh coriander (cilantro) leaves

NUTRITIONAL NOTES	
Per Portion	
Energy	169Kcals/706KJ
Fat	8.13g
Saturated Fat	2.71g
Carbohydrate	10.01g
Fibre	1.32g

COOK'S TIP

Leaving the strips of lamb to marinate for an hour in the spicy yogurt mixture allows the flavour to penetrate right through the meat and also makes it beautifully tender, so it cooks quickly.

1 Using a sharp knife, remove any excess fat from the lamb and cut the meat into even-size strips.

2 In a bowl, mix the yogurt, cardamom, ginger, garlic, chilli powder and garam masala. Stir in the salt. Add the lamb and leave for about 1 hour to marinate.

3 Heat the oil in a karahi, wok or heavy pan and fry the onions for 3-5 minutes until golden.

4 Add the bay leaf, then add the lamb with the yogurt and spice mixture. Stir-fry for 2–3 minutes.

5 Pour over the water, cover and cook for 15–20 minutes over a low heat, checking occasionally. Once the water has evaporated, stir-fry the mixture for 1 further minute.

6 Stir in the red and green chillies and the fresh coriander. Spoon into a serving dish and serve hot.

Spicy Lamb and Potato Stew

Indian spices transform a simple lamb and potato stew into a dish fit for princes.

INGREDIENTS

Serves 6

675g/1½lb lean lamb fillet (tenderloin)
15ml/1 tbsp oil
1 onion, finely chopped
2 bay leaves
1 fresh green chilli, seeded and
   finely chopped
2 garlic cloves, finely chopped
10ml/2 tsp ground coriander
5ml/1 tsp ground cumin
2.5ml/½ tsp ground turmeric
2.5ml/½ tsp chilli powder
2.5ml/½ tsp salt
2 tomatoes, peeled and chopped
600ml/1 pint/2½ cups chicken stock
2 large potatoes, cut in large chunks
chopped fresh coriander (cilantro),
   to garnish

NUTRITIONAL NOTES	
Per Portion	
Energy	283Kcals/1187KJ
Fat	12.40g
Saturated Fat	5.02g
Carbohydrate	17.20g
Fibre	1.70g

1 Remove any visible fat from the lamb and cut the meat into neat 2.5cm/1in cubes.

2 Heat the oil in a large heavy pan and fry the onion, bay leaves, chilli and garlic for 5 minutes.

3 Add the meat and cook for about 6–8 minutes until lightly browned.

4 Add the ground coriander, ground cumin, ground turmeric, chilli powder and salt and cook the spices for 3–4 minutes, stirring all the time to prevent the spices from sticking to the bottom of the pan.

5 Add the tomatoes and stock and simmer for 5 minutes. Bring to the boil, cover and simmer for 1 hour.

6 Add the bitesize chunks of potato to the simmering mixture, stir in, and cook for a further 30–40 minutes, or until the meat is tender and much of the excess juices have been absorbed, leaving a thick but minimal sauce. Garnish with chopped fresh coriander and serve piping hot.

COOK'S TIP

This stew is absolutely delicious served with warm, freshly made chapatis and a cucumber raita.

Lamb Dhansak

About 13 centuries ago, a small group of Persians fled their country to avoid religious persecution and landed in the state of Gujarat. They became known as Parsis. This is one of their traditional dishes. It is time-consuming to make, but the excellent flavour is just reward.

INGREDIENTS

Serves 4–6
90ml/6 tbsp vegetable oil
5 fresh green chillies, chopped
2.5cm/1in piece fresh root ginger, grated
3 garlic cloves, crushed, plus 1 garlic clove, sliced
2 bay leaves
5cm/2in piece cinnamon stick
900g/2lb lean lamb, cut into large pieces
600ml/1 pint/2½ cups water
175g/6oz/¾ cup whole red lentils, washed and drained
50g/2oz/¼ cup each chana dhal or yellow split peas, husked moong dhal and split red lentils, washed and drained
2 potatoes, diced, soaked in water
1 aubergine (eggplant), chopped, soaked in water
4 onions, finely sliced, deep-fried and drained
50g/2oz fresh spinach, trimmed, washed and chopped
25g/1oz fresh or dried fenugreek leaves
2 carrots, sliced
115g/4oz fresh coriander (cilantro), chopped
50g/2oz fresh mint, chopped
30ml/2 tbsp dhansak masala
30ml/2 tbsp sambhar masala
5ml/1 tsp salt
10ml/2 tsp soft brown sugar
60ml/4 tbsp tamarind juice

1 Heat 45ml/3 tbsp of the oil in a wok, karahi or large pan, and gently fry the fresh chillies, ginger, crushed garlic, bay leaves and cinnamon for 2 minutes. Add the lamb pieces and the measured water. Bring to the boil, then simmer, covered, until the lamb is half cooked.

2 Drain the meat stock into another pan and put the lamb aside. Add the whole red lentils, chana dhal or split peas, moong dhal and split red lentils to the stock and cook gently for 25–30 minutes at a low temperature until they are tender. Mash the lentils with the back of a spoon.

3 Drain the potatoes and aubergine and add to the lentils. Reserve a little of the deep-fried onions and stir the remainder into the pan, along with the spinach, fenugreek and carrot.

4 Add some hot water to the pan if the mixture seems too thick. Cook until the vegetables are tender, then mash again with a spoon, keeping the vegetables a little coarse.

5 Heat 15ml/1 tbsp of the remaining oil in a large frying pan. Reserve a few coriander and mint leaves to use as a garnish, and gently fry the remaining leaves with the dhansak and sambhar masala, salt and sugar. Add the lamb pieces and fry gently for 5 minutes.

6 Add the lamb and spices to the lentil mixture and stir. Cover, reduce the heat to low and cook until the lamb is tender. The lentils will absorb liquid, so add more water if needed. Mix in the tamarind juice.

7 Heat the remaining vegetable oil in a small pan and fry the sliced garlic until golden brown.

8 Sprinkle the fried garlic slices over the dhansak. Garnish with the remaining deep-fried onion and the reserved fresh coriander and mint leaves. Serve the dish hot, with caramelized basmati rice if you like.

NUTRITIONAL NOTES	
Per Portion	
Energy	720Kcals/3017KJ
Fat	34.8g
Saturated Fat	10g
Carbohydrate	58.6g
Fibre	7.6g

Lahore-style Lamb Curry

Named after Lahore, a former Indian city which has been in Pakistan since the Independence, this hearty dish has a wonderfully aromatic flavour imparted by the winter spices such as cloves, black peppercorns and cinnamon.

INGREDIENTS

Serves 4

60ml/4 tbsp vegetable oil
1 bay leaf
2 cloves
4 black peppercorns
1 onion, sliced
450g/1lb lean boneless lamb, cubed
1.5ml/¼ tsp ground turmeric
7.5ml/1½ tsp chilli powder
5ml/1 tsp crushed coriander seeds
2.5cm/1in piece cinnamon stick
5ml/1 tsp crushed garlic
7.5ml/1½ tsp salt
1.5 litres/2½ pints/6 cups water
50g/2oz/⅓ cup chana dhal (yellow
    split peas)
2 tomatoes, quartered
2 fresh green chillies, chopped
15ml/1 tbsp chopped fresh
    coriander (cilantro)

1 Heat the oil in a karahi, wok or large pan. Lower the heat slightly and add the bay leaf, cloves, peppercorns and onion. Fry for about 5 minutes, or until the onion is golden brown.

2 Add the cubed lamb, turmeric, chilli powder, coriander seeds, cinnamon stick, garlic and most of the salt, and stir-fry for about 5 minutes over a medium heat.

3 Pour in 900ml/1½ pints/3¾ cups of the water and cover the pan with a lid or foil, making sure the foil does not come into contact with the food. Simmer for 35–40 minutes or until the lamb is tender.

4 Put the chana dhal into a large pan with the remaining measured water and a good pinch of salt and boil for 12–15 minutes, or until the water has almost evaporated and the dhal is soft enough to be mashed. If the mixture is too thick, add up to 150ml/¼ pint/⅔ cup water.

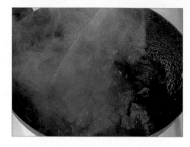

5 When the lamb is tender, remove the lid or foil and stir-fry the mixture using a wooden spoon, until some free oil begins to appear on the sides of the pan.

6 Add the cooked lentils to the lamb and mix together well. Stir in the tomatoes, chillies and chopped fresh coriander and serve.

NUTRITIONAL NOTES	
Per Portion	
Energy	362Kcals/1508KJ
Fat	24g
Saturated Fat	7.3g
Carbohydrate	11.5g
Fibre	1.6g

Hot and Sour Lamb and Lentil Curry

This dish has a hot, sweet-and-sour flavour, through which should rise the slightly bitter flavour of fenugreek.

INGREDIENTS

Serves 4–6

90ml/6 tbsp vegetable oil
2 fresh red chillies, chopped
2 fresh green chillies, chopped
2.5cm/1in piece fresh ginger, crushed
3 garlic cloves crushed
2 bay leaves
5cm/2in piece cinnamon stick
900g/2lb lean lamb, cubed
600ml/1 pint/2½ cups water
350g/12oz/2 cups mixed lentils
  (see Cook's Tip)
2 potatoes, cubed
1 aubergine (eggplant), cubed
2 courgettes (zucchini), cubed
4 onions, thinly sliced, deep-fried
  and drained
115g/4oz frozen spinach, thawed
  and drained
25g/1oz fenugreek leaves, fresh or dried
115g/4oz pumpkin, cubed
115g/4oz/4 cups fresh coriander
  (cilantro), chopped
50g/2oz/2 cups fresh mint, chopped,
  or 15ml/1 tbsp mint sauce
45ml/3 tbsp garam masala
salt, to taste
10ml/2 tsp brown sugar
lemon juice, to taste
1 garlic clove, sliced

1 Heat 45ml/3 tbsp of the oil in a pan, wok or karahi and fry the chillies, ginger and garlic for 2 minutes. Add the bay leaves, cinnamon, lamb and water. Bring to the boil, then reduce the heat and simmer until the lamb is half cooked.

2 Drain the water into another pan and put the lamb aside. Add the lentils to the water and cook until they are tender. Mash the lentils with the back of a spoon.

3 Add the cubes of potatoes and aubergines and stir into the mashed lentils, then add the courgette cubes and deep-fried onions. Stir in the spinach, fenugreek and pumpkin. Add some hot water if the mixture is too thick. Cook until the vegetables are tender, then mash again with a spoon, keeping the vegetables a little coarse.

4 Heat 15ml/1 tbsp of the oil in a frying pan, and gently fry the fresh coriander and mint (saving a little to garnish) with the masala, salt and sugar. Add the reserved lamb and fry gently for about 5 minutes.

5 Return the lamb and spices to the lentil and vegetable mixture and stir well. If the mixture seems dry, add more water. Heat gently until the lamb is fully cooked.

6 Add the lemon juice and mix well. Heat the remaining oil and fry the sliced clove of garlic until golden brown. Pour over the curry. Garnish with the remaining deep-fried onion slices and the reserved coriander and mint. Serve hot.

COOK'S TIP

India has dozens of different lentils and it is worth visiting an Indian market or grocer to familiarize yourself with some of the most popular. For this recipe, you might like to include bengal gram (a type of chick-pea), moong dhal (small split yellow lentils) and masoor dhal (red split lentils). Cooking times will depend on the types chosen.

NUTRITIONAL NOTES
Per Portion

Energy	1040Kcals/4359KJ
Fat	53.5g
Saturated Fat	14.9g
Carbohydrate	73.5g
Fibre	9.8g

Fragrant Lamb Curry with Cardamom-spiced Rice

Wonderfully aromatic, this Indian-style lamb biriani, with the meat and rice cooked together in a clay pot, is a delicious meal in itself.

INGREDIENTS

Serves 4

1 large onion, quartered
2 garlic cloves
1 fresh green chilli, halved and seeded
5cm/2in piece fresh root ginger
15ml/1 tbsp ghee
15ml/1 tbsp vegetable oil
675 g/1½lb boned shoulder or leg of lamb, cut into chunks
15ml/1 tbsp ground coriander
10ml/2 tsp ground cumin
1 cinnamon stick, broken into 3 pieces
150ml/¼ pint/⅔ cup thick natural (plain) yogurt
150ml/¼ pint/⅔ cup water
75g/3oz/⅓ cup ready-to-eat dried apricots, cut into chunks
salt and black pepper

FOR THE RICE

250g/9oz/1¼ cups basmati rice
6 cardamom pods, split open
25g/1oz/2 tbsp butter, cut into small pieces
45ml/3 tbsp toasted cashew nuts or flaked (sliced) almonds

FOR THE GARNISH

1 onion, sliced and fried until golden
a few sprigs of fresh coriander (cilantro)

1 Soak a large clay pot or chicken brick in cold water for 20 minutes, then drain. Place the onion, garlic, chilli and ginger in a food processor or blender and process with 15ml/1 tbsp water, to a smooth paste.

2 Heat the ghee and vegetable oil in a heavy frying pan. Fry the lamb chunks in batches over a high heat until golden brown. Remove from the pan using a slotted spoon and set aside.

3 Scrape the onion paste into the remaining oil left in the frying pan, stir in the ground coriander and cumin, add the cinnamon stick pieces and fry for 1–2 minutes, stirring constantly with a wooden spoon.

4 Return the meat to the frying pan, then gradually add the yogurt, a spoonful at a time, stirring well between each addition with a wooden spoon. Season the meat well with plenty of salt and pepper and stir in the water.

5 Transfer the contents of the frying pan to the prepared clay pot, cover with the lid and place in an unheated oven. Set the oven to 180°C/350°F/Gas 4 and cook for 45 minutes.

6 Meanwhile prepare the basmati rice. Place it in a bowl, cover with cold water and leave to soak for 20 minutes. Drain the rice and place it in a large pan of boiling salted water, bring back to the boil and cook for 10 minutes. Drain and stir in the split cardamom pods.

7 Remove the clay pot from the oven and stir in the chopped ready-to-eat apricots. Pile the cooked rice on top of the lamb and dot with the butter. Drizzle over 60ml/4 tbsp water, then sprinkle the cashew nuts or flaked almonds on top. Cover the pot, reduce the oven temperature to 150°C/300°F/Gas 2 and cook the meat and rice for 30 minutes.

8 Remove the lid from the pot and fluff up the rice with a fork. Spoon into warmed individual bowls, then sprinkle over the fried onion slices and garnish with the sprigs of fresh coriander.

NUTRITIONAL NOTES	
Per Portion	
Energy	427Kcals/1784KJ
Fat	25.3g
Saturated Fat	11.3g
Carbohydrate	14.4g
Fibre	2g

Creamy Lamb Korma

A heritage of the talented cooks who served the Mogul emperors, this is a rich and luxurious dish. Mild in flavour, it is ideal for serving when you are unsure about how hot your guests like their curries to be.

INGREDIENTS

Serves 4–6

15ml/1 tbsp white sesame seeds
15ml/1 tbsp white poppy seeds
50g/2oz/½ cup blanched almonds
2 fresh green chillies, seeded
6 garlic cloves, sliced
5cm/2in piece fresh root ginger, sliced
1 onion, finely chopped
45ml/3 tbsp ghee or vegetable oil
6 green cardamom pods
5cm/2in piece cinnamon stick
4 cloves
900g/2lb lean lamb, boned and cubed
5ml/1 tsp ground cumin
5ml/1 tsp ground coriander
300ml/½ pint/1¼ cups double (heavy)
    cream mixed with 2.5ml/½ tsp
    cornflour (cornstarch)
salt
roasted sesame seeds, to garnish

NUTRITIONAL NOTES	
Per Portion	
Energy	939Kcals/3892KJ
Fat	80.8g
Saturated Fat	38.3g
Carbohydrate	5.1g
Fibre	1.5g

COOK'S TIP

If white poppy seeds are not available, use sunflower seeds instead.

1 Preheat a karahi, wok or large pan over a medium heat without any fat, and add the first seven ingredients. Stir until they begin to change colour. They should go just a shade darker.

2 Leave the mixture to cool, then grind to a fine paste using a pestle and mortar or in a food processor. Heat the ghee or oil in the pan over a low heat.

3 Fry the cardamoms, cinnamon and cloves until the cloves swell. Add the lamb, ground cumin and coriander and the prepared paste, and season with salt, to taste. Increase the heat to medium and stir well. Reduce the heat to low, then cover the pan and cook until the lamb is almost done.

4 Remove from the heat, leave to cool a little and gradually fold in the cream, reserving 5ml/1 tsp to garnish.

5 When ready to serve, gently reheat the lamb, uncovered. Spoon into a warmed dish and garnish with the sesame seeds and the reserved cream. This korma is very good served with pilau rice.

Rojan Josh

This is one of the most popular lamb dishes to have originated in Kashmir. Traditionally, fatty meat on the bone is slow cooked until most of the fat is separated from the meat. The fat that escapes from the meat in this way is known as rogan and josh refers to the rich red colour.

INGREDIENTS

Serves 4–6
45ml/3 tbsp lemon juice
250ml/8fl oz/1 cup natural (plain) yogurt
5ml/1 tsp salt
2 garlic cloves, crushed
2.5cm/1in piece fresh root ginger,
    finely grated
900g/2lb lean lamb fillet
    (tenderloin), cubed
60ml/4 tbsp vegetable oil
2.5ml/½ tsp cumin seeds
2 bay leaves
4 green cardamom pods
1 onion, finely chopped
10ml/2 tsp ground coriander
10ml/2 tsp ground cumin
5ml/1 tsp chilli powder
400g/14oz can chopped tomatoes
30ml/2 tbsp tomato purée (paste)
150ml/¼ pint/⅔ cup water
toasted cumin seeds and bay leaves,
    to garnish
plain boiled rice, to serve

1 In a large bowl, mix together the lemon juice, yogurt, salt, half the crushed garlic and the ginger. Add the lamb, cover and marinate in the refrigerator overnight.

2 Heat the oil in a karahi, wok or large pan and fry the cumin seeds for 2 minutes. Add the bay leaves and cardamom pods and fry for 2 minutes.

3 Add the onion and remaining garlic and fry for 5 minutes. Add the coriander, cumin and chilli powder. Fry for 2 minutes.

4 Add the marinated lamb to the pan and cook for a further 5 minutes, stirring occasionally to prevent the mixture from sticking to the base of the pan and starting to burn.

5 Stir in the tomatoes, tomato purée and water. Cover and simmer for 1–1½ hours. Garnish with toasted cumin seeds and bay leaves, and serve with the rice.

NUTRITIONAL NOTES	
Per Portion	
Energy	566Kcals/2362KJ
Fat	37g
Saturated Fat	13.3g
Carbohydrate	10.7g
Fibre	1.2g

Rezala

Essentially a Muslim dish, this delectable recipe comes from Bengal where there is a tradition of Muslim cooking. This is a legacy from the Muslim rulers of the Mogul era.

INGREDIENTS

Serves 4

1 large onion, roughly chopped
10ml/2 tsp grated fresh root ginger
10ml/2 tsp crushed garlic
4–5 cloves
2.5ml/½ tsp black peppercorns
6 green cardamom pods
5cm/2in piece cinnamon stick, halved
8 lamb rib chops
60ml/4 tbsp vegetable oil
1 large onion, finely sliced
175ml/6fl oz/¾ cup natural (plain) yogurt
50g/2oz/¼ cup butter
2.5ml/1 tsp salt
2.5ml/½ tsp ground cumin
2.5ml/½ tsp hot chilli powder
nutmeg
2.5ml/½ tsp granulated sugar
15ml/1 tbsp lime juice
pinch of saffron, steeped in 15ml/1 tbsp
   hot water for 10–15 minutes
15ml/1 tbsp rose water
rose petals, to garnish

1 Process the onion in a blender or food processor. Add a little water if necessary to form a purée.

2 Put the purée in a glass bowl and add the grated ginger, crushed garlic, cloves, peppercorns, cardamom pods and cinnamon. Mix well.

3 Put the lamb chops in a large shallow glass dish and add the spice mixture. Mix thoroughly, cover the bowl and leave the lamb to marinate for 3–4 hours or overnight in the refrigerator. Bring back to room temperature before cooking.

4 In a karahi, wok or large pan, heat the oil over a medium-high heat and fry the sliced onion for 6–7 minutes, until golden brown. Remove the onion slices with a slotted spoon, squeezing out as much oil as possible on the side of the pan. Drain the onions on kitchen paper.

5 In the remaining oil, fry the marinated lamb chops for 4–5 minutes, stirring frequently. Reduce the heat to low, cover and cook for 5–7 minutes.

6 Meanwhile, mix the yogurt and butter together in a small pan and place over a low heat. Cook for 5–6 minutes, stirring constantly, then stir into the lamb chops along with the salt. Add the cumin and chilli powder and cover the pan. Cook for 45–50 minutes until the chops are tender.

7 Using a nutmeg grater, or the finest cutting surface on a large, stainless steel grater, grate about 2.5ml/ ½ tsp nutmeg.

8 Add the nutmeg and sugar to the pan containing the lamb, cook for 1–2 minutes and add the lime juice, saffron and rose water. Stir and mix well, simmer for 2–3 minutes and remove from the heat. Spoon into a dish and garnish with the fried onion and rose petals. Serve with naan bread or boiled basmati rice, if you like.

COOK'S TIP

If you don't have whole nutmegs in your pantry, use ground nutmeg. The flavour will not be as strong so you may need to use a little more than if using fresh.

NUTRITIONAL NOTES
Per Portion

Energy	637Kcals/2630KJ
Fat	57.4g
Saturated Fat	25.7g
Carbohydrate	12.8g
Fibre	1.7g

Lamb with Peas and Mint

A simple dish for a family meal, this is easy to prepare and very versatile. It is equally delicious whether served with plain boiled rice or chapatis. Another excellent use for the lamb mixture is as a filling for samosas, or even in meat pies or pasties.

INGREDIENTS

Serves 4

15ml/1 tbsp oil
1 medium onion, chopped
2.5ml/½ tsp crushed garlic
2.5ml/½ tsp grated fresh root ginger
2.5ml/½ tsp chilli powder
1.5ml/¼ tsp ground turmeric
5ml/1 tsp ground coriander
5ml/1 tsp salt
2 medium tomatoes, sliced
275g/10oz lean leg of lamb,
    minced (ground)
1 large carrot, sliced or cut into batons
75g/3oz/½ cup petit pois (baby peas)
15ml/1 tbsp chopped fresh mint
15ml/1 tbsp chopped fresh coriander
1 fresh green chilli, chopped
fresh coriander (cilantro), to garnish

NUTRITIONAL NOTES	
Per Portion	
Energy	178Kcals/742KJ
Fat	9.40g
Saturated Fat	3.32g
Carbohydrate	7.20g
Fibre	2.10g

_____ COOK'S TIP _____

To cut the carrot into batons, first cut it into 5cm/2in lengths and square up the sides. Slice the carrot lengthways, then cut the pieces again at the identical width to make strips.

1 In a deep heavy frying pan, heat the oil and fry the chopped onion over a medium heat for 5 minutes until golden.

2 Meanwhile, in a small mixing bowl, mix the garlic, ginger, chilli powder, turmeric, ground coriander and salt. Stir well.

3 Add the sliced tomatoes and the spice mixture to the onions in the frying pan and fry for 2–3 minutes, stirring continuously.

4 Add the minced lamb to the mixture and stir-fry for about 7–10 minutes to seal.

5 Break up any lumps of meat which may form in the pan, using a potato masher if necessary.

6 Finally add the carrot, petit pois, chopped fresh mint and coriander and the chopped green chilli and mix together well.

7 Cook, stirring for 2–3 minutes until the carrot slices or batons and the petit pois are cooked, then serve immediately, garnished with fresh coriander sprigs.

Minced Lamb with Curry Leaves and Chilli

The whole chillies pack quite a punch, but can be removed from the dish before serving.

Ingredients

Serves 4

10ml/2 tsp oil
2 medium onions, chopped
10 curry leaves
6 fresh green chillies
350g/12oz lean minced (ground) lamb
5ml/1 tsp crushed garlic
5ml/1 tsp grated fresh root ginger
5ml/1 tsp chilli powder
1.5ml/¼ tsp ground turmeric
5ml/1 tsp salt
2 tomatoes, peeled and quartered
15ml/1 tbsp chopped fresh
    coriander (cilantro)

1 Heat the oil in a karahi, wok or heavy pan and fry the onions with the curry leaves and 3 of the whole green chillies.

_____ Cook's Tip _____

This curry also makes a terrific brunch if served with fried eggs.

2 Put the lamb into a bowl. Mix with the garlic, ginger and spices.

3 Add the lamb and salt to the onions and stir-fry for 7–10 minutes.

4 Add the tomatoes, coriander and remaining chillies and stir-fry for 2 minutes. Serve hot.

Nutritional Notes	
Per Portion	
Energy	197Kcals/821KJ
Fat	9.37g
Saturated Fat	3.59g
Carbohydrate	8.57g
Fibre	1.63g

Lamb with Apricots

Lamb is combined with apricots and traditional Indian spices to produce a rich, spicy curry with a hint of sweetness.

INGREDIENTS

Serves 6

900g/2lb lean stewing lamb
15ml/1 tbsp oil
2.5cm/1in cinnamon stick
4 green cardamom pods
1 onion, chopped
15ml/1 tbsp curry paste
5ml/1 tsp ground cumin
5ml/1 tsp ground coriander
1.5ml/¼ tsp salt
175g/6oz/²⁄₃ cup ready-to-eat
   dried apricots
350ml/12fl oz/1½ cups lamb stock
fresh coriander (cilantro), to garnish
yellow rice and mango chutney,
   to serve

1 Remove all the fat from the lamb and cut into 2.5cm/1in cubes.

NUTRITIONAL NOTES	
Per Portion	
Energy	327Kcals/1368KJ
Fat	16.00g
Saturated Fat	6.59g
Carbohydrate	13.30g
Fibre	2.70g

2 Heat the oil in a large heavy pan and fry the cinnamon stick and cardamoms for 2 minutes. Add the onion and gently fry for about 6–8 minutes, stirring occasionally.

3 Add the curry paste and fry for 2 minutes. Stir in the cumin, coriander and salt and stir-fry for a further 2–3 minutes.

4 Add the meat, apricots and the stock. Cover and cook for 1–1½ hours. Serve, garnished with fresh coriander, on yellow rice, with the chutney in a separate bowl.

Spicy Spring Lamb Roast

Coating leg of lamb with a spicy, fruity rub gives it a wonderful flavour. During the initial cooking process, the flavours permeate the meat, which remains moist inside its foil parcel. Later, the foil is removed to allow the roast to brown beautifully.

INGREDIENTS

Serves 6

1.5kg/3–3½lb lean leg of spring lamb
5ml/1 tsp chilli powder
5ml/1 tsp crushed garlic
5ml/1 tsp ground coriander
5ml/1 tsp ground cumin
5ml/1 tsp salt
15ml/1 tbsp dried breadcrumbs
45ml/3 tbsp natural (plain) low
 fat yogurt
30ml/2 tbsp lemon juice
30ml/2 tbsp sultanas (golden raisins)
15ml/1 tbsp oil

For the garnish
mixed salad leaves
fresh coriander (cilantro)
2 tomatoes, quartered
1 large carrot, shredded
lemon wedges

NUTRITIONAL NOTES	
Per Portion	
Energy	265Kcals/1109KJ
Fat	13.40g
Saturated Fat	5.59g
Carbohydrate	8.90g
Fibre	0.70g

1 Preheat the oven to 180°C/350°F/ Gas 4. Trim any excess fat from the lamb. Rinse the joint, pat it dry and set aside on a sheet of foil large enough to enclose it completely.

2 In a medium bowl, mix together the chilli powder, garlic, ground coriander, ground cumin and salt.

3 Mix together in a food processor the breadcrumbs, yogurt, lemon juice and sultanas.

4 Add the contents of the food processor to the spice mixture together with the oil and mix together well. Pour this on to the leg of lamb and rub all over the meat.

5 Enclose the meat in the foil and place in an ovenproof dish. Cook in the oven for about 1½ hours.

6 Remove the lamb from the oven, open the foil and, using the back of a spoon, spread the mixture evenly over the meat. Return the lamb, uncovered, to the oven for another 45 minutes or until it is cooked right through and tender.

7 Slice the meat and serve with the mixed salad leaves, fresh coriander, tomatoes, carrot and lemon wedges.

——————— COOK'S TIP ———————

Make sure that the spice mixture is rubbed all over the leg of lamb so that its flavour penetrates all parts of the joint.

Mughlai-style Leg of Lamb

In India, there are different names for this style of cooking a leg of lamb, two of which are *shahi raan* and *peshawari raan*. Legend has it that roasting a whole leg of lamb was first popularized by the Mongolian warrior Genghis Khan.

INGREDIENTS

Serves 4–6
4 large onions, chopped
4 garlic cloves
5cm/2in piece fresh root ginger, chopped
45ml/3 tbsp ground almonds
10ml/2 tsp ground cumin
10ml/2 tsp ground coriander
10ml/2 tsp ground turmeric
10ml/2 tsp garam masala
4–6 fresh green chillies
juice of 1 lemon
300ml/½ pint/1¼ cups natural (plain) yogurt, beaten
1.8kg/4lb leg of lamb
8–10 cloves
salt
15ml/1 tbsp flaked (sliced) almonds, to garnish
4 firm tomatoes, halved and grilled (broiled), to serve

1 Preheat the oven to 190°C/375°F/ Gas 5. Place the onions, garlic, ginger, ground almonds, dry spices, chillies and lemon juice in a food processor or blender. Add salt to taste, and process to a smooth paste. Gradually add the yogurt and blend briefly to mix. Grease a large, deep roasting pan.

NUTRITIONAL NOTES	
Per Portion	
Energy	852Kcals/3549KJ
Fat	51.2g
Saturated Fat	17g
Carbohydrate	25.4g
Fibre	3.5g

2 Remove most of the fat and skin from the lamb. Using a sharp knife, make deep pockets above the bone at each side of the thick end. Make deep diagonal gashes on both sides of the lamb.

3 Push the cloves firmly into the meat, spaced evenly on all sides.

4 Push some of the spice mixture into the pockets and gashes and spread the remainder evenly all over the meat. Place the meat on the roasting pan and loosely cover the whole pan with foil. Roast for 2–2½ hours, or until the meat is cooked, removing the foil for the last 10 minutes of cooking time.

5 Remove from the oven and leave to rest for about 10 minutes before carving. Garnish the roast with the almonds and serve with the tomatoes.

--- COOK'S TIP ---

If time permits, leave the lamb to stand at room temperature for a couple of hours before putting it in the oven.

Madras Beef Curry

Although Madras is renowned for the best vegetarian food in India, meat-based recipes such as this one are also extremely popular.

INGREDIENTS

Serves 4–6
60ml/4 tbsp vegetable oil
1 large onion, finely sliced
3–4 cloves
4 green cardamoms
2 whole star anise
4 fresh green chillies, chopped
2 fresh or dried red chillies, chopped
45ml/3 tbsp Madras masala paste
5ml/1 tsp ground turmeric
450g/1lb lean beef, cubed
60ml/4 tbsp tamarind juice
granulated sugar, to taste
salt
a few fresh coriander (cilantro) leaves, chopped, to garnish

1 Heat the oil in a karahi, wok or large pan over a medium heat and fry the onion slices for about 8 minutes until they turn golden brown. Lower the heat, add all the spice ingredients, and fry for a further 2–3 minutes.

2 Add the beef and mix well. Cover and cook over a low heat until the beef is tender and fully cooked. Cook uncovered on a higher heat for the last few minutes to reduce any excess liquid.

NUTRITIONAL NOTES	
Per Portion	
Energy	317Kcals/1318KJ
Fat	21.6g
Saturated Fat	5.6g
Carbohydrate	4.8g
Fibre	0.9g

3 Fold in the tamarind juice, sugar and salt. Reheat the dish and garnish with the chopped coriander leaves. Pulao rice and a tomato and onion salad would make excellent accompaniments for this dish.

_____ COOK'S TIP _____

To tenderize the meat, add 60ml/4 tbsp white wine vinegar in step 2, along with the meat, and omit the tamarind juice.

Spicy Meat Loaf

This mixture is baked in the oven and provides a hearty meal on cold winter days.

INGREDIENTS

Serves 4-6
5 eggs
450g/1lb lean minced (ground) beef
30ml/2 tbsp grated fresh root ginger
30ml/2 tbsp crushed garlic
6 fresh green chillies, chopped
2 small onions, finely chopped
2.5ml/½ tsp ground turmeric
50g/2oz/2 cups fresh coriander
    (cilantro), chopped
175g/6oz potato, grated
salt, to taste
salad leaves, to serve
lemon twist, to garnish

1 Preheat the oven to 180°C/350°F/ Gas 4. Beat 2 eggs until fluffy and pour into a greased 900g/2lb loaf pan.

2 Knead together the meat, ginger and garlic, 4 green chillies, 1 chopped onion, 1 beaten egg, the turmeric, fresh coriander, potato and salt. Pack into the loaf pan and smooth the surface. Cook in the preheated oven for 45 minutes.

3 Meanwhile, beat the remaining eggs and fold in with the remaining green chillies and onion. Remove the loaf pan from the oven and pour the mixture all over the meat.

4 Return to the oven and cook until the eggs have set. Serve hot on a bed of salad leaves, garnished with a twist of lemon.

NUTRITIONAL NOTES	
Per Portion	
Energy	394Kcals/1637KJ
Fat	25.4g
Saturated Fat	9.8g
Carbohydrate	10.1g
Fibre	1g

Beef Koftas

Serve these tasty treats piping hot with naan bread, raita and light salad. Leftover koftas can be chopped coarsely and packed into pitta bread.

INGREDIENTS

Makes 20–25
450g/1lb lean minced (ground) beef
30ml/2 tbsp grated fresh root ginger
30ml/2 tbsp crushed garlic
4 fresh green chillies, finely chopped
1 small onion, finely chopped
1 egg
2.5ml/½ tsp ground turmeric
5ml/1 tsp garam masala
50g/2oz/2 cups fresh coriander
    (cilantro), chopped
4–6 fresh mint leaves, chopped
175g/6oz potato
salt, to taste
vegetable oil, for deep-frying

1 Mix the meat, ginger, garlic, chillies, onion, egg, spices and herbs in a large bowl. Grate the potato into the bowl, and season with salt. Knead together to blend well and form a soft dough.

2 Shape the mixture into portions the size of golf balls. Place on a plate, cover and leave the koftas to rest for about 25 minutes.

NUTRITIONAL NOTES	
Per Portion	
Energy	63Kcals/263KJ
Fat	4g
Saturated Fat	1.7g
Carbohydrate	1.8g
Fibre	0.2g

3 In a karahi, wok or frying pan, heat the oil to medium-hot and fry the koftas in small batches until they are golden brown in colour. Drain well and serve hot.

VARIATION
Use lamb instead of the beef, if you prefer.

Beef Vindaloo

A fiery dish originally from Goa, a "vindaloo" curry is made using a unique blend of hot aromatic spices and vinegar to give it a distinctive flavour.

INGREDIENTS

Serves 6

15ml/1 tbsp cumin seeds
4 dried red chillies
5ml/1 tsp black peppercorns
seeds from 5 green cardamom pods
5ml/1 tsp fenugreek seeds
5ml/1 tsp black mustard seeds
2.5ml/½ tsp salt
2.5ml/½ tsp demerara sugar
60ml/4 tbsp white wine vinegar
30ml/2 tbsp oil
1 large onion, finely chopped
900g/2lb lean stewing beef, cut
     into 2.5cm/1in cubes
2.5cm/1in piece fresh root ginger,
     finely chopped
1 garlic clove, crushed
10ml/2 tsp ground coriander
2.5ml/½ tsp ground turmeric
plain and yellow rice, see Cook's Tip,
     to serve

1 Put the cumin seeds, chillies, peppercorns, cardamom seeds, fenugreek seeds and mustard seeds into a spice grinder (or a pestle and mortar) and grind to a fine powder.

2 Spoon into a bowl, add the salt, sugar and white wine vinegar and mix to a thin paste. Heat 15ml/1 tbsp of the oil in a large heavy pan and fry the onion for 10 minutes.

3 Put the onions and the spice mixture into a food processor or blender and process to a coarse paste.

4 Heat the remaining oil in the frying pan and fry the meat cubes for about 10 minutes until lightly browned. Remove with a slotted spoon.

5 Add the ginger and garlic to the oil remaining in the pan and fry for 2 minutes. Stir in the ground coriander and turmeric and fry for a further 2 minutes.

6 Add the spice and onion paste and fry for about 5 minutes.

7 Return the beef cubes to the pan with 300ml/½ pint/1¼ cups water. Cover and simmer for about 1–1½ hours or until the meat is tender. Serve with plain and yellow rice.

NUTRITIONAL NOTES	
Per Portion	
Energy	269Kcals/1127KJ
Fat	11.60g
Saturated Fat	3.28g
Carbohydrate	7.30g
Fibre	0.60g

COOK'S TIP

To make plain and yellow rice, infuse a pinch of saffron strands or dissolve a little ground turmeric in 15ml/1 tbsp hot water. Stir into half the cooked rice until uniformly yellow. Mix the yellow rice into the plain rice.

Beef with Green Beans

Green beans cooked with beef is a variation on the traditional recipe using lamb. The sliced red pepper provides a contrast to the colour of the beans and chillies, and adds extra flavour.

INGREDIENTS

Serves 4

275g/10oz fine green beans, cut into
   2.5cm/1in pieces
15ml/1 tbsp oil
1 medium onion, sliced
5ml/1 tsp grated fresh root ginger
5ml/1 tsp crushed garlic
5ml/1 tsp chilli powder
6.5ml/1¼ tsp salt
1.5ml/¼ tsp ground turmeric
2 tomatoes, chopped
450g/1lb lean beef, cubed
475ml/16fl oz/2 cups water
1 red (bell) pepper, seeded and sliced
15ml/1 tbsp chopped fresh
   coriander (cilantro)
2 fresh green chillies, chopped
warm chapatis, to serve (optional)

NUTRITIONAL NOTES	
Per Portion	
Energy	242Kcals/1012KJ
Fat	11.60g
Saturated Fat	2.91g
Carbohydrate	9.30g
Fibre	3.00g

COOK'S TIP

Blanching the beans in boiling water helps to preserve their bright green colour. Rinsing them under cold water arrests the cooking process. Drain them well.

1 Blanch the beans in boiling water for 3–4 minutes, then rinse under cold running water, drain and set aside.

2 Heat the oil in a large heavy pan and gently fry the onion slices until golden brown.

3 In a bowl, mix the ginger pulp, garlic, chilli powder, salt, turmeric and chopped tomatoes. Spoon the ginger and garlic mixture into the pan and stir-fry with the onion for 5–7 minutes.

4 Add the beef and stir-fry for a further 3 minutes. Pour in the water, bring to the boil and lower the heat. Half cover the pan and cook for 1–1¼ hours until most of the water has evaporated and the meat is tender.

5 Add the green beans and mix everything together well.

6 Finally, add the red pepper, fresh coriander and green chillies. Cook the mixture, stirring, for a further 7–10 minutes, or until the beans are tender.

7 Spoon into a large bowl or individual plates. Serve the beef hot, with warm chapatis if you like.

Citrus Beef Curry

This superbly aromatic curry is not exceptionally hot but it is full of flavour.

INGREDIENTS

Serves 4

450g/1lb rump (round) steak
30ml/2 tbsp vegetable oil
30ml/2 tbsp medium curry paste
2 bay leaves
400ml/14fl oz/1⅔ cups coconut milk
300ml/½ pint/1¼ cups beef stock
30ml/2 tbsp lemon juice
grated rind and juice of ½ orange
15ml/1 tbsp granulated sugar
115g/4oz baby (pearl) onions, peeled
  but left whole
225g/8oz new potatoes, halved
115g/4oz/1 cup unsalted roasted
  peanuts, roughly chopped
115g/4oz fine green beans, halved
1 red (bell) pepper, seeded and
  thinly sliced
unsalted roasted peanuts, to
  garnish (optional)

4 Stir in the bay leaves, coconut milk, stock, lemon juice, orange rind and juice and sugar, and bring to the boil, stirring frequently.

5 Add the onions and potatoes, then bring back to the boil, reduce the heat and simmer, uncovered, for 5 minutes.

6 Stir in the peanuts, beans and pepper and simmer for a further 10 minutes, or until the beef and potatoes are tender. Serve in shallow bowls, with a spoon and fork, to enjoy all the rich and creamy juices. Sprinkle with extra unsalted roasted peanuts, if you like.

1 Trim any fat from the beef and cut the meat into 5cm/2in strips.

2 Heat the vegetable oil in a large, heavy pan, add the curry paste and cook over a medium heat for 30 seconds, stirring constantly.

3 Add the beef and cook, stirring, for 2 minutes until it is beginning to brown and is thoroughly coated with the spices.

NUTRITIONAL NOTES	
Per Portion	
Energy	444Kcals/1858KJ
Fat	24.2g
Saturated Fat	5.4g
Carbohydrate	23.5g
Fibre	4.2g

Steak and Kidney with Spinach

When this dish is cooked in India, the spinach is often pulverized. Here, it is coarsely chopped and added in at the last stages of cooking, which retains the nutritional value of the spinach and gives the dish a lovely appearance.

INGREDIENTS

Serves 4–6
5cm/2in piece fresh ginger
30ml/2 tbsp vegetable oil
1 large onion, finely chopped
4 garlic cloves, crushed
60ml/4 tbsp mild curry paste, or
  60ml/4 tbsp mild curry powder
1.5ml/¼ tsp ground turmeric
salt, to taste
900g/2lb steak and kidney, cubed
450g/1lb fresh spinach, trimmed,
  washed and chopped or 450g/1lb
  frozen spinach, thawed and drained
60ml/4 tbsp tomato purée (paste)
2 large tomatoes, finely chopped

1 Using a sharp knife or vegetable peeler, remove the skin from the ginger. Grate it on the fine side of a metal cheese grater.

___ COOK'S TIP ___

Root ginger freezes very easily, and is actually much easier to grate when frozen. There's no need to defrost the ginger before adding it to the spicy onion mixture, as it will thaw instantly upon contact with heat.

2 Heat the oil in a frying pan, wok or karahi and fry the onion, ginger and garlic until the onion is soft and the ginger and garlic turn golden brown.

3 Lower the heat and add the curry paste or powder, turmeric and salt. Add the steak and kidney to the pan and mix well. Cover and cook, stirring frequently to prevent the mixture from sticking to the pan, for 20–30 minutes over a medium heat, until the meat is just tender.

4 Add the spinach and tomato purée and mix well. Cook uncovered until the spinach is softened and most of the liquid evaporated.

5 Fold in the chopped tomatoes. Increase the heat, as the tomatoes will have a cooling effect on the other ingredients, and cook the mixture for a further 5 minutes, until they are soft.

6 Dish into shallow bowls and serve piping hot with a simple accompaniment to offset the rich, gamey flavour of the dish, like plain boiled basmati rice. Go easy on any side portions though, as this is a very rich and filling dish.

NUTRITIONAL NOTES
Per Portion

Energy	362Kcals/1515KJ
Fat	13.5g
Saturated Fat	3.5g
Carbohydrate	11.7g
Fibre	4.4g

Beef Biryani

This biryani, which uses beef, is a speciality of the Muslim community. The recipe may seem long, but biryani is one of the easiest and most relaxing ways of cooking, especially when you are entertaining. Once the dish is assembled and placed in the oven, it looks after itself and you can get on with greeting your guests.

INGREDIENTS

Serves 4

2 large onions
2 garlic cloves, chopped
2.5cm/1in piece fresh root ginger, peeled and roughly chopped
½–1 fresh green chilli, seeded and chopped
small bunch of fresh coriander (cilantro)
60ml/4 tbsp flaked (sliced) almonds
30–45ml/2–3 tbsp water
15ml/1 tbsp ghee or butter, plus 25g/1oz/2 tbsp butter for the rice
45ml/3 tbsp vegetable oil
30ml/2 tbsp sultanas (golden raisins)
500g/1¼lb braising or stewing steak, cubed
5ml/1 tsp ground coriander
15ml/1 tbsp ground cumin
2.5ml/½ tsp ground turmeric
2.5ml/½ tsp ground fenugreek
good pinch of ground cinnamon
175ml/6fl oz/¾ cup natural (plain) yogurt, whisked
275g/10oz/1½ cups basmati rice
about 1.2 litres/2 pints/5 cups hot chicken stock or water
salt and black pepper
2 hard-boiled eggs, quartered, to garnish
chapatis, to serve

COOK'S TIP

Place a piece of buttered greaseproof (waxed) paper on the rice. This will help to keep the top layer moist in the oven.

---

1 Roughly chop one onion and place it in a food processor or blender. Add the garlic, ginger, chilli, fresh coriander and half the flaked almonds. Pour in the water and process to a smooth paste. Transfer the paste to a small bowl and set aside.

2 Finely slice the remaining onion into rings or half rings. Heat half the ghee or butter with half the oil in a heavy flameproof casserole and fry the onion rings for 10–15 minutes until they are a deep golden brown. Transfer to a plate with a slotted spoon.

3 Fry the remaining flaked almonds briefly until golden and set aside with the onion rings, then quickly fry the sultanas until they swell. Transfer to the plate.

4 Heat the remaining ghee or butter in the casserole with a further 15ml/1 tbsp of the oil. Fry the cubed meat, in batches, until evenly browned on all sides. Transfer the meat to a plate and set aside.

5 Wipe the casserole clean with kitchen paper, heat the remaining oil and pour in the onion, spice and coriander paste made earlier. Cook over a medium heat for 2–3 minutes, stirring all the time, until the mixture begins to brown lightly. Stir in all the additional spices, season with salt and ground black pepper and cook for 1 minute more.

6 Lower the heat, then stir in the yogurt, a little at a time. When all of it has been incorporated into the spice mixture, return the meat to the casserole. Stir to coat, cover tightly and simmer over a gentle heat for 40–45 minutes until the meat is tender. Meanwhile, soak the rice in a bowl of cold water for 15–20 minutes.

7 Preheat the oven to 160°C/325°F/ Gas 3. Drain the rice, place in a pan and add the hot chicken stock or water, together with a little salt. Bring back to the boil, cover and cook for 5 minutes.

8 Drain the rice, and pile it in a mound on top of the meat in the casserole. Using the handle of a spoon, make a hole through the rice and meat mixture, to the bottom of the pan. Place the fried onions, almonds and sultanas over the top and dot with butter. Cover the casserole tightly with a double layer of foil and secure with a lid.

9 Cook the biryani in the preheated oven for 30–40 minutes. To serve, spoon the mixture on to a warmed serving platter and garnish with the quartered hard-boiled eggs. Serve with chapatis.

NUTRITIONAL NOTES	
Per Portion	
Energy	741Kcals/3090KJ
Fat	29.3g
Saturated Fat	10.9g
Carbohydrate	79.1g
Fibre	3.1g

Chilli Beef with Basil

This is a dish for chilli lovers! It is very easy to prepare – all you need is a karahi or a wok.

INGREDIENTS

Serves 2

about 90ml/6 tbsp vegetable oil
16–20 large fresh basil leaves
275g/10oz rump steak
30ml/2 tbsp Worcestershire sauce
5ml/1 tsp dark brown soft sugar
1–2 fresh red chillies, sliced into rings
3 garlic cloves, chopped
5ml/1 tsp chopped fresh root ginger
1 shallot, thinly sliced
30ml/2 tbsp finely chopped fresh basil
  leaves, plus extra to garnish
squeeze of lemon juice
salt and black pepper
rice, to serve

1 Heat the oil in a karahi or wok. Add the whole basil leaves and fry for about 1 minute until crisp and golden. Drain on kitchen paper. Remove the pan from the heat and pour off all but 30ml/2 tbsp of the oil.

-------------------- COOK'S TIP --------------------

Although Worcestershire sauce is often thought of as archetypally English, it is actually based on an Indian recipe. Ingredients include molasses, anchovies and tamarind extract.

2 Cut the steak across the grain into thin strips. Mix the Worcestershire sauce and sugar in a bowl. Add the beef, mix well, then cover and leave to marinate for about 30 minutes.

3 Reheat the oil until hot, add the chilli, garlic, ginger and shallot and stir-fry for 30 seconds. Add the beef and chopped basil, then stir-fry for about 3 minutes. Flavour with lemon juice and salt and pepper to taste.

4 Transfer the chilli beef to a warmed serving plate, scatter over the basil leaves to garnish and serve immediately with rice.

NUTRITIONAL NOTES	
Per Portion	
Energy	469Kcals/1943KJ
Fat	38.6g
Saturated Fat	9g
Carbohydrate	0g
Fibre	0g

Portuguese Pork

This dish displays the influence
of Portuguese cooking on
Indian cuisine.

INGREDIENTS

Serves 4–6

115g/4oz deep-fried onions, crushed
4 fresh red chillies
60ml/4 tbsp vindaloo curry paste
90ml/6 tbsp white wine vinegar
90ml/6 tbsp tomato purée (paste)
2.5ml/½ tsp fenugreek seeds
5ml/1 tsp ground turmeric
5ml/1 tsp crushed mustard seeds, or
    2.5ml/½ tsp mustard powder
salt, to taste
7.5ml/1½ tsp granulated sugar
900g/2lb boneless pork spareribs, cubed
250ml/8fl oz/1 cup water
plain boiled rice, to serve

1 Place the crushed onions, chillies,
curry paste, vinegar, tomato purée,
fenugreek seeds, turmeric and mustard
seeds or powder in a bowl, with the salt
and sugar.

2 Add the pork cubes and mix well.
Cover and marinate for 2 hours,
then tip into a large, heavy pan.

3 Stir in the water. Bring to the boil
and simmer gently for 2 hours.
Serve hot with the rice.

NUTRITIONAL NOTES
Per Portion

Energy	322Kcals/1349KJ
Fat	12.2g
Saturated Fat	3.6g
Carbohydrate	4.1g
Fibre	0.9g

Chilli Pork with Curry Leaves

Curry leaves and chillies are two of the hallmark ingredients used in the southern states of India. This recipe is from the state of Andhra Pradesh, where the hottest chillies, known as *guntur* after the region where they are produced, are grown in abundance.

INGREDIENTS

Serves 4–6
30ml/2 tbsp vegetable oil
1 large onion, finely sliced
5cm/2in piece fresh root ginger, grated
4 garlic cloves, crushed
12 curry leaves
45ml/3 tbsp extra hot curry paste, or
   60ml/4 tbsp hot curry powder
15ml/1 tbsp chilli powder
5ml/1 tsp five-spice powder
5ml/1 tsp ground turmeric
900g/2lb lean lamb, beef or pork,
   cubed
175ml/6fl oz/¾ cup thick coconut
   milk
salt
red onion, finely sliced, to garnish
Indian bread and fruit raita, to serve

1 Heat the oil in a karahi, wok or large, pan, and fry the onion, ginger, garlic and curry leaves until the onion is soft. Add the curry paste or powder, chilli and five-spice powder, turmeric and salt. Stir well.

2 Add the meat and stir well over a medium heat to seal and evenly brown the meat pieces. Keep stirring until the oil separates. Cover the pan and cook for about 20 minutes.

NUTRITIONAL NOTES	
Per Portion	
Energy	484Kcals/2018KJ
Fat	31g
Saturated Fat	12.5g
Carbohydrate	6.9g
Fibre	0.9g

_____ COOK'S TIP _____

For extra flavour, reserve half the curry leaves and add in step 3, along with the coconut milk.

3 Stir in the coconut milk and simmer, covered, until the meat is cooked. Towards the end of cooking, uncover the pan to reduce the excess liquid. Garnish with onions and serve with any Indian bread, and with fruit raita, for a cooling effect.

Pork Balchao

Pork and beef dishes are not very common in India, but Goa, on the west coast of the country, has several of both. This spicy stew is flavoured with vinegar and sugar, a combination that immediately identifies it as Goan.

INGREDIENTS

Serves 4

60ml/4 tbsp vegetable oil
15ml/1 tbsp grated fresh root ginger
15ml/1 tbsp crushed garlic
2.5cm/1in piece cinnamon stick, broken up
2–4 dried red chillies, chopped or torn
4 cloves
10ml/2 tsp cumin seeds
10 black peppercorns
675g/1½lb cubed leg of pork, crackling and visible fat removed
5ml/1 tsp ground turmeric
200ml/7fl oz/scant 1 cup warm water
25ml/1½ tbsp tomato purée (paste)
2.5ml/½ tsp chilli powder (optional)
1 large onion, finely sliced
5ml/1 tsp salt
5ml/1 tsp granulated sugar
10ml/2 tbsp cider vinegar
fresh chillies, to garnish

1 Heat 30ml/2 tbsp of the oil in a karahi, wok or large pan, and add the ginger and garlic. Fry for 30 seconds.

2 Grind the cinnamon stick, dried chillies, cloves, cumin seeds and peppercorns to a fine powder, using a spice mill or coffee grinder reserved for spices.

3 Add the spice mix to the pan and fry for a further 30 seconds, stirring.

4 Add the pork and turmeric and increase the heat slightly. Fry for 5–6 minutes or until the meat starts to release its juices, stirring regularly.

5 Add the water, tomato purée and chilli powder, if using, and bring to the boil. Cover the pan and simmer gently for 35–40 minutes.

6 Heat the remaining oil and fry the onion for 8–9 minutes until browned, stirring regularly.

7 Add the fried onion to the pork along with the salt, sugar and vinegar. Stir, cover and simmer for 30–35 minutes or until the pork is tender. Remove from the heat and spoon into a serving dish. Garnish with chillies and serve.

NUTRITIONAL NOTES	
Per Portion	
Energy	326Kcals/1361KJ
Fat	17.9g
Saturated Fat	3.7g
Carbohydrate	4.8g
Fibre	0.9g

Lentils with Venison and Tomatoes

Venison curries well and tastes good in this simple dish. Serve it with pilau rice, naan or bhaturas. Spinach with mushrooms and peppers would make a colourful accompaniment.

INGREDIENTS

Serves 4
60ml/4 tbsp corn oil
1 bay leaf
2 cloves
4 black peppercorns
1 medium onion, sliced
450g/1lb diced venison
2.5ml/½ tsp ground turmeric
7.5ml/1½ tsp chilli powder
5ml/1 tsp garam masala
5ml/1 tsp crushed coriander seeds
2.5cm/1in cinnamon stick
5ml/1 tsp crushed garlic
5ml/1 tsp grated fresh root ginger
7.5ml/1½ tsp salt
1.5 litres/2½ pints/6 cups water
50g/2oz/⅓ cup split red lentils
2 medium tomatoes, quartered
2 fresh green chillies, chopped
15ml/1 tbsp chopped fresh
   coriander (cilantro)

1 Heat the oil in a karahi, wok or deep pan. Lower the heat slightly and add the bay leaf, cloves, peppercorns and onion slices. Fry for about 5 minutes, or until the onions are golden brown, stirring occasionally.

2 Add the diced venison, turmeric, chilli powder, garam masala, coriander seeds, cinnamon stick, garlic, ginger and most of the salt, and stir-fry for about 5 minutes over a medium heat.

3 Pour in 900ml/1½ pints/3¾ cups of the water and cover the pan with a lid. Simmer over a low heat for about 35–40 minutes, or until the water has evaporated and the meat is tender.

4 Put the lentils into a pan with 600ml/1 pint/2½ cups water and boil for about 12–15 minutes, or until the water has almost evaporated and the lentils are soft enough to mash. If the lentils are too thick, add up to 150ml/¼ pint/⅔ cup water to loosen the mixture.

5 When the meat is tender, stir-fry the mixture using a wooden spoon, until some free oil begins to appear on the sides of the pan.

6 Add the cooked lentils to the venison and mix together well.

7 Add the tomatoes, chillies and fresh coriander and serve.

COOK'S TIP

Cubed boneless chicken can be used in place of the venison. At step 3, reduce the amount of water to 300ml/½ pint/ 1¼ cups and cook uncovered, stirring occasionally, for 10–15 minutes or until the water has evaporated and the chicken is cooked through.

NUTRITIONAL NOTES
Per Portion

Energy	277Kcals/1160KJ
Fat	13.9g
Saturated Fat	2.6g
Carbohydrate	11.6g
Fibre	1.6g

Balti Dishes

THERE IS some confusion about the origins of Balti, but absolutely no doubt as to its popularity. This style of cooking may well have originated in Kashmir, but it was perfected, developed and adapted for Western tastes in the British city of Birmingham.

Balti-style of cooking draws heavily on the traditional recipes and cooking methods from the north of the Indian subcontinent, but happily adopts ingredients from elsewhere. What distinguishes Balti dishes is their autonomy. Whereas many traditional Indian dishes are bit-players, sharing the limelight with numerous other dishes at the table, the Balti meal is a solo star.

Everything is cooked and served in a single pan, and many Balti dishes need only be served with a simple accompaniment, such as naan bread. They are easy to cook, even for the novice, are subtly spiced, and work equally well with either meat, poultry, fish, shellfish or fresh vegetables as their base.

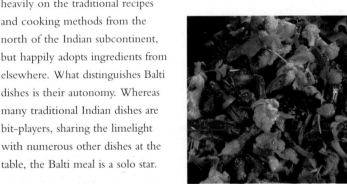

Chunky Fish Balti with Peppers

Try to find peppers in different colours to make this dish as colourful as possible.

INGREDIENTS

Serves 2–4

450g/1lb cod, or any other firm, white
   fish, such as haddock
7.5ml/1½ tsp ground cumin
10ml/2 tsp amchur (dried
   mango powder)
5ml/1 tsp ground coriander
2.5ml/½ tsp chilli powder
5ml/1 tsp salt
5ml/1 tsp grated fresh root ginger
45ml/3 tbsp cornflour (cornstarch)
150ml/¼ pint/⅔ cup corn oil
1 each green, orange and red (bell)
   peppers, seeded and chopped
8–10 cherry tomatoes

1 Skin the fish and cut into small cubes. Put the cubes into a large mixing bowl and add the ground cumin, mango powder, ground coriander, chilli powder, salt, ginger and cornflour. Mix together thoroughly until the fish is well coated.

2 Heat the oil in a karahi, wok or large, deep pan. Lower the heat slightly and add the fish pieces, 3 or 4 at a time. Fry for about 3 minutes, turning constantly.

3 Drain the fish pieces on kitchen paper and transfer to a serving dish. Keep hot while you fry the remaining fish pieces.

4 Fry the chopped peppers in the oil remaining in the pan for about 2 minutes. They should still be slightly crisp. Drain on kitchen paper.

5 Add the cooked peppers to the fish and garnish with the cherry tomatoes. Serve.

NUTRITIONAL NOTES	
Per Portion	
Energy	495Kcals/2058KJ
Fat	30g
Saturated Fat	3.8g
Carbohydrate	13.3g
Fibre	3.4g

Balti Fish Fillets in Spicy Coconut Sauce

Although coconut milk is a familiar ingredient in Indian fish dishes, it is quite unusual to find shredded coconut in a starring role. It makes for a delicious and unusual dish.

INGREDIENTS

Serves 4

30ml/2 tbsp corn oil
5ml/1 tsp onion seeds
4 dried red chillies
3 garlic cloves, sliced
1 medium onion, sliced
2 medium tomatoes, sliced
30ml/2 tbsp desiccated (dry
    unsweetened shredded) coconut
5ml/1 tsp salt
5ml/1 tsp ground coriander
4 flatfish fillets, such as plaice, sole or
    flounder, each about 75g/3oz
150ml/¼ pint/⅔ cup water
15ml/1 tbsp lime juice
15ml/1 tbsp chopped fresh
    coriander (cilantro)

1 Heat the oil in a karahi, wok or deep pan. Lower the heat slightly and add the onion seeds, dried red chillies, garlic slices and onion. Cook for 3–4 minutes, stirring once or twice.

COOK'S TIP

Use fresh fish fillets to make this dish if you can, as the flavour and texture will probably be superior. If you must use frozen fillets, ensure that they are completely thawed before cooking.

2 Add the tomatoes, coconut, salt and coriander and stir thoroughly.

NUTRITIONAL NOTES
Per Portion

Energy	175Kcals/731KJ
Fat	11.4g
Saturated Fat	5g
Carbohydrate	4.9g
Fibre	2g

3 Cut each fish fillet into 3 pieces. Drop the fish pieces into the mixture and turn them over gently until they are well coated.

4 Cook for 5–7 minutes, lowering the heat if necessary. Add the water, lime juice and fresh coriander and cook for a further 3–5 minutes until most of the water has evaporated. Serve immediately, with rice, if you like.

Seafood Balti with Vegetables

In this dish, the spicy seafood is cooked separately and combined with the vegetables at the last minute to give a truly delicious combination of flavours.

INGREDIENTS

Serves 4

225g/½lb cod, or any other firm, white fish
225g/½lb cooked prawns (shrimp)
6 seafood sticks, halved lengthways, or 115g/4oz white crab meat
15ml/1 tbsp lemon juice
5ml/1 tsp ground coriander
5ml/1 tsp chilli powder
5ml/1 tsp salt
5ml/1 tsp ground cumin
60ml/4 tbsp cornflour (cornstarch)
150ml/¼ pint/⅔ cup corn oil

For the vegetables

150ml/¼ pint/⅔ cup corn oil
2 medium onions, chopped
5ml/1 tsp onion seeds
½ medium cauliflower, cut into florets
115g/4oz French (green) beans, cut into 2.5cm/1in lengths
175g/6oz/1 cup sweetcorn
5ml/1 tsp shredded fresh root ginger
5ml/1 tsp chilli powder
5ml/1 tsp salt
4 fresh green chillies, sliced
30ml/2 tbsp chopped fresh coriander (cilantro)
lime slices

1 Skin the fish and cut into small cubes. Put into a medium mixing bowl with the prawns and seafood sticks or crab meat.

2 In a separate bowl, mix together the lemon juice, ground coriander, chilli powder, salt and ground cumin. Pour this over the seafood and mix together thoroughly, using your hands.

3 Sprinkle on the cornflour and mix again until the seafood is well coated. Place in the refrigerator for about 1 hour to allow the flavours to develop.

4 To make the vegetable mixture, heat the oil in a karahi, wok or deep pan. Add the onions and the onion seeds, and stir-fry until lightly browned.

5 Add the cauliflower, green beans, corn, ginger, chilli powder, salt, green chillies and fresh coriander. Stir-fry for about 7–10 minutes over a medium heat, making sure that the pieces of cauliflower retain their shape.

6 Spoon the fried vegetables around the edge of a shallow dish, leaving a space in the middle for the seafood, and keep hot.

7 Wash and dry the pan, then heat the oil to fry the seafood pieces. Fry the seafood pieces in 2–3 batches, until they turn a golden brown. Remove with a slotted spoon and drain on kitchen paper.

8 Arrange the seafood in the middle of the dish of vegetables and keep hot while you fry the remaining seafood. Garnish with lime slices and serve. Plain boiled rice and raita make ideal accompaniments.

COOK'S TIP

Cover the seafood closely when leaving it to stand in the refrigerator, or the spicy flavour will permeate the other foods stored there.

NUTRITIONAL NOTES
Per Portion

Energy	279Kcals/1165KJ
Fat	11g
Saturated Fat	1.6g
Carbohydrate	18.5g
Fibre	4g

Sizzling Balti Prawns in Hot Sauce

This sizzling prawn dish is cooked in a fiery hot and spicy sauce. This sauce not only contains chilli powder, but is further enhanced by the addition of ground green chillies mixed with other spices. If the heat seems extreme, offer raita to moderate the piquant flavour.

INGREDIENTS

Serves 4

2 medium onions, roughly chopped
30ml/2 tbsp tomato purée (paste)
5ml/1 tsp ground coriander
1.5ml/¼ tsp ground turmeric
5ml/1 tsp chilli powder
2 fresh green chillies
45ml/3 tbsp chopped fresh
    coriander (cilantro)
30ml/2 tbsp lemon juice
5ml/1 tsp salt
45ml/3 tbsp corn oil
16 cooked king prawns (jumbo shrimp)
sliced green chillies, to garnish, optional

1 Put the onions, tomato purée, ground coriander, turmeric, chilli powder, 2 whole green chillies, 30ml/2 tbsp of the fresh coriander, the lemon juice and salt into the bowl of a food processor. Process for about 1 minute. If the mixture seems too thick, add a little water to loosen it.

2 Heat the oil in a karahi, wok or deep pan. Lower the heat slightly and add the spice mixture. Fry the mixture for 3–5 minutes or until the sauce has thickened slightly.

_____ COOK'S TIP _____

Don't overcook the prawns (shrimp) or they will become tough.

3 Add the prawns and stir-fry briefly over a medium heat.

4 As soon as the prawns are heated through, transfer them to a serving dish, Garnish with the rest of the fresh coriander and the chopped green chilli, if using. Serve immediately.

NUTRITIONAL NOTES	
Per Portion	
Energy	139Kcals/578KJ
Fat	8.7g
Saturated Fat	1.3g
Carbohydrate	5.9g
Fibre	1.1g

Karahi Prawns and Fenugreek

The black-eyed peas, prawns and paneer in this recipe ensure that it is rich in protein. The combination of both ground and fresh fenugreek makes this a very fragrant and delicious dish. When preparing fresh fenugreek, use the leaves whole, but discard the stalks which would add a bitter flavour to the dish.

INGREDIENTS

Serves 4-6

60ml/4 tbsp corn oil
2 medium onions, sliced
2 medium tomatoes, sliced
7.5ml/1½ tsp crushed garlic
5ml/1 tsp chilli powder
5ml/1 tsp grated fresh root ginger
5ml/1 tsp ground cumin
5ml/1 tsp ground coriander
5ml/1 tsp salt
150g/5oz paneer, cubed
5ml/1 tsp ground fenugreek
1 bunch fresh fenugreek leaves
115g/4oz cooked prawns (shrimp)
2 fresh red chillies, sliced
30ml/2 tbsp chopped fresh
   coriander (cilantro)
50g/2oz/⅓ cup canned black-eyed
   beans (peas), drained
15ml/1 tbsp lemon juice

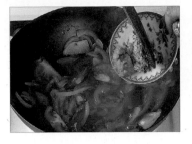

2 Add the garlic, chilli powder, ginger, ground cumin, ground coriander, salt, paneer and the ground and fresh fenugreek. Lower the heat and stir-fry for about 2 minutes.

NUTRITIONAL NOTES	
Per Portion	
Energy	206Kcals/858KJ
Fat	13g
Saturated Fat	2.6g
Carbohydrate	10.7g
Fibre	2.3g

3 Add the prawns, red chillies, fresh coriander and the black-eyed beans and mix well. Toss over the heat for a further 3–5 minutes, or until the prawns are heated through. Sprinkle on the lemon juice and serve.

--- COOK'S TIP ---

If you cannot locate paneer, beancurd (tofu) makes a good substitute.

1 Heat the oil in a karahi, wok or deep pan. Lower the heat slightly and add the onions and tomatoes. Fry for about 3 minutes.

Prawn and Vegetable Balti

This makes a delicious light lunch or supper, and is ideal for those vegetarians who eat seafood.

INGREDIENTS

Serves 4

175g/6oz frozen cooked peeled
  prawns (shrimp)
30ml/2 tbsp oil
1.5ml/¼ tsp onion seeds
4–6 curry leaves
115g/4oz/1 cup frozen peas
115g/4oz/²⁄₃ cup frozen sweetcorn
1 large courgette (zucchini), sliced
1 medium red (bell) pepper, seeded and
  roughly diced
5ml/1 tsp crushed coriander seeds
5ml/1 tsp crushed dried red chillies
1.5ml/½ tsp salt
15ml/1 tbsp lemon juice
15ml/1 tbsp fresh coriander (cilantro)
  leaves, to garnish

NUTRITIONAL NOTES	
Per Portion	
Energy	171Kcals/714KJ
Fat	7.70g
Saturated Fat	1.05g
Carbohydrate	11.8g
Fibre	2.80g

COOK'S TIP

The best way to crush whole seeds is to use an electric spice grinder or a small marble pestle and mortar.

1 Thaw the prawns and drain them of any excess liquid.

2 Heat the oil with the onion seeds and curry leaves in a karahi, wok or heavy frying pan.

3 Add the prawns to the spicy mixture in the wok and stir-fry until the liquid has evaporated.

4 Next, add the peas, sweetcorn, courgette and red pepper. Continue to stir for 3–5 minutes.

5 Finally, add the crushed coriander seeds and chillies, salt to taste and the lemon juice.

6 Serve immediately, garnished with fresh coriander leaves.

Paneer Balti with Prawns

Paneer is a protein food and makes an excellent substitute for red meat. Here it is combined with king prawns to make a dish with unforgettable flavour.

INGREDIENTS

Serves 4

12 cooked king prawns
   (jumbo shrimp)
175g/6oz paneer
30ml/2 tbsp tomato purée (paste)
60ml/4 tbsp Greek yogurt (US strained
   plain yogurt)
7.5ml/1½ tsp garam masala
5ml/1 tsp chilli powder
5ml/1 tsp crushed garlic
5ml/1 tsp salt
10ml/2 tsp amchur (mango powder)
5ml/1 tsp ground coriander
115g/4oz/½ cup butter
15ml/1 tbsp vegetable oil
3 fresh green chillies, chopped
45ml/3 tbsp chopped fresh
   coriander (cilantro)
150ml/¼ pint/⅔ cup single (light) cream

1 Peel the king prawns (jumbo shrimp) and cube the paneer.

2 Put the tomato purée, yogurt, garam masala, chilli powder, garlic, salt, mango powder and ground coriander in a mixing bowl. Mix to a paste and set aside.

3 Melt the butter with the oil in a karahi, wok or deep pan. Lower the heat slightly and quickly fry the paneer and prawns for about 2 minutes. Remove with a slotted spoon and drain on kitchen paper.

4 Pour the spice paste into the fat left in the pan and cook for about 1 minute, stirring constantly.

5 Add the paneer and prawns, and cook for 7–10 minutes, stirring occasionally, until the prawns are heated through.

6 Add the fresh chillies and most of the coriander, and pour in the cream. Heat through for about 2 minutes, garnish with the remaining coriander and serve.

VARIATIONS

• For a less costly dish, substitute regular peeled prawns (shelled shrimp). You will need about 225g/8oz.
• Beancurd (tofu) can be used instead of paneer. It is a highly nutritious ingredient and absorbs the flavour of the spices extremely well. You can make it at home by bringing 1 litre/1¾ pints/4 cups milk to boil over a low heat, then adding 2 tbsp lemon juice and stirring continuously until the milk thickens and begins to curdle. Strain the curdled milk through a sieve (strainer) lined with muslin (cheesecloth), and set aside under a heavy weight for 1½ –2 hours to press the curd to a flat shape about 1cm/½in thick. It will keep for about one week in the refrigerator.

NUTRITIONAL NOTES
Per Portion

Energy	416Kcals/1720KJ
Fat	36g
Saturated Fat	21.2g
Carbohydrate	5.4g
Fibre	0g

Basic Balti Chicken

This recipe has a beautifully delicate flavour, and is probably the most popular of all Balti dishes. Choose a young chicken as it will be more flavoursome.

INGREDIENTS

Serves 4-6

1–1½kg/2½–3lb chicken
45ml/3 tbsp corn oil
3 medium onions, sliced
3 medium tomatoes, halved and sliced
2.5cm/1in cinnamon stick
2 large black cardamom pods
4 black peppercorns
2.5ml/½ tsp black cumin seeds
5ml/1 tsp grated root ginger
5ml/1 tsp crushed garlic
5ml/1 tsp garam masala
5ml/1 tsp chilli powder
5ml/1 tsp salt
30ml/2 tbsp natural (plain) yogurt
60ml/4 tbsp lemon juice
30ml/2 tbsp chopped fresh
   coriander (cilantro)
2 fresh green chillies, chopped

1 Skin the chicken, then use a sharp knife or cleaver to cut it into 8 pieces. Wash and trim the chicken pieces, and set to one side.

2 Heat the oil in a large karahi, wok or deep pan. Add the onions and fry until they are golden brown. Add the tomatoes and stir well.

3 Add the piece of cinnamon stick, cardamoms, peppercorns, black cumin seeds, ginger, garlic, garam masala, chilli powder and salt. Lower the heat and stir-fry for 3–5 minutes.

4 Add the chicken pieces, 2 at a time, and stir-fry for at least 7 minutes or until the spice mixture has completely penetrated the chicken pieces and they are beginning to brown.

5 Add the yogurt to the chicken and mix well.

6 Lower the heat and cover the pan with a piece of foil, making sure that the foil does not touch the food. Cook very gently for about 15 minutes, checking once to make sure the food is not catching on the bottom of the pan.

7 Finally, add the lemon juice, fresh coriander and green chillies. Serve at once, from the cooking pan.

NUTRITIONAL NOTES	
Per Portion	
Energy	569Kcals/2362KJ
Fat	38.2g
Saturated Fat	9.5g
Carbohydrate	13.2g
Fibre	2.3g

—— COOK'S TIP ——

Chicken cooked on the bone is both tender and flavoursome. However, do substitute the whole chicken with 675g/1½lb boned and cubed chicken, if you like. Chicken that has been taken off the bone will cook quickly, so check it frequently and take care not to overcook. The cooking time can be reduced at step 6, too.

Sweet and Sour Balti Chicken

This dish combines a sweet-and-sour flavour with a creamy texture. It is delicious served with pulao rice or naan bread.

INGREDIENTS

Serves 4

45ml/3 tbsp tomato purée (paste)
30ml/2 tbsp Greek (US strained plain) yogurt
7.5ml/1½ tsp garam masala
5ml/1 tsp chilli powder
5ml/1 tsp crushed garlic
30ml/2 tbsp mango chutney
5ml/1 tsp salt
2.5ml/½ tsp granulated sugar
60ml/4 tbsp corn oil
675g/1½lb skinless, boneless chicken, cubed
150ml/¼ pint/⅔ cup water
2 fresh green chillies, chopped
30ml/2 tbsp chopped fresh coriander (cilantro)
30ml/2 tbsp single (light) cream

1 Mix the tomato purée, yogurt, garam masala, chilli powder, garlic, mango chutney, salt and sugar in a medium mixing bowl. Stir well.

NUTRITIONAL NOTES	
Per Portion	
Energy	227Kcals/957KJ
Fat	4.2g
Saturated Fat	1.7g
Carbohydrate	6.7g
Fibre	0.3g

2 Heat the oil in a karahi, wok or deep pan. Lower the heat slightly and pour in the spice mixture. Bring to the boil and cook for about 2 minutes, stirring occasionally.

3 Add the chicken pieces and stir until they are well coated.

4 Stir in the water to thin the sauce slightly. Continue cooking for 5–7 minutes, or until the chicken is fully cooked and tender.

5 Finally add the fresh chillies, coriander and cream, cook for a further 2 minutes over a low heat, then serve.

Balti Chicken Pasanda

Yogurt and cream give this tasty dish its characteristic richness. Serve it with Peshwari naan to complement the almonds.

INGREDIENTS

Serves 4

60ml/4 tbsp Greek (US strained plain) yogurt
2.5ml/½ tsp black cumin seeds
4 cardamom pods
6 whole black peppercorns
10ml/2 tsp garam masala
2.5cm/1in cinnamon stick
15ml/1 tbsp ground almonds
5ml/1 tsp crushed garlic
5ml/1 tsp grated fresh root ginger
5ml/1 tsp chilli powder
5ml/1 tsp salt
675g/1½lb skinless, boneless chicken, cubed
75ml/5 tbsp corn oil
2 medium onions, diced
3 fresh green chillies, chopped
30ml/2 tbsp chopped fresh coriander (cilantro)
120ml/4fl oz/½ cup single (light) cream

3 Tip in the chicken mixture and stir until it is well blended with the onions.

4 Cook for 12–15 minutes over a medium heat until the sauce thickens and the chicken is cooked through.

5 Add the green chillies and fresh coriander, and pour in the cream. Bring to the boil, stirring constantly, and serve garnished with more coriander, if you like.

NUTRITIONAL NOTES	
Per Portion	
Energy	453Kcals/1888KJ
Fat	26.8g
Saturated Fat	8.7g
Carbohydrate	10.9g
Fibre	1.1g

1 Mix the yogurt, cumin seeds, cardamoms, peppercorns, garam masala, cinnamon stick, ground almonds, garlic, ginger, chilli powder and salt in a medium mixing bowl. Add the chicken pieces, stir to coat, and leave to marinate for 2 hours.

2 Heat the oil in a large karahi, wok or deep pan. Add the onions and fry for 2–3 minutes.

Khara Masala Balti Chicken

Whole spices (khara) are used in this recipe, giving it a wonderful, rich flavour. This is a dry dish so it is best served with plenty of creamy raita.

INGREDIENTS

Serves 4
3 curry leaves
1.5ml/¼ tsp mustard seeds
1.5ml/¼ tsp fennel seeds
1.5ml/¼ tsp onion seeds
2.5ml/½ tsp crushed dried red chillies
2.5ml/½ tsp white cumin seeds
1.5ml/¼ tsp fenugreek seeds
2.5ml/½ tsp crushed pomegranate seeds
5ml/1 tsp salt
5ml/1 tsp shredded fresh root ginger
3 garlic cloves, sliced
60ml/4 tbsp corn oil
4 fresh green chillies, slit
1 large onion, sliced
1 medium tomato, sliced
675g/1½lb skinless, boneless chicken, cubed
15ml/1 tbsp chopped fresh coriander (cilantro)

2 Add the shredded ginger and garlic cloves.

5 Finally add the tomato and chicken pieces, and cook over a medium heat for about 7 minutes. The chicken should be cooked through and the sauce reduced.

3 Heat the oil in a medium karahi, wok or deep pan. Add the spice mixture, then tip in the green chillies.

6 Stir everything together over the heat for a further 3–5 minutes. Serve from the pan, garnished with chopped fresh coriander.

1 Mix together the curry leaves, mustard seeds, fennel seeds, onion seeds, crushed red chillies, cumin seeds, fenugreek seeds, crushed pomegranate seeds and salt in a large bowl.

4 Spoon the sliced onion into the pan and fry over a medium heat for 5–7 minutes, stirring constantly to flavour the onion with the spices.

NUTRITIONAL NOTES	
Per Portion	
Energy	313Kcals/1310KJ
Fat	13.7g
Saturated Fat	2.3g
Carbohydrate	8.1g
Fibre	2.3g

Chicken and Tomato Balti

If you like tomatoes, you will love this chicken recipe. It makes a semi-dry Balti and is good served with a lentil dish and plain boiled rice.

INGREDIENTS

Serves 4

60ml/4 tbsp corn oil
6 curry leaves
2.5ml/½ tsp mixed onion and
    mustard seeds
8 medium tomatoes, sliced
5ml/1 tsp ground coriander
5ml/1 tsp chilli powder
5ml/1 tsp salt
5ml/1 tsp ground cumin
5ml/1 tsp crushed garlic
675g/1½lb skinless, boneless
    chicken, cubed
150ml/¼ pint/⅔ cup water
15ml/1 tbsp sesame seeds, roasted
15ml/1 tbsp chopped fresh
    coriander (cilantro)

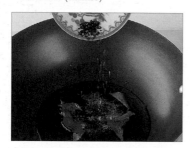

1 Heat the oil in a karahi, wok or deep round-bottomed frying pan. Add the curry leaves and mixed onion and mustard seeds and toss over the heat for 1–2 minutes so that they become fragrant. Do not let the seeds burn.

2 Lower the heat slightly and add the tomatoes.

3 While the tomatoes are gently cooking, mix together the ground coriander, chilli powder, salt, ground cumin and garlic in a bowl. Tip the spices onto the tomatoes.

4 Add the chicken pieces and stir well. Stir-fry for about 5 minutes more.

5 Stir in the water and continue cooking, stirring occasionally, until the sauce thickens and the chicken is fully cooked.

6 Sprinkle the sesame seeds and fresh coriander over the Balti. Serve immediately, from the pan.

COOK'S TIP

Sesame seeds are available from Asian and health food stores. There are two types – unroasted seeds, which are white, and roasted ones, which are lightly browned. To roast sesame seeds at home, simply tip a quantity into a frying pan and place the pan over a high heat for about 1 minute. Shake the pan constantly to prevent the seeds burning. Use immediately or cool, then store in a screw-topped jar.

NUTRITIONAL NOTES
Per Portion

Energy	360Kcals/1508KJ
Fat	18.3g
Saturated Fat	3g
Carbohydrate	8.6g
Fibre	2.3g

Balti Chicken Pieces with Cumin and Coriander

The potatoes are tossed in spices and cooked separately in the oven before being added to the chicken.

INGREDIENTS

Serves 4

150ml/¼ pint/⅔ cup natural (plain)
  low fat yogurt
25g/1oz/¼ cup ground almonds
7.5ml/1½ tsp ground coriander
2.5ml/½ tsp chilli powder
5ml/1 tsp garam masala
15ml/1 tbsp coconut milk
5ml/1 tsp crushed garlic
5ml/1 tsp grated fresh root ginger
30ml/2 tbsp chopped fresh coriander
1 fresh red chilli, seeded and chopped
225g/8oz skinless, boneless chicken
  breast portions, cubed
15ml/1 tbsp oil
2 medium onions, sliced
3 green cardamom pods
2.5cm/1in cinnamon stick
2 cloves

For the potatoes

15ml/1 tbsp oil
8 baby potatoes, thickly sliced
1.5ml/¼ tsp cumin seeds
15ml/1 tbsp finely chopped fresh
  coriander (cilantro)

NUTRITIONAL NOTES	
Per Portion	
Energy	2783Kcals/1166KJ
Fat	10.76g
Saturated Fat	1.58g
Carbohydrate	27.43g
Fibre	2.78g

—————— COOK'S TIP ——————

Any variety of fresh mint may also be added to the potatoes. The flavour goes well with the spices.

1 In a large bowl, mix together the yogurt, ground almonds, ground coriander, chilli powder, garam masala, coconut milk, garlic, ginger, half the fresh coriander and half the red chilli.

2 Place the chicken pieces in the mixture, mix well, then cover and leave to marinate for about 2 hours.

3 Meanwhile, start to prepare the spicy potatoes. Heat the oil in a karahi, wok or heavy pan. Add the sliced potatoes, cumin seeds and fresh coriander and quickly stir-fry for 2–3 minutes.

4 Preheat the oven to 180°C/350°F/ Gas 4. Spoon the potatoes into a baking dish, cover and bake for about 30 minutes or until they are cooked through.

5 Halfway through the potatoes' cooking time, heat the oil and fry the onions, cardamoms, cinnamon and cloves for 1½ minutes.

6 Add the chicken mixture to the onions and stir-fry for 5–7 minutes. Lower the heat, cover and cook for 5–7 minutes. Top with the potatoes and garnish with coriander and red chilli.

Balti Chicken in a Spicy Lentil Sauce

Traditionally, this dish is made with lamb, but it is equally delicious made with chicken. The lentils are flavoured with a traditional *tarka*, which is poured over the dish just before serving.

INGREDIENTS

Serves 4

30ml/2 tbsp chana dhal or yellow split peas
50g/2oz/¼ cup masoor dhal or red split peas
15ml/1 tbsp oil
2 medium onions, chopped
5ml/1 tsp crushed garlic
5ml/1 tsp grated fresh root ginger
2.5ml/½ tsp ground turmeric
7.5ml/1½ tsp chilli powder
5ml/1 tsp garam masala
2.5ml/½ tsp ground coriander
7.5ml/1½ tsp salt
175g/6oz skinless chicken breast fillets, cubed
45ml/3 tbsp fresh coriander (cilantro) leaves
1–2 fresh green chillies, seeded and chopped
30-45ml/2–3 tbsp lemon juice
300ml/½ pint/1¼ cups water
2 tomatoes, peeled and halved

For the *tarka*

5ml/1 tsp oil
2.5ml/½ tsp cumin seeds
2 garlic cloves
2 dried red chillies
4 curry leaves

NUTRITIONAL NOTES	
Per Portion	
Energy	207Kcals/868KJ
Fat	7.07g
Saturated Fat	1.03g
Carbohydrate	20.37g
Fibre	2.84g

1 Put the pulses in a pan with water and bring to the boil. Cook for 30–45 minutes until soft and mushy. Drain and set aside.

2 Heat the oil in a karahi, wok or heavy frying pan and fry the onions until soft and golden brown. Stir in the garlic, ginger, turmeric, chilli powder, garam masala, ground coriander and salt.

3 Next, add the chicken pieces and fry for 5–7 minutes, stirring constantly over a medium heat to seal in the juices and lightly brown the meat.

4 Add half the fresh coriander, the green chillies, lemon juice and water and cook for a further 3–5 minutes. Stir in the cooked pulses, then add the tomatoes.

5 Sprinkle over the remaining coriander leaves. Take the pan off the heat and set aside.

6 To make the *tarka*, heat the oil and add the cumin seeds, whole garlic cloves, dried chillies and curry leaves. Heat for about 30 seconds then pour over the top of the dhal. Serve immediately.

Balti Chicken with Paneer and Peas

This is rather an unusual combination, but it really works well. Serve with plain boiled rice.

INGREDIENTS

Serves 4

1 small chicken, about 675g/1½lb
30ml/2 tbsp tomato purée (paste)
45ml/3 tbsp natural (plain) low fat yogurt
7.5ml/1½ tsp garam masala
5ml/1 tsp crushed garlic
5ml/1 tsp grated fresh root ginger
pinch of ground cardamom
15ml/1 tbsp chilli powder
1.5ml/¼ tsp ground turmeric
5ml/1 tsp salt
5ml/1 tsp granulated sugar
10ml/2 tsp oil
2.5cm/1in cinnamon stick
2 black peppercorns
300ml/½ pint/1¼ cups water
115g/4oz paneer
2 fresh green chillies, seeded and chopped
30ml/2 tbsp fresh coriander (cilantro) leaves
50g/2oz low fat fromage frais or ricotta cheese
75g/3oz/¾ cup frozen peas, thawed

1 Skin the chicken and cut it into 6–8 equal pieces.

2 Mix the tomato purée, yogurt, garam masala, garlic, ginger, cardamom, chilli powder, turmeric, salt and sugar in a bowl.

3 Heat the oil with the whole spices in a karahi, wok or heavy pan, then pour the yogurt mixture into the oil. Lower the heat and cook gently for about 3 minutes, then pour in the water and bring to a simmer.

4 Cut the paneer into cubes. Chop the chillies, discarding the seeds if you like.

5 Add the chicken pieces to the pan. Stir-fry for 2 minutes, then cover the pan and cook over a medium heat for about 10 minutes.

6 Add the paneer cubes to the pan, followed by half the coriander and half the green chillies. Mix well and cook for a further 5–7 minutes.

7 Stir in the fromage frais or ricotta and peas, heat through and serve with the reserved coriander and chillies.

COOK'S TIP

Paneer is an Indian whole milk cheese and provides a good source of protein.

NUTRITIONAL NOTES
Per Portion

Energy	233Kcals/977KJ
Fat	10.28g
Saturated Fat	4.64g
Carbohydrate	8.14g
Fibre	1.49g

Balti Chicken with Green and Red Chillies

Minced or ground chicken is seldom cooked in Indian homes. However, it works very well in this recipe.

INGREDIENTS

Serves 4

275g/10oz skinless chicken breast
  fillet, cubed
2 plump fresh red chillies
3 plump fresh green chillies
30ml/2 tbsp oil
6 curry leaves
3 medium onions, sliced
7.5ml/1½ tsp crushed garlic
7.5ml/1½ tsp ground coriander
7.5ml/1½ tsp grated fresh root ginger
5ml/1 tsp chilli powder
5ml/1 tsp salt
15ml/1 tbsp lemon juice
30ml/2 tbsp chopped fresh
  coriander (cilantro)
chapatis and lemon wedges, to serve

1 Cook the chicken in a pan of water for about 10 minutes until soft and cooked through. Remove with a slotted spoon and place in the bowl of a food processor fitted with a metal blade.

_____ COOK'S TIP _____

Taste this dish during cooking as it is quite mild, especially if you seed the chillies, and you may find that it needs some additional spices to suit your palate.

2 Process the cooked chicken mince or grind it roughly.

3 Cut the chillies in half lengthways and remove the seeds, if you like. Cut the flesh into strips and set aside.

4 Heat the oil in a karahi, wok or heavy pan and fry the curry leaves and onions until the onions are a soft golden brown. Lower the heat and stir in the garlic, ground coriander, ginger, chilli powder and salt.

5 Add the minced (ground) chicken and stir-fry for 3–5 minutes.

6 Add the lemon juice, the prepared chilli strips and most of the fresh coriander. Stir-fry for a further 3–5 minutes, then serve, garnished with the remaining fresh coriander and accompanied by warm chapatis and lemon wedges.

NUTRITIONAL NOTES	
Per Portion	
Energy	184Kcals/767KJ
Fat	8.40g
Saturated Fat	1.57g
Carbohydrate	10.10g
Fibre	1.30g

Balti Chicken with Leeks

This dish has rather an unusual combination of flavours. Mango powder gives it a deliciously tangy flavour.

INGREDIENTS

Serves 4–6
2 medium leeks
75g/3oz/½ cup chana dhal or yellow
  split peas
60ml/4 tbsp corn oil
6 large dried red chillies
4 curry leaves
5ml/1 tsp mustard seeds
10ml/2 tsp mango powder (amchur)
2 medium tomatoes, chopped
2.5ml/½ tsp chilli powder
5ml/1 tsp ground coriander
5ml/1 tsp salt
450g/1lb skinless, boneless
  chicken, cubed
15ml/1 tbsp chopped fresh
  coriander (cilantro)

1 Using a sharp knife, slice the leeks thinly into rounds. Separate the slices, rinse them in a colander under cold water to wash away any grit, then drain well.

2 Wash the chana dhal or split peas carefully and remove any stones.

3 Put the pulses into a pan with enough water to cover, and boil for about 10 minutes until they are soft but not mushy. Drain and set to one side in a bowl.

4 Heat the oil in a karahi, wok or deep pan. Lower the heat slightly and add the leeks, dried red chillies, curry leaves and mustard seeds. Stir-fry gently for a few minutes.

5 Add the mango powder, tomatoes, chilli powder, ground coriander, salt and chicken, and stir-fry for 7–10 minutes.

6 Mix in the cooked chana dhal or split peas and fry for a further 2 minutes, or until you are sure that the chicken is cooked right through.

7 Garnish with fresh coriander and serve immediately, from the pan.

COOK'S TIPS

• Chana dhal, a split yellow lentil, is available from Asian stores. However, yellow split peas are a good substitute.
• Dried mango powder is made from sun-dried green mangoes and has a sour taste. You may find it under the name *amchur*.

NUTRITIONAL NOTES
Per Portion

Energy	309Kcals/1295KJ
Fat	13.4g
Saturated Fat	2.2g
Carbohydrate	16.1g
Fibre	2.8g

Balti Butter Chicken

Butter Chicken is one of the most popular Balti chicken dishes, especially in the West. Cooked in butter, with aromatic spices, cream and almonds, this mild dish will be enjoyed by everyone. Serve with pulao rice.

INGREDIENTS

Serves 4

150ml/¼ pint/⅔ cup natural
  (plain) yogurt
50g/2oz/½ cup ground almonds
7.5ml/1½ tsp chilli powder
1.5ml/¼ tsp crushed bay leaves
1.5ml/¼ tsp ground cloves
1.5ml/¼ tsp ground cinnamon
5ml/1 tsp garam masala
4 green cardamom pods
5ml/1 tsp grated fresh root ginger
5ml/1 tsp crushed garlic
400g/14oz/2 cups canned tomatoes
7.5ml/1¼ tsp salt
1kg/2¼lb skinless, boneless
  chicken, cubed
75g/3oz/6 tbsp butter
15ml/1 tbsp corn oil
2 medium onions, sliced
30ml/2 tbsp chopped fresh
  coriander (cilantro)
60ml/4 tbsp single (light) cream
coriander (cilantro) sprigs, to garnish

1 Put the yogurt into a bowl and add the ground almonds, chilli powder, crushed bay leaves, ground cloves, cinnamon, garam masala, cardamoms, ginger and garlic.

2 Chop the tomatoes and add them to the bowl with the salt. Mix thoroughly.

3 Put the chicken into a large mixing bowl and pour over the yogurt mixture. Set aside.

4 Melt together the butter and oil in a karahi, wok or deep pan. Add the onions and fry for about 3 minutes.

5 Add the chicken mixture and stir-fry for 7–10 minutes.

6 Sprinkle over about half of the coriander and mix well.

7 Pour over the cream and stir in well. Heat through and serve, garnished with the remaining chopped coriander and coriander sprigs.

COOK'S TIP

Substitute natural (plain) yogurt with Greek (US strained plain) yogurt for an even richer and creamier flavour.

NUTRITIONAL NOTES
Per Portion

Energy	592Kcals/2474KJ
Fat	32.2g
Saturated Fat	13.7g
Carbohydrate	12.1g
Fibre	1.6g

Balti Chicken in Hara Masala Sauce

This chicken dish can be served as an accompaniment to any of the rice dishes in this book.

INGREDIENTS

Serves 4

1 crisp green eating apple, peeled, cored and cut into small cubes
60ml/4 tbsp fresh coriander leaves
30ml/2 tbsp fresh mint leaves
120ml/4fl oz/½ cup natural (plain) low fat yogurt
45ml/3 tbsp low fat fromage frais or ricotta cheese
2 fresh green chillies, seeded and chopped
1 bunch spring onions (scallions), chopped
5ml/1 tsp salt
5ml/1 tsp granulated sugar
5ml/1 tsp crushed garlic
5ml/1 tsp grated fresh root ginger
15ml/1 tbsp oil
225g/8oz skinless chicken breast fillets, cubed
25g/1oz/⅙ cup sultanas (golden raisins)

1 Place the apple, 45ml/3 tbsp of the coriander, the mint, yogurt, fromage frais or ricotta, chillies, spring onions, salt, sugar, garlic and ginger in a food processor and pulse for about 1 minute.

NUTRITIONAL NOTES	
Per Portion	
Energy	158Kcals/666KJ
Fat	4.37g
Saturated Fat	1.69g
Carbohydrate	14.54g
Fibre	1.08g

2 Heat the oil in a karahi, wok or heavy pan, pour in the yogurt mixture and cook over a low heat for about 2 minutes.

3 Next, add the chicken pieces and blend everything together. Cook over a medium/low heat for 12–15 minutes or until the chicken is fully cooked.

4 Stir in the sultanas and remaining 15ml/1 tbsp fresh coriander leaves and serve.

COOK'S TIP

This dish makes an attractive centrepiece for a dinner-party.

Balti Chicken in Thick Creamy Coconut Sauce

If you like the flavour of coconut, you will really love this aromatic curry.

INGREDIENTS

Serves 4

15ml/1 tbsp ground almonds
15ml/1 tbsp desiccated (dry unsweetened shredded) coconut
75ml/3fl oz/¹⁄₃ cup coconut milk
175g/6oz/²⁄₃ cup low fat fromage frais or ricotta cheese
7.5ml/1½ tsp ground coriander
5ml/1 tsp chilli powder
5ml/1 tsp crushed garlic
7.5ml/1½ tsp grated fresh root ginger
5ml/1 tsp salt
15ml/1 tbsp oil
225g/8oz skinless, boneless chicken, cubed
3 green cardamom pods
1 bay leaf
1 dried red chilli, crushed
30ml/2 tbsp chopped fresh coriander (cilantro)

1 Using a heavy pan, dry-roast the ground almonds and desiccated coconut, stirring frequently, until they turn just a shade darker. Transfer the nut mixture to a mixing bowl.

NUTRITIONAL NOTES	
Per Portion	
Energy	166Kcals/696KJ
Fat	8.30g
Saturated Fat	2.84g
Carbohydrate	6.38g
Fibre	0.95g

2 Add the coconut milk, fromage frais or ricotta, ground coriander, chilli powder, garlic, ginger and salt to the mixing bowl.

3 Heat the oil in a karahi, wok or heavy pan and add the chicken cubes, cardamoms and bay leaf. Stir-fry for about 2 minutes to seal the chicken but not cook it.

4 Pour in the coconut milk mixture and blend everything together. Lower the heat, add the chilli and fresh coriander, cover and cook for 10–12 minutes, stirring occasionally. Uncover, then stir and cook for a further 2 minutes before serving, making sure the chicken is cooked.

Balti Chicken in Saffron Sauce

This is a beautifully aromatic chicken dish that is partly cooked in the oven. It contains saffron, the most expensive spice in the world, and is sure to impress your guests.

INGREDIENTS

Serves 4

50g/2oz/¼ cup butter
30ml/2 tbsp corn oil
1–1½kg/2½–3lb chicken, skinned and
    cut into 8 pieces
1 medium onion, chopped
5ml/1 tsp crushed garlic
2.5ml/½ tsp crushed black peppercorns
2.5ml/½ tsp crushed cardamom pods
2.5ml/¼ tsp ground cinnamon
7.5ml/1½ tsp chilli powder
150ml/¼ pint/⅔ cup natural
    (plain) yogurt
50g/2oz/½ cup ground almonds
15ml/1 tbsp lemon juice
5ml/1 tsp salt
5ml/1 tsp saffron strands
150ml/¼ pint/⅔ cup water
150ml/¼ pint/⅔ cup single
    (light) cream
30ml/2 tbsp chopped fresh
    coriander (cilantro)

1 Preheat the oven to 180°C/350°F/ Gas 4. Melt the butter with the oil in a karahi, wok or deep pan. Add the chicken pieces and fry until lightly browned. This will take about 5 minutes. Remove the chicken using a slotted spoon, leaving behind as much of the fat as possible.

2 Add the onion to the same pan, and fry over a medium heat. Meanwhile, mix together the garlic, black peppercorns, cardamom, cinnamon, chilli powder, yogurt, ground almonds, lemon juice, salt and saffron strands in a mixing bowl.

3 When the onions are lightly browned, pour the spice mixture into the pan and stir-fry for about 1 minute.

4 Add the chicken pieces, and continue to fry for a further 2 minutes stirring constantly. Pour in the water and bring to a simmer.

5 Transfer the contents of the pan to a casserole and cover with a lid, or, if using a karahi with heatproof handles, cover with foil. Transfer to the oven and cook for 30–35 minutes.

6 Once you are sure that the chicken is cooked right through, remove it from the oven. Transfer the mixture to a frying pan or place the karahi on the hob (stovetop) and stir in the cream.

7 Reheat gently for about 2 minutes. Garnish with fresh coriander and serve with a fruity pulao or plain boiled rice.

COOK'S TIP

There is no substitute for saffron, so don't be tempted to use turmeric instead. It is well worth buying just a small amount of saffron – either strands or in powdered form – to create this dish for a treat.

NUTRITIONAL NOTES
Per Portion

Energy	525Kcals/2190KJ
Fat	33g
Saturated Fat	13.3g
Carbohydrate	11g
Fibre	1.5g

Balti Chicken with Vegetables

This is an excellent recipe for making a small amount of chicken go a long way. The vegetables add colour and boost the nutritional value.

INGREDIENTS

Serves 4-6

60ml/4 tbsp corn oil
2 medium onions, sliced
4 garlic cloves, thickly sliced
450g/1lb skinless chicken breast fillets, cut into strips
5ml/1 tsp salt
30ml/2 tbsp lime juice
3 fresh green chillies, chopped
2 medium carrots, cut into batons
2 medium potatoes, peeled and cut into 1cm/½in strips
1 medium courgette (zucchini), cut into batons
4 lime slices
15ml/1 tbsp chopped fresh coriander (cilantro)
2 fresh green chillies, cut into strips (optional)

1 Heat the oil in a large karahi, wok or deep pan. Lower the heat slightly and add the onions. Fry until the onions are lightly browned.

2 Add half the garlic slices and fry for a few seconds before adding the chicken and salt. Cook everything together, stirring, until all the moisture has evaporated and the chicken is lightly browned.

3 Add the lime juice, green chillies and all the vegetables to the pan. Increase the heat and add the rest of the garlic. Stir-fry for 7–10 minutes, or until the chicken is cooked through and the vegetables are just tender.

4 Transfer to a serving dish and garnish with the lime slices, fresh coriander and green chilli strips, if wished. Serve immediately.

NUTRITIONAL NOTES	
Per Portion	
Energy	308Kcals/1289KJ
Fat	13.1g
Saturated Fat	2.1g
Carbohydrate	20.1g
Fibre	2.8g

Balti Chilli Chicken

Hot and spicy would be the best way of describing this mouth-watering Balti dish. The smell of the fresh chillies cooking is irresistible.

INGREDIENTS

Serves 4-6

75ml/5 tbsp corn oil
8 large fresh green chillies, slit
2.5ml/½ tsp mixed onion seeds and cumin seeds
4 curry leaves
5ml/1 tsp grated fresh root ginger
5ml/1 tsp chilli powder
5ml/1 tsp ground coriander
5ml/1 tsp crushed garlic
5ml/1 tsp salt
2 medium onions, chopped
675g/1½ lb skinless, boneless chicken, cubed
15ml/1 tbsp lemon juice
15ml/1 tbsp roughly chopped fresh mint
15ml/1 tbsp roughly chopped fresh coriander (cilantro)
8–10 cherry tomatoes

1 Heat the oil in a karahi, wok or deep pan. Lower the heat slightly and add the slit green chillies. Fry until the skin starts to change colour.

2 Add the onion seeds and cumin seeds, curry leaves, ginger, chilli powder, ground coriander, garlic, salt and onions, and fry for a few seconds, stirring continuously.

3 Add the chicken pieces to the pan. Stir-fry over a medium heat for 7–10 minutes, or until the chicken is cooked right through. Do not overcook the chicken or it will become tough in texture.

NUTRITIONAL NOTES	
Per Portion	
Energy	346Kcals/1448KJ
Fat	16.5g
Saturated Fat	2.7g
Carbohydrate	9.9g
Fibre	1.3g

4 Sprinkle on the lemon juice and add the roughly chopped fresh mint and coriander.

5 Dot with the cherry tomatoes and serve from the pan.

Balti Baby Chicken in Tamarind Sauce

The tamarind in this recipe gives the dish a sweet-and-sour flavour; this is also quite a hot Balti.

INGREDIENTS

Serves 4–6

60ml/4 tbsp tomato ketchup
15ml/1 tbsp tamarind paste
60ml/4 tbsp water
7.5ml/1½ tsp chilli powder
7.5ml/1½ tsp salt
15ml/1 tbsp granulated sugar
7.5ml/1½ tsp grated fresh root ginger
7.5ml/1½ tsp crushed garlic
30ml/2 tbsp desiccated (dry unsweetened shredded) coconut
30ml/2 tbsp sesame seeds
5ml/1 tsp poppy seeds
5ml/1 tsp ground cumin
7.5ml/1½ tsp ground coriander
2 × 450g/1lb baby chickens, skinned and cut into 6–8 pieces each
75ml/5 tbsp corn oil
120ml/8 tbsp curry leaves
2.5ml/½ tsp onion seeds
3 large dried red chillies
2.5ml/½ tsp fenugreek seeds
10–12 cherry tomatoes
45ml/3 tbsp chopped fresh coriander (cilantro)
2 fresh green chillies, chopped

1 Put the tomato ketchup, tamarind paste and water into a large mixing bowl and use a fork to blend everything together.

2 Add the chilli powder, salt, sugar, ginger, garlic, coconut, sesame and poppy seeds, cumin and coriander to the mixture. Stir to mix.

3 Add the chicken pieces and stir until they are well coated with the spice mixture. Set aside.

4 Heat the oil in a karahi, wok or deep pan. Add the curry leaves, onion seeds, dried red chillies and fenugreek seeds and fry for about 1 minute.

5 Lower the heat to medium and add 2 or 3 chicken pieces at a time, with their sauce, mixing as you go. When all the pieces have been added to the pan, stir well, using a slotted spoon.

6 Simmer gently for about 12–15 minutes, or until the chicken is thoroughly cooked.

7 Finally, add the tomatoes, fresh coriander and green chillies, and serve from the pan.

NUTRITIONAL NOTES	
Per Portion	
Energy	348Kcals/1454KJ
Fat	19.9g
Saturated Fat	6.4g
Carbohydrate	11.9g
Fibre	1.5g

Balti Chicken Madras

This is a fairly hot chicken curry which is good served with either plain boiled rice, pilau rice or naan bread.

INGREDIENTS

Serves 4

275g/10oz skinless chicken breast fillets
45ml/3 tbsp tomato purée (paste)
large pinch of ground fenugreek
1.5ml/¼ tsp ground fennel seeds
5ml/1 tsp grated fresh root ginger
7.5ml/1½ tsp ground coriander
5ml/1 tsp crushed garlic
5ml/1 tsp chilli powder
1.5ml/¼ tsp ground turmeric
30ml/2 tbsp lemon juice
5ml/1 tsp salt
300ml/½ pint/1¼ cups water
15ml/1 tbsp oil
2 medium onions, diced
2–4 curry leaves
2 fresh green chillies, seeded and chopped
15ml/1 tbsp fresh coriander (cilantro) leaves

NUTRITIONAL NOTES	
Per Portion	
Energy	141Kcals/591KJ
Fat	4.11g
Saturated Fat	0.60g
Carbohydrate	8.60g
Fibre	1.53g

COOK'S TIP

Always take care not to be over-generous when you are using ground fenugreek as it can be quite bitter.

1 Remove any visible fat from the chicken breasts and cut the meat into bite-size cubes.

2 Mix the tomato purée in a bowl with the fenugreek, fennel seeds, ginger, coriander, garlic, chilli powder, turmeric, lemon juice, salt and water.

3 Heat the oil in a karahi, wok or heavy pan and fry the onions together with the curry leaves until the onions are golden brown.

4 Add the chicken pieces to the onions and stir over the heat for about 1 minute to seal the meat.

5 Next, pour in the prepared spice mixture and continue to stir the chicken for about 2 minutes.

6 Lower the heat and cook for 8–10 minutes, stirring frequently to prevent the mixture from catching on the bottom of the pan. Add the chillies and fresh coriander and serve at once.

Balti Chicken Vindaloo

This version of a popular dish from Goa is not as fiery as some, but will still suit those who like their curry to have a definite impact.

INGREDIENTS

Serves 4

1 large potato
150ml/¼ pint/⅔ cup malt vinegar
7.5ml/1½ tsp crushed coriander seeds
5ml/1 tsp crushed cumin seeds
7.5ml/1½ tsp chilli powder
1.5ml/¼ tsp ground turmeric
5ml/1 tsp crushed garlic
5ml/1 tsp grated fresh root ginger
5ml/1 tsp salt
7.5ml/1½ tsp paprika
15ml/1 tbsp tomato purée (paste)
large pinch of ground fenugreek
300ml/½ pint/1¼ cups water
225g/8oz skinless chicken breast
    fillets, cubed
15ml/1 tbsp oil
2 medium onions, sliced
4 curry leaves
2 fresh green chillies, chopped

1 Peel the potato, cut it into large, irregular shapes, place these in a bowl of water and set aside.

COOK'S TIP

The best thing to drink with a hot curry is either iced water or a yogurt-based lassi.

2 In a bowl, mix the vinegar, coriander, cumin, chilli powder, turmeric, garlic, ginger, salt, paprika, tomato purée, fenugreek and water.

3 Pour this spice mixture over the chicken, stir and set aside.

4 Heat the oil in a karahi, wok or heavy pan and quickly fry the onions with the curry leaves for 3–4 minutes without burning.

5 Lower the heat and add the chicken mixture to the pan with the spices. Continue to stir-fry for a further 2 minutes.

6 Drain the potato pieces and add to the pan. Cover with a lid and cook over a medium to low heat for 5–7 minutes or until the sauce has thickened slightly and the chicken and potatoes are cooked through.

7 Stir in the chopped green chillies and serve.

NUTRITIONAL NOTES
Per Portion

Energy	168Kcals/704KJ
Fat	4.20g
Saturated Fat	0.60g
Carbohydrate	17.65g
Fibre	2.04g

Balti Lamb Tikka

This is a traditional tikka recipe, in which the lamb is marinated in yogurt and spices. The lamb is usually cut into cubes, but the cooking time can be halved by cutting it into strips instead.

INGREDIENTS

Serves 4

450g/1lb lean boneless lamb, cut
  into strips
175ml/6fl oz/³/₄ cup natural
  (plain) yogurt
5ml/1 tsp ground cumin
5ml/1 tsp ground coriander
5ml/1 tsp chilli powder
5ml/1 tsp crushed garlic
5ml/1 tsp salt
5ml/1 tsp garam masala
30ml/2 tbsp chopped fresh
  coriander (cilantro)
30ml/2 tbsp lemon juice
30ml/2 tbsp corn oil
15ml/1 tbsp tomato purée (paste)
1 large green (bell) pepper, seeded
  and sliced
3 large fresh red chillies

1 Put the lamb strips, yogurt, ground cumin, ground coriander, chilli powder, garlic, salt, garam masala, fresh coriander and lemon juice into a large mixing bowl and stir thoroughly. Cover and marinate at cool room temperature for 1 hour.

NUTRITIONAL NOTES Per Portion	
Energy	289Kcals/1207KJ
Fat	18.7g
Saturated Fat	6.9g
Carbohydrate	6.1g
Fibre	0.7g

2 Heat the oil in a karahi, wok or deep pan. Lower the heat slightly and stir in the tomato purée.

3 Add the lamb strips to the pan, a few at a time, leaving any excess marinade behind in the bowl.

4 Cook the lamb, stirring frequently, for 7–10 minutes or until it is well browned.

5 Finally, add the green pepper slices and the whole red chillies. Heat through, checking that the lamb is fully cooked, spoon into a serving dish and serve hot.

Balti Lamb with Potatoes and Fenugreek

The combination of lamb with fresh fenugreek works very well in this dish, which is delicious accompanied by plain boiled rice and mango pickle. Only use the fenugreek leaves, as the stalks can be rather bitter. This dish is traditionally served with rice.

INGREDIENTS

Serves 4

450g/1lb lean minced (ground) lamb
5ml/1 tsp grated fresh root ginger
5ml/1 tsp crushed garlic
7.5ml/1½ tsp chilli powder
5ml/1 tsp salt
1.5ml/¼ tsp turmeric
45ml/3 tbsp corn oil
2 medium onions, sliced
2 medium potatoes, peeled, par-boiled
  and roughly diced
1 bunch fresh fenugreek, chopped
2 tomatoes, chopped
50g/2oz/½ cup frozen peas
30ml/2 tbsp chopped fresh
  coriander (cilantro)
3 fresh red chillies, seeded and sliced

3 Add the minced lamb and fry over a medium heat for 5–7 minutes, stirring.

4 Stir in the potatoes, chopped fenugreek, tomatoes and peas and cook for a further 5–7 minutes, stirring continuously.

5 Just before serving, stir in the fresh coriander. Spoon into a large dish or on to individual plates and serve hot. Garnish with fresh red chillies.

NUTRITIONAL NOTES	
Per Portion	
Energy	386Kcals/1610KJ
Fat	23.7g
Saturated Fat	8.2g
Carbohydrate	20.3g
Fibre	2.5g

1 Put the minced lamb, grated ginger, garlic, chilli powder, salt and turmeric into a large bowl, and mix together thoroughly. Set to one side.

2 Heat the oil in a karahi, wok or deep pan. Add the onion slices and fry for about 5 minutes until golden brown.

Balti Lamb Koftas with Vegetables

These koftas look very attractive served on their bed of vegetables, especially if you make them quite small.

INGREDIENTS

Serves 4

450g/1lb lean minced (ground) lamb
5ml/1 tsp garam masala
5ml/1 tsp ground cumin
5ml/1 tsp ground coriander
5ml/1 tsp crushed garlic
5ml/1 tsp chilli powder
5ml/1 tsp salt
15ml/1 tbsp chopped fresh
  coriander (cilantro)
1 small onion, finely diced
150ml/¼ pint/⅔ cup corn oil

For the vegetables

45ml/3 tbsp corn oil
1 bunch spring onions (scallions),
  roughly chopped
½ large red (bell) pepper, seeded
  and chopped
½ large green (bell) pepper, seeded
  and chopped
175g/6oz/1 cup corn
225g/8oz/1½ cups canned butter
  (lima) beans
½ small cauliflower, cut into florets
4 fresh green chillies, chopped

To garnish

5ml/1 tsp chopped fresh mint
15ml/1 tbsp chopped fresh
  coriander (cilantro)
15ml/1 tbsp shredded ginger
lime slices
15ml/1 tbsp lemon juice

NUTRITIONAL NOTES	
Per Portion	
Energy	515Kcals/2146KJ
Fat	35g
Saturated Fat	9.9g
Carbohydrate	22g
Fibre	5.7g

1 Put the minced lamb into a food processor or blender and process for about 1 minute.

2 Transfer the lamb to a medium bowl. Add the dry spices, garlic, chilli powder, salt, fresh coriander and onion, and use your fingers to blend the kofta mixture thoroughly. Cover and set aside in the refrigerator.

3 Heat the oil for the vegetables in a karahi, wok or deep pan. Add the spring onions and stir-fry for 2 minutes.

4 Add the peppers, corn, butter beans, cauliflower and green chillies, and stir-fry over a high heat for about 2 minutes. Set to one side.

5 Using your hands, roll small pieces of the kofta mixture into golf-ball size portions. You should have between 12 and 16 koftas.

6 Heat the oil for the koftas in a frying pan. Lower the heat slightly and add the koftas, a few at a time. Shallow-fry each batch, turning the koftas, until they are evenly browned. Remove from the oil with a slotted spoon, and drain on kitchen paper.

7 Put the vegetable mixture back over a medium heat, and add the cooked koftas. Stir the mixture gently for about 5 minutes, or until everything is heated through.

8 Garnish with the mint, coriander, shredded ginger and lime slices. Just before serving, sprinkle over the lemon juice.

Balti Mini Lamb Kebabs with Baby Onions

This is rather an unusual Balti dish as the meat patties are cooked on skewers before being added to the karahi to be mixed with the vegetables.

INGREDIENTS

Serves 6

450g/1lb lean minced (ground) lamb
1 medium onion, finely chopped
5ml/1 tsp garam masala
5ml/1 tsp crushed garlic
2 medium fresh green chillies, finely chopped
30ml/2 tbsp chopped fresh coriander (cilantro)
5ml/1 tsp salt
15ml/1 tbsp plain (all-purpose) flour
60ml/4 tbsp corn oil
12 baby onions
4 fresh green chillies, sliced
12 cherry tomatoes
30ml/2 tbsp chopped fresh coriander (cilantro)

1 Mix the lamb, onion, garam masala, garlic, green chillies, fresh coriander, salt and flour in a medium bowl. Use your hands to make sure that all the ingredients are thoroughly mixed together.

2 Transfer the mixture to a food processor and process for about 1 minute, to make the mixture even finer in texture.

3 Put the mixture back into the bowl. Break off small pieces, about the size of a lime, and wrap them around skewers to form small sausage shapes. Put about 2 of these shapes on each skewer.

4 Continue making up the sausage shapes until you have used up all the mixture. Preheat the grill (broiler) to its maximum setting. Baste the meat with 15ml/1 tbsp of the oil and grill (broil) the kebabs for 12–15 minutes, turning and basting occasionally, until the meat is evenly browned.

5 Heat the remaining 45ml/3 tbsp of the oil in a karahi, wok or deep pan. Lower the heat slightly and add the whole baby onions. As soon as they start to darken, add the fresh chillies and tomatoes.

6 Slide the lamb patties from their skewers and add them to the onion and tomato mixture. Stir gently for about 3 minutes to heat them through.

7 Transfer to a serving dish and garnish with fresh coriander.

NUTRITIONAL NOTES	
Per Portion	
Energy	252Kcals/1047KJ
Fat	17.6g
Saturated Fat	5.7g
Carbohydrate	8.5g
Fibre	1.2g

___ COOK'S TIP ___

In India, these shaped meat patties are called kababs. They are sometimes cooked and served on skewers, like the kebabs from which they are derived, but are often served simply as rounds or sausage shapes.

Balti Lamb with Cauliflower

Cauliflower and lamb go very well together. This tasty curry is given a final *tarka*, a dressing of oil, cumin seeds and curry leaves, to enhance the flavour.

INGREDIENTS

Serves 4
10ml/2 tsp oil
2 medium onions, sliced
7.5ml/1½ tsp grated fresh root ginger
5ml/1 tsp chilli powder
5ml/1 tsp crushed garlic
1.5ml/¼ tsp ground turmeric
2.5ml/½ tsp ground coriander
30ml/2 tbsp fresh fenugreek leaves
275g/10oz boneless lean spring lamb, cut into strips
1 small cauliflower, cut into small florets
300ml/½ pint/1¼ cups water
30ml/2 tbsp fresh coriander (cilantro) leaves
½ red (bell) pepper, seeded and sliced
15ml/1 tbsp lemon juice

For the *tarka*
10ml/2 tsp oil
2.5ml/½ tsp cumin seeds
4–6 curry leaves

1 Heat the oil in a karahi, wok or heavy pan and gently fry the onions until they are golden brown. Lower the heat and then add the ginger, chilli powder, garlic, turmeric and ground coriander. Stir well to combine all the ingredients, then add the fresh fenugreek leaves and mix well.

2 Add the lamb strips to the wok and stir-fry until the lamb is completely coated with the spices. Add half the cauliflower florets and stir the mixture well.

3 Pour in the water, cover the wok, lower the heat and cook for 5–7 minutes until the cauliflower and lamb are almost cooked through.

4 Add the remaining cauliflower, half the fresh coriander, the red pepper and lemon juice and stir-fry for about 5 minutes, ensuring the sauce does not catch on the bottom of the pan.

5 Check that the lamb is completely cooked, then remove the pan from the heat and set it aside.

6 To make the *tarka*, heat the oil and fry the seeds and curry leaves for about 30 seconds. While it is still hot, pour the seasoned oil over the cauliflower and lamb and serve garnished with the remaining fresh coriander leaves.

NUTRITIONAL NOTES	
Per Portion	
Energy	202Kcals/839KJ
Fat	9.88g
Saturated Fat	3.24g
Carbohydrate	10.86g
Fibre	2.88g

COOK'S TIP

Groundnut or peanut oil is an excellent oil to use for curries.

Balti Bhoona Lamb

Bhooning is a very traditional way of stir-frying which simply involves semi-circular movements, scraping the bottom of the pan each time in the centre. Serve this dish with freshly made chapatis.

INGREDIENTS

Serves 4

225–275g/8–10oz boneless lean spring lamb
3 medium onions
15ml/1 tbsp oil
15ml/1 tbsp tomato purée (paste)
5ml/1 tsp crushed garlic
7.5ml/1½ tsp finely grated ginger
5ml/1 tsp salt
1.5ml/¼ tsp ground turmeric
600ml/1 pint/2½ cups water
15ml/1 tbsp lemon juice
15ml/1 tbsp shredded fresh root ginger
15ml/1 tbsp chopped fresh coriander (cilantro)
15ml/1 tbsp chopped fresh mint
1 fresh red chilli, chopped

1 Using a sharp knife remove any excess fat from the lamb and cut the meat into small cubes.

COOK'S TIP

Bhooning ensures that the meat becomes well-coated and combined with the spice mixture before the cooking liquid is added. The action of stirring the mixture can be satisfying, like cooking a risotto.

2 Dice the onions finely. Heat the oil in a karahi, wok or heavy pan and fry the onions until soft.

3 Meanwhile, mix together the tomato purée, garlic and ginger, salt and turmeric. Pour the spice mixture on to the onions in the pan and stir-fry for a few seconds.

4 Add the lamb and continue to stir-fry for about 2–3 minutes. Stir in the water, lower the heat, cover the pan and cook for 15–20 minutes, stirring occasionally.

5 When the water has almost evaporated, start bhooning over a medium heat (see the introduction above left), making sure that the sauce does not catch on the bottom of the pan. Continue for 5–7 minutes.

6 Pour in the lemon juice, followed by the shredded ginger, coriander, mint and red chilli. Stir to mix, then serve from the pan.

NUTRITIONAL NOTES	
Per Portion	
Energy	198Kcals/825KJ
Fat	10.37g
Saturated Fat	3.24g
Carbohydrate	11.05g
Fibre	1.84g

Balti Lamb with Peas and Potatoes

Fresh mint leaves are used in this dish, but if they are unobtainable, use ready-minted frozen peas to bring an added freshness. Serve with plain rice.

INGREDIENTS

Serves 4

225g/8oz boneless lean spring lamb
120ml/4fl oz/½ cup natural (plain)
   low fat yogurt
1 cinnamon stick
2 green cardamom pods
3 black peppercorns
5ml/1 tsp crushed garlic
5ml/1 tsp grated fresh root ginger
5ml/1 tsp chilli powder
5ml/1 tsp garam masala
5ml/1 tsp salt
30ml/2 tbsp roughly chopped
   fresh mint
15ml/1 tbsp oil
2 medium onions, sliced
300ml/½ pint/1¼ cups water
1 large potato, diced
115g/4oz/1 cup frozen peas
1 firm tomato, peeled, seeded
   and diced

1 Using a sharp knife, trim any excess fat from the lamb and cut the meat into strips. Place it in a bowl.

2 Add the yogurt, cinnamon, cardamoms, peppercorns, garlic, ginger, chilli powder, garam masala, salt and half the mint. Stir well, cover the bowl and leave in a cool place to marinate for about 2 hours.

3 Heat the oil in a karahi, wok or heavy pan and fry the onions until golden brown. Stir in the lamb and the marinade and stir-fry for about 3 minutes.

NUTRITIONAL NOTES
Per Portion

Energy	231Kcals/968KJ
Fat	8.47g
Saturated Fat	2.79g
Carbohydrate	22.72g
Fibre	3.73g

4 Pour in the water, lower the heat and cook for about 15 minutes until the meat is cooked right through. Meanwhile, cook the potato in boiling water until just soft, but not mushy.

5 Add the peas and potato to the lamb and stir gently to mix.

6 Finally, add the remaining mint and the tomato and cook for a further 5 minutes before serving.

─────── COOK'S TIP ───────

This dish will improve in flavour if cooked a day ahead and kept in the refrigerator.

Balti Lamb in Yogurt and Garam Masala Sauce

The lamb is first marinated then cooked slowly in a hot yogurt sauce and it is served with dried apricots which have been lightly sautéed in ghee with cinnamon and cardamom.

INGREDIENTS

Serves 4

15ml/1 tbsp tomato purée (paste)
175ml/6fl oz/³/₄ cup natural (plain) low fat yogurt
5ml/1 tsp garam masala
1.5ml/¹/₄ tsp cumin seeds
5ml/1 tsp salt
5ml/1 tsp crushed garlic
5ml/1 tsp grated fresh root ginger
5ml/1 tsp chilli powder
225g/8oz boneless lean spring lamb, cut into strips
15ml/1 tbsp oil
2 medium onions, finely sliced
25g/1oz/2 tbsp ghee or unsalted (sweet) butter
2.5cm/1in cinnamon stick
2 green cardamom pods
5 dried apricots, quartered
15ml/1 tbsp fresh coriander (cilantro) leaves, to garnish

1 In a bowl blend together the tomato purée, yogurt, garam masala, cumin seeds, salt, garlic, ginger and chilli powder.

2 Add the lamb to the sauce and mix well. Cover and leave to marinate in a cool place for about 1 hour.

3 Heat 10ml/2 tsp of the oil in a wok or heavy-based frying pan and fry the onions over a medium heat until they are crisp and golden brown.

4 Remove the onions using a slotted spoon, allow to cool and then grind down by processing briefly in a food processor or with a pestle and mortar. Reheat the oil remaining in the pan and return the onions to the wok.

NUTRITIONAL NOTES	
Per Portion	
Energy	221Kcals/922KJ
Fat	11.20g
Saturated Fat	3.64g
Carbohydrate	14.60g
Fibre	1.80g

―――――― COOK'S TIP ――――――

If you want this curry to be slightly hotter, increase the quantity of garam masala and chilli powder to 7.5ml/1½ tsp each.

5 Add the lamb and stir-fry for about 2 minutes. Cover with a lid, lower the heat and cook, stirring occasionally, for about 15 minutes or until the meat is cooked through. If required, add about 150ml/¹/₄ pint/ ²/₃ cup water during the cooking. Remove from the heat and set aside.

6 Heat the ghee or butter with the remaining 5ml/1 tsp of oil and drop in the cinnamon stick and cardamoms. Add the dried apricots and stir over a low heat for about 2 minutes. Pour this over the lamb.

7 Serve garnished with the fresh coriander leaves.

Balti Lamb with Stuffed Vegetables

Aubergines and peppers make an excellent combination. Here they are stuffed with an aromatic lamb filling and served on a bed of sautéed onions. The presentation is very attractive.

INGREDIENTS

Serves 4-6
3 small aubergines (eggplant)
1 each red, green and yellow
   (bell) peppers

Stuffing
45ml/3 tbsp corn oil
3 medium onions, sliced
5ml/1 tsp chilli powder
1.5ml/¼ tsp ground turmeric
5ml/1 tsp ground coriander
5ml/1 tsp ground cumin
5ml/1 tsp grated fresh root ginger
5ml/1 tsp crushed garlic
5ml/1 tsp salt
450g/1lb lean minced (ground) lamb
3 fresh green chillies, chopped
30ml/2 tbsp chopped fresh
   coriander (cilantro)

For the sautéed onions
45ml/3 tbsp corn oil
5ml/1 tsp mixed onion, mustard,
   fenugreek and white cumin seeds
4 dried red chillies
3 medium onions, roughly chopped
5ml/1 tsp salt
5ml/1 tsp chilli powder
2 medium tomatoes, sliced
2 fresh green chillies, chopped
30ml/2 tbsp chopped fresh
   coriander (cilantro)

NUTRITIONAL NOTES	
Per Portion	
Energy	606Kcals/2521KJ
Fat	40.8g
Saturated Fat	10.6g
Carbohydrate	35g
Fibre	7.4g

1 Prepare the vegetables. Slit the aubergines lengthways up to the stalks; keep the stalks intact. Cut the tops off the peppers and remove the seeds.

2 Make the stuffing. Heat the oil in a medium pan. Add the onions and fry for about 3 minutes. Lower the heat and add the chilli powder, turmeric, ground coriander, ground cumin, ginger, garlic and salt, and stir-fry for about 1 minute. Add the lamb to the pan and increase the heat.

3 Stir-fry for 7–10 minutes or until the lamb is cooked, using a wooden spoon to scrape the bottom of the pan. Add the green chillies and fresh coriander towards the end. Remove from the heat, cover and set to one side.

4 Make the sautéed onions. Heat the oil in a karahi, wok or deep pan and add the mixed onion, mustard, fenugreek and white cumin seeds. Stir in the dried red chillies, and fry for about 1 minute. Add the onions and fry for about 2 minutes or until soft.

5 Add the salt, chilli powder, tomatoes, green chillies and fresh coriander. Cook for a further minute. Remove from the heat and set to one side.

6 The minced lamb should by now be cool enough to stuff the prepared aubergines and peppers. Fill the vegetables quite loosely with the meat mixture.

7 As you stuff the vegetables, place them on top of the sautéed onions in the karahi. Cover with foil, making sure the foil doesn't touch the food, and cook over a low heat for about 15 minutes.

8 The dish is ready as soon as the aubergines and peppers are tender. Serve with a dish of plain boiled rice or colourful pulao rice.

_____ COOK'S TIP _____

You can retain the pepper tops and use them as "lids" after the vegetables have been stuffed, if you like.

Balti Lamb Chops with Potatoes

These chops are marinated before being cooked in a deliciously spicy sauce. They are ideal for a family meal, served with a simple mixed salad.

INGREDIENTS

Serves 6–8

8 lamb chops (about 50–75g/
   2–3oz each)
30ml/2 tbsp olive oil
150ml/¼ pint/⅔ cup lemon juice
5ml/1 tsp salt
15ml/1 tbsp chopped fresh mint and
   coriander (cilantro)
150ml/¼ pint/⅔ cup corn oil
fresh mint sprigs
lime slices

For the sauce

45ml/3 tbsp corn oil
8 medium tomatoes, roughly chopped
1 bay leaf
5ml/1 tsp garam masala
30ml/2 tbsp natural (plain) yogurt
5ml/1 tsp crushed garlic
5ml/1 tsp chilli powder
5ml/1 tsp salt
2.5ml/½ tsp black cumin seeds
3 black peppercorns
2 medium potatoes, peeled, roughly
   chopped and boiled

1 Put the chops into a large bowl. Mix together the olive oil, lemon juice, salt and fresh mint and coriander.

2 Pour the oil mixture over the chops and rub it in well with your fingers. Cover and leave to marinate for at least 3 hours in the refrigerator.

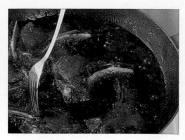

3 To make the sauce, heat the corn oil in a karahi, wok or deep pan. Lower the heat and add the chopped tomatoes. Stir-fry for about 2 minutes.

4 Add the bay leaf, garam masala, yogurt, garlic, chilli powder, salt, black cumin seeds and black peppercorns, and stir-fry for a further 2–3 minutes.

5 Lower the heat again and add the cooked potatoes, mixing everything together well. Remove from the heat and set to one side.

6 Heat 150ml/¼ pint/⅔ cup corn oil in a separate frying pan. Lower the heat slightly and fry the marinated chops until they are cooked through. This will take about 10–12 minutes. Remove with a slotted spoon and drain the cooked chops on kitchen paper.

7 Heat the sauce in the karahi, bringing it to the boil. Add the chops and lower the heat. Simmer for 5–7 minutes.

8 Transfer to a warmed serving dish and garnish with the mint sprigs and lime slices.

NUTRITIONAL NOTES	
Per Portion	
Energy	327Kcals/1367KJ
Fat	18.7g
Saturated Fat	6.3g
Carbohydrate	14.8g
Fibre	2g

Balti Beef

There's no marinating involved with this simple recipe, which can be prepared and cooked in under an hour.

INGREDIENTS

Serves 4

1 red (bell) pepper
1 green (bell) pepper
15ml/1 tbsp oil
5ml/1 tsp cumin seeds
2.5ml/½ tsp fennel seeds
1 onion, cut into thick wedges
1 garlic clove, crushed
2.5cm/1in piece fresh root ginger, finely chopped
1 fresh red chilli, finely chopped
15ml/1 tbsp curry paste
2.5ml/½ tsp salt
675g/1½lb lean rump or fillet steak (beef tenderloin), cut into thick strips
naan bread, to serve

1 Cut the red and green peppers into 2.5cm/1in chunks.

2 Heat the oil in a karahi, wok or frying pan and fry the cumin and fennel seeds for 2 minutes or until they begin to splutter. Add the onion, garlic, ginger and chilli and fry for a further 5 minutes.

3 Stir in the curry paste and salt and fry for a further 3–4 minutes.

4 Add the peppers and toss over the heat for about 5 minutes. Stir in the beef strips and continue to fry for 10–12 minutes or until the meat is tender. Serve from the pan, with warm naan bread.

NUTRITIONAL NOTES	
Per Portion	
Energy	278Kcals/1166KJ
Fat	11.60g
Saturated Fat	3.52g
Carbohydrate	7.70g
Fibre	2.50g

Balti Potatoes with Aubergines

Using baby potatoes adds to the attractiveness of this dish. Choose the smaller variety of aubergines, too, as they are far tastier than the large ones, which contain a lot of water and little flavour. Small aubergines are readily available from specialist grocers.

INGREDIENTS

Serves 4

10–12 baby potatoes
6 small aubergines (eggplant)
1 medium red (bell) pepper
15ml/1 tbsp oil
2 medium onions, sliced
4–6 curry leaves
2.5ml/½ tsp onion seeds
5ml/1 tsp crushed coriander seeds
2.5ml/½ tsp cumin seeds
5ml/1 tsp grated fresh root ginger
5ml/1 tsp crushed garlic
5ml/1 tsp crushed dried red chillies
15ml/1 tbsp chopped fresh
    fenugreek leaves
5ml/1 tsp chopped fresh
    coriander (cilantro)
15ml/1 tbsp natural (plain) low
    fat yogurt
fresh coriander (cilantro) leaves,
    to garnish

1 Cook the unpeeled potatoes in a pan of boiling water until they are just soft, but still whole.

2 Cut the aubergines into quarters, or eighths if using large aubergines.

3 Cut the pepper in half, remove the seeds and ribs, then slice the flesh into thin even-size strips.

4 Heat the oil in a karahi, wok or heavy pan and fry the sliced onions, curry leaves, onion seeds, crushed coriander seeds and cumin seeds until the onion slices are a soft golden brown, stirring constantly.

5 Add the ginger, garlic, crushed chillies and fenugreek, followed by the aubergines and potatoes. Stir everything together and cover the pan with a lid. Lower the heat and cook the vegetables for 5–7 minutes.

6 Remove the lid, add the fresh coriander followed by the yogurt and stir well. Serve garnished with coriander leaves.

NUTRITIONAL NOTES	
Per Portion	
Energy	183Kcals/773KJ
Fat	4.42g
Saturated Fat	0.70g
Carbohydrate	33.02g
Fibre	5.43g

——— COOK'S TIP ———

Remember to whisk yogurt before adding it to a hot dish to prevent it from curdling.

Balti Stir-fried Vegetables with Cashew Nuts

This quick and versatile stir-fry will accommodate most other combinations of vegetables – you do not have to use the selection suggested here.

INGREDIENTS

Serves 4

2 medium carrots
1 medium red (bell) pepper, seeded
1 medium green (bell) pepper, seeded
2 courgettes (zucchini)
115g/4oz green beans
1 medium bunch spring
    onions (scallions)
15ml/1 tbsp oil
4–6 curry leaves
2.5ml/½ tsp cumin seeds
4 dried red chillies
10–12 cashew nuts
5ml/1 tsp salt
30ml/2 tbsp lemon juice
fresh mint leaves, to garnish

1 Prepare the vegetables: cut the carrots, peppers and courgettes into matchsticks, halve the beans and chop the spring onions. Set aside.

NUTRITIONAL NOTES	
Per Portion	
Energy	98Kcals/406KJ
Fat	5.28g
Saturated Fat	0.88g
Carbohydrate	10.3g
Fibre	3.94g

2 Heat the oil in a karahi, wok or heavy pan and fry the curry leaves, cumin seeds and dried chillies for about 1 minute.

3 Add the vegetables and nuts and stir them around gently. Add the salt and lemon juice. Continue to stir and cook for about 3–5 minutes.

4 Transfer the vegetables to a serving dish, garnish with fresh mint leaves and serve immediately.

Karahi Potatoes with Whole Spices

The potato is transformed into something quite exotic when it is cooked like this with a delicious mixture of spices.

INGREDIENTS

Serves 4

15ml/1 tbsp oil
5ml/1 tsp cumin seeds
3 curry leaves
5ml/1 tsp crushed dried red chillies
2.5ml/½ tsp mixed onion, mustard and fenugreek seeds
2.5ml/½ tsp fennel seeds
3 garlic cloves, sliced
2.5cm/1in piece fresh root ginger, grated
2 onions, sliced
6 new potatoes, thinly sliced
15ml/1 tbsp chopped fresh coriander (cilantro)
1 fresh red chilli, seeded and sliced
1 fresh green chilli, seeded and sliced

―――――― COOK'S TIP ――――――

Choose a waxy variety of new potato for this fairly hot vegetable dish; if you use a very soft potato, it will not be possible to cut it into thin slices without it breaking up. Suitable varieties are often labelled "salad potatoes" when sold at supermarkets. Leave the skin on for a tastier result.

NUTRITIONAL NOTES
Per Portion

Energy	110Kcals/462KJ
Fat	3.60g
Saturated Fat	0.39g
Carbohydrate	17.1g
Fibre	1.60g

1 Heat the oil in a karahi, wok or heavy pan. Lower the heat slightly and add the cumin seeds, curry leaves, dried red chillies, mixed onion, mustard and fenugreek seeds, fennel seeds, garlic slices and ginger. Fry for 1 minute.

2 Add the onions and fry for a further 5 minutes, or until the onions are golden brown.

3 Add the potatoes, fresh coriander and fresh red and green chillies and mix well. Cover the pan tightly with a lid or foil; if using foil, make sure that it does not touch the food. Cook over a very low heat for about 7 minutes or until the potatoes are tender.

4 Remove the pan from the heat, and take off the lid or foil cover. Serve hot straight from the pan.

Balti Mushrooms in a Creamy Garlic Sauce

This is a simple and delicious Balti recipe which could be accompanied by one of the rice side dishes from this book.

INGREDIENTS

Serves 4

350g/12oz/4½ cups button (white) mushrooms
15ml/1 tbsp oil
1 bay leaf
3 garlic cloves, roughly chopped
2 green chillies, seeded and chopped
225g/8oz/1 cup low fat fromage frais or ricotta cheese
15ml/1 tbsp chopped fresh mint
15ml/1 tbsp chopped fresh coriander (cilantro)
5ml/1 tsp salt
fresh mint and coriander leaves, to garnish

1 Cut the mushrooms in half, or in quarters if large, and set aside.

NUTRITIONAL NOTES	
Per Portion	
Energy	76Kcals/321KJ
Fat	3.40g
Saturated Fat	0.55g
Carbohydrate	5.20g
Fibre	1.10g

2 Heat the oil in a karahi, wok or heavy pan, then add the bay leaf, garlic and chillies and quickly stir-fry for about 1 minute.

3 Add the mushrooms. Stir-fry for another 2 minutes.

4 Remove from the heat and stir in the fromage frais or ricotta cheese, followed by the mint, coriander and salt. Return to the heat and stir-fry for 2–3 minutes, then transfer to a warmed serving dish and garnish with mint and coriander leaves.

Balti Sweetcorn with Cauliflower

This quick and tasty vegetable side dish can be made with frozen sweetcorn so it is an excellent storecupboard standby. If you do not have any cauliflower, substitute broccoli or another vegetable.

INGREDIENTS

Serves 4

3 small onions
1 fresh red chilli
15ml/1 tbsp oil
4 curry leaves
1.5ml/¼ tsp onion seeds
175g/6oz/1 cup frozen sweetcorn
½ small cauliflower, separated into florets
3–7 mint leaves

NUTRITIONAL NOTES	
Per Portion	
Energy	124Kcals/519KJ
Fat	3.89g
Saturated Fat	0.58g
Carbohydrate	19.31g
Fibre	2.56g

COOK'S TIP

It is best to cook this dish immediately before serving and eating, as the flavour tends to spoil if it is kept warm.

2 Heat the oil in a karahi, wok or heavy pan and stir-fry the curry leaves and the onion seeds for about 30 seconds.

4 Add the chilli, frozen sweetcorn and cauliflower florets and stir-fry for 5–8 minutes.

1 Using a sharp knife dice the onions finely. Slit the chilli, scrape out the seeds and then slice the chilli thinly.

3 Add the onions and fry them for 5–8 minutes until golden brown.

5 Toss with the mint leaves and serve immediately.

Balti Dhal with Spring Onions and Tomatoes

This rich-tasting dish is made using toor dhal, a shiny, yellow split lentil which resembles chana dhal. Fresh fenugreek leaves impart a stunning aroma.

INGREDIENTS

Serves 4

115g/4oz/½ cup toor dhal or yellow
    split peas
30ml/2 tbsp oil
1.5ml/¼ tsp onion seeds
1 medium bunch spring onions
    (scallions), roughly chopped
5ml/1 tsp crushed garlic
1.5ml/¼ tsp ground turmeric
7.5ml/1½ tsp grated fresh root ginger
5ml/1 tsp chilli powder
30ml/2 tbsp fresh fenugreek leaves
5ml/1 tsp salt
150ml/¼ pint/⅔ cup water
6-8 cherry tomatoes
30ml/2 tbsp fresh coriander
    (cilantro) leaves
½ green (bell) pepper, seeded and sliced
15ml/1 tbsp lemon juice
shredded spring onion tops and fresh
    coriander (cilantro) leaves, to garnish

COOK'S TIP

Fresh fenugreek leaves are too bitter to use as a vegetable on their own but they are excellent mixed with pulses. If you cannot get fresh fenugreek leaves, use dried leaves which are available in most Indian shops.

NUTRITIONAL NOTES
Per Portion

Energy	152Kcals/640KJ
Fat	6.1g
Saturated Fat	0.9g
Carbohydrate	17.8g
Fibre	2.1g

1 Cook the dhal in a pan of boiling water for 40–45 minutes until soft and mushy. Drain and set aside.

2 Heat the oil with the onion seeds in a karahi, wok or heavy pan for a few seconds until hot.

3 Add the drained dhal to the wok or frying pan and stir-fry with the onion seeds for about 3 minutes.

4 Add the spring onions followed by the garlic, turmeric, ginger, chilli powder, fenugreek leaves and salt and continue to stir-fry for 5–7 minutes.

5 Pour in just enough of the water to loosen the mixture.

6 Add the whole cherry tomatoes, coriander leaves, green pepper and lemon juice. Stir well and serve garnished with shredded spring onion tops and some extra coriander leaves.

Balti Baby Vegetables

There is a wide and wonderful selection of baby vegetables available in supermarkets these days, and this simple recipe does full justice to their delicate flavour and attractive appearance. Serve as part of a main meal or even as a light appetizer.

INGREDIENTS

Serves 4–6
10 new potatoes, halved
12–14 baby carrots
12–14 baby courgettes (zucchini)
30ml/2 tbsp corn oil
15 baby onions
30ml/2 tbsp chilli sauce
5ml/1 tsp crushed garlic
5ml/1 tsp grated fresh root ginger
5ml/1 tsp salt
400g/14oz/2 cups drained
   canned chickpeas
10 cherry tomatoes
5ml/1 tsp crushed dried red chillies
30ml/2 tbsp sesame seeds

1 Bring a medium pan of salted water to the boil and add the potatoes and carrots. Cook for 12–15 minutes, then add the courgettes and boil for a further 5 minutes or until all the vegetables are just tender. Take care not to overcook the vegetables, as they will be given a brief additional cooking time later.

2 Drain the vegetables well and put them in a bowl. Set aside.

3 Heat the oil in a karahi, wok or deep pan and add the baby onions. Fry until the onions turn golden brown. Lower the heat and add the chilli sauce, garlic, ginger and salt, taking care not to burn the mixture.

4 Stir in the chickpeas and stir-fry over a medium heat until the moisture has been absorbed.

5 Add the cooked vegetables and cherry tomatoes and stir over the heat with a slotted spoon for about 2 minutes.

6 Sprinkle the crushed red chillies and sesame seeds evenly over the vegetable mixture as a garnish and serve.

VARIATION

By varying the vegetables chosen and experimenting with different combinations, this recipe can form the basis for a wide variety of vegetable accompaniments. Try baby corn cobs, French (green) beans, mange-tout (snow peas), cauliflower florets, and okra too.

NUTRITIONAL NOTES
Per Portion

Energy	311Kcals/1306KJ
Fat	8.5g
Saturated Fat	1.3g
Carbohydrate	48.7g
Fibre	8.4g

Vegetarian Main Dishes

THE COMPLAINT that there's nothing suitable on the menu for vegetarian diners never applies in India, where many sections of the population eat neither meat, fish nor eggs as a matter of religious principle. The following dishes prove just how versatile vegetables can be, whether stuffed with spices, layered with rice, or roasted on skewers. Some dishes are light and easy to digest; others bulked with lentils or chickpeas to make a substantial lunch or supper.

Careful spicing transforms the most ordinary ingredients into tasty treats. Spinach and potatoes, for instance, take on tremendous flavour when cooked with mustard seeds, ginger and chilli. Sweetcorn and Pea Curry is another winning combination, as is Okra with Green Mango and Lentils. Most of the dishes in this chapter are quick and easy to prepare, making them ideal for those occasions when a son or daughter announces that they have just become vegetarian.

Stuffed Aubergines in Seasoned Tamarind Juice

The traditional way of cooking with tamarind is in a terracotta dish, which brings out the full fruity tartness of the tamarind. This spicy aubergine dish will add a refreshing tang to any meal.

INGREDIENTS

Serves 4

12 baby aubergines (eggplant)
30ml/2 tbsp vegetable oil
1 small onion, chopped
10ml/2 tsp grated fresh root ginger
10ml/2 tsp crushed garlic
5ml/1 tsp coriander seeds
5ml/1 tsp cumin seeds
10ml/2 tsp white poppy seeds
10ml/2 tsp sesame seeds
10ml/2 tsp desiccated (dry unsweetened shredded) coconut
15ml/1 tbsp dry-roasted skinned peanuts
2.5–5ml/½–1 tsp chilli powder
5ml/1 tsp salt
6–8 curry leaves
1–2 dried red chillies, chopped
2.5ml/½ tsp concentrated tamarind paste

1 Make three deep slits lengthways on each aubergine, without cutting through, then soak in salted water for 20 minutes.

2 Heat half the oil in a pan and sauté the onion for 3–4 minutes. Add the ginger and garlic and cook for 30 seconds.

3 Add the coriander and cumin seeds and sauté for 30 seconds, then add the poppy seeds, sesame seeds and coconut. Sauté for 1 minute, stirring constantly. Leave to cool slightly, then grind the spices in a food processor, adding 105ml/7 tbsp warm water. The mixture should resemble a thick, slightly coarse paste.

4 Mix the peanuts, chilli powder and salt into the spice paste. Drain the aubergines and dry on kitchen paper. Stuff each of the slits with the spice paste and reserve any remaining paste.

5 Heat the remaining oil in a wok, karahi or large pan over a medium heat and add the curry leaves and chillies. Let the chillies blacken, then add the aubergines and the tamarind blended with 105ml/7 tbsp hot water. Add any remaining spice paste and stir to mix.

6 Cover the pan and simmer gently for 15–20 minutes or until the aubergines are tender. Serve with chapatis and a meat or poultry dish, if you like.

NUTRITIONAL NOTES	
Per Portion	
Energy	141Kcals/585KJ
Fat	12g
Saturated Fat	1.7g
Carbohydrate	5.1g
Fibre	3.3g

Potatoes Stuffed with Spicy Cottage Cheese

For this recipe, it is important to choose a variety of potato recommended for baking, as the texture of the potato should not be too dry. This makes an excellent low fat snack at any time of the day.

INGREDIENTS

Serves 4

4 medium baking potatoes
225g/8oz/1 cup low fat cottage cheese
10ml/2 tsp tomato purée
2.5ml/½ tsp ground cumin
2.5ml/½ tsp ground coriander
2.5ml/½ tsp chilli powder
2.5ml/½ tsp salt
15ml/1 tbsp oil
2.5ml/½ tsp mixed onion and
    mustard seeds
3 curry leaves
30ml/2 tbsp water

For the garnish
mixed salad leaves
fresh coriander (cilantro) sprigs
lemon wedges
2 tomatoes, quartered

1 Preheat the oven to 180°C/350°F/ Gas 4. Wash each potato and pat dry. Make a slit in the middle of each potato. Prick the potatoes a few times with a fork or skewer, then wrap them individually in foil. Bake in the oven directly on the shelf for about 1 hour, or until soft.

2 Put the cottage cheese into a heatproof dish and set aside.

3 In a separate bowl, mix the tomato purée, ground cumin, ground coriander, chilli powder and salt.

4 Heat the oil in a small pan for about 1 minute. Add the mixed onion and mustard seeds and the curry leaves and tilt the pan so the oil covers all the seeds and leaves.

_____ COOK'S TIP _____

This recipe can also be used as a basis for a tangy vegetable accompaniment to a main meal. Instead of using baked potatoes, boil some small new potatoes in their skins, then cut each one in half. Add the cooked potatoes to the spicy cottage cheese mixture, mix together well and serve.

5 When the curry leaves turn a shade darker and you can smell their beautiful aroma, pour the tomato purée mixture into the pan and turn the heat immediately to low. Add the water and mix well. Cook for a further minute, then pour the spicy tomato mixture on to the cottage cheese and stir together well.

6 Check that the baked potatoes are cooked right through, by inserting a knife or skewer into the middle of the flesh. If it is soft, unwrap the potatoes from the foil and divide the cottage cheese equally between them.

7 Garnish the filled potatoes with mixed salad leaves, fresh coriander sprigs, lemon wedges and tomato quarters and serve hot.

NUTRITIONAL NOTES	
Per Portion	
Energy	175Kcals/740KJ
Fat	4.30g
Saturated Fat	0.43g
Carbohydrate	24.40g
Fibre	1.90g

Stuffed Baby Vegetables

The combination of potatoes and aubergines is popular in Indian cooking. This recipe uses small vegetables, which are stuffed with a dry, spicy masala paste.

INGREDIENTS

Serves 4
12 small potatoes
8 baby aubergines (eggplant)

For the stuffing
15ml/1 tbsp sesame seeds
30ml/2 tbsp ground coriander
30ml/2 tbsp ground cumin
2.5ml/½ tsp salt
1.5ml/¼ tsp chilli powder
2.5ml/½ tsp ground turmeric
10ml/2 tsp granulated sugar
1.5ml/¼ tsp garam masala
15ml/1 tbsp gram flour
2 garlic cloves, crushed
15ml/1 tbsp lemon juice
30ml/2 tbsp chopped fresh
    coriander (cilantro)

For the sauce
15ml/1 tbsp oil
2.5ml/½ tsp black mustard seeds
400g/14oz can chopped tomatoes
30ml/2 tbsp chopped fresh
    coriander (cilantro)
150ml/¼ pint/⅔ cup water

1 Preheat the oven to 200°C/400°F/ Gas 6. Make slits in the potatoes and aubergines, ensuring that you do not cut right through.

2 Mix all the ingredients for the stuffing together on a plate.

3 Carefully spoon the spicy stuffing mixture into each of the slits in the potatoes and aubergines.

4 Arrange the stuffed potatoes and aubergines in a greased ovenproof dish, filling side up.

COOK'S TIP

Make sure that the potatoes are all about the same size and the baby aubergines (eggplant) are a similar size, so that they all cook evenly. Baby aubergines are often on sale in supermarkets, but if you find it difficult to obtain them, try an Asian market or Indian grocer.

5 For the sauce, heat the oil in a heavy pan and fry the mustard seeds for 2 minutes until they begin to splutter, then add the canned tomatoes, chopped coriander and any leftover stuffing. Stir in the water. Bring to the boil and simmer for 5 minutes until the sauce thickens.

6 Pour the sauce over the potatoes and aubergines. Cover and bake in the oven for 25–30 minutes until the potatoes and aubergines are soft.

NUTRITIONAL NOTES	
Per Portion	
Energy	259Kcals/1088KJ
Fat	7.60g
Saturated Fat	0.73g
Carbohydrate	41.30g
Fibre	4.00g

Mushroom and Okra Curry with Mango Relish

The sliced okra not only flavours this unusual curry, but thickens it, too. Mushrooms are an excellent addition, but it is the mango relish that really pulls this dish together, adding an inspired touch of spicy sweetness.

INGREDIENTS

Serves 4

4 garlic cloves, roughly chopped
2.5cm/1in piece fresh root ginger,
    peeled and roughly chopped
1–2 fresh red chillies, seeded and
    chopped
175ml/6fl oz/¾ cup cold water
15ml/1 tbsp sunflower oil
5ml/1 tsp coriander seeds
5ml/1 tsp cumin seeds
5ml/1 tsp ground cumin
seeds from 2 green cardamom
    pods, ground
pinch of ground turmeric
400g/14oz can chopped tomatoes
450g/1lb/6 cups mushrooms, quartered
    if large
225g/8oz okra, trimmed and sliced
30ml/2 tbsp chopped fresh
    coriander (cilantro)
basmati rice, to serve

For the mango relish

1 large ripe mango, about 500g/1¼lb
1 small garlic clove, crushed
1 small onion, finely chopped
10ml/2 tsp grated fresh root ginger
1 fresh red chilli, seeded and
    finely chopped
pinch each of salt and sugar

NUTRITIONAL NOTES	
Per Portion	
Energy	152Kcals/645KJ
Fat	4.4g
Saturated Fat	0.7g
Carbohydrate	24.2g
Fibre	8g

1 Make the mango relish. Peel the mango, cut the flesh off the stone and chop it finely. Put it in a bowl.

2 Mash the mango with a fork and mix in the garlic, onion, ginger, chilli, salt and sugar. Set aside.

3 Put the garlic, ginger, chillies and 45ml/3 tbsp of the water in a blender or food processor and blend to a smooth paste.

4 Heat the oil in a large pan. Add the whole coriander and cumin seeds and let them sizzle for a few seconds. Add the ground cumin, ground cardamom and turmeric and cook for 1 minute more, until aromatic.

5 Scrape in the garlic paste, then add the tomatoes, mushrooms and okra. Pour in the remaining water. Stir to mix well, and bring to the boil. Reduce the heat, cover and simmer the curry for 5 minutes.

6 Remove the lid, increase the heat slightly and cook for 5-10 minutes more, until the okra is tender. Stir in the fresh coriander and serve with the rice and the mango relish.

_____ COOK'S TIP _____

Stir the mango relish just before serving it.

Cumin-scented Vegetable Curry with Toasted Almonds

Cabbage is widely enjoyed in India. Baby corn cobs and mangetouts are less well known, except in the larger cities. This is therefore an example of a modern fusion curry, applying traditional cooking methods to what, for some, are exotic ingredients.

INGREDIENTS

Serves 4

15ml/1 tbsp vegetable oil
50g/2oz/¼ cup butter
2.5ml/½ tsp crushed coriander seeds
2.5ml/½ tsp white cumin seeds
6 dried red chillies
1 small savoy cabbage, shredded
12 mangetouts (snow peas)
3 fresh red chillies, seeded and sliced
12 baby corn cobs, halved
salt
25g/1oz/¼ cup flaked (sliced) almonds, toasted and 15ml/1 tbsp chopped fresh coriander (cilantro), to garnish

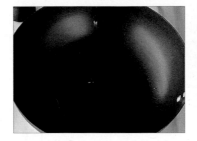

1 Heat the oil and butter in a wok, karahi or large pan and add the crushed coriander seeds, white cumin seeds and dried red chillies.

--------- COOK'S TIP ---------

Julienne strips of other vegetables will make this dish visually more appealing, and will add superb taste at the same time. Try julienne carrots and leeks instead of mangetouts and baby corn. Add the cabbage and carrots together, and add the leeks in step 3.

2 Add the shredded cabbage and mangetouts to the spices in the pan and stir-fry briskly for about 5 minutes, until the cabbage starts to turn crisp.

3 Add the fresh red chillies and baby corn cobs to the pan and season with salt to taste. Stir-fry for 3 minutes more.

4 Garnish with the toasted almonds and fresh coriander, and serve hot. This dish would go well with any meat curry and with a classic pulao.

NUTRITIONAL NOTES	
Per Portion	
Energy	133Kcals/550KJ
Fat	12.2g
Saturated Fat	6.1g
Carbohydrate	3.6g
Fibre	2.1g

Spicy Potato and Tomato Curry

Diced potatoes are cooked gently in a fresh tomato sauce, which is flavoured with curry leaves and green chillies.

INGREDIENTS

Serves 4

2 medium potatoes
15ml/1 tbsp oil
2 medium onions, finely chopped
4 curry leaves
1.5ml/¼ tsp onion seeds
1 fresh green chilli, seeded
  and chopped
4 tomatoes, sliced
5ml/1 tsp grated fresh root ginger
5ml/1 tsp crushed garlic
5ml/1 tsp chilli powder
5ml/1 tsp ground coriander
1.5ml/¼ tsp salt
5ml/1 tsp lemon juice
15ml/1 tbsp chopped fresh
  coriander (cilantro)
3 hard-boiled eggs, to garnish

1 Peel the potatoes and cut them into small cubes.

NUTRITIONAL NOTES
Per Portion

Energy	188Kcals/790KJ
Fat	7.62g
Saturated Fat	1.66g
Carbohydrate	23.41g
Fibre	3.10g

2 Heat the oil in a karahi, wok or heavy pan and stir-fry the onions, curry leaves, onion seeds and green chilli for about 40 seconds.

3 Add the tomatoes and cook for about 2 minutes over a low heat.

4 Add the ginger and garlic, chilli powder, ground coriander and salt to taste. Continue to stir-fry for 1–2 minutes, then add the potatoes and cook over a low heat for 5–7 minutes until the potatoes are tender.

5 Add the lemon juice and fresh coriander and stir to mix together.

6 Shell the hard-boiled eggs, cut into quarters, and add as a garnish to the finished dish.

COOK'S TIPS

• Drain the hard-boiled eggs and cool them under cold running water, then tap the shells and leave the eggs until cold. This prevents a discoloured rim from forming round the outside of the yolk and enables the shell to be removed easily.
• Discoloration can also be a problem if the potatoes are cubed and left to stand before being cooked. Prepare them just before frying the onion mixture.

Spinach and Potato Curry

Spinach, potatoes and traditional Indian spices are the main ingredients in this simple but authentic curry.

INGREDIENTS

Serves 4

450g/1lb spinach
15ml/1 tbsp oil
5ml/1 tsp black mustard seeds
1 onion, thinly sliced
2 garlic cloves, crushed
2.5cm/1in piece fresh root ginger, finely chopped
675g/1½lb potatoes, cut into 2.5cm/1in chunks
5ml/1 tsp chilli powder
5ml/1 tsp salt
120ml/4fl oz/½ cup water

NUTRITIONAL NOTES	
Per Portion	
Energy	203Kcals/851KJ
Fat	4.60g
Saturated Fat	0.65g
Carbohydrate	34.40g
Fibre	5.10g

COOK'S TIPS

• To make certain that the spinach is completely dry, put it in a clean dishtowel, roll up tightly and squeeze gently to remove any excess liquid.
• Use a waxy variety of potato for this dish so that the pieces do not break up during cooking.
• When frying the mustard seeds, put a lid on the pan so that when they splutter they do not escape.

1 Wash and trim the spinach, then blanch it in a pan of boiling water for about 3–4 minutes.

2 Drain the spinach thoroughly and set aside. When it is cool enough to handle, use your hands to squeeze out any remaining liquid (see Cook's Tip) and set aside.

3 Heat the oil in a large heavy pan and fry the mustard seeds for 2 minutes or until they splutter.

4 Add the sliced onion, garlic cloves and chopped ginger to the mustard seeds and fry for 5 minutes, stirring.

5 Add the potato chunks, chilli powder, salt and water and stir-fry for a further 8 minutes.

6 Add the drained spinach. Cover the pan with a lid and simmer for 10–15 minutes or until the potatoes are tender. Serve hot.

Okra with Green Mango and Lentils

If you like okra, you'll love this spicy tangy dish.

INGREDIENTS

Serves 4

115g/4oz/½ cup toor dhal or yellow
   split peas
450g/1lb okra
15ml/1 tbsp oil
2.5ml/½ tsp onion seeds
2 onions, sliced
2.5ml/½ tsp ground fenugreek
1.5ml/¼ tsp ground turmeric
5ml/1 tsp ground coriander
7.5ml/1½ tsp chilli powder
5ml/1 tsp grated fresh root ginger
5ml/1 tsp crushed garlic
1 green mango, peeled and sliced
7.5ml/1½ tsp salt
2 red chillies, seeded and sliced
30ml/2 tbsp chopped fresh
   coriander
1 tomato, sliced

1 Wash the toor dhal thoroughly to remove any grit and place in a large saucepan with enough cold water to cover. Bring to the boil and cook for 30–45 minutes until soft but not mushy.

2 Trim the okra and cut the pods into 1cm/½in pieces.

3 Heat the oil in a karahi, wok or heavy pan and fry the onion seeds until they begin to pop. Add the onions and fry until golden brown. Lower the heat and stir in the ground fenugreek, turmeric and coriander, and the chilli powder, ginger and garlic.

4 Add the mango slices and the okra pieces. Stir well and then add the salt, red chillies and fresh coriander. Stir-fry for 3–4 minutes or until the okra is well cooked and tender.

5 Finally, add the cooked dhal and sliced tomato and cook for a further 3 minutes. Serve hot.

COOK'S TIP

When buying okra, always choose small, bright green ones with no brown patches. If cooking whole, trim off the conical cap, taking care not to pierce through to the seed pod where there are tiny edible seeds and a sticky juice.

NUTRITIONAL NOTES
Per Portion

Energy	229Kcals/963KJ
Fat	5.00g
Saturated Fat	0.55g
Carbohydrate	36.00g
Fibre	8.10g

Broad Bean and Cauliflower Curry

This is a hot and spicy vegetable curry, tasty when served with cooked rice (especially a brown basmati variety), a few small poppadums and cucumber raita.

INGREDIENTS

Serves 4

2 garlic cloves, chopped
2.5cm/1in piece fresh root ginger
1 fresh green chilli, seeded
  and chopped
30ml/2 tbsp oil
1 onion, sliced
1 large potato, chopped
15ml/1 tbsp curry powder, mild or hot
1 cauliflower, cut into small florets
600ml/1 pint/2½ cups vegetable stock
salt and black pepper
275g/10oz can broad (fava) beans
juice of ½ lemon, optional
fresh coriander (cilantro) sprig,
  to garnish
plain rice, to serve

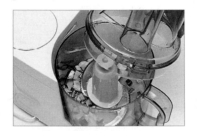

1 Blend the garlic, ginger, chilli and 15ml/1 tbsp of the oil in a food processor or blender until the mixture forms a smooth paste.

2 In a large heavy pan, fry the onion and potato in the remaining oil for 5 minutes, then stir in the spice paste and curry powder. Cook for another minute.

3 Add the cauliflower florets to the onion and potato and stir well until they are thoroughly combined with the spicy mixture, then pour in the stock and bring to the boil over a medium to high heat.

4 Season well, cover and simmer for 10 minutes. Add the beans with the liquid from the can and cook, uncovered, for a further 10 minutes.

5 Check the seasoning and adjust if necessary. Add a good squeeze of lemon juice, if liked, and serve hot, garnished with coriander and accompanied by plain boiled rice.

_____ COOK'S TIP _____

Other root vegetables, such as parsnips and carrots, can be used in this recipe.

NUTRITIONAL NOTES
Per Portion

Energy	216Kcals/906KJ
Fat	7.70g
Saturated Fat	0.75g
Carbohydrate	25.80g
Fibre	7.90g

Lentils Seasoned with Fried Spices

A simple supper dish for family or friends.

INGREDIENTS

Serves 4-6

115g/4oz/½ cup red gram or pigeon peas
50g/2oz/¼ cup bengal gram
4 fresh green chillies
5ml/1 tsp ground turmeric
1 large onion, sliced
salt, to taste
400g/14oz can chopped tomatoes
60ml/4 tbsp vegetable oil
2.5ml/½ tsp mustard seeds
2.5ml/½ tsp cumin seeds
1 garlic clove, crushed
6 curry leaves
2 dried red chillies
deep-fried onions and fresh coriander
  (cilantro), to garnish

1 Place the red gram or pigeon peas and bengal gram in a heavy pan and pour in 350ml/12fl oz/1½ cups water. Add the chillies, turmeric and onion slices and bring to the boil. Simmer, covered, until the lentils are soft and the water has evaporated.

2 Mash the lentils with the back of a spoon. When nearly smooth, add the salt and tomatoes and mix well. If necessary, thin with hot water.

3 Heat the oil in a frying pan. Fry the remaining ingredients until the garlic browns. Pour the oil and spices over the lentils and cover. After 5 minutes, mix well, garnish, and serve.

NUTRITIONAL NOTES	
Per Portion	
Energy	268Kcals/1124KJ
Fat	11.8g
Saturated Fat	1.4g
Carbohydrate	31g
Fibre	3.6g

South Indian Lentils and Vegetables

Pulses are perfect for easy, inexpensive meals.

INGREDIENTS

Serves 4-6

60ml/4 tbsp vegetable oil
2.5ml/½ tsp mustard seeds
2.5ml/½ tsp cumin seeds
2 dried red chillies
1.5ml/¼ tsp asafoetida
6–8 curry leaves
2 garlic cloves, crushed
30ml/2 tbsp desiccated (dry
  unsweetened shredded) coconut
225g/8oz/1 cup masoor dhal or
  red split lentils
10ml/2 tsp sambhar masala or
  garam masala
2.5ml/½ tsp ground turmeric
450g/1lb mixed vegetables
60ml/4 tbsp tamarind juice
4 firm tomatoes, quartered
60ml/4 tbsp vegetable oil
2 garlic cloves, finely sliced
handful fresh coriander (cilantro), chopped

1 Heat the oil in a heavy pan. Fry the next 7 ingredients until the coconut browns. Mix in the lentils, sambhar masala and turmeric. Stir in 450ml/¾ pint/scant 2 cups water.

2 Simmer until the lentils are mushy. Add the vegetables, tamarind juice and tomatoes. Cook so the vegetables are crunchy.

3 In the oil, fry the garlic slices and fresh coriander. Pour over the lentils and vegetables. Mix at the table before serving.

NUTRITIONAL NOTES	
Per Portion	
Energy	459Kcals/1917KJ
Fat	28.1g
Saturated Fat	7g
Carbohydrate	37.3g
Fibre	5.8g

Lentil Dhal with Roasted Garlic and Whole Spices

This spicy lentil dhal makes a sustaining and comforting meal when served with rice or Indian breads and any dry-spiced dish, particularly a cauliflower or potato dish. The spicy garnish offers a contrast in texture and flavour.

INGREDIENTS

Serves 4–6

40g/1½oz/3 tbsp butter or ghee
1 onion, chopped
2 fresh green chillies, seeded and chopped
15ml/1 tbsp chopped fresh root ginger
225g/8oz/1 cup yellow or red lentils
900ml/1½ pints/3¾ cups water
45ml/3 tbsp roasted garlic purée
5ml/1 tsp ground cumin
5ml/1 tsp ground coriander
200g/7oz tomatoes, peeled and diced
a little lemon juice
salt and black pepper
30–45ml/2–3 tbsp coriander (cilantro) sprigs, to garnish

For the spicy garnish

30ml/2 tbsp groundnut (peanut) oil
4–5 shallots, sliced
2 garlic cloves, thinly sliced
15g/½oz/1 tbsp butter or ghee
5ml/1 tsp cumin seeds
5ml/1 tsp mustard seeds
3–4 small dried red chillies
8–10 fresh curry leaves

1 First begin the spicy garnish. Heat the oil in a large, heavy pan. Add the shallots and fry them over a medium heat, stirring occasionally, until they are crisp and browned. Add the garlic and cook, stirring frequently, for a moment or two until the garlic colours slightly. Use a slotted spoon to remove the mixture from the pan and set it aside in a bowl.

2 Melt the butter or ghee in the pan and cook the onion, chillies and ginger for 10 minutes, until golden.

3 Stir in the lentils and water, then bring to the boil, reduce the heat and part-cover the pan. Simmer, stirring occasionally, for 50–60 minutes, until similar to a very thick soup.

4 Stir in the roasted garlic purée, cumin and ground coriander, then season with salt and pepper to taste. Cook for a further 10–15 minutes, uncovered, stirring frequently.

5 Stir in the tomatoes and then adjust the seasoning, adding a little lemon juice to taste if necessary.

6 Finish the spicy garnish. Melt the butter or ghee in a frying pan. Add the cumin and mustard seeds and fry until the mustard seeds pop. Stir in the chillies, curry leaves and the shallot mixture, then immediately swirl the mixture into the cooked dhal. Garnish with coriander and serve.

NUTRITIONAL NOTES	
Per Portion	
Energy	340Kcals/1424KJ
Fat	16.3g
Saturated Fat	7.5g
Carbohydrate	36.3g
Fibre	3.8g

—————— COOK'S TIP ——————

Ghee is type of clarified butter that has had all the milk solids removed by heating – it was originally made to extend the keeping qualities of butter in India. It is the main cooking fat used in Indian cooking. Because the milk solids have been removed, ghee has a high smoking point and can therefore be cooked at higher temperatures than ordinary butter. Look for it in Indian and Asian stores.

Black-Eyed Beans and Potato Curry

A nutritious supper dish for a
chilly evening.

INGREDIENTS

Serves 4-6

225g/8oz/1⅓ cups black-eyed beans
  (peas), soaked overnight and drained
1.5ml/¼ tsp bicarbonate of soda
  (baking soda)
5ml/1 tsp five-spice powder
1.5ml/¼ tsp asafoetida
2 onions, finely chopped
2.5cm/1in piece fresh root ginger, crushed
few fresh mint leaves
450ml/¾ pint/scant 2 cups water
60ml/4 tbsp vegetable oil
2.5ml/½ tsp each, turmeric, ground cumin,
  ground coriander and chilli powder
4 fresh green chillies, chopped
75ml/5 tbsp tamarind juice
2 potatoes, cubed and boiled
115g/4oz/4 cups fresh coriander
  (cilantro), chopped
2 firm tomatoes, chopped
salt, to taste

1 Place the black-eyed beans with the
first 7 ingredients in a heavy pan.
Simmer until the beans are soft.
Remove any excess water and reserve.

2 Heat the oil in a frying pan. Gently
fry the spices, chillies and tamarind
juice, until they are well blended. Pour
over the black-eyed beans and mix.

3 Add the potatoes, fresh coriander,
tomatoes and salt. Mix well, and if
necessary thin with a little reserved
water. Reheat and serve.

NUTRITIONAL NOTES	
Per Portion	
Energy	362Kcals/1526KJ
Fat	12.4g
Saturated Fat	1.6g
Carbohydrate	49.6g
Fibre	6.6g

Bengal Gram and Bottle Gourd Curry

Tamarind gives this pulse and
vegetable dish a lemony flavour.

INGREDIENTS

Serves 4-6

175g/6oz/⅔ cup bengal gram
scant 60ml/4 tbsp vegetable oil
2 fresh green chillies, chopped
1 onion, chopped
2 garlic cloves, crushed
5cm/2in piece fresh ginger, crushed
6–8 curry leaves
5ml/1 tsp chilli powder
5ml/1 tsp ground turmeric
salt, to taste
450g/1lb bottle gourd, marrow (large
  zucchini), peeled, pithed and sliced
60ml/4 tbsp tamarind juice
2 tomatoes, chopped
chopped fresh coriander (cilantro)

1 Put the lentils in a pan with 450ml/
¾ pint/scant 2 cups water, cook the
lentils in the water until the grains are
tender but not mushy. Put aside without
draining away any excess water.

3 Add the lentils and any water
remaining in the pan. Bring to the
boil. Stir in the tamarind juice,
tomatoes and fresh coriander. Simmer
gently until the gourd is cooked. Serve
hot with a dry meat curry.

2 Heat the oil and fry the chillies,
onion, garlic and spices. Add the
gourd and cook until soft.

NUTRITIONAL NOTES	
Per Portion	
Energy	280Kcals/1173KJ
Fat	12.2g
Saturated Fat	1.6g
Carbohydrate	31.1g
Fibre	4.2g

Aubergine Curry

A simple and delicious way of cooking aubergines which retains their full flavour.

INGREDIENTS

Serves 4

2 large aubergines (eggplant)
115g/4oz/1½ cups button
   (white) mushrooms
15ml/1 tbsp oil
2.5ml/½ tsp black mustard seeds
1 bunch spring onions (scallions),
   finely chopped
2 garlic cloves, crushed
1 fresh red chilli, finely chopped
2.5ml/½ tsp chilli powder
5ml/1 tsp ground cumin
5ml/1 tsp ground coriander
1.5ml/¼ tsp ground turmeric
5ml/1 tsp salt
400g/14oz can chopped tomatoes
15ml/1 tbsp chopped fresh coriander
   (cilantro), plus a sprig to garnish

1 Preheat the oven to 200°C/400°F/ Gas 6. Wrap each aubergine in foil and bake for 1 hour or until soft. Unwrap and leave to cool.

2 Cut the mushrooms in half, or in quarters, if large, and set aside.

3 While the aubergines are baking, heat the oil in a heavy pan and fry the mustard seeds for 2 minutes until they begin to splutter. Add the spring onions, mushrooms, garlic and chilli and fry for 5 minutes. Stir in the chilli powder, cumin, ground coriander, turmeric and salt and fry for 3–4 minutes. Add the tomatoes and simmer for 5 minutes.

4 Cut each of the aubergines in half lengthways and scoop out the soft flesh into a mixing bowl. Mash the flesh roughly with a fork.

5 Add the mashed aubergines and chopped fresh coriander to the saucepan. Bring to the boil and simmer for 5 minutes or until the sauce thickens. Serve garnished with a fresh coriander sprig.

NUTRITIONAL NOTES	
Per Portion	
Energy	99Kcals/413KJ
Fat	4.60g
Saturated Fat	0.45g
Carbohydrate	10.40g
Fibre	6.00g

_____ COOK'S TIP _____

This curry can be served as a vegetarian main course or as an accompaniment to a lamb or chicken dish. If preferred, you can use four large courgettes (zucchini) in place of the aubergines used here.

Mushroom Curry

This is a delicious way of cooking mushrooms. It goes well with meat dishes, but is also great served on its own.

INGREDIENTS

Serves 4

30ml/2 tbsp oil
2.5ml/½ tsp cumin seeds
1.5ml/¼ tsp black peppercorns
4 green cardamom pods
1.5ml/¼ tsp ground turmeric
1 onion, finely chopped
5ml/1 tsp ground cumin
5ml/1 tsp ground coriander
2.5ml/½ tsp garam masala
1 fresh green chilli, finely chopped
2 garlic cloves, crushed
2.5cm/1in piece fresh root
    ginger, grated
400g/14oz can chopped tomatoes
1.5ml/¼ tsp salt
450g/1lb/6 cups button (white)
    mushrooms, halved
chopped fresh coriander (cilantro),
    to garnish

NUTRITIONAL NOTES
Per Portion

Energy	113Kcals/469KJ
Fat	6.90g
Saturated Fat	0.88g
Carbohydrate	8.80g
Fibre	2.50g

COOK'S TIP

The distinctive flavour of mushrooms goes well with this mixture of spices. If you don't want to use button mushrooms, you can substitute any other mushrooms. Dried mushrooms can be added, if you like. Their intense flavour holds its own against the taste of the curry spices. Soak dried mushrooms before using, and add them to the recipe with the tomatoes.

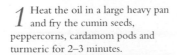

1 Heat the oil in a large heavy pan and fry the cumin seeds, peppercorns, cardamom pods and turmeric for 2–3 minutes.

2 Add the onion and fry for about 5 minutes until golden. Stir in the cumin, ground coriander and garam masala and fry for a further 2 minutes.

3 Add the chilli, garlic and ginger and fry for 2–3 minutes, stirring all the time to prevent the spices from sticking to the pan. Add the tomatoes and salt. Bring to the boil and simmer for 5 minutes.

4 Add the mushrooms. Cover and simmer over a low heat for 10 minutes. Garnish with chopped fresh coriander before serving.

Corn Cob Curry

Corn cobs are rubbed with lemon juice, salt and chilli powder and then roasted over charcoal in India. In season, the aroma of these treats tempts everyone to buy.

INGREDIENTS

Serves 4-6

4 whole corn cobs, fresh, canned
  or frozen
vegetable oil, for frying
1 large onion, finely chopped
2 garlic cloves, crushed
5cm/2in piece fresh root
  ginger, crushed
2.5ml/½ tsp ground turmeric
2.5ml/½ tsp onion seeds
2.5ml/½ tsp cumin seeds
2.5ml/½ tsp five-spice powder
chilli powder, to taste
6–8 curry leaves
2.5ml/½ tsp granulated sugar
200ml/7fl oz/scant 1 cup natural
  (plain) yogurt

1 Cut each corn cob in half, using a sharp, heavy knife or cleaver to make clean cuts and limit damage to the kernels.

2 Heat the oil in a large frying pan and fry the corn pieces until golden brown on all sides. Remove the corn-cobs and set aside.

3 Remove any excess oil, leaving about 30ml/2 tbsp in the pan. Grind the onion, garlic and ginger to a paste using a pestle and mortar or food processor. Remove and mix in all the spices, curry leaves and sugar.

4 Reheat the oil gently and fry the onion mixture until all the spices have blended well and the oil separates from the paste.

5 Cool the mixture and gradually fold in the yogurt. Mix well until you have a smooth sauce. Add the corn to the mixture and mix well so all the pieces are evenly covered with the sauce. Gently reheat for about 10 minutes or until the corn is tender. Serve hot.

NUTRITIONAL NOTES	
Per Portion	
Energy	214Kcals/888KJ
Fat	15.1g
Saturated Fat	2g
Carbohydrate	15.9g
Fibre	1.5g

Curried Stuffed Peppers

Hot, spicy and delicious, these peppers are often prepared for weddings in Hyderabad.

INGREDIENTS

Serves 4–6

15ml/1 tbsp sesame seeds
15ml/1 tbsp white poppy seeds
5ml/1 tsp coriander seeds
60ml/4 tbsp desiccated (dry unsweetened shredded) coconut
½ onion, sliced
2.5cm/1in piece fresh ginger, sliced
4 garlic cloves, sliced
handful of fresh coriander (cilantro)
6 fresh green chillies
60ml/4 tbsp vegetable oil
2 potatoes, boiled and coarsely mashed
salt, to taste
2 each, green, red and yellow (bell) peppers
30ml/2 tbsp sesame oil
5ml/1 tsp cumin seeds
60ml/4 tbsp tamarind juice

NUTRITIONAL NOTES	
Per Portion	
Energy	390Kcals/1617KJ
Fat	27.3g
Saturated Fat	10.4g
Carbohydrate	31.1g
Fibre	7.8g

1 In a frying pan, dry-fry the sesame, poppy and coriander seeds, then add the coconut and continue to roast until the coconut turns golden brown.

2 Add the onion, ginger, garlic, coriander (cilantro), and 2 of the chillies and roast for a further 5 minutes. Cool, and grind to a paste using a pestle and mortar or food processor. Put aside.

3 Heat 30ml/2 tbsp of the oil in a frying pan and fry the ground paste for 4–5 minutes. Add the potatoes and salt and stir well until the spices have blended evenly into the potatoes.

4 Trim the bases of the peppers so they stand, then slice off the tops and reserve. Remove the seeds and any white pith. Fill the peppers with equal amounts of the potato mixture and replace the tops.

5 Slit the remaining chillies and remove the seeds, if you like. Heat the sesame oil and remaining vegetable oil in a frying pan and fry the cumin seeds and the slit green chillies.

6 When the chillies turn white, add the tamarind juice and bring to the boil. Place the peppers over the mixture, cover the pan and cook until the peppers are just tender. Serve at once.

Sweetcorn and Pea Curry

Tender sweetcorn cooked in a spicy tomato sauce makes a flavoursome curry.

INGREDIENTS

Serves 4

6 frozen corn cobs, thawed
15ml/1 tbsp oil
2.5ml/½ tsp cumin seeds
1 onion, finely chopped
2 garlic cloves, crushed
1 fresh green chilli, finely chopped
15ml/1 tbsp curry paste
5ml/1 tsp ground coriander
5ml/1 tsp ground cumin
1.5ml/¼ tsp ground turmeric
2.5ml/½ tsp salt
2.5ml/½ tsp granulated sugar
400g/14oz can chopped tomatoes
15ml/1 tbsp tomato purée (paste)
150ml/¼ pint/⅔ cup water
115g/4oz/1 cup frozen peas, thawed
30ml/2 tbsp chopped fresh
    coriander (cilantro)
chapatis, to serve, optional

NUTRITIONAL NOTES	
Per Portion	
Energy	159Kcals/669KJ
Fat	5.20g
Saturated Fat	0.48g
Carbohydrate	23.00g
Fibre	4.60g

1 Using a sharp knife, cut each piece of corn in half crossways to make 12 equal pieces in total.

2 Bring a large pan of water to the boil and cook the corn cob pieces for 10–12 minutes. Drain well.

3 Heat the oil in a large heavy pan and fry the cumin seeds for 2 minutes or until they begin to splutter. Add the onion, garlic and chilli and fry for about 5–6 minutes until the onion is golden.

4 Add the curry paste and fry for 2 minutes. Stir in the remaining spices, salt and sugar and fry for a further 2–3 minutes, adding some water if the mixture is too dry.

5 Add the chopped tomatoes and tomato purée together with the water and simmer for 5 minutes or until the sauce thickens. Add the peas and cook for a further 5 minutes.

6 Stir in the pieces of corn and the fresh coriander and cook for 6–8 minutes more, until the corn and peas are tender. Serve with chapatis, for mopping up the rich sauce, if you like.

VARIATION

If you don't like peas you can replace them with the same quantity of thawed frozen broad (fava) beans.

Courgette Curry

Thickly sliced courgettes are combined with authentic Indian spices for a tasty vegetable curry.

INGREDIENTS

Serves 4

675g/1½lb courgettes (zucchini)
30ml/2 tbsp oil
2.5ml/½ tsp cumin seeds
2.5ml/½ tsp mustard seeds
1 onion, thinly sliced
2 garlic cloves, crushed
1.5ml/¼ tsp ground turmeric
1.5ml/¼ tsp chilli powder
5ml/1 tsp ground coriander
5ml/1 tsp ground cumin
2.5ml/½ tsp salt
15ml/1 tbsp tomato purée (paste)
400g/14oz can chopped tomatoes
150ml/¼ pint/⅔ cup water
15ml/1 tbsp chopped fresh
  coriander (cilantro)
5ml/1 tsp garam masala

1 Trim the ends from the courgettes and then cut them evenly into 1cm/½in thick slices.

COOK'S TIP

You can use medium-sized courgettes or the slightly larger ones for this dish; the very large ones have less flavour. Whichever size you choose, look for smooth, shiny courgettes without blemishes.

2 Heat the oil in a large heavy pan and fry the cumin and the mustard seeds for 2 minutes until they begin to splutter.

3 Add the onion and garlic and fry for about 5–6 minutes.

4 Add the turmeric, chilli powder, ground coriander, cumin and salt and fry for 2–3 minutes.

5 Add the sliced courgettes all at once, and cook for 5 minutes, stirring so they do not burn.

6 Mix together the tomato purée and chopped tomatoes and add to the pan with the water. Cover and simmer for 10 minutes until the sauce thickens.

7 Stir in the fresh coriander and garam masala, then cook for 5 minutes or until the courgettes are tender.

NUTRITIONAL NOTES	
Per Portion	
Energy	133Kcals/550KJ
Fat	7.20g
Saturated Fat	0.91g
Carbohydrate	11.60g
Fibre	2.80g

Mixed Vegetable Curry

A good all-round vegetable curry that goes well with most Indian meat dishes. You can use any combination of vegetables that are in season for this basic recipe.

INGREDIENTS

Serves 4

15ml/1 tbsp oil
2.5ml/½ tsp black mustard seeds
2.5ml/½ tsp cumin seeds
1 onion, thinly sliced
2 curry leaves
1 fresh green chilli, finely chopped
2.5cm/1in piece fresh root ginger, finely chopped
30ml/2 tbsp curry paste
1 small cauliflower, broken into florets
1 large carrot, thickly sliced
115g/4oz French (green) beans, cut into 2.5cm/1in lengths
1.5ml/¼ tsp ground turmeric
1.5ml/¼ tsp chilli powder
2.5ml/½ tsp salt
2 tomatoes, finely chopped
50g/2oz/½ cup frozen peas, thawed
150ml/¼ pint/⅔ cup vegetable stock
fresh curry leaves, to garnish

NUTRITIONAL NOTES	
Per Portion	
Energy	130Kcals/540KJ
Fat	6.20g
Saturated Fat	0.61g
Carbohydrate	12.30g
Fibre	6.20g

VARIATION

To turn this dish into a non-vegetarian main course, add some prawns (shrimp) or cubes of cooked chicken with the stock.

1 Heat the oil in a large heavy pan and fry the mustard seeds and cumin seeds for 2 minutes until they begin to splutter. If they are very lively, put a lid on the pan.

2 Add the onion and the curry leaves and fry for 5 minutes.

3 Add the chopped chilli and fresh ginger and fry for 2 minutes. Stir in the curry paste, mix well and fry for 3–4 minutes.

4 Add the cauliflower florets, sliced carrot and beans and cook for 4–5 minutes. Add the turmeric, chilli powder, salt and tomatoes and cook for 2–3 minutes.

5 Tip in the thawed peas and cook for a further 2–3 minutes.

6 Add the stock. Cover and simmer over a low heat for 10–15 minutes until all the vegetables are tender. Serve garnished with curry leaves.

Vegetable Korma

Careful blending of spices is an ancient art in India. Here the aim is to produce a subtle, aromatic curry rather than an assault on the senses.

INGREDIENTS

Serves 4

50g/2oz/¼ cup butter
2 onions, sliced
2 garlic cloves, crushed
2.5cm/1in piece fresh root ginger, grated
5ml/1 tsp ground cumin
15ml/1 tbsp ground coriander
6 cardamom pods
5cm/2in piece of cinnamon stick
5ml/1 tsp ground turmeric
1 fresh red chilli, seeded and
    finely chopped
1 potato, peeled and cut into
    2.5cm/1in cubes
1 small aubergine (eggplant), chopped
115g/4oz/1½ cups mushrooms,
    thickly sliced
175ml/6fl oz/¾ cup water
115g/4oz/1 cup green beans, cut into
    2.5cm/1in lengths
60ml/4 tbsp natural (plain) yogurt
150ml/¼ pint/⅔ cup double
    (heavy) cream
5ml/1 tsp garam masala
salt and black pepper
fresh coriander (cilantro) sprigs,
    to garnish
boiled rice and poppadums, to serve

----------- COOK'S TIP -----------

Try using canned chickpeas or butter (lima) beans to really bulk out this curry.

NUTRITIONAL NOTES
Per Portion

Energy	361Kcals/1494KJ
Fat	31.3g
Saturated Fat	19.3g
Carbohydrate	16.7g
Fibre	3.2g

1 Melt the butter in a heavy pan. Add the onions and cook for 5 minutes until soft. Add the garlic and ginger and cook for 2 minutes, then stir in the cumin, coriander, cardamom pods, cinnamon stick, turmeric and finely chopped chilli. Cook, stirring constantly, for 30 seconds.

2 Add the potato cubes, aubergine and mushrooms and the water. Cover the pan, bring to the boil, then lower the heat and simmer for 15 minutes.

3 Add the beans and cook, uncovered, for 5 minutes. With a slotted spoon, remove the vegetables to a warmed serving dish and keep hot.

4 Allow the cooking liquid to bubble up until it has reduced a little. Season with salt and pepper, then stir in the yogurt, cream and garam masala. Pour the sauce over the vegetables and garnish with fresh coriander. Serve with boiled rice and poppadums.

Sweet and Sour Vegetables with Paneer

The cheese used in this recipe is Indian paneer, which can be bought at some Asian stores; tofu can be used in its place.

INGREDIENTS

Serves 4

1 green (bell) pepper, seeded and cut into squares
1 yellow (bell) pepper, seeded and cut into squares
8 cherry tomatoes
8 cauliflower florets
8 pineapple chunks
8 cubes paneer
plain, boiled rice, to serve

For the seasoned oil

15ml/1 tbsp oil
30ml/2 tbsp lemon juice
5ml/1 tsp salt
5ml/1 tsp crushed black peppercorns
15ml/1 tbsp clear honey
30ml/2 tbsp chilli sauce

NUTRITIONAL NOTES	
Per Portion	
Energy	75Kcals/311KJ
Fat	3.30g
Saturated Fat	0.38g
Carbohydrate	9.90g
Fibre	2.10g

1 Preheat the grill (broiler) to hot. Thread the pepper squares, cherry tomatoes, cauliflower florets, pineapple chunks and paneer cubes on to four skewers, alternating the ingredients. Place the skewers on a flameproof dish or in a grill (broiler) pan.

2 In a small bowl, combine all the ingredients for the seasoned oil. If too thick, add 15ml/1 tbsp water.

--- COOK'S TIP ---

Metal skewers are ideal for this recipe. Some of the traditional Indian ones are very pretty, and will enhance the colour of the dish. Wooden or bamboo skewers can be used instead, but remember to soak them in water for at least 30 minutes before threading them with the vegetables and paneer, or the exposed tips may burn under the heat.

3 Brush the vegetables with the seasoned oil. Grill (broil) for about 10 minutes until the vegetables begin to darken slightly, turning the skewers regularly to cook evenly. Serve on a bed of plain boiled rice.

Spiced Vegetable Curry with Yogurt

This is a very delicately spiced vegetable dish that makes an appetizing snack when served with plain yogurt. It is also a good accompaniment to a main meal of heavily spiced curries.

INGREDIENTS

Serves 4-6

350g/12oz mixed vegetables, eg beans, peas, potatoes, cauliflower, carrots, cabbage, mangetouts (snow peas) and mushrooms
30ml/2 tbsp vegetable oil
5ml/1 tsp cumin seeds, freshly roasted
2.5ml/½ tsp mustard seeds
2.5ml/½ tsp onion seeds
5ml/1 tsp ground turmeric
2 garlic cloves, crushed
6–8 curry leaves
1 dried red chilli
salt, to taste
5ml/1 tsp granulated sugar
150ml/¼ pint/⅔ cup natural (plain) yogurt mixed with 1 tsp cornflour (cornstarch)

1 Prepare all the vegetables you have chosen: string the beans; thaw the peas, if frozen; cube the potatoes; cut the cauliflower into florets; dice the carrots; shred the cabbage; top and tail the mangetouts; wash the mushrooms and leave whole.

2 Heat a large pan with enough water to cook all the vegetables and bring to the boil. First add the potatoes and carrots and cook until nearly tender then add all the other vegetables and cook until crisp-tender. All the vegetables should be crunchy except the potatoes. Drain.

NUTRITIONAL NOTES	
Per Portion	
Energy	99Kcals/411KJ
Fat	6.1g
Saturated Fat	0.9g
Carbohydrate	6.5g
Fibre	2g

3 Heat the oil in a frying pan and fry the cumin, mustard and onion seeds, the turmeric, garlic, curry leaves and dried chilli gently until the garlic is golden brown and the chilli nearly burnt. Reduce the heat.

4 Fold in the drained vegetables, add the sugar and salt and gradually add the yogurt and cornflour mixture. When hot, serve at once.

Spicy Omelette

Another popular contribution by the Parsis, this irresistible omelette is known to them as *poro*. Parsi cuisine offers some unique flavours, which appeal to both Eastern and Western palates.

INGREDIENTS

Serves 4–6

30ml/2 tbsp vegetable oil
1 onion, finely chopped
2.5ml/½ tsp ground cumin
1 garlic clove, crushed
1 or 2 fresh green chillies, finely chopped
a few coriander (cilantro) sprigs,
  chopped, plus extra, to garnish
1 firm tomato, chopped
1 small potato, cubed and boiled
25g/1oz/¼ cup cooked peas
25g/1oz/¼ cup cooked corn,
  or drained canned corn
2 eggs, beaten
25g/1oz/¼ cup grated Cheddar cheese
  or Monterey Jack
salt and black pepper

1 Heat the oil in a karahi, wok or omelette pan, and add the onion, cumin, garlic, chillies, coriander, tomato, potato, peas and corn. Mix well.

NUTRITIONAL NOTES	
Per Portion	
Energy	167Kcals/694KJ
Fat	11.3g
Saturated Fat	3g
Carbohydrate	9.7g
Fibre	1.5g

2 Cook over a medium heat, stirring, for 5 minutes, until the potato and tomato are almost tender. Season well.

3 Preheat the grill (broiler) to high. Increase the heat under the pan and pour in the beaten eggs. Reduce the heat, cover and cook until the bottom layer is brown. Turn the omelette over and sprinkle with the grated cheese. Place under the hot grill (broiler) and cook until the egg sets and the cheese has melted.

4 Garnish the omelette with sprigs of coriander and serve with salad for a light lunch. If you prefer, serve it for breakfast, in the typical Parsi style.

—————— VARIATION ——————

You can use any vegetable with the potatoes. Try thickly sliced button (white) mushrooms, which can be added in step 1.

Eggs on Chipsticks

This is an unusual and delicious way of combining eggs with potato sticks, and is known as *sali pur eeda* in the Parsi language. The potato sticks are cooked with chillies and spices. Eggs are then placed on top of the potato mixture and gently cooked.

INGREDIENTS

Serves 4–6

225g/8oz salted chipsticks
2 fresh green chillies, finely chopped
a few coriander (cilantro) sprigs,
  chopped
1.5ml/¼ tsp ground turmeric
60ml/4 tbsp vegetable oil
75ml/5 tbsp water
6 eggs
3 spring onions (scallions),
  finely chopped
salt and black pepper

1 In a large bowl, mix the salted chipsticks with the chopped chillies, coriander and turmeric. Heat 30ml/2 tbsp of the oil in a heavy frying pan. Add the chipstick mixture and water. Cook until the chipsticks turn soft, and then crisp.

2 Place a dinner plate over the frying pan, and hold in place as you turn the pan over and carefully transfer the chipstick "pancake" on to the plate. Heat the remaining oil in the pan and slide the "pancake" back into the frying pan to brown the other side. Do this very gently, so no chipsticks break off.

3 Gently break the eggs over the top, cover the frying pan and leave the eggs to set over a low heat. Season well and sprinkle with spring onions. Cook until the base is crisp. Serve hot for breakfast in the Parsi style, or with chapatis and a salad for lunch or supper.

COOK'S TIP

As the chipsticks cook, the starch they contain will cause them to stick together. To encourage this, use a spoon to press them down.

NUTRITIONAL NOTES
Per Portion

Energy	482Kcals/2008KJ
Fat	33.3g
Saturated Fat	6.8g
Carbohydrate	36.6g
Fibre	1.6g

Cauliflower and Coconut Milk Curry

A delicious vegetable stew which combines coconut milk with spices and is perfect as a vegetarian main course or as part of a buffet.

INGREDIENTS

Serves 4
1 cauliflower
2 medium tomatoes
1 onion, chopped
2 garlic cloves, crushed
1 fresh green chilli, seeded
2.5ml/½ tsp ground turmeric
30ml/2 tbsp sunflower oil
400ml/14fl oz coconut milk
250ml/8fl oz/1 cup water
5ml/1 tsp granulated sugar
5ml/1 tsp tamarind pulp, soaked in
   45ml/3 tbsp warm water
salt

1 Trim the stalk from the cauliflower and divide into tiny florets. Peel the tomatoes if you like, then chop them into 1–2.5cm/½–1in pieces.

2 Grind the chopped onion, garlic, green chilli and ground turmeric to a paste in a food processor.

3 Heat the oil in a karahi, wok or large frying pan and fry the spice paste to bring out the aromatic flavours, without allowing it to brown.

4 Add the cauliflower florets and toss well to coat in the spices. Stir in the coconut milk, water, sugar and salt to taste. Simmer for 5 minutes. Strain the tamarind and reserve the juice.

5 Add the tamarind juice and chopped tomatoes to the pan then cook for 2–3 minutes only. Taste and check the seasoning and serve.

NUTRITIONAL NOTES	
Per Portion	
Energy	119Kcals/495KJ
Fat	6.7g
Saturated Fat	1.1g
Carbohydrate	11.5g
Fibre	2.3g

Scrambled Eggs with Chilli

This is a lovely way to liven up scrambled eggs. Prepare all the ingredients ahead so that the vegetables can be cooked quickly and retain crunch and colour.

INGREDIENTS

Serves 4
30ml/2 tbsp sunflower oil
1 onion, finely sliced
225g/8oz Chinese leaves, finely sliced
   or cut in diamonds
200g/7oz can corn kernels
1 small fresh red chilli, seeded and
   finely sliced
30ml/2 tbsp water
2 eggs, beaten
salt and black pepper
deep-fried onions, to garnish

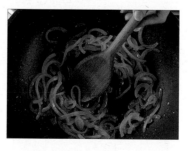

1 Heat a karahi, wok or deep pan. Add the oil and, when it is hot, fry the onion, until soft but not browned.

2 Add the Chinese leaves and toss over the heat until well mixed.

3 Add the corn, chilli and water. Cover with a lid and cook for 2 minutes.

4 Remove the lid and stir in the beaten eggs and seasoning. Stir constantly until the eggs are creamy and just set. Serve on warmed plates, scattered with crisp deep-fried onions.

NUTRITIONAL NOTES	
Per Portion	
Energy	171Kcals/711KJ
Fat	10.3g
Saturated Fat	1.8g
Carbohydrate	13.7g
Fibre	2.1g

Masala Chana

Chickpeas are used and cooked in a variety of ways all over the Indian subcontinent. Tamarind adds a sharp, tangy flavour.

INGREDIENTS

Serves 4

225g/8oz/1¼ cups dried chickpeas
50g/2oz tamarind stick
120ml/4fl oz/½ cup boiling water
30ml/2 tbsp oil
2.5ml/½ tsp cumin seeds
1 onion, finely chopped
2 garlic cloves, crushed
2.5cm/1in piece fresh root
   ginger, grated
1 fresh green chilli, finely chopped
5ml/1 tsp ground cumin
5ml/1 tsp ground coriander
1.5ml/¼ tsp ground turmeric
2.5ml/½ tsp salt
225g/8oz tomatoes, peeled and
   finely chopped
2.5ml/½ tsp garam masala
chopped fresh chillies and chopped
   onion, to garnish

2 Drain the chickpeas and place in a large pan with double the volume of cold water. Bring to the boil and boil vigorously for 10 minutes.

3 Skim off any scum that has risen to the surface of the liquid, using a slotted spoon. Lower the heat, cover the pan and simmer for 1½–2 hours or until the chickpeas are soft.

4 Meanwhile, break up the tamarind and soak in the boiling water for about 15 minutes. Rub the tamarind through a sieve into a bowl, discarding any stones and fibre left behind in the strainer.

5 Heat the oil in a large heavy pan and fry the cumin seeds for 2 minutes until they splutter. Add the onion, garlic, ginger and chilli and fry for 5 minutes.

6 Stir in the cumin and coriander, with the turmeric and salt and fry for 3–4 minutes. Add the chopped tomatoes. Bring to the boil and then simmer for 5 minutes.

7 Drain the chickpeas and add to the tomato mixture together with the garam masala and tamarind pulp. Cover and simmer gently for about 15 minutes. Garnish with the chopped chillies and onion before serving.

1 Put the chickpeas in a large bowl and cover with plenty of cold water. Leave to soak overnight.

--- COOK'S TIP ---

Tamarind is usually sold as compressed blocks of pulp and seeds. To use, break off a small piece and soak it in a few spoonfuls of hot water for 15 minutes. Strain off the water, pressing some of the pulp through the sieve. Discard the rest of the pulp.

NUTRITIONAL NOTES
Per Portion

Energy	313Kcals/1317KJ
Fat	9.40g
Saturated Fat	0.77g
Carbohydrate	44.60g
Fibre	1.50g

Vegetable Kashmiri

This is a wonderful vegetable curry, in which fresh mixed vegetables are cooked in a spicy aromatic yogurt sauce. The spicing is quite gentle, so it will appeal to most palates.

INGREDIENTS

Serves 4

10ml/2 tsp cumin seeds
8 black peppercorns
seeds from 2 green cardamom pods
5cm/2in piece of cinnamon stick
2.5ml/½ tsp grated nutmeg
30ml/2 tbsp oil
1 fresh green chilli, chopped
2.5cm/1in piece fresh root
 ginger, grated
5ml/1 tsp chilli powder
2.5ml/½ tsp salt
2 large potatoes, cut into 2.5cm/
 1in chunks
225g/8oz cauliflower, broken
 into florets
225g/8oz okra, trimmed and
 thickly sliced
150ml/¼ pint/⅔ cup natural (plain)
 low fat yogurt
150ml/¼ pint/⅔ cup vegetable stock
toasted flaked almonds and fresh
 coriander (cilantro) sprigs,
 to garnish

1 Grind the cumin seeds and peppercorns, cardamom seeds, cinnamon stick and nutmeg to a fine powder using a spice blender or a pestle and mortar.

2 Heat the oil in a large heavy pan and fry the chilli and ginger for 2 minutes, stirring all the time.

3 Add the chilli powder, salt and ground spice mixture and fry for about 2–3 minutes, stirring all the time to prevent the spices from sticking to the bottom of the pan.

NUTRITIONAL NOTES	
Per Portion	
Energy	220Kcals/920KJ
Fat	8.20g
Saturated Fat	1.02g
Carbohydrate	29.10g
Fibre	4.70g

COOK'S TIP

Instead of the vegetable mixture used here, try cooking other ones of your choice in this lovely yogurt sauce.

4 Stir in the potatoes, cover and cook for 10 minutes over a low heat, stirring from time to time.

5 Add the cauliflower and okra and cook for 5 minutes.

6 Add the yogurt and stock. Bring to the boil, then reduce the heat. Cover and simmer for 20 minutes, or until all the vegetables are tender. Garnish with the toasted almonds and the coriander sprigs.

Basmati Rice and Peas with Curry Leaves

This is a very simple rice dish, but it is full of flavour.

INGREDIENTS

Serves 4

300g/11oz/1½ cups basmati rice
15ml/1 tbsp oil
6–8 curry leaves
1.5ml/¼ tsp mustard seeds
1.5ml/¼ tsp onion seeds
30ml/2 tbsp fresh fenugreek leaves
5ml/1 tsp crushed garlic
5ml/1 tsp grated fresh root ginger
5ml/1 tsp salt
115g/4oz/1 cup frozen peas
475ml/16fl oz/2 cups water

COOK'S TIP

Curry leaves freeze very well, so it is worth keeping a stock in the freezer.

1 Wash the rice well and leave it to soak in water for 30 minutes.

NUTRITIONAL NOTES	
Per Portion	
Energy	336Kcals/1425KJ
Fat	5.96g
Saturated Fat	1.09g
Carbohydrate	67.67g
Fibre	1.83g

2 Heat the oil in a heavy pan and add the curry leaves, mustard seeds, onion seeds, fenugreek leaves, garlic, ginger and salt and stir-fry for 2–3 minutes.

3 Drain the rice, add it to the pan and stir gently.

4 Add the frozen peas and water and bring to the boil. Lower the heat, cover with a lid and cook for 15–20 minutes. Remove from the heat and leave to stand, still covered, for 10 minutes.

5 When ready to serve, fluff up the rice with a fork. Spoon the mixture onto serving plates.

Tomato Biryani

Although generally served as an accompaniment to meat, poultry or fish dishes, this tasty rice dish can also be eaten as a complete meal on its own.

INGREDIENTS

Serves 4

400g/14oz/2 cups basmati rice
15ml/1 tbsp oil
2.5ml/½ tsp onion seeds
1 medium onion, sliced
2 medium tomatoes, sliced
1 orange or yellow (bell) pepper,
   seeded and sliced
5ml/1 tsp grated fresh root ginger
5ml/1 tsp crushed garlic
5ml/1 tsp chilli powder
30ml/2 tbsp chopped fresh
   coriander (cilantro)
1 medium potato, diced
7.5ml/1½ tsp salt
50g/2oz/½ cup frozen peas
750ml/1¼ pints/3 cups water

1 Wash the rice well and leave it to soak in water for 30 minutes. Heat the oil in a heavy pan and fry the onion seeds for about 30 seconds. Add the sliced onion and fry for 5 minutes, stirring occasionally to prevent the slices from sticking to the pan.

COOK'S TIP

Plain rice can look a bit dull; it is greatly enhanced by adding colourful ingredients such as tomatoes, peppers and peas.

2 Add the sliced tomatoes and peppers, ginger, garlic and chilli powder. Stir-fry for 2 minutes.

3 Add the fresh coriander, potato, salt and peas and stir-fry over a medium heat for a further 5 minutes.

4 Tip the rice into a colander and drain it thoroughly. Add it to the spiced tomato and potato mixture and stir-fry for 1–2 minutes.

5 Pour in the water and bring to the boil, then lower the heat to medium. Cover and cook the rice for 12–15 minutes. Leave to stand for 5 minutes and then serve.

NUTRITIONAL NOTES	
Per Portion	
Energy	409Kcals/1710KJ
Fat	3.70g
Saturated Fat	0.44g
Carbohydrate	89.70g
Fibre	2.40g

Vegetable Biryani

This is a good-tempered dish made from everyday ingredients, and thus indispensable for the cook catering for an unexpected vegetarian guest. It is extremely low in fat, but packed full of exciting flavours.

INGREDIENTS

Serves 4–6

175g/6oz/scant 1 cup long-grain rice
2 whole cloves
seeds from 2 cardamom pods
450ml/¾ pint/scant 2 cups
   vegetable stock
2 garlic cloves
1 small onion, roughly chopped
5ml/1 tsp cumin seeds
5ml/1 tsp ground coriander
2.5ml/½ tsp ground turmeric
2.5ml/½ tsp chilli powder
salt and black pepper
1 large potato, cut into 2.5cm/
   1in cubes
2 carrots, sliced
½ cauliflower, broken into florets
50g/2oz green beans, cut into 2.5cm/
   1in lengths
30ml/2 tbsp chopped fresh coriander
   (cilantro), plus extra to garnish
30ml/2 tbsp lime juice

NUTRITIONAL NOTES	
Per Portion (6)	
Energy	260Kcals/1100KJ
Fat	1.90g
Saturated Fat	0.07g
Carbohydrate	55.80g
Fibre	3.20g

___ VARIATIONS ___

Substitute other vegetables for the ones chosen here, if you like. Courgettes (zucchini), broccoli, parsnip and sweet potatoes would all be excellent choices. Or add some toasted almond slices.

1 Wash the rice and put it with the cloves and cardamom seeds into a large heavy pan. Pour over the stock and bring to the boil.

2 Reduce the heat, cover the pan and simmer for 20 minutes or until all the stock has been absorbed.

3 Meanwhile, put the garlic cloves, onion, cumin seeds, ground coriander, turmeric, chilli powder and seasoning into a blender or food processor together with 30ml/2 tbsp water. Blend to a smooth paste. Scrape the paste into a flameproof casserole which is large enough to hold all the vegetables.

4 Preheat the oven to 180°C/350°F/ Gas 4. Cook the spicy paste in the casserole over a low heat for 2 minutes, stirring occasionally.

5 Add the potato cubes, carrots, cauliflower, beans and 90ml/6 tbsp water. Cover and cook over a low heat for 12 minutes, stirring occasionally. Add the chopped fresh coriander.

6 Remove the cloves from the rice. Spoon the rice over the vegetables. Sprinkle with the lime juice. Cover and cook in the oven for 25 minutes or until the vegetables are tender. Fluff up the rice with a fork before serving and garnish with more coriander.

Pea and Mushroom Pulao

Tiny white mushrooms and petits pois or baby peas look great in this delectable rice dish.

INGREDIENTS

Serves 6

450g/1lb/2¼ cups basmati rice
15ml/1 tbsp oil
2.5ml/½ tsp cumin seeds
2 black cardamom pods
2 cinnamon sticks
3 garlic cloves, sliced
5ml/1 tsp salt
1 medium tomato, sliced
50g/2oz/²⁄³ cup button
   (white) mushrooms
75g/3oz/¾ cup petits pois (baby peas)
750ml/1¼ pints/3 cups water

1 Wash the rice well and leave it to soak in water for 30 minutes.

2 In a medium heavy pan, heat the oil and add the spices, garlic and salt.

3 Add the tomato and mushrooms and stir-fry for 2–3 minutes.

4 Tip the rice into a colander and drain it thoroughly. Add it to the pan with the peas. Stir gently, making sure that you do not break up the grains of rice.

5 Add the water and bring to the boil. Lower the heat, cover and continue to cook for 15–20 minutes. Just before serving, remove the lid from the pan and fluff up the rice with a fork. Spoon into a dish and serve immediately.

NUTRITIONAL NOTES	
Per Portion	
Energy	423Kcals/1768KJ
Fat	3.80g
Saturated Fat	0.39g
Carbohydrate	92.90g
Fibre	1.30g

——— COOK'S TIP ———

Petits pois are small green peas, picked when very young. The tender, sweet peas inside the immature pods are ideal for this delicately flavoured rice dish. However, if you can't find petit pois, garden peas can be used instead.

Nut Pulao

Versions of this rice dish are cooked throughout Asia, always with the best-quality long grain rice. In India, basmati rice is the natural choice. In this particular interpretation of the recipe, walnuts and cashews are added. Serve the pulao with a raita or a bowl of yogurt.

INGREDIENTS

Serves 4

15–30ml/1–2 tbsp vegetable oil
1 onion, chopped
1 garlic clove, crushed
1 large carrot, coarsely grated
225g/8oz/generous 1 cup basmati rice,
   soaked for 20–30 minutes
5ml/1 tsp cumin seeds
10ml/2 tsp ground coriander
10ml/2 tsp black mustard
   seeds
4 green cardamom pods
450ml/¾ pint/scant 2 cups
   vegetable stock
1 bay leaf
75g/3oz/¾ cup unsalted walnuts and
   cashew nuts
salt and black pepper
fresh coriander (cilantro) sprigs,
   to garnish

1 Heat the oil in a karahi, wok or large pan. Fry the onion, garlic and carrot for 3–4 minutes. Drain the rice and add with the spices. Cook for 2 minutes, stirring to coat the grains in oil.

2 Pour in the vegetable stock, stirring. Add the bay leaf and season well.

3 Bring to the boil, lower the heat, cover and simmer very gently for 10–12 minutes without stirring.

4 Remove the pan from the heat without lifting the lid. Leave to stand for 5 minutes, then check the rice. If it is cooked, there will be small steam holes on the surface of the rice. Discard the bay leaf and the cardamom pods.

5 Stir in the walnuts and cashew nuts and check the seasoning. Spoon on to a warmed platter, garnish with the fresh coriander and serve.

NUTRITIONAL NOTES	
Per Portion	
Energy	376Kcals/1562KJ
Fat	16g
Saturated Fat	1.4g
Carbohydrate	50g
Fibre	1.6g

Lentils and Rice

Lentils are cooked with whole and ground spices, potato, rice and onion to produce a tasty and nutritious meal.

INGREDIENTS

Serves 4

150g/5oz/¾ cup tuvar dhal or red split lentils
115g/4oz/½ cup basmati rice
1 large potato
1 large onion
30ml/2 tbsp oil
4 whole cloves
1.5ml/¼ tsp cumin seeds
1.5ml/¼ tsp ground turmeric
10ml/2 tsp salt
300ml/½ pint/1¼ cups water

1 Wash the tuvar dhal or red split lentils and rice in several changes of cold water. Put into a bowl and cover with water. Leave to soak for 15 minutes, then tip into a strainer and drain well.

NUTRITIONAL NOTES
Per Portion

Energy	332Kcals/1396KJ
Fat	6.70g
Saturated Fat	0.76g
Carbohydrate	58.60g
Fibre	3.40g

2 Peel the potato, then cut it into 2.5cm/1in chunks.

3 Using a sharp knife, thinly slice the onion and set aside for later.

4 Heat the oil in a large heavy pan and fry the cloves and cumin seeds for 2 minutes until the seeds are beginning to splutter.

5 Add the onion and potato chunks and fry for 5 minutes. Add the lentils, rice, turmeric and salt and fry for a further 3 minutes.

6 Add the water. Bring to the boil, cover and simmer gently for 15–20 minutes until all the water has been absorbed and the potato chunks are tender. Leave to stand, covered, for about 10 minutes before serving.

COOK'S TIP

Red split lentils are widely available in most supermarkets. Before cooking they are salmon-coloured and they turn a pale, dull yellow during cooking. They have a mild, pleasant, nutty flavour. Soaking them in water speeds up the cooking process but isn't strictly necessary.

Rice Layered with Bengal Gram

Bhori Muslims in India have their own special style of cooking and have adapted many of the traditional dishes from other Indian communities. This rice and lentil dish is served with a gourd curry, or *palida*, which is prominently flavoured with fenugreek and soured with dried mangosteen (kokum). Lemon juice will provide the same effect.

INGREDIENTS

Serves 4-6

175g/6oz/²⁄₃ cup bengal gram or
   lentils of own choice
600ml/1 pint/2¹⁄₂ cups water
2.5ml/¹⁄₂ tsp ground turmeric
50g/2oz deep-fried onions, crushed
45ml/3 tbsp green masala paste
few fresh mint and coriander (cilantro)
   leaves, chopped
salt, to taste
350g/12oz/1³⁄₄ cups basmati rice, cooked
30ml/2 tbsp ghee

For the curry

60ml/4 tbsp vegetable oil
1.5ml/¹⁄₄ tsp fenugreek seeds
15g/¹⁄₂oz dried fenugreek leaves
2 garlic cloves, crushed
5ml/1 tsp ground coriander
5ml/1 tsp cumin seeds
5ml/1 tsp chilli powder
60ml/4 tbsp gram flour mixed with
   60ml/4 tbsp water
450g/1lb bottle gourd, peeled, pith
   and seeds removed and cut into
   bite-size pieces, or marrow (large
   zucchini) or firm courgettes (zucchini) prepared in the same way
175ml/6fl oz/³⁄₄ cup tomato juice
6 dried mangosteen (kokum), or juice
   of 3 lemons
salt, to taste

1 For the rice, boil the bengal gram in the water with the turmeric until the grains are soft but not mushy. Drain and reserve the water for the curry.

2 Toss the bengal gram gently with the deep-fried onions, green masala paste, chopped mint and coriander. Stir in salt to taste.

3 Grease a heavy pan and place a layer of rice in the bottom. Add the bengal gram mixture and another layer of the remaining rice. Place small knobs of ghee on top, sprinkle with a little water and heat gently until steam rises from the mixture.

4 To make the curry, heat the oil in a pan and fry the fenugreek seeds and leaves and garlic until the garlic turns golden brown.

5 Mix the ground coriander, cumin and chilli powder to a paste with a little water. Add to the pan and simmer until all the water has evaporated.

6 Add the gram flour paste, with the gourd or alternative vegetable. Pour in the tomato juice and add the mangosteen and salt. Cook until the gourd is soft and transparent. Serve hot with the rice.

NUTRITIONAL NOTES	
Per Portion	
Energy	536Kcals/2250KJ
Fat	14g
Saturated Fat	1.8g
Carbohydrate	82.3g
Fibre	4.9g

Root Vegetable Gratin with Indian Spices

Subtly spiced with curry powder, turmeric, coriander and mild chilli powder, this rich gratin is substantial enough to serve on its own for lunch or supper. It also makes a good accompaniment to a vegetable or bean curry.

INGREDIENTS

Serves 4

2 large potatoes, total weight about
  450g/1lb
2 sweet potatoes, total weight about
  275g/10oz
175g/6oz celeriac
15ml/1 tbsp unsalted (sweet) butter
5ml/1 tsp curry powder
5ml/1 tsp ground turmeric
2.5ml/½ tsp ground coriander
5ml/1 tsp mild chilli powder
3 shallots, chopped
150ml/¼ pint/⅔ cup single
  (light) cream
150ml/¼ pint/⅔ cup milk
salt and black pepper
chopped fresh flat leaf parsley,
  to garnish

1 Peel the potatoes, sweet potatoes and celeriac and cut into thin, even slices using a sharp knife or the slicing attachment on a food processor. Immediately place the vegetables in a bowl of cold water to prevent them from discolouring.

2 Preheat the oven to 180°C/350°F/ Gas 4. Heat half the butter in a heavy pan, add the curry powder, ground turmeric and coriander and half the chilli powder. Cook for 2 minutes, then leave to cool slightly. Drain the vegetables, then pat them dry with kitchen paper. Place in a bowl, add the spice mixture and the shallots and mix well.

3 Arrange the vegetables in a shallow baking dish, seasoning well with salt and pepper between the layers. Mix together the cream and milk, pour the mixture over the vegetables, then sprinkle the remaining chilli powder on top.

4 Cover the dish with baking parchment and bake for 45 minutes. Remove the baking parchment, dot the vegetables with the remaining butter and bake for a further 50 minutes, or until the top is golden brown. Serve the gratin garnished with chopped parsley.

NUTRITIONAL NOTES	
Per Portion	
Energy	205Kcals/863KJ
Fat	5.1g
Saturated Fat	2.9g
Carbohydrate	36.9g
Fibre	4.7g

Rice and Vegetable Side Dishes and Light Salads

ALTHOUGH DEFINED as side dishes, the recipes in this chapter play an important role in Indian cuisine, and their size makes them especially versatile. They can be served alongside curries, as simple snacks, or enjoyed as main courses. Tomato and Spinach Pulao, for instance, makes a satisfying supper, whether served solo or in the company of another curry, such as Masala Okra or Bombay Potatoes.

Some dishes simply refuse to be sidelined. Stuffed Bananas, for instance, is a real showstopper. A popular Indian treat, they taste as intriguing as they look, and would make an excellent centrepiece for a special occasion meal.

Also included in this chapter are several light and tasty salads. While not all are authentically Indian, they have been selected for their cooling qualities, and are the perfect partners for spicy dishes. Vegetables, fruits and nuts all feature, and there's even a recipe for Coronation Chicken.

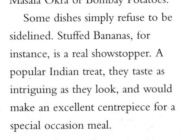

Saffron Rice

The saffron crocus is a perennial bulb that only flowers for two weeks of the year, and each stigma has to be removed by hand and dried with care. Consequently, saffron is said to be worth its weight in gold. Kashmir in the northern region of India is a major producer, so it isn't surprising that the subcontinent has some wonderful recipes for the spice.

INGREDIENTS

Serves 6
450g/1lb/2⅓ cups basmati rice
750ml/1¼ pints/3 cups water
3 green cardamom pods
2 cloves
5ml/1 tsp salt
45ml/3 tbsp semi-skimmed
  (low-fat) milk
2.5ml/½ tsp saffron threads, crushed

NUTRITIONAL NOTES	
Per Portion	
Energy	273Kcals/1141KJ
Fat	0.5g
Saturated Fat	0.1g
Carbohydrate	60.2g
Fibre	0g

1 Wash the rice, put it in a bowl and pour over water to cover. Leave to soak for 20 minutes.

2 Drain the basmati rice and put it in a large pan with the measured water. Add the cardamoms, cloves and salt. Stir, then bring to the boil. Lower the heat and cover tightly, and simmer for 5 minutes.

3 Meanwhile, place the milk in a small pan. Add the saffron threads and heat through gently.

4 Pour the saffron milk over the rice and stir. Cover again and continue cooking over a low heat for 5–6 minutes.

5 Remove the pan from the heat without lifting the lid. Leave the rice to stand for about 5 minutes, then fork through just before serving.

COOK'S TIP

Washing and soaking the rice before cooking makes it fluffier.

Caramelized Basmati Rice

This dish is the traditional accompaniment to a dhansak curry. Sugar is caramelized in hot oil before the rice is added, along with a few whole spices.

INGREDIENTS

Serves 4

225g/8oz/generous 1 cup basmati rice
45ml/3 tbsp vegetable oil
20ml/4 tsp granulated sugar
4–5 green cardamom pods, bruised
2.5cm/1in piece cinnamon stick
4 cloves
1 bay leaf, crumpled
½ tsp salt
475ml/16fl oz/2 cups hot water

1 Wash the rice, put it in a bowl and pour over water to cover. Leave to soak for 20 minutes.

2 Drain the rice in a colander, shaking it a little as you do so. Run the washed grains through your fingers to check that there is no excess water trapped between them. Set aside.

3 In a large pan, heat the vegetable oil over a medium heat. When the oil is hot, sprinkle the granulated sugar over the surface and wait until it has caramelized. Do not stir.

4 Reduce the heat to low and add the spices and bay leaf. Let sizzle for about 15–20 seconds, then add the rice and salt. Fry gently, stirring, for 2–3 minutes.

5 Pour in the water and bring to the boil. Let it boil steadily for 2 minutes then reduce the heat to very low. Cover the pan and cook for 8 minutes.

6 Remove the rice from the heat and let it stand for 6–8 minutes. Gently fluff up the rice with a fork and transfer to a warmed dish to serve.

NUTRITIONAL NOTES	
Per Portion	
Energy	276Kcals/1150KJ
Fat	8.5g
Saturated Fat	1g
Carbohydrate	44.9g
Fibre	0g

Sultana and Cashew Pulao

The secret of a perfect pulao is to wash the rice thoroughly, then soak it briefly. This softens and moistens the grains, enabling the rice to absorb moisture during cooking, which results in fluffier rice.

INGREDIENTS

Serves 4

600ml/1 pint/2½ cups hot chicken or vegetable stock
generous pinch of saffron threads
50g/2oz/¼ cup butter
1 onion, chopped
1 garlic clove, crushed
2.5cm/1in piece cinnamon stick
6 green cardamom pods
1 bay leaf
250g/9oz/1⅓ cups basmati rice, soaked in water for 20–30 minutes
50g/2oz/⅓ cup sultanas (golden raisins)
15ml/1 tbsp vegetable oil
50g/2oz/½ cup cashew nuts
naan bread and tomato and onion salad, to serve

1 Pour the hot chicken stock into a jug (pitcher). Stir in the saffron threads and set aside.

2 Heat the butter in a pan and fry the onion and garlic for 5 minutes. Stir in the cinnamon stick, cardamoms and bay leaf and cook for 2 minutes.

3 Drain the rice and add to the pan, then cook, stirring, for 2 minutes more. Pour in the saffron stock and add the sultanas. Bring to the boil, stir, then lower the heat, cover and cook gently for 10 minutes or until the rice is tender and all the liquid has been absorbed.

4 Meanwhile, heat the oil in a wok, karahi or large pan and fry the cashew nuts until browned. Drain on kitchen paper, then sprinkle the cashew nuts over the rice. Serve with naan bread and tomato and onion salad.

COOK'S TIP

Saffron powder can be used instead of saffron threads, if you prefer. Dissolve it in the hot stock.

NUTRITIONAL NOTES

Per Portion

Energy	462Kcals/1922KJ
Fat	19.5g
Saturated Fat	8g
Carbohydrate	63.9g
Fibre	1.2g

Tomato and Spinach Pulao

A tasty and nourishing dish for vegetarians and meat eaters alike. Serve it with another vegetable curry, or with tandoori chicken, marinated fried fish or shammi kabab. Add a cooling fruit raita for a completely balanced meal.

INGREDIENTS

Serves 4

30ml/2 tbsp vegetable oil
15ml/1 tbsp ghee or unsalted
  (sweet) butter
1 onion, chopped
2 garlic cloves, crushed
3 tomatoes, peeled and chopped
225g/8oz/generous 1 cup brown
  basmati rice
10ml/2 tsp dhana jeera powder or
  5ml/1 tsp ground coriander and
  5ml/1 tsp ground cumin
2 carrots, coarsely grated
900ml/1½ pints/3¾ cups
  vegetable stock
275g/10oz young spinach leaves
50g/2oz/½ cup unsalted cashew nuts
salt and black pepper
naan bread, to serve

1 Wash the basmati rice. Place it in a bowl, cover with cold water and leave to soak for 20 minutes.

2 Drain the rice and place it in a large pan of boiling salted water, bring back to the boil and cook for 10 minutes.

3 Heat the oil and ghee or butter in a karahi, wok or large pan, and fry the onion and garlic for 4–5 minutes until soft. Add the tomatoes and cook for 3–4 minutes, stirring, until the mixture thickens.

4 Drain the rice, add it to the pan and cook for a further 1–2 minutes, stirring, until the grains of rice are coated.

5 Stir in the dhana jeera powder or coriander and cumin, then add the carrots. Season with salt and pepper. Pour in the stock and stir well to mix.

6 Bring to the boil, then cover tightly and simmer over a very gentle heat for 20–25 minutes, until the rice is tender.

7 Lay the spinach on the surface of the rice, cover again, and cook for a further 2–3 minutes, until the spinach has wilted. Fold the spinach into the rest of the rice.

8 Fry the cashew nuts until lightly browned and sprinkle over the rice mixture. Serve with naan bread.

NUTRITIONAL NOTES	
Per Portion	
Energy	402Kcals/1687KJ
Fat	17.1g
Saturated Fat	4.4g
Carbohydrate	56.4g
Fibre	4.8g

Basmati Rice with Vegetables

Serve this delectable dish with roast chicken, lamb cutlets or pan-fried fish. Add the vegetables near the end of cooking so that they remain crisp.

Ingredients

Serves 4

350g/12oz/1¾ cups basmati rice
45ml/3 tbsp vegetable oil
1 onion, chopped
2 garlic cloves, crushed
750ml/1¼ pints/3 cups water or
   vegetable stock
115g/4oz/⅔ cup fresh or drained
   canned corn
1 red or green (bell) pepper, seeded
   and chopped
1 large carrot, grated
fresh chervil sprigs, to garnish

1 Wash the rice in a sieve, soak in cold water for 20 minutes, then drain very thoroughly.

2 Heat the oil in a large pan and fry the onion for a few minutes over a medium heat until it starts to soften.

Nutritional Notes	
Per Portion	
Energy	454Kcals/1897KJ
Fat	9.7g
Saturated Fat	1.2g
Carbohydrate	82.7g
Fibre	2.3g

3 Add the rice to the pan and fry for about 10 minutes, stirring constantly to prevent the rice from sticking to the base of the pan. Stir in the crushed garlic.

4 Pour in the water or stock and stir well. Bring to the boil, then lower the heat. Cover and simmer for 10 minutes.

5 Sprinkle the corn over the rice, spread the chopped pepper on top and sprinkle over the grated carrot. Cover tightly and steam over a low heat until the rice is tender, then mix with a fork. Pile on to a serving plate and garnish with chervil.

Basmati Rice with Potato

Rice is eaten at all meals in Indian and Pakistani homes. There are several ways of cooking rice and mostly whole spices are used. Always choose a good-quality basmati rice.

INGREDIENTS

Serves 4

300g/11oz/1½ cups basmati rice
15ml/1 tbsp oil
1 small cinnamon stick
1 bay leaf
1.5ml/¼ tsp black cumin seeds
3 green cardamom pods
1 medium onion, sliced
5ml/1 tsp grated fresh root ginger
5ml/1 tsp crushed garlic
1.5ml/¼ tsp ground turmeric
7.5ml/1½ tsp salt
1 large potato, roughly diced
475ml/16fl oz/2 cups water
15ml/1 tbsp chopped fresh
  coriander (cilantro)

1 Wash the rice well and leave it to soak in water for 20 minutes. Heat the oil in a heavy pan, add the cinnamon, bay leaf, black cumin seeds, cardamoms and onion and cook for about 2 minutes.

2 Add the ginger, garlic, turmeric, salt and potato and cook for 1 minute.

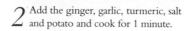

3 Drain the rice very well. Add it to the potato and spices in the pan.

4 Stir to mix, then pour in the water followed by the coriander. Cover the pan with a lid and cook for 15–20 minutes. Remove from the heat and leave to stand, still covered, for 5–10 minutes before serving.

COOK'S TIP

It is important to observe the standing time of this dish before serving. Use a slotted spoon to serve the rice and potato mixture and handle it gently to avoid breaking the delicate grains of rice.

NUTRITIONAL NOTES	
Per Portion	
Energy	371Kcals/1572KJ
Fat	5.72g
Saturated Fat	1.03g
Carbohydrate	77.36g
Fibre	1.62g

Tricolour Pulao

Most Indian restaurants in the West serve this popular vegetable pulao, which has three different vegetables. The effect is easily achieved with canned or frozen vegetables, but for entertaining or a special occasion dinner, you may prefer to use fresh produce.

INGREDIENTS

Serves 4–6

225g/8oz/1 cup basmati rice
30ml/2 tbsp vegetable oil
2.5ml/½ tsp cumin seeds
2 dried bay leaves
4 green cardamom pods
4 cloves
1 onion, finely chopped
1 carrot, finely diced
50g/2oz/½ cup frozen peas, thawed
50g/2oz/⅓ cup frozen
   corn, thawed
25g/1oz/¼ cup cashew nuts,
   lightly fried
475ml/16fl oz/2 cups water
1.5ml/¼ tsp ground cumin
salt

1 Wash the rice, then soak it in cold water for 20 minutes.

2 Heat the oil in a karahi, wok, or large pan over a medium heat, and fry the cumin seeds for 2 minutes. Add the bay leaves, cardamoms and cloves, and fry gently for 2 minutes more, stirring the spices from time to time.

3 Add the onion and fry until lightly browned. Stir in the diced carrot and cook, stirring, for 3–4 minutes.

4 Drain the soaked basmati rice and add to the contents in the pan. Stir well to mix. Add the peas, corn and fried cashew nuts.

5 Add the measured water and the ground cumin, and stir in salt to taste. Bring to the boil, cover and simmer for 15 minutes over a low heat until all the water is absorbed.

6 Leave to stand, covered, for 10 minutes. Fluff up the rice with a fork, transfer to a warmed dish and serve.

NUTRITIONAL NOTES
Per Portion

Energy	331Kcals/1378KJ
Fat	9.4g
Saturated Fat	1.4g
Carbohydrate	54.1g
Fibre	2g

Green Lentils and Rice

Also known as continental lentils, green lentils retain their shape and colour when cooked.

INGREDIENTS

Serves 4-6

350g/12oz/1¾ cups patna rice
175g/6oz/⅔ cup green split lentils
50g/2oz/¼ cup ghee
1 onion, finely chopped
2 garlic cloves, crushed
2.5cm/1in piece ginger, shredded
4 fresh green chillies, chopped
4 cloves
2.5cm/1in piece cinnamon stick
4 green cardamom pods
5ml/1 tsp ground turmeric
salt, to taste
600ml/1 pint/2½ cups water

1 Wash the rice and lentils, then soak them in a bowl of cold water for 20 minutes.

2 Gently heat the ghee in a large heavy pan with a tight-fitting cover and fry the onion, garlic, ginger, chillies, cloves, cinnamon, cardamoms, turmeric and salt until the onion is soft and translucent.

3 Drain the rice and lentils, add to the spices; sauté for 2–3 minutes. Add the water and bring to the boil. Reduce the heat, cover and cook for about 20–25 minutes or until all the water has been absorbed.

4 Take the pan off the heat and leave to rest with the lid on for 5 minutes. Just before serving gently toss the mixture with a flat spatula.

NUTRITIONAL NOTES	
Per Portion	
Energy	669Kcals/2793KJ
Fat	23.5g
Saturated Fat	15g
Carbohydrate	97.4g
Fibre	2.7g

Courgettes with Split Lentils

This recipe also works well with split red lentils.

INGREDIENTS

Serves 4-6

225g/8oz courgettes (zucchini), cut into wedges
175g/6oz/⅔ cup mung dhal or yellow split peas
2.5ml/½ tsp ground turmeric
60ml/4 tbsp vegetable oil
1 large onion, finely sliced
2 garlic cloves, crushed
2 fresh green chillies, chopped
2.5ml/½ tsp mustard seeds
2.5ml/½ tsp cumin seeds
1.5ml/¼ tsp asafoetida
few fresh coriander (cilantro) and mint leaves, chopped
6–8 curry leaves
salt, to taste
2.5ml/½ tsp granulated sugar
200g/7oz can chopped tomatoes
60ml/4 tbsp lemon juice

1 In a pan, simmer the lentils and turmeric in 300ml/½ pint/1¼ cups water, until cooked but not mushy.

2 Heat the oil in a frying pan and fry the remaining ingredients except the lemon juice. Cover and cook until the courgettes are nearly tender but still crunchy.

3 Fold in the drained lentils and the lemon juice. If the dish is too dry, add some of the cooking water. Reheat and serve.

NUTRITIONAL NOTES	
Per Portion	
Energy	278Kcals/1165KJ
Fat	12g
Saturated Fat	1.5g
Carbohydrate	31.9g
Fibre	3.9g

Creamy Black Lentils

Black lentils or urad dhal are available whole, split, and skinned and split. Generally, both split, and skinned and split versions are used in west and south Indian cooking, whereas whole black lentils are a typical ingredient in the north.

INGREDIENTS

Serves 4–6

175g/6oz/¾ cup black lentils, soaked
50g/2oz/¼ cup red split lentils
120ml/4fl oz/½ cup double
 (heavy) cream
120ml/4fl oz/½ cup natural
 (plain) yogurt
5ml/1 tsp cornflour (cornstarch)
40g/1½oz/3 tbsp ghee or vegetable oil
1 onion, finely chopped
5cm/2in piece fresh root
 ginger, crushed
4 fresh green chillies, chopped
1 tomato, chopped
2.5ml/½ tsp chilli powder
2.5ml/½ tsp ground turmeric
2.5ml/½ tsp ground cumin
2 garlic cloves, sliced
salt
coriander (cilantro) sprigs and sliced
 fresh red chilli, to garnish

NUTRITIONAL NOTES	
Per Portion	
Energy	431Kcals/1800KJ
Fat	26.5g
Saturated Fat	16.2g
Carbohydrate	35g
Fibre	2.9g

1 Drain the black lentils and place in a large pan with the red lentils. Cover with water and bring to the boil. Reduce the heat, cover the pan and simmer until tender. Mash with a spoon, and cool.

2 In a bowl, mix together the cream, yogurt and cornflour, and stir into the lentils in the pan.

3 Heat 15g/½oz/1 tbsp of the ghee or oil in a karahi, wok or large pan, and fry the onion, ginger, 2 green chillies and the tomato until the onion is soft.

4 Add the ground spices and salt and fry for a further 2 minutes. Stir into the lentil mixture and mix well. Reheat, transfer to a heatproof serving dish and keep warm.

5 Heat the remaining ghee or oil in a frying pan over a low heat and fry the garlic slices and remaining chillies until the garlic slices are golden brown.

6 Pour over the lentils and fold in the garlic and chilli just before serving. Place extra cream on the table so that diners can add more as they eat, if they wish.

Lentils Seasoned with Garlic-infused Oil

This dish is popular in southern India, where there are numerous variations. A single vegetable can be added to the lentils, or a combination of two or more. It is traditionally served with steamed rice dumplings or stuffed rice pancakes. The garlic-flavoured lentils are also extremely satisfying with plain boiled rice.

INGREDIENTS

Serves 4–6

120ml/4fl oz/½ cup vegetable oil
2.5ml/½ tsp mustard seeds
2.5ml/½ tsp cumin seeds
2 dried red chillies
1.5ml/¼ tsp asafoetida
6–8 curry leaves
2 garlic cloves, crushed, plus 2 garlic cloves, sliced
30ml/2 tbsp desiccated (dry unsweetened shredded) coconut
225g/8oz/1 cup red lentils, washed and drained
10ml/2 tsp sambhar masala or other curry powder
2.5ml/½ tsp ground turmeric
450ml/¾ pint/scant 2 cups water
450g/1lb mixed vegetables, such as okra, courgettes (zucchini), aubergine (eggplant) cauliflower, shallots and (bell) peppers
60ml/4 tbsp tamarind juice
4 firm tomatoes, quartered
a few coriander (cilantro) leaves, chopped

NUTRITIONAL NOTES	
Per Portion	
Energy	477Kcals/1994KJ
Fat	28.7g
Saturated Fat	7.1g
Carbohydrate	38.6g
Fibre	6.8g

1 Heat half the oil in a karahi, wok, or large pan, and stir-fry the next seven ingredients until the coconut begins to brown.

2 Stir in the prepared red lentils with the masala and turmeric. Stir-fry for 2–3 minutes and add the water. Bring it to the boil and reduce the heat to low.

3 Cover the pan and leave to simmer for 25–30 minutes, until the lentils are mushy. Add the mixed vegetables, tamarind juice and tomato quarters. Cook until the vegetables are just tender.

4 Heat the remaining oil in a small pan over a low heat, and fry the garlic slices until golden. Stir in the coriander leaves, then pour over the lentils and vegetables. Mix at the table before serving.

Spinach Dhal

Many different types of dhal are eaten in India and each region has its own speciality. This is a delicious, lightly spiced dish with a mild nutty flavour from the yellow lentils, which combine well with the spinach.

INGREDIENTS

Serves 4

175g/6oz/1 cup chana dhal or
    yellow split peas
175ml/6fl oz/¾ cup water
15ml/1 tbsp oil
1.5ml/¼ tsp black mustard seeds
1 onion, thinly sliced
2 garlic cloves, crushed
2.5cm/1in piece fresh root ginger, grated
1 fresh red chilli, finely chopped
275g/10oz frozen spinach, thawed
1.5ml/¼ tsp chilli powder
2.5ml/½ tsp ground coriander
2.5ml/½ tsp garam masala
2.5ml/½ tsp salt

1 Wash the chana dhal or split peas in several changes of cold water. Put into a bowl and cover with plenty of water. Leave to soak for 30 minutes.

2 Drain the pulses and put them in a large pan with the water. Bring to the boil, cover and simmer for 20–25 minutes until soft.

NUTRITIONAL NOTES	
Per Portion	
Energy	183Kcals/778KJ
Fat	2.00g
Saturated Fat	0.44g
Carbohydrate	30.30g
Fibre	4.90g

3 Meanwhile, heat the oil in a large heavy pan and fry the mustard seeds for 2 minutes until they begin to splutter. Add the onion, garlic, ginger and chilli and fry for 5–6 minutes. Add the spinach and cook for 10 minutes or until the spinach is dry and the liquid has been absorbed. Stir in the remaining spices and salt and cook for 2–3 minutes.

4 Drain the split peas, add to the spinach and cook for about 5 minutes. Serve at once.

Tarka Dhal

Tarka Dhal is probably the most popular Indian lentil dish and is found today in most Indian and Pakistani restaurants.

INGREDIENTS

Serves 4

115g/4oz/½ cup masoor dhal
(red split lentils)
50g/2oz/¼ cup mung dhal or yellow
split peas
600ml/1 pint/2½ cups water
5ml/1 tsp grated fresh root ginger
5ml/1 tsp crushed garlic
1.5ml/¼ tsp ground turmeric
2 fresh green chillies, chopped
7.5ml/1½ tsp salt

For the tarka
30ml/2 tbsp oil
1 onion, sliced
1.5ml/¼ tsp mixed mustard and
onion seeds
4 dried red chillies
1 tomato, sliced

For the garnish
15ml/1 tbsp chopped fresh
coriander (cilantro)
1–2 fresh green chillies, seeded and sliced
15ml/1 tbsp chopped fresh mint

1 Boil all the pulses in the water with the ginger and garlic, turmeric and chopped green chillies for 15–20 minutes until soft.

2 Pound the mixture with a rolling pin or mash with a fork until it has the consistency of a creamy chicken soup.

3 If the lentil mixture looks too dry, add a little more water. Season with the salt. To prepare the tarka, heat the oil in a heavy pan and fry the onion with the mustard and onion seeds, dried red chillies and tomato for 2 minutes.

4 Spoon the mashed lentils into a serving dish and pour the tarka over. Garnish with fresh coriander, green chillies and mint. Serve immediately.

NUTRITIONAL NOTES	
Per Portion	
Energy	162Kcals/681KJ
Fat	6.60g
Saturated Fat	0.74g
Carbohydrate	18.70g
Fibre	3.20g

COOK'S TIP

Dried red chillies are available in many different sizes. If the ones you have are large, or if you want a less spicy flavour, reduce the quantity specified to 1–2.

Vegetables with Almonds

Yogurt gives this dish a tangy flavour and also makes it creamy.

INGREDIENTS

Serves 4

30ml/2 tbsp oil
2 medium onions, sliced
5cm/2in piece fresh root
  ginger, shredded
5ml/1 tsp crushed black peppercorns
1 bay leaf
1.5ml/¼ tsp ground turmeric
5ml/1 tsp ground coriander
5ml/1 tsp salt
2.5ml/½ tsp garam masala
175g/6oz/2½ cups mushrooms,
  thickly sliced
1 medium courgette (zucchini),
  thickly sliced
50g/2oz green beans, cut into
  2.5cm/1in lengths
15ml/1 tbsp roughly chopped fresh mint
150ml/¼ pint/⅔ cup water
30ml/2 tbsp natural (plain) low
  fat yogurt
25g/1oz/¼ cup flaked (sliced) almonds

1 Heat the oil in a heavy pan, and fry the onions, ginger, peppercorns and bay leaf for 3–5 minutes.

NUTRITIONAL NOTES
Per Portion

Energy	140Kcals/579KJ
Fat	9.80g
Saturated Fat	1.13g
Carbohydrate	9.00g
Fibre	2.20g

2 Lower the heat and stir in the turmeric, coriander, salt and garam masala. Gradually add the sliced mushrooms, courgette, green beans and mint. Stir gently to coat the vegetables, being careful not to break them up.

3 Pour in the water and bring to a simmer, then lower the heat and cook until the water has been totally absorbed by the vegetables.

4 Beat the yogurt lightly with a fork, then pour it on to the vegetables in the pan and mix together well until the vegetables are coated.

5 Cook the vegetables for a further 2–3 minutes, stirring occasionally. Spoon into a large serving dish or on to individual plates. Serve immediately, garnished with the flaked almonds.

Vegetables and Beans with Curry Leaves

Bright, shiny green curry leaves look like small bay leaves, though they are not as tough. A popular seasoning ingredient in Indian cooking, curry leaves add a spicy flavour to dishes such as this dry vegetable and bean curry.

INGREDIENTS

Serves 4

3 fresh green chillies
15ml/1 tbsp oil
6 curry leaves
3 garlic cloves, sliced
3 dried red chillies
1.5ml/¼ tsp onion seeds
1.5ml/¼ tsp fenugreek seeds
115g/4oz/½ cup drained canned red
   kidney beans
1 medium carrot, cut into strips
50g/2oz green beans, sliced diagonally
1 medium red (bell) pepper, seeded and
   cut into strips
5ml/1 tsp salt
30ml/2 tbsp lemon juice

NUTRITIONAL NOTES *Per Portion*	
Energy	79Kcals/331KJ
Fat	3.30g
Saturated Fat	0.37g
Carbohydrate	9.70g
Fibre	2.60g

3 When these ingredients turn a shade darker, add the chillies, kidney beans, carrot strips, green beans and pepper strips, stirring constantly.

4 Stir in the salt and the lemon juice. Lower the heat, cover and cook for about 5 minutes.

5 Transfer the hot curry to a serving dish and serve immediately.

1 Cut the chillies in half lengthways. Remove the membranes and seeds and chop the flesh.

2 Heat the oil in a karahi, wok or deep heavy pan. Add the curry leaves, garlic cloves, dried chillies, and onion and fenugreek seeds.

Spiced Coconut Mushrooms

Here is a simple and delicious way to cook mushrooms. They can be served with almost any Indian meal as well as with traditional western grilled or roasted meats and poultry.

INGREDIENTS

Serves 4

30ml/2 tbsp groundnut oil
2 garlic cloves, finely chopped
2 fresh red chillies, seeded and sliced
   into rings
3 shallots, finely chopped
225g/8oz/3 cups brown-cap
   mushrooms, thickly sliced
150ml/¼ pint/²/₃ cup coconut milk
30ml/2 tbsp chopped fresh
   coriander (cilantro)
salt and black pepper

1 Heat a karahi, wok or shallow pan until hot, add the oil and swirl it round. Add the garlic and chillies, then stir-fry for a few seconds.

— COOK'S TIP —

Use snipped fresh chives instead of chopped fresh coriander (cilantro), if you wish.

2 Add the shallots and stir-fry them for 2–3 minutes until softened. Add the mushrooms and stir-fry for 3 minutes.

3 Pour in the coconut milk and bring to the boil. Boil rapidly over a high heat until the liquid has reduced by about half and coats the mushrooms. Season to taste with salt and pepper.

4 Sprinkle over the chopped coriander and toss the mushrooms gently to mix. Serve at once.

NUTRITIONAL NOTES	
Per Portion	
Energy	67Kcals/280KJ
Fat	5.9g
Saturated Fat	1.2g
Carbohydrate	2.4g
Fibre	0.8g

Courgettes with Mushrooms in a Yogurt Sauce

Yogurt makes a creamy sauce which is delicious with cooked mushrooms and courgettes.

INGREDIENTS

Serves 4
15ml/1 tbsp oil
1 medium onion, roughly chopped
5ml/1 tsp ground coriander
5ml/1 tsp ground cumin
5ml/1 tsp salt
2.5ml/½ tsp chilli powder
225g/8oz/3 cups mushrooms, sliced
2 courgettes (zucchini), sliced
45ml/3 tbsp natural (plain) low
   fat yogurt
15ml/1 tbsp chopped fresh coriander

1 Heat the oil in a heavy pan and fry the onion until golden brown. Lower the heat to medium, add the ground coriander, cumin, salt and chilli powder and stir together well.

2 Once the onion and the spices are well blended, add the mushrooms and courgettes and stir-fry gently for about 5 minutes until soft. If the mixture is too dry, add just a little water to loosen.

3 Finally add the yogurt and mix it well into the vegetables.

4 Sprinkle with chopped fresh coriander and serve immediately.

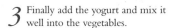

NUTRITIONAL NOTES
Per Portion

Energy	64Kcals/265KJ
Fat	3.70g
Saturated Fat	0.58g
Carbohydrate	4.80g
Fibre	1.40g

COOK'S TIP

Yogurt has a great affinity with stir-fried vegetables and this lovely combination of sliced courgettes (zucchini) and mushrooms would make a tasty accompaniment to serve with poultry or lamb dishes. If preferred, you could use aubergines (eggplant) or mushrooms instead.

Mung Beans with Potatoes

Mung beans are one of the quicker-cooking pulses. They do not require soaking and are very easy and convenient to use. In this recipe they are cooked with potatoes and Indian spices to give a tasty nutritious dish.

INGREDIENTS

Serves 4

175g/6oz/1 cup mung beans
750ml/1¼ pints/3 cups water
225g/8oz potatoes, cut into
   2cm/¾in chunks
30ml/2 tbsp oil
2.5ml/½ tsp cumin seeds
1 fresh green chilli, finely chopped
1 garlic clove, crushed
2.5cm/1in piece fresh root ginger,
   finely chopped
1.5ml/¼ tsp ground turmeric
2.5ml/½ tsp chilli powder
5ml/1 tsp salt
5ml/1 tsp granulated sugar
4 curry leaves
5 tomatoes, peeled and finely chopped
15ml/1 tbsp tomato purée (paste)
curry leaves, to garnish
plain rice, to serve

1 Wash the beans. Pour the water into a pan, add the beans and bring to the boil. Boil hard for 15 minutes, then reduce the heat, cover the pan and simmer until soft, about 30 minutes cooking time. Drain.

3 Heat the oil in a heavy pan and fry the cumin seeds until they splutter. Add the chilli, garlic and ginger and fry for 3–4 minutes.

5 Add the 4 curry leaves, chopped tomatoes and tomato purée and simmer for about 5 minutes until the sauce thickens. Mix the tomato sauce and the potatoes with the mung beans and heat through. Garnish with the extra curry leaves and serve with plain boiled rice.

2 In a separate pan, par-boil the potatoes in boiling water for 10 minutes, then drain well.

4 Add the turmeric, chilli powder, salt and sugar and cook for 2 minutes, stirring to prevent the mixture from sticking to the pan.

NUTRITIONAL NOTES	
Per Portion	
Energy	254Kcals/1070KJ
Fat	6.80g
Saturated Fat	0.89g
Carbohydrate	36.90g
Fibre	6.30g

Madras Sambal

There are many variations of this popular dish but it is regularly cooked in one form or another in almost every south-Indian home. You can use any combination of vegetables that are in season.

INGREDIENTS

Serves 4

225g/8oz/1 cup tuvar dhal or red split lentils
600ml/1 pint/2½ cups water
2.5ml/½ tsp ground turmeric
2 large potatoes, cut into 2.5cm/ 1in chunks
30ml/2 tbsp oil
2.5ml/½ tsp black mustard seeds
1.5ml/¼ tsp fenugreek seeds
4 curry leaves
1 onion, thinly sliced
115g/4oz green beans, cut into 2.5cm/1in lengths
5ml/1 tsp salt
2.5ml/½ tsp chilli powder
15ml/1 tbsp lemon juice
toasted coconut, to garnish
coriander chutney, to serve

NUTRITIONAL NOTES	
Per Portion	
Energy	335Kcals/1414KJ
Fat	6.10g
Saturated Fat	1.98g
Carbohydrate	55.70g
Fibre	5.60g

1 Wash the tuvar dhal or lentils in several changes of water. Place in a heavy pan with the measured water and the turmeric. Bring to the boil, then reduce the heat, cover the pan and simmer for 30–35 minutes until the lentils are soft.

2 Par-cook the potatoes in a large pan of boiling water for 10 minutes. Drain well and set aside.

3 Heat the oil in a large frying pan and fry the mustard and fenugreek seeds and curry leaves for 2–3 minutes until the seeds begin to splutter. Add the sliced onion and the green beans and stir-fry for 7–8 minutes. Add the par-boiled potatoes and cook for a further 2 minutes.

4 Drain the lentils. Stir them into the potato mixture with the salt, chilli powder and lemon juice. Simmer for 2 minutes or until heated through. Garnish with toasted coconut and serve with freshly made coriander chutney.

Okra in Yogurt

This tangy vegetable dish can be served as an accompaniment, but it also makes an excellent vegetarian meal if served with *Tarka Dhal* and warm, freshly made chapatis.

INGREDIENTS

Serves 4
450g/1lb okra
15ml/1 tbsp oil
2.5ml/½ tsp onion seeds
3 medium fresh green chillies, chopped
1 medium onion, sliced
1.5ml/¼ tsp ground turmeric
2.5ml/½ tsp salt
15ml/1 tbsp natural (plain) low fat yogurt
2 medium tomatoes, sliced
15ml/1 tbsp chopped fresh coriander (cilantro)
chapatis, to serve

NUTRITIONAL NOTES	
Per Portion	
Energy	82Kcals/342KJ
Fat	4.20g
Saturated Fat	0.41g
Carbohydrate	7.60g
Fibre	5.30g

1 Wash, top and tail the okra, cut into 1cm/½ in pieces and place in a bowl. Set aside.

2 Heat the oil in a medium heavy pan, add the onion seeds, green chillies and onion and fry for about 5 minutes until the onion has turned golden brown.

3 Reduce the heat. Add the ground turmeric and salt to the onions and fry for about 1 minute.

4 Next, add the prepared okra, turn the heat to medium-high and quickly stir-fry the okra for a few minutes until they are lightly golden.

5 Stir in the yogurt, tomatoes and, finally, the coriander. Cook for a further 2 minutes.

6 Transfer the okra to a serving dish and serve immediately with freshly made chapatis.

COOK'S TIP

Take care when preparing the chillies. Many people forget that they can be a strong irritant, due to the capsaicin they contain. If you rub your eyes after handling, and especially chopping, chillies, or touch another sensitive part of your anatomy, the burning sensation will be very unpleasant. It is wise to take simple precautionary measures such as wearing gloves when cutting up chillies, if possible, or wash your hands several times and very thoroughly in soapy water afterwards. In particular, if you wear contact lenses, make sure your fingers have been thoroughly cleansed before attempting to remove the lenses from your eyes.

Masala Okra

Okra, or "ladies' fingers", are a very popular Indian vegetable. Here the pods are stir-fried with a dry masala mixture to make a tasty side dish.

INGREDIENTS

Serves 4

450g/1lb okra
2.5ml/½ tsp ground turmeric
5ml/1 tsp chilli powder
15ml/1 tbsp ground cumin
15ml/1 tbsp ground coriander
1.5ml/¼ tsp salt
1.5ml/¼ tsp granulated sugar
15ml/1 tbsp lemon juice
30ml/2 tbsp chopped fresh
   coriander (cilantro)
15ml/1 tbsp oil
2.5ml/½ tsp cumin seeds
2.5ml/½ tsp black mustard seeds
chopped fresh tomatoes, to garnish
poppadums, to serve

1 Wash, dry and trim the okra and set aside. In a bowl, mix together the turmeric, chilli powder, cumin, ground coriander, salt, sugar, lemon juice and fresh coriander.

2 Heat the oil in a large heavy pan. Add the cumin seeds and mustard seeds and fry for about 2 minutes or until they start to splutter.

—————— COOK'S TIP ——————

When buying okra, choose firm, brightly coloured pods that are less than 10cm/ 4in long; larger ones can be stringy.

3 Scrape in the spice mixture and continue to fry for 2 minutes.

4 Add the okra, cover and cook over a low heat for 10 minutes, or until tender. Garnish with chopped fresh tomatoes and serve with poppadums.

NUTRITIONAL NOTES	
Per Portion	
Energy	102Kcals/424KJ
Fat	5.4g
Saturated Fat	0.4g
Carbohydrate	8.6g
Fibre	4.7g

Spicy Bitter Gourds

Bitter gourds are widely used in Indian cooking, often combined with other vegetables in a curry.

INGREDIENTS

Serves 4

675g/1½lb bitter gourds
15ml/1 tbsp oil
2.5ml/½ tsp cumin seeds
6 spring onions (scallions),
    finely chopped
5 tomatoes, finely chopped
2.5cm/1in piece fresh root ginger,
    finely chopped
2 garlic cloves, crushed
2 fresh green chillies, finely chopped
2.5ml/½ tsp salt
2.5ml/½ tsp chilli powder
5ml/1 tsp ground coriander
5ml/1 tsp ground cumin
45ml/3 tbsp soft dark brown sugar
15ml/1 tbsp gram flour
fresh coriander (cilantro) sprigs,
    to garnish

1 Bring a large pan of lightly salted water to the boil. Peel the bitter gourds and halve them. Discard the seeds. Cut into 2cm/¾in pieces, then cook in the boiling water for about 10–15 minutes or until just tender. Drain well.

2 Heat the oil in a large heavy pan and fry the cumin seeds for 2 minutes until they begin to splutter.

3 Add the spring onions and fry for 3–4 minutes. Add the tomatoes, ginger, garlic and chillies and cook the mixture, stirring occasionally, for a further 5 minutes.

4 Add the salt, remaining spices and sugar to the pan and cook for a further 2–3 minutes. Add the bitter gourds to the pan and mix well.

5 Sprinkle over the gram flour. Cover and simmer over a low heat for 5–8 minutes or until all of the gram flour has been absorbed into the sauce. Stir well, then serve garnished with fresh coriander sprigs.

NUTRITIONAL NOTES	
Per Portion	
Energy	120Kcals/490KJ
Fat	3.50g
Saturated Fat	0.41g
Carbohydrate	9.20g
Fibre	0.40g

_____ COOK'S TIP _____

Bitter gourds, which are also known as karelas, resemble small cucumbers with a warty skin. True to their name, they are extremely bitter. The medium-size ones (about 10cm/4in long) are usually slightly less bitter than the tiny ones.

Corn on the Cob in Rich Onion Sauce

Corn is grown extensively in the Punjab region, where it is used in many delicacies. Corn bread, *makki ki roti*, along with spiced mustard greens, *sarson ka saag*, is a combination that is hard to beat and it is what the Punjabis thrive on. Here, corn is cooked in a thick rich onion sauce, in another classic Punjabi dish. It is excellent served with naan bread.

INGREDIENTS

Serves 4–6
4 corn cobs, thawed if frozen
vegetable oil, for frying
1 large onion, finely chopped
2 garlic cloves, crushed
5cm/2in piece fresh root
 ginger, crushed
2.5ml/½ tsp ground turmeric
2.5ml/½ tsp onion seeds
2.5ml/½ tsp cumin seeds
2.5ml/½ tsp chilli powder
6–8 curry leaves
2.5ml/½ tsp granulated sugar
200ml/7fl oz/scant 1 cup natural
 (plain) yogurt
chilli powder, to taste

1 Cut each corn cob in half, using a heavy knife or cleaver to make clean cuts. Heat the oil in a karahi, wok or large pan and fry the corn until golden brown. Remove the corn and set aside. Remove any excess oil, leaving 30ml/2 tbsp in the wok.

2 Grind the onion, garlic and ginger to a paste using a pestle and mortar or in a food processor. Transfer the paste to a bowl and mix in the spices, curry leaves and granulated sugar.

3 Heat the oil and fry the onion paste mixture over a low heat for 8–10 minutes until all the spices have blended well and the oil separates from the sauce.

4 Cool the mixture and fold in the yogurt. Mix to a smooth sauce. Add the corn and mix well, so that all the pieces are covered with the sauce. Reheat gently for about 10 minutes. Serve hot.

NUTRITIONAL NOTES	
Per Portion	
Energy	214Kcals/888KJ
Fat	15.1g
Saturated Fat	2g
Carbohydrate	15.9g
Fibre	1.5g

Stir-fried Indian Cheese with Mushrooms and Peas

Indian cheese, known as *paneer*, is a very versatile ingredient. It is used in both sweet and savoury dishes. Indian housewives generally make this cheese at home, although in recent years it has become available commercially. It is a useful source of protein for those people in the north of the subcontinent who are vegetarian.

INGREDIENTS

Serves 4–6
90ml/6 tbsp ghee or vegetable oil
225g/8oz paneer, cubed
1 onion, finely chopped
a few fresh mint leaves, chopped, plus
    extra sprigs to garnish
50g/2oz chopped fresh coriander
    (cilantro)
3 fresh green chillies, chopped
3 garlic cloves
2.5cm/1in piece fresh root ginger, sliced
5ml/1 tsp ground turmeric
5ml/1 tsp chilli powder, optional
5ml/1 tsp garam masala
225g/8oz/3 cups tiny button (white)
    mushrooms, washed
225g/8oz/2 cups frozen peas, thawed
175ml/6fl oz/¾ cup natural (plain)
    yogurt, mixed with 5ml/1 tsp
    cornflour (cornstarch)
salt

1 Heat the ghee or oil in a karahi, wok or large pan, and fry the paneer cubes until they are golden brown on all sides. Remove and drain on kitchen paper.

2 Grind the onion, mint, coriander, chillies, garlic and ginger with a pestle and mortar or in a food processor to a fairly smooth paste. Remove and mix in the turmeric, chilli powder, if using, and garam masala, with salt to taste.

3 Remove excess ghee or oil from the pan, leaving about 15ml/1 tbsp. Heat and fry the paste over a medium heat for 8–10 minutes, or until the raw onion smell disappears and the oil separates.

4 Add the mushrooms, thawed peas and paneer and mix well. Cool the mixture slightly and gradually fold in the yogurt.

5 Simmer for about 10 minutes, until the vegetables are tender and the flavours are well mixed. Remove to a serving dish, garnish with sprigs of fresh mint and serve immediately.

----------- COOK'S TIP -----------

If paneer is not available, use beancurd (tofu) or substitute grilled (broiled) goat's cheese, adding it just before the garnish.

NUTRITIONAL NOTES
Per Portion

Energy	280Kcals/1162KJ
Fat	19.9g
Saturated Fat	3.7g
Carbohydrate	11.7g
Fibre	3.7g

Spinach and Potatoes and Red Chillies

India is blessed with over 18 varieties of spinach. If you have access to an Indian or Chinese grocer, look out for some of the more unusual varieties.

INGREDIENTS

Serves 4-6

60ml/4 tbsp vegetable oil
225g/8oz potatoes
2.5cm/1in piece fresh root
    ginger, crushed
4 garlic cloves, crushed
1 onion, chopped
2 fresh green chillies, chopped
2 dried red chillies, chopped
5ml/1 tsp cumin seeds
salt, to taste
225g/8oz fresh spinach, trimmed,
    washed and chopped or 225g/8oz
    frozen spinach, thawed and drained
2 firm tomatoes, roughly chopped,
    to garnish

1 Wash the potatoes and cut into quarters. If using small new potatoes, leave them whole. Heat the oil in a frying pan and fry the potatoes until brown on all sides. Remove and put aside.

2 Remove the excess oil, leaving about 15ml/1 tbsp in the pan. Fry the ginger, garlic, onion, green chillies, dried chillies and cumin seeds until the onion is golden brown.

3 Add the potatoes and salt and stir well. Cover the pan and cook over a medium heat, stirring occasionally, until the potatoes are tender when pierced with a sharp knife.

4 Add the spinach and stir well. Using two wooden spoons or spatulas, toss the mixture over the heat until the spinach is tender and all the excess fluid has evaporated.

5 Spoon into a heated serving dish or onto individual plates and garnish with the chopped tomatoes. Serve hot.

VARIATION

This also tastes very good if you substitute sweet potatoes for ordinary potatoes. Slice them just before cooking, or they may discolour.

NUTRITIONAL NOTES	
Per Portion	
Energy	177Kcals/734KJ
Fat	11.8g
Saturated Fat	1.4g
Carbohydrate	15g
Fibre	2.9g

Spinach with Mushrooms

A tasty vegetable that is often overlooked, spinach is highly nutritious. Cooked in this way it tastes wonderful. Serve with chapatis.

INGREDIENTS

Serves 4

450g/1lb fresh or frozen spinach, thawed
30ml/2 tbsp oil
2 medium onions, diced
6-8 curry leaves
1.5ml/¼ tsp onion seeds
5ml/1 tsp crushed garlic
5ml/1 tsp grated fresh root ginger
5ml/1 tsp chilli powder
5ml/1 tsp salt
7.5ml/1½ tsp ground coriander
1 large red (bell) pepper, seeded
　and sliced
115g/4oz/1½ cups mushrooms,
　roughly chopped
225g/8oz/1 cup low fat fromage frais
　or ricotta cheese
30ml/2 tbsp fresh coriander
　(cilantro) leaves

1 If using fresh spinach, blanch it briefly in boiling water and drain thoroughly. If using frozen spinach, drain well. Set aside.

2 Heat the oil in a karahi, wok or heavy pan and fry the onions with the curry leaves and the onion seeds for 1–2 minutes. Add the garlic, ginger, chilli powder, salt and ground coriander. Stir-fry for a further 2–3 minutes.

3 Add half the red pepper slices and all the mushrooms and continue to stir-fry for 2–3 minutes.

4 Add the spinach and stir-fry for 4–6 minutes, then add the fromage frais or ricotta and half the fresh coriander, followed by the remaining red pepper slices. Stir-fry for a further 2–3 minutes before serving, garnished with the remaining coriander.

NUTRITIONAL NOTES
Per Portion

Energy	188Kcals/778KJ
Fat	11.57g
Saturated Fat	5.99g
Carbohydrate	14.71g
Fibre	4.68g

--- COOK'S TIP ---

Whether you use fresh or frozen spinach, make sure it is well drained, otherwise the stir-fried mixture will be too wet when you add the fromage frais or ricotta. It is a good idea to tip the spinach into a colander, and press it against the sides of the colander with a wooden spoon to extract as much liquid as possible.

Carrot and Cauliflower Stir-fry

Slicing the carrots thinly into thin batons helps them cook quickly. This dish has a crunchy texture and only a few whole spices.

INGREDIENTS

Serves 4

2 large carrots
1 small cauliflower
15ml/1 tbsp oil
1 bay leaf
2 cloves
1 small cinnamon stick
2 cardamom pods
3 black peppercorns
5ml/1 tsp salt
50g/2oz/½ cup frozen peas, thawed
10ml/2 tsp lemon juice
15ml/1 tbsp chopped fresh coriander
   (cilantro), plus fresh leaves,
   to garnish

1 Cut the carrots into thin batons about 2.5cm/1in long. Separate the cauliflower into small florets.

NUTRITIONAL NOTES	
Per Portion	
Energy	84Kcals/349KJ
Fat	3.75g
Saturated Fat	0.60g
Carbohydrate	9.05g
Fibre	3.67g

2 Heat the oil in a karahi, wok or heavy pan and add the bay leaf, cloves, cinnamon stick, cardamom pods and peppercorns. Quickly stir-fry over a medium heat for 30–35 seconds, then add the salt.

3 Next add the carrot batons and cauliflower florets and continue to stir-fry for 3–5 minutes.

4 Add the peas, lemon juice and chopped coriander and cook for a further 4–5 minutes. Serve garnished with the whole coriander leaves.

--- COOK'S TIP ---

As both carrots and cauliflower can be eaten raw, they need only minimal cooking or they will lose their crunchy texture.

Cauliflower and Potato Curry

Cauliflower and potatoes are encrusted with Indian spices in this delicious recipe.

INGREDIENTS

Serves 4

450g/1lb potatoes, cut into 2.5cm/
  1in chunks
30ml/2 tbsp oil
5ml/1 tsp cumin seeds
1 fresh green chilli, finely chopped
450g/1lb cauliflower, broken into florets
5ml/1 tsp ground coriander
5ml/1 tsp ground cumin
1.5ml/¼ tsp chilli powder
2.5ml/½ tsp ground turmeric
2.5ml/½ tsp salt
chopped fresh coriander (cilantro),
  to garnish
tomato and onion salad and pickle,
  to serve

1 Par-cook the potatoes in a large pan of boiling water for about 10 minutes. Drain well and set aside.

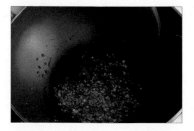

2 Heat the oil in a large heavy pan. Add the cumin seeds and fry them for 2 minutes until they begin to splutter. Add the chilli and fry for a further 1 minute.

3 Add the cauliflower florets and fry, stirring, for 5 minutes.

NUTRITIONAL NOTES	
Per Portion	
Energy	189Kcals/791KJ
Fat	7.40g
Saturated Fat	0.77g
Carbohydrate	24.60g
Fibre	3.50g

4 Add the potatoes and the ground spices and salt and cook for a further 7–10 minutes, or until both the vegetables are tender. Garnish with fresh coriander and serve with tomato and onion salad and pickle.

COOK'S TIP

Use sweet potatoes instead of ordinary potatoes for a curry with a sweeter flavour.

Masala Beans with Fenugreek

The term *masala* refers to the blending of several spices to achieve a distinctive taste, with different spice-combinations being used to complement specific ingredients. Households will traditionally create their own blends, and many are unique.

INGREDIENTS

Serves 4

1 onion
5ml/1 tsp ground cumin
5ml/1 tsp ground coriander
5ml/1 tsp sesame seeds
5ml/1 tsp chilli powder
2.5ml/½ tsp crushed garlic
1.5ml/¼ tsp ground turmeric
5ml/1 tsp salt
30ml/2 tbsp vegetable oil
1 tomato, quartered
225g/8oz/1½ cups green
 beans, blanched
1 bunch fresh fenugreek leaves,
 stems discarded
60ml/4 tbsp chopped fresh
 coriander (cilantro)
15ml/1 tbsp lemon juice

1 Roughly chop the onion. Mix together the cumin and coriander, sesame seeds, chilli powder, garlic, turmeric and salt.

2 Put the chopped onion and spice mixture into a food processor or blender, and process for 30–45 seconds until you have a rough paste.

3 In a karahi, wok or large pan, heat the oil over a medium heat and fry the spice paste for about 5 minutes, stirring the mixture occasionally.

4 Add the tomato quarters, blanched green beans, fresh fenugreek and chopped coriander.

5 Stir-fry the contents of the pan for about 5 minutes, then sprinkle in the lemon juice and serve.

VARIATION

Instead of fresh fenugreek, you can also use 15ml/1 tbsp dried fenugreek for this recipe. Dried fenugreek is readily available from Indian stores and markets.

NUTRITIONAL NOTES	
Per Portion	
Energy	80Kcals/331KJ
Fat	5.9g
Saturated Fat	0.8g
Carbohydrate	5.4g
Fibre	2g

Green Beans with Corn

Frozen green beans are useful for this dish, as they are quick to cook. It makes an excellent vegetable accompaniment.

INGREDIENTS

Serves 4

15ml/1 tbsp oil
1.5ml/¼ tsp mustard seeds
1 medium red onion, diced
50g/2oz/⅓ cup frozen corn
50g/2oz/¼ cup canned red kidney beans, drained
175g/6oz frozen green beans
1 fresh red chilli, seeded and diced
1 garlic clove, chopped
2.5cm/1in piece fresh root ginger, finely chopped
15ml/1 tbsp chopped fresh coriander (cilantro)
5ml/1 tsp salt
1 medium tomato, seeded and diced, to garnish

1 Heat the oil in a karahi, wok or heavy pan for about 30 seconds, then add the mustard seeds and onion. Stir-fry for 2–3 minutes.

NUTRITIONAL NOTES	
Per Portion	
Energy	84Kcals/349KJ
Fat	3.44g
Saturated Fat	0.50g
Carbohydrate	11.13g
Fibre	2.70g

2 Add the corn, red kidney beans and green beans. Stir-fry for 3–5 minutes.

3 Add the red chilli, chopped garlic and ginger, coriander and salt and stir-fry for 2–3 minutes.

4 Remove the pan from the heat. Transfer the vegetables to a serving dish and garnish with the diced tomato.

COOK'S TIP

This is a good stand-by dish as it uses frozen and canned ingredients. To make sure you have always got a chilli available for making this dish, or others like it, freeze whole fresh chillies, washed but not blanched.

Fiery Spiced Potatoes

The quantity of red chillies used here may be too fiery for some palates. For a milder version, seed the chillies, use fewer, or substitute them with a roughly chopped red pepper.

INGREDIENTS

Serves 4

12–14 baby new potatoes, peeled
   and halved
2.5ml/½ tsp salt
15ml/1 tbsp oil
2.5ml/½ tsp crushed dried red chillies
2.5ml/½ tsp cumin seeds
2.5ml/½ tsp fennel seeds
2.5ml/½ tsp crushed coriander seeds
1 medium onion, sliced
3–4 fresh red chillies, chopped
15ml/1 tbsp chopped fresh
   coriander (cilantro)

1 Boil the potatoes in a pan of salted water until just cooked but still firm. Remove from the heat and drain off the water.

NUTRITIONAL NOTES	
Per Portion	
Energy	122Kcals/513KJ
Fat	3.50g
Saturated Fat	0.37g
Carbohydrate	21.20g
Fibre	1.50g

2 In a karahi, wok or deep pan, heat the oil quickly over a high heat, then turn down the heat to medium. Add the crushed chillies, cumin, fennel and coriander seeds and a little salt and quickly stir-fry for about 30–40 seconds.

3 Add the onion and fry gently until golden brown. Then add the new potatoes, fresh red chillies and fresh coriander.

4 Cover and cook for 5–7 minutes over a very low heat. Serve hot.

Potatoes with Roasted Poppy Seeds

Poppy seeds are used in Indian cooking as thickening agents, and to lend a nutty taste to sauces. It is the creamy white variety of poppy seed that is used here, rather than the ones with a blue-grey hue that are used for baking.

INGREDIENTS

Serves 4

45ml/3 tbsp white poppy seeds
45–60ml/3–4 tbsp vegetable oil
675g/1½lb potatoes, peeled and cut
 into 1cm/½in cubes
2.5ml/½ tsp black mustard seeds
2.5ml/½ tsp onion seeds
2.5ml/½ tsp cumin seeds
2.5ml/½ tsp fennel seeds
1–2 dried red chillies, chopped or
 broken into small pieces
2.5ml/½ tsp ground turmeric
2.5ml/½ tsp salt
150ml/¼ pint/⅔ cup warm water
fresh coriander (cilantro) sprigs,
 to garnish
pooris and natural (plain) yogurt,
 to serve

1 Peel the potatoes and cut into small cubes.

2 Preheat a karahi, wok or large pan over a medium setting. When the pan is hot, reduce the heat slightly and add the poppy seeds. Stir them around in the pan until they are just a shade darker. Remove from the pan and leave to cool.

3 In the pan, heat the vegetable oil over a medium heat and fry the cubes of potato until they are light brown. Remove them with a slotted spoon and drain on kitchen paper.

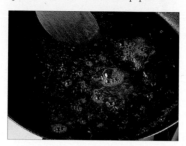

4 To the same oil, add the mustard seeds. As soon as they begin to pop, add the onion, cumin and fennel seeds and the chillies. Let the chillies blacken, but remove them from the pan before they burn.

5 Stir in the turmeric and follow quickly with the fried potatoes and salt. Stir well and add the warm water. Cover the pan with the lid and reduce the heat to low. Cook for 8–10 minutes, or until the potatoes are tender.

6 Grind the cooled poppy seeds in a pestle and mortar or coffee grinder. Stir the ground seeds into the potatoes. It should form a thick paste which should cling to the potatoes. If there is too much liquid, continue to stir over a medium heat until you have the right consistency. Transfer to a serving dish. Garnish with coriander and serve with pooris and natural yogurt.

NUTRITIONAL NOTES	
Per Portion	
Energy	201Kcals/842KJ
Fat	13.5g
Saturated Fat	1.6g
Carbohydrate	29g
Fibre	2.2g

Potatoes in Chilli Tamarind Sauce

In this favourite potato dish from the state of Karnataka, the combination of chilli and tamarind awakens the taste buds immediately. This version adapts the traditional recipe slightly, to reduce the customary pungency and enhance the fiery appearance of this delicious combination.

INGREDIENTS

Serves 4–6

450g/1lb small new potatoes, washed
  and dried
25g/1oz whole dried red chillies,
  preferably Kashmiri
7.5ml/1½ tsp cumin seeds
4 garlic cloves, chopped
90ml/6 tbsp vegetable oil
60ml/4 tbsp thick tamarind juice
30ml/2 tbsp tomato purée (paste)
4 curry leaves
5ml/1 tsp granulated sugar
1.5ml/¼ tsp asafoetida
salt
coriander (cilantro) sprigs and lemon
  wedges, to garnish

NUTRITIONAL NOTES	
Per Portion	
Energy	227Kcals/945KJ
Fat	16.8g
Saturated Fat	2.1g
Carbohydrate	18.1g
Fibre	1.1g

VARIATION

Chunks of large potatoes can be used as an alternative to new potatoes. Alternatively, try this with sweet potatoes. The spicy sweet and sour taste works very well in this variation.

1 Boil the potatoes until they are fully cooked, ensuring they do not break. To test, insert a thin sharp knife into the potatoes. It should come out clean when the potatoes are fully cooked. Drain and cool the potatoes in iced water to prevent further cooking.

2 Soak the chillies for 5 minutes in warm water. Drain and grind with the cumin seeds and garlic to a coarse paste, either using a pestle and mortar or in a food processor.

3 Heat the oil and fry the paste, tamarind juice, tomato purée, curry leaves, sugar, asafoetida and salt until the oil can be seen to have separated from the spice paste.

4 Add the potatoes and stir to coat. Reduce the heat, cover and simmer for 5 minutes. Garnish and serve.

Golden Chunky Potatoes with Spinach and Mustard Seeds

The combination of spinach and potato is a common one in India and there are numerous versions using the same or similar ingredients. This recipe is from Bengal, where it is known as *palong saaker ghonto.*

INGREDIENTS

Serves 4–6
450g/1lb spinach
30ml/2 tbsp vegetable oil
5ml/1 tsp black mustard seeds
1 onion, thinly sliced
2 garlic cloves, crushed
2.5cm/1in piece fresh root ginger, finely chopped
675g/1½lb firm potatoes, cut into 2.5cm/1in chunks
5ml/1 tsp chilli powder
5ml/1 tsp salt
120ml/4fl oz/½ cup water

1 Blanch the spinach in a pan of boiling water for 3–4 minutes, then drain in a colander and leave to cool. When it is cool enough to handle, squeeze out any remaining liquid using the back of a wooden spoon or with your hands.

2 Heat the oil in a large pan over a medium heat and fry the mustard seeds until they begin to splutter.

3 Add the sliced onion, crushed garlic and chopped ginger and fry for about 5 minutes, stirring.

4 Stir in the potatoes, chilli powder and salt. Pour in the measure of water and cook for 8 minutes, stirring occasionally.

5 Add the spinach to the pan. Cover and simmer for 10–15 minutes until the potatoes are tender. Serve.

VARIATION

For an excellent alternative to spinach, use 450g/1lb spring greens or collard greens. Whether you use spinach or an alternative, choose young vegetables.

NUTRITIONAL NOTES	
Per Portion	
Energy	209Kcals/878KJ
Fat	7g
Saturated Fat	1g
Carbohydrate	31.9g
Fibre	4.6g

Potatoes in Yogurt Sauce

It is nice to use tiny new potatoes with the skins on for this recipe. The yogurt adds a tangy flavour to this fairly spicy dish, which is delicious served with plain or wholemeal chapatis.

INGREDIENTS

Serves 4

small bunch fresh coriander (cilantro)
12 new potatoes, halved
275g/10oz/1¼ cups natural low
   fat yogurt
300ml/½ pint/1¼ cups water
1.5ml/¼ tsp ground turmeric
5ml/1 tsp chilli powder
5ml/1 tsp ground coriander
2.5ml/½ tsp ground cumin
5ml/1 tsp soft brown sugar
1.5ml/¼ tsp salt
15ml/1 tbsp oil
5ml/1 tsp cumin seeds
2 green chillies, sliced

_____ COOK'S TIP _____

If new potatoes are unavailable, use 450g/ 1lb ordinary potatoes instead. Peel them and cut into large chunks, then cook as described above.

1 Cut off the roots and any thick stalks from the coriander and chop the leaves finely. Set aside.

2 Boil the potatoes in salted water with their skins on until they are just tender, then drain and set aside.

3 Mix together the yogurt, water, turmeric, chilli powder, ground coriander, ground cumin, sugar and salt in a bowl. Set aside.

4 Heat the oil in a medium heavy pan and stir in the cumin seeds. Fry for 1 minute.

5 Reduce the heat, stir in the spicy yogurt mixture and cook for about 3 minutes over a medium heat.

6 Add the chopped fresh coriander, green chillies and cooked potatoes. Blend everything together and cook for a further 5–7 minutes, stirring from time to time. Serve hot.

NUTRITIONAL NOTES
Per Portion

Energy	169Kcals/712KJ
Fat	4.30g
Saturated Fat	0.78g
Carbohydrate	27.60g
Fibre	1.20g

Masala Mashed Potatoes

This delightfully simple variation on the popular Western side dish can be used as an accompaniment to just about any main course dish, not just Indian food. There are easily attainable alternatives to mango powder if you cannot get hold of any (see Cook's Tip).

INGREDIENTS

Serves 4

3 medium potatoes
15ml/1 tbsp chopped fresh mint and coriander (cilantro), mixed
5ml/1 tsp mango powder (amchur)
5ml/1 tsp salt
5ml/1 tsp crushed black peppercorns
1 fresh red chilli, chopped
1 fresh green chilli, chopped
50g/2oz/¼ cup butter

1 Boil the potatoes until soft then mash them down using a masher.

2 Stir the remaining ingredients together in a small bowl.

3 Stir the spice mixture into the mashed potatoes. Mix together thoroughly with a fork and serve warm as an accompaniment.

COOK'S TIP

Mango powder, also known as *amchur*, is the unripe green fruit of the mango tree ground to a powder. The sour mangoes are sliced and dried in the sun, turning a light brown, before they are ground. Mango powder adds a fruity sharpness, and a slightly resinous bouquet, to a dish. It is widely used with vegetables and is usually added towards the end of the cooking time. If mango powder is unavailable, the nearest substitute is lemon or lime juice, in double or treble quantity.

NUTRITIONAL NOTES
Per Portion

Energy	100Kcals/416KJ
Fat	5.30g
Saturated Fat	1.25g
Carbohydrate	11.40g
Fibre	0.80g

Spicy Cabbage

Another spicy twist on a Western favourite. This nutritious side dish is a great way to jazz up the flavour of cabbage for those not usually keen on the vegetable. Note the colourful variations.

INGREDIENTS

Serves 4

50g/2oz/¼ cup ghee or butter
2.5ml/½ tsp white cumin seeds
3–8 dried red chillies, to taste
1 small onion, sliced
225g/8oz/2½ cups cabbage, shredded
2 medium carrots, grated
2.5ml/½ tsp salt
30ml/2 tbsp lemon juice

1 Melt the ghee or butter in a medium pan and fry the cumin seeds and dried chillies for about 30 seconds.

2 Add the onion and fry for about 2 minutes. Add the cabbage and carrots and stir-fry for a further 5 minutes or until the cabbage is soft.

3 Finally, stir in the salt and lemon juice and serve at once.

VARIATION

Try this with red onion and red cabbage for a colourful alternative.

NUTRITIONAL NOTES
Per Portion

Energy	91Kcals/376KJ
Fat	5.50g
Saturated Fat	1.27g
Carbohydrate	8.50g
Fibre	2.40g

Spiced Potatoes and Carrots Parisienne

Ready prepared "parisienne" vegetables have recently become available in many supermarkets. These are simply root vegetables that have been peeled and cut into perfectly spherical shapes. This dish looks extremely fresh and appetizing and is delicious.

INGREDIENTS

Serves 4

175g/6oz carrots parisienne
175g/6oz potatoes parisienne
115g/4oz green beans, sliced
75g/3oz/6 tbsp butter
15ml/1 tbsp vegetable oil
1.5ml/¼ tsp onion seeds
1.5ml/¼ tsp fenugreek seeds
4 dried red chillies
2.5ml/½ tsp mustard seeds
6 curry leaves
1 medium onion, sliced
5ml/1 tsp salt
4 garlic cloves, sliced
4 fresh red chillies
15ml/1 tbsp chopped fresh
  coriander (cilantro)
15ml/1 tbsp chopped fresh mint, plus
  1 mint sprig to garnish

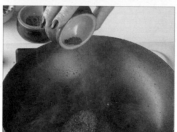

1 Drop the carrots, potatoes and green beans into a pan of boiling water, and cook for about 7 minutes, or until they are just tender but not overcooked. Drain in a colander, then refresh under cold water to arrest the cooking process. Drain again and set to one side.

2 Heat the butter and oil in a deep frying pan or a large karahi and add the onion seeds, fenugreek seeds, dried red chillies, mustard seeds and curry leaves. When these have sizzled for a few seconds, add the onion and fry for 3–5 minutes, stirring the mixture occasionally.

3 Add the salt, garlic and fresh chillies, followed by the cooked vegetables, and stir gently for about 5 minutes, over a medium heat.

4 Add the fresh coriander and mint and serve hot, garnished with a sprig of mint.

NUTRITIONAL NOTES	
Per Portion	
Energy	232Kcals/961KJ
Fat	18.6g
Saturated Fat	10.2g
Carbohydrate	15g
Fibre	2.7g

COOK'S TIP

If you can't locate "parisienne" vegetables, you can simply dice the potatoes and carrots yourself, or cut them into batons.

Karahi Shredded Cabbage with Cumin

This is one of the best ways to cook cabbage, stir-fried with butter and crushed spices. This mild side dish makes a wonderful accompaniment to many other meats or vegetables.

INGREDIENTS

Serves 4

15ml/1 tbsp corn oil
50g/2oz/¼ cup ghee or butter
2.5ml/½ tsp crushed coriander seeds
2.5ml/½ tsp white cumin seeds
6 dried red chillies
1 small savoy cabbage, shredded
12 mange-tout (snow peas)
3 fresh red chillies, seeded and sliced
12 baby corn cobs
salt, to taste
25g/1oz/¼ cup flaked (slivered)
    almonds, toasted
15ml/1 tbsp chopped fresh
    coriander (cilantro)

1 Heat the oil and butter in a deep round-bottomed frying pan or a karahi and add the crushed coriander seeds, white cumin seeds and dried red chillies.

2 Add the shredded cabbage and mange-tout and stir-fry for about 5 minutes.

3 Add the sliced fresh red chillies, baby corn cobs and salt, and fry for a further 3 minutes.

4 Garnish with the toasted almonds and fresh coriander and serve hot.

NUTRITIONAL NOTES	
Per Portion	
Energy	184Kcals/759KJ
Fat	16.9g
Saturated Fat	7.2g
Carbohydrate	4.3g
Fibre	3g

Potatoes in Red Sauce

This is a lightly spiced dish, perfect for children or those who like mild curries.

INGREDIENTS

Serves 4–6

450g/1lb small new potatoes
7.5ml/1½ tsp coriander seeds
7.5ml/1½ tsp cumin seeds
4 garlic cloves
90ml/6 tbsp vegetable oil
45ml/3 tbsp thick tamarind juice
60ml/4 tbsp tomato purée (paste)
4 curry leaves
salt, to taste
5ml/1 tsp granulated sugar
coriander (cilantro) sprig, to garnish

1 Boil the potatoes until they are fully cooked but still retain their shape. To test, insert a thin sharp knife into the potatoes. It should come out clean when the potatoes are fully cooked. Drain well.

2 Grind the coriander seeds with the cumin seeds and garlic to a coarse paste using a pestle and mortar or food processor.

3 Heat the oil in a karahi, wok or frying pan. Fry the paste, tamarind juice, tomato purée, curry leaves, salt and sugar until the oil separates.

4 Add the potatoes and stir to coat them in the spicy tomato mixture. Reduce the heat, cover and simmer for about 5 minutes. Garnish and serve.

NUTRITIONAL NOTES	
Per Portion	
Energy	231Kcals/962KJ
Fat	16.8g
Saturated Fat	2.1g
Carbohydrate	19.2g
Fibre	1.1g

Cucumber Curry

Served hot, this is good with fish dishes and can also be served cold with cooked meats.

INGREDIENTS

Serves 4–6

120ml/4fl oz/½ cup water
115g/4oz creamed coconut or
    120ml/4fl oz/½ cup coconut cream
2.5ml/½ tsp ground turmeric
salt, to taste
5ml/1 tsp sugar
1 large cucumber, cut into small pieces
1 large red (bell) pepper, cut into
    small pieces
50g/2oz/½ cup salted peanuts, crushed
60ml/4 tbsp vegetable oil
2 dried red chillies
5ml/1 tsp cumin seeds
5ml/1 tsp mustard seeds
4–6 curry leaves
4 garlic cloves, crushed
a few whole salted peanuts, to garnish

1 Bring the water to the boil in a heavy pan and add the creamed coconut, turmeric, salt and sugar. Simmer until the coconut dissolves and the mixture becomes a smooth, thick sauce.

2 Add the cucumber, red pepper and crushed peanuts and simmer for about 5 minutes. Transfer to a heat-proof serving dish and keep hot.

3 Heat the oil in a karahi, wok or frying pan. Fry the chillies and cumin with the mustard seeds until they start to pop.

4 Reduce the heat, add the curry leaves and garlic and fry for 2 minutes. Pour over the cucumber mixture and stir well. Garnish with whole peanuts and serve hot.

NUTRITIONAL NOTES	
Per Portion	
Energy	385Kcals/1588KJ
Fat	37.6g
Saturated Fat	19.6g
Carbohydrate	6.4g
Fibre	1.7g

Potatoes in Tomato Sauce

This curry makes an excellent accompaniment to almost any other savoury dish, but goes particularly well with Balti dishes. Served with rice, it makes a great vegetarian main course.

INGREDIENTS

Serves 4

10ml/2 tsp oil
1.5ml/¼ tsp onion seeds
4 curry leaves
2 medium onions, diced
400g/14oz can tomatoes
5ml/1 tsp ground cumin
7.5ml/1½ tsp ground coriander
5ml/1 tsp chilli powder
5ml/1 tsp grated fresh root ginger
5ml/1 tsp crushed garlic
1.5ml/¼ tsp ground turmeric
5ml/1 tsp salt
15ml/1 tbsp lemon juice
15ml/1 tbsp chopped fresh
  coriander (cilantro)
2 medium potatoes, diced

1 Heat the oil in a karahi, wok or heavy pan and fry the onion seeds, curry leaves and onions over a medium heat for a few minutes, being careful not to burn the onions.

2 Meanwhile, place the canned tomatoes in a bowl and add the cumin, ground coriander, chilli powder, ginger, garlic, turmeric, salt, lemon juice and fresh coriander. Mix together until well blended.

3 Pour this mixture into the pan and stir for about 1 minute to mix thoroughly with the onions.

4 Finally, add the diced potatoes, cover the pan and cook gently for 7–10 minutes over a low heat. Check that the potatoes are properly cooked through, then serve.

VARIATIONS

This curry is also delicious if you add a few cauliflower or broccoli florets with the potatoes, or if you substitute diced parsnips for the potatoes. To emphasize the tomato flavour, stir in 15ml/1 tbsp tomato purée (paste).

NUTRITIONAL NOTES
Per Portion

Energy	119Kcals/502KJ
Fat	2.27g
Saturated Fat	0.24g
Carbohydrate	22.91g
Fibre	2.88g

Kidney Bean Curry

This is a popular Punjabi-style dish using red kidney beans. You can substitute the same quantity of other pulses, if you prefer.

INGREDIENTS

Serves 4

225g/8oz/1 cup dried red kidney beans
30ml/2 tbsp oil
2.5ml/½ tsp cumin seeds
1 onion, thinly sliced
1 fresh green chilli, finely chopped
2 garlic cloves, crushed
2.5cm/1in piece fresh root ginger, grated
30ml/2 tbsp curry paste
5ml/1 tsp ground cumin
5ml/1 tsp ground coriander
2.5ml/½ tsp chilli powder
2.5ml/½ tsp salt
400g/14oz can chopped tomatoes
30ml/2 tbsp chopped fresh
    coriander (cilantro)

1 Leave the kidney beans to soak overnight in a bowl of cold water.

2 Drain the beans and put in a large saucepan with double the volume of water. Boil vigorously for 10 minutes. Skim off any scum. Cover and cook for 1–1½ hours or until the beans are soft.

3 Meanwhile, heat the oil in a large heavy frying pan and fry the cumin seeds for 2 minutes until they begin to splutter. Add the onion, chilli, garlic and ginger and fry for 5 minutes. Stir in the curry paste, cumin, ground coriander, chilli powder and salt and cook for 5 minutes.

4 Add the tomatoes and simmer for 5 minutes. Drain the beans and stir them in with the fresh coriander, reserving a little for the garnish. Cover and cook for 15 minutes, adding a little water if necessary. Serve garnished with the reserved fresh coriander.

NUTRITIONAL NOTES	
Per Portion	
Energy	258Kcals/1087KJ
Fat	7.80g
Saturated Fat	0.86g
Carbohydrate	33.70g
Fibre	11.70g

———— COOK'S TIP ————

If you want to reduce the cooking time, cook the beans in a pressure cooker for 20–25 minutes after boiling them vigorously for 10 minutes. Alternatively, replace the dried beans with canned beans. Use a 400g/14oz can and drain it well.

Bombay Potatoes

This authentic dish belongs to the Gujarati, a totally vegetarian people and the largest population group in Mumbai.

INGREDIENTS

Serves 4–6
450g/1lb new potatoes
salt, to taste
5ml/1 tsp turmeric
60ml/4 tbsp vegetable oil
2 dried red chillies
6–8 curry leaves
2 onions, finely chopped
2 fresh green chillies, finely chopped
50g/2oz/2 cups fresh coriander
 (cilantro), coarsely chopped
1.5ml/¼ tsp asafoetida
2.5ml/½ tsp each, cumin, mustard,
 onion, fennel and nigella seeds
lemon juice, to taste

1 Scrub the potatoes under cold running water and cut them into small pieces. Boil the potatoes in water with a little salt and ½ tsp of the turmeric for 10–15 minutes, or until tender. Drain the potatoes well then mash them and set aside.

2 Heat the oil in a frying pan and fry the dried chillies and curry leaves until the chillies are nearly burnt.

3 Add the onions, green chillies, fresh coriander, remaining turmeric and spice seeds to the pan and cook until the onions are soft.

4 Fold in the potatoes and add a few drops of water. Cook over a low heat for about 10 minutes, stirring well to ensure the spices are evenly mixed. Add lemon juice to taste, and serve.

NUTRITIONAL NOTES	
Per Portion	
Energy	207Kcals/865KJ
Fat	11.6g
Saturated Fat	1.4g
Carbohydrate	24.3g
Fibre	2.2g

Curried Cauliflower

In this dish the creamy coconut sauce complements the flavour of the spiced cauliflower.

INGREDIENTS

Serves 4–6
15ml/1 tbsp gram flour (besan)
120ml/4fl oz/½ cup water
5ml/1 tsp chilli powder
15ml/1 tbsp ground coriander
5ml/1 tsp ground cumin
5ml/1 tsp mustard powder
5ml/1 tsp ground turmeric
salt, to taste
60ml/4 tbsp vegetable oil
6–8 curry leaves
5ml/1 tsp cumin seeds
1 cauliflower, broken into florets
175ml/6fl oz/¾ cup thick coconut milk
juice of 2 lemons
lime wedges, to serve

1 Put the gram flour in a small bowl and stir in enough of the water to make a smooth paste. Add the chilli, coriander, cumin, mustard, turmeric and salt. Add the remaining water and keep mixing to blend all the ingredients well.

2 Heat the oil in a frying pan (skillet), add the curry leaves and cumin seeds. Add the spice paste and simmer for about 5 minutes. If the sauce has become too thick, add a little hot water.

3 Add the cauliflower and coconut milk. Bring to the boil, reduce the heat, cover and cook until the cauliflower is tender but crunchy. Cook longer if you prefer. Add the lemon juice, mix well and serve hot with the lime wedges.

NUTRITIONAL NOTES	
Per Portion	
Energy	160Kcals/663KJ
Fat	12.1g
Saturated Fat	1.6g
Carbohydrate	9g
Fibre	2g

VARIATION
This sauce also goes well with broccoli. For a pretty presentation use whole miniature vegetables.

Peppers Filled with Spiced Vegetables

Nigella, or kalonji as it is also known, is a tiny black seed. It is widely used in Indian cooking, especially sprinkled over breads or in potato dishes. It has a mild, slightly nutty flavour and is best toasted for a few seconds in a dry or lightly oiled frying pan over a medium heat before being used in a recipe. This helps to bring out its flavour.

INGREDIENTS

Serves 6

6 large evenly shaped red or yellow
  (bell) peppers
500g/1¼lb waxy potatoes
1 small onion, chopped
4–5 garlic cloves, chopped
5cm/2in piece fresh root
  ginger, chopped
1–2 fresh green chillies, seeded
  and chopped
105ml/7 tbsp water
90–105ml/6–7 tbsp vegetable oil
1 aubergine (eggplant), diced
10ml/2 tsp cumin seeds
5ml/1 tsp nigella seeds
2.5ml/½ tsp ground turmeric
5ml/1 tsp ground coriander
5ml/1 tsp ground toasted cumin seeds
cayenne pepper
about 30ml/2 tbsp lemon juice
sea salt and black pepper
30ml/2 tbsp chopped fresh coriander
  (cilantro), to garnish

1 Cut the tops off the red or yellow peppers, then remove and discard the seeds. Cut a thin slice off the base of any wobbly peppers so that they stand upright.

> **COOK'S TIP**
>
> The hottest part of a chilli is the white membrane that connects the seeds to the flesh. Removing the seeds and membrane before cooking gives a milder flavour.

2 Bring a large pan of lightly salted water to the boil. Add the peppers and cook for 5–6 minutes. Drain and leave them upside down in a colander.

3 Cook the potatoes in lightly salted, boiling water for 10–12 minutes until just tender. Drain, cool and peel, then cut into 1cm/½in dice.

4 Put the onion, garlic, ginger and green chillies in a food processor or blender with 60ml/4 tbsp of the water and process to a purée.

5 Heat 45ml/3 tbsp of the vegetable oil in a large, deep frying pan and cook the diced aubergine, stirring occasionally, until it is evenly browned on all sides. Remove the aubergine from the pan using a slotted spoon and set aside.

6 Add another 30ml/2 tbsp of the vegetable oil to the pan, add the diced potatoes and cook until lightly browned on all sides. Remove the potatoes from the pan and set aside.

7 If necessary, add another 15ml/ 1 tbsp sunflower oil to the pan, then add the cumin and nigella seeds. Fry briefly until the seeds darken, then add the turmeric, coriander and ground cumin. Cook for 15 seconds. Stir in the onion and garlic purée and fry, scraping the pan with a spatula, until the onions begin to brown.

8 Return the potatoes and aubergine to the pan, season with salt, pepper and 1–2 pinches of cayenne. Add the remaining water and 15ml/1 tbsp lemon juice and then cook, stirring, until the liquid evaporates. Preheat the oven to 190°C/375°F/Gas 5.

9 Fill the peppers with the spiced vegetable mixture and place on a lightly greased baking tray. Brush the peppers with a little oil and bake for 30–35 minutes until they are cooked. Leave to cool a little, then sprinkle with a little more lemon juice. Garnish with the coriander and serve.

NUTRITIONAL NOTES	
Per Portion	
Energy	221Kcals/923KJ
Fat	12.1g
Saturated Fat	1.6g
Carbohydrate	26.1g
Fibre	4.4g

Stuffed Bananas

Bananas are cooked with spices in many different ways in southern India. Some recipes contain large quantities of chillies, but the taste is skilfully mellowed by adding coconut milk and tamarind juice. Green bananas are available from Indian stores, or you can use plantains or unripe eating bananas that are firm to the touch.

INGREDIENTS

Serves 4

1 bunch fresh coriander (cilantro)
4 green bananas or plantains
30ml/2 tbsp ground coriander
15ml/1 tbsp ground cumin
5ml/1 tsp chilli powder
2.5ml/½ tsp salt
1.5ml/¼ tsp ground turmeric
5ml/1 tsp granulated sugar
15ml/1 tbsp gram flour
90ml/6 tbsp vegetable oil
1.5ml/¼ tsp cumin seeds
1.5ml/¼ tsp black mustard seeds

NUTRITIONAL NOTES	
Per Portion	
Energy	265Kcals/1110KJ
Fat	16.8g
Saturated Fat	2.1g
Carbohydrate	29.4g
Fibre	1.3g

_____ COOK'S TIP _____

Baby courgettes (zucchini) would make a delicious alternative to bananas.

1 Set aside two or three coriander sprigs for the garnish. If necessary, remove the roots and any thick stems from the remaining coriander, then chop the leaves finely.

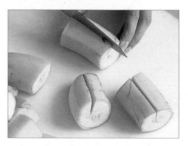

2 Trim the bananas or plantains and cut each crossways into three equal pieces, leaving the skin on. Make a lengthwise slit along each piece of banana, without cutting all the way through the flesh.

3 On a plate mix together the ground coriander, cumin, chilli powder, salt, turmeric, sugar, gram flour, chopped fresh coriander and 15ml/1 tbsp of the oil. Use your fingers to combine well.

4 Carefully stuff each piece of banana with the spice mixture, taking care not to break the bananas in half.

5 Heat the remaining oil in a wok, karahi or large pan, and fry the cumin and mustard seeds for 2 minutes or until they begin to splutter. Add the bananas and toss gently in the oil.

6 Cover and simmer over a low heat for 15 minutes, stirring from time to time, until the bananas are soft but not mushy.

7 Garnish with the fresh coriander sprigs, and serve with warm chapatis, if you like.

Chilli and Mustard Flavoured Pineapple

Pineapple is cooked with coconut milk and a blend of spices in this South Indian dish, which could be served with any meat, fish or vegetable curry. The chilli adds heat, and the mustard seeds lend a rich, nutty flavour that complements the sharpness of the pineapple, while the coconut milk provides a delectable creamy sweetness.

INGREDIENTS

Serves 4
1 pineapple
50ml/2fl oz/¼ cup water
150ml/¼ pint/⅔ cup coconut milk
2.5ml/½ tsp ground turmeric
2.5ml/½ tsp crushed dried chillies
5ml/1 tsp salt
10ml/2 tsp granulated sugar
15ml/1 tbsp groundnut (peanut) oil
2.5ml/½ tsp mustard seeds
2.5ml/½ tsp cumin seeds
1 small onion, finely chopped
1–2 dried red chillies, broken
6–8 fresh curry leaves

1 Using a sharp knife halve the pineapple lengthways, then cut each half into two, so that you end up with four boat-shaped wedges. Peel them and remove the eyes and the central core. Cut into bitesize pieces.

2 Put the pineapple in a karahi, wok or large pan and add the measured water, with the coconut milk, turmeric and crushed chillies. Bring to a slow simmer over a low heat, and cook, covered, for 10–12 minutes, or until the pineapple is soft, but not mushy.

3 Add the salt and sugar, and cook, uncovered, until the sauce thickens.

4 Heat the oil in a second pan, and add the mustard seeds. As soon as they begin to pop, add the cumin seeds and the onion. Fry for 6–7 minutes, stirring regularly, until the onion is soft.

5 Add the chillies and curry leaves. Fry for 1–2 minutes more, then pour the entire contents over the pineapple. Stir well, then remove from the heat. Serve hot or cold, but not chilled.

COOK'S TIP

Use canned pineapple in natural juice to save time. You will need approximately 500g/1¼lb drained pineapple.

NUTRITIONAL NOTES
Per Portion

Energy	60Kcals/252KJ
Fat	3g
Saturated Fat	0.6g
Carbohydrate	8.3g
Fibre	0.8g

Yogurt Salad

If this salad looks and tastes familiar, it isn't surprising. It is very similar to coleslaw, except that yogurt is used instead of mayonnaise, and cashew nuts are added.

INGREDIENTS

Serves 4

350ml/12fl oz/1½ cups natural (plain) low fat yogurt
10ml/2 tsp clear honey
2 medium carrots, thickly sliced
2 spring onions (scallions), roughly chopped
115g/4oz cabbage, finely shredded
50g/2oz/⅓ cup sultanas (golden raisins)
50g/2oz/½ cup cashew nuts, optional
16 white grapes, halved
2.5ml/½ tsp salt
5ml/1 tsp chopped fresh mint

1 Using a fork, beat the yogurt in a bowl with the honey.

2 In a separate bowl, which will be suitable for serving the salad, mix together the carrots, spring onions, cabbage, sultanas, cashew nuts (if you are using them), grapes, salt and chopped mint.

3 Pour the sweetened yogurt mixture over the salad, mix well and serve.

NUTRITIONAL NOTES	
Per Portion	
Energy	119Kcals/503KJ
Fat	0.90g
Saturated Fat	0.49g
Carbohydrate	23.40g
Fibre	1.80g

Spicy Baby Vegetable Salad

This warm vegetable salad makes an excellent accompaniment.

INGREDIENTS

Serves 6

10 baby potatoes, halved
15 baby carrots
10 baby courgettes (zucchini)
115g/4oz/1½ cups button (white) mushrooms

For the dressing

45ml/3 tbsp lemon juice
25ml/1½ tbsp oil
15ml/1 tbsp chopped fresh coriander (cilantro)
5ml/1 tsp salt
2 fresh green chillies, finely sliced

1 Boil the potatoes, carrots and courgettes in water until tender. Drain them and place in a serving dish with the mushrooms.

2 Make the dressing in a separate bowl. Mix together the lemon juice, oil, fresh coriander, salt and chillies.

3 Toss the vegetables in the dressing and serve immediately.

NUTRITIONAL NOTES	
Per Portion	
Energy	73Kcals/308KJ
Fat	3.10g
Saturated Fat	0.39g
Carbohydrate	10.10g
Fibre	1.50g

_____ COOK'S TIP _____

As well as looking extremely attractive, the tiny baby vegetables give this salad a lovely flavour. Other baby vegetables, such as leeks, miniature corn cobs or egg-size cauliflowers can be used just as well.

Spinach and Mushroom Salad

This salad is especially good served with glazed garlic prawns or any other seafood curry.

INGREDIENTS

Serves 4
10 baby corn cobs
115g/4oz/3 cups mushrooms
2 medium tomatoes
20 small spinach leaves
8-10 onion rings
salt and black pepper
fresh coriander (cilantro) sprigs and
  lime slices, to garnish, optional

1 Halve the baby corn cobs and slice the mushrooms and tomatoes.

2 Arrange all the salad ingredients in a bowl. Season with salt and pepper and garnish with fresh coriander and lime slices, if wished.

_____ COOK'S TIP _____

Baby corn can be eaten whole or sliced in half lengthways. Don't overcook them or they will lose their sweetness and be tough. To use in salads, cook for about 3 minutes.

NUTRITIONAL NOTES	
Per Portion	
Energy	25Kcals/103KJ
Fat	0.60g
Saturated Fat	0.09g
Carbohydrate	2.80g
Fibre	1.80g

Nutty Salad

The smooth creamy dressing is perfect with the crunchy nuts.

INGREDIENTS

Serves 4
150g/5oz can red kidney beans, drained
1 medium onion, cut into 12 rings
1 medium green courgette
  (zucchini), sliced
1 medium yellow courgette
  (zucchini), sliced
50g/2oz/⅔ cup pasta shells, cooked
50g/2oz/½ cup cashew nuts
25g/1oz/¼ cup peanuts
fresh coriander (cilantro) and lime
  wedges, to garnish

For the dressing
115g/4oz low fat fromage frais or
  ricotta cheese
30ml/2 tbsp natural (plain) low
  fat yogurt
1 fresh green chilli, chopped
15ml/1 tbsp chopped fresh
  coriander (cilantro)
salt and pepper
2.5ml/½ tsp crushed dried red chillies
15ml/1 tbsp lemon juice

1 Drain the kidney beans. Arrange them with the onion rings, kidney beans, courgette slices and pasta in a salad dish and sprinkle the cashew nuts and peanuts over the top.

2 In a separate bowl, mix together the fromage frais or ricotta cheese, yogurt, green chilli, fresh coriander and salt. Beat well using a fork until all the ingredients are thoroughly combined. You may find it easier to add the coriander leaves a few at a time and mix in, to allow their flavour to permeate the mixture and ensure the resulting dressing is smooth in texture.

3 Sprinkle the crushed peppercorns, red chillies and lemon juice over the dressing. Garnish the salad with fresh coriander and lime wedges and serve with the dressing.

NUTRITIONAL NOTES	
Per Portion	
Energy	199Kcals/829KJ
Fat	11.60g
Saturated Fat	2.63g
Carbohydrate	15.20g
Fibre	2.90g

_____ COOK'S TIP _____

Make the dressing just before serving the salad, when the flavour of the coriander will be at its most intense.

Sweet Potato and Carrot Salad

This warm salad has a piquant flavour. As a main course, it will serve two.

INGREDIENTS

Serves 4

1 medium sweet potato
2 carrots, cut into thick diagonal slices
3 medium tomatoes
8–10 iceberg lettuce leaves
75g/3oz/½ cup drained
   canned chickpeas

For the dressing
15ml/1 tbsp clear honey
90ml/6 tbsp natural (plain) low
   fat yogurt
2.5ml/½ tsp salt
5ml/1 tsp coarsely ground black pepper

For the garnish
15ml/1 tbsp walnuts
15ml/1 tbsp sultanas (golden raisins)
1 small onion, cut into rings

1 Peel and dice the sweet potato. Cook in boiling water until soft but not mushy, remove from the heat, cover the pan and set aside.

NUTRITIONAL NOTES	
Per Portion	
Energy	127Kcals/532KJ
Fat	3.70g
Saturated Fat	0.47g
Carbohydrate	20.60g
Fibre	3.10g

2 Cook the carrots in a pan of boiling water for just a few minutes, making sure that they remain crunchy. Add the carrots to the sweet potatoes.

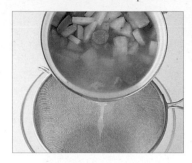

3 Drain the water from the sweet potatoes and carrots and mix them together in a bowl.

4 Slice the tops off the tomatoes, then scoop out and discard the seeds. Roughly chop the flesh.

COOK'S TIP

The skin of sweet potatoes may be pink or orangey yellow and the flesh can range from mealy to moist and from almost white to deep yellow in colour. It is best to boil or bake sweet potatoes in their skins if possible, as some varieties turn a dullish colour if boiled unpeeled.

5 Line a glass bowl with the lettuce leaves. Add the carrots, chickpeas and tomatoes to the potatoes and carrots. Mix lightly, then spoon the mixture into the lettuce-lined bowl.

6 Mix together all the dressing ingredients and beat using a fork.

7 Garnish the salad with the walnuts, sultanas and onion rings. Pour the dressing over the salad or serve it in a separate bowl.

Carrot and Orange Salad

A fruit and a vegetable that could have been made for each other form the basis of this wonderful, fresh-tasting salad.

INGREDIENTS

Serves 4
450g/1lb carrots
2 large oranges
15ml/1 tbsp olive oil
30ml/2 tbsp lemon juice
pinch of granulated sugar, optional
30ml/2 tbsp chopped pistachio nuts or
    toasted pine nuts
salt and black pepper

1 Peel the carrots and grate them into a large bowl.

2 Peel the oranges with a sharp knife and cut into segments, catching the juice in a small bowl.

3 Mix together the olive oil, lemon juice and orange juice. Season with a little salt and pepper to taste, and sugar if you like.

4 Toss the orange segments together with the carrots and pour the dressing over. Scatter the salad with the pistachio nuts or pine nuts before serving.

COOK'S TIP

Squeeze the orange pulp after removing the segments, to extract the maximum amount of juice.

NUTRITIONAL NOTES	
Per Portion	
Energy	148Kcals/618KJ
Fat	7.4g
Saturated Fat	1.1g
Carbohydrate	18.4g
Fibre	5g

Fennel Coleslaw

Another variation on traditional coleslaw in which the aniseed flavour of fennel plays a major role.

INGREDIENTS

Serves 4

175g/6oz fennel
2 spring onions (scallions)
175g/6oz white cabbage
115g/4oz celery
175g/6oz carrots
50g/2oz/⅓ cup sultanas
   (golden raisins)
2.5ml/½ tsp caraway seeds
15ml/1 tbsp chopped fresh parsley
45ml/3 tbsp extra-virgin olive oil
5ml/1 tsp lemon juice
shreds of spring onion (scallion),
   to garnish

1 Using a sharp knife, cut the fennel and spring onions into thin slices.

2 Slice the cabbage and celery finely and cut the carrots into fine strips. Place in a bowl with the fennel and spring onions. Add the sultanas and caraway seeds, and toss lightly to mix.

3 Stir in the chopped parsley, olive oil and lemon juice and mix all the ingredients very thoroughly. Cover and chill for 3 hours to allow the flavours to mingle. Serve garnished with shreds of spring onion.

<hr>
VARIATION
<hr>

Use sour cream instead of olive oil for a creamier dressing.

<hr>
NUTRITIONAL NOTES
Per Portion

Energy	146Kcals/607KJ
Fat	8.7g
Saturated Fat	1.2g
Carbohydrate	15.9g
Fibre	3.8g

Spicy Potato Salad

This tasty salad is quick to prepare, and makes a satisfying accompaniment to grilled or barbecued meat or fish.

INGREDIENTS

Serves 6
900g/2lb potatoes
2 red (bell) peppers
2 celery sticks
1 shallot
2 or 3 spring onions (scallions)
1 fresh green chilli
1 garlic clove, crushed
10ml/2 tsp finely snipped fresh chives
10ml/2 tsp finely chopped fresh basil
15ml/1 tbsp finely chopped
    fresh parsley
30ml/2 tbsp single (light) cream
45ml/3 tbsp mayonnaise
5ml/1 tsp prepared mild mustard
7.5ml/1½ tsp granulated sugar
salt
chopped fresh chives, to garnish

3 Mix the cream, mayonnaise, mustard and sugar in a small bowl, stirring until the mixture is well combined.

4 Pour the dressing over the salad and stir gently to coat evenly. Serve, garnished with the chopped chives.

NUTRITIONAL NOTES	
Per Portion	
Energy	185Kcals/777KJ
Fat	6.7g
Saturated Fat	1.3g
Carbohydrate	29.3g
Fibre	2.6g

1 Peel the potatoes. Boil in salted water for 10–12 minutes, until tender. Drain and cool, then cut into cubes and place in a large mixing bowl.

2 Halve the peppers, cut away and discard the core and seeds and cut the flesh into small pieces. Finely chop the celery, shallot and spring onions and slice the chilli very thinly, discarding the seeds. Add the vegetables to the potatoes together with the garlic and herbs.

Coronation Chicken

The connection between this recipe and traditional Indian cooking is tenuous, but coronation chicken is such a popular dish that it would have been churlish to leave it out.

INGREDIENTS

Serves 6
450g/1lb new potatoes
45ml/3 tbsp French dressing
3 spring onions (scallions), chopped
6 eggs, hard-boiled and halved
frilly lettuce leaves
¼ cucumber, cut into thin strips
6 large radishes, sliced
salad cress, optional
salt and pepper

For the coronation dressing
30ml/2 tbsp olive oil
1 small onion, chopped
15ml/1 tbsp mild curry powder or
  korma spice mix
10ml/2 tsp tomato purée (paste)
30ml/2 tbsp lemon juice
30ml/2 tbsp sherry
300ml/½ pint/1¼ cups mayonnaise
150ml/¼ pint/⅔ cup natural
  (plain) yogurt

1 Boil the potatoes in salted water until tender. Drain them, transfer to a large bowl and toss in the French dressing while they are still warm.

2 Stir in the spring onions and the salt and pepper, and leave to cool thoroughly.

3 Meanwhile, make the coronation dressing. Heat the oil in a small pan. Fry the onion for 3 minutes, until soft. Stir in the curry powder or spice mix and fry for a further 1 minute. Remove from the heat and mix in all the other dressing ingredients.

4 Stir the dressing into the potatoes, add the eggs, then chill.

5 Line a serving platter with lettuce leaves and pile the salad in the centre. Scatter over the cucumber and radishes with the cress, if using.

NUTRITIONAL NOTES	
Per Portion	
Energy	597Kcals/2468KJ
Fat	53g
Saturated Fat	8.8g
Carbohydrate	15.2g
Fibre	1.2g

Peppery Bean Salad

This pretty salad uses canned beans for speed and convenience.

INGREDIENTS

Serves 4–6

425g/15oz can red kidney beans
425g/15oz can black-eyed beans (peas)
425g/15oz can chickpeas
¼ red (bell) pepper
¼ green (bell) pepper
6 radishes
15ml/1 tbsp chopped spring
   onion (scallion)

For the dressing

5ml/1 tsp ground cumin
15ml/1 tbsp tomato ketchup
30ml/2 tbsp olive oil
15ml/1 tbsp white wine vinegar
1 garlic clove, crushed
2.5ml/½ tsp hot pepper sauce

1 Drain the red kidney beans, black-eyed beans and chickpeas and rinse under cold running water. Shake off the excess water and tip them into a large bowl.

2 Core, seed and chop the peppers. Trim the radishes and slice thinly. Add the peppers, radishes and spring onion to the bowl.

3 Make the dressing. Mix together the cumin, tomato ketchup, oil, vinegar and garlic in a small bowl. Add a little salt and hot pepper sauce to taste and stir again thoroughly.

4 Pour the dressing over the salad and mix. Cover the salad and chill for at least 1 hour before serving, garnished with the sliced spring onion.

COOK'S TIP

Look out for cans of mixed beans at the supermarket. These contain a colourful medley and would be perfect for this salad.

NUTRITIONAL NOTES
Per Portion

Energy	430Kcals/1814KJ
Fat	9.3g
Saturated Fat	1.3g
Carbohydrate	64.8g
Fibre	19.8g

Mango, Tomato and Red Onion Salad

This salad makes an appetizing starter. The under-ripe mango blends well with the tomato.

INGREDIENTS

Serves 4

1 firm under-ripe mango
2 large tomatoes or 1 beef
   tomato, sliced
½ red onion, sliced into rings
½ cucumber, peeled and thinly sliced
chopped chives, to garnish

For the dressing

30 ml/2 tbsp vegetable oil
15 ml/1 tbsp lemon juice
1 garlic clove, crushed
2.5 ml/½ tsp hot pepper sauce
salt and black pepper

1 Have the mango lengthways, cutting either side of the stone. Cut the flesh into slices and peel the skin away neatly.

2 Arrange the mango, tomatoes, onion and cucumber on a large serving plate.

3 Make the dressing. Blend the oil, lemon juice, garlic, pepper sauce and seasoning in a blender or food processor, or shake vigorously in a small screw-top jar.

NUTRITIONAL NOTES	
Per Portion	
Energy	89Kcals/370KJ
Fat	5.8g
Saturated Fat	0.7g
Carbohydrate	8.6g
Fibre	1.9g

4 Spoon the dressing over the salad. Garnish with the chopped chives and serve.

Relishes
and Chutneys

ONE OF the delights of dining out on Indian food is the dazzling selection of relishes and chutneys that always accompanies the meal. Unlike bottled chutneys, which are slow-cooked and tend to be jam-like in consistency, these are usually freshly made mixtures, where each of the component flavours can be easily discerned.

Relishes and chutneys have a variety of purposes at the table. Raita cools the palate, while Hot Lime Pickle has the opposite effect. Fresh Coriander Relish is ideal for providing lovely colour and fresh flavour, and works perfectly with spicy kebabs and samosas. Mango Chutney is an old favourite, often served as a sweet and fruity dip with poppadums, as well as in its more traditional role as a tangy accompaniment for curries. Finally, there's Bombay Duck pickle, one of the curiosities of the culinary world. Made with salted fish rather than fowl, it's a special and unique contribution to Indian cuisine.

Spiced Yogurt

Yogurt is always a welcome accompaniment to hot curries. This is topped with a hot spice mixture to provide a contrast in both taste and temperature.

INGREDIENTS

Makes 450ml/³/₄ pint/scant 2 cups

450ml/³/₄ pint/scant 2 cups natural (plain) yogurt
2.5ml/¹/₂ tsp freshly ground fennel seeds
salt, to taste
2.5ml/¹/₂ tsp granulated sugar
60ml/4 tbsp vegetable oil
1 dried red chilli
1.5ml/¹/₄ tsp mustard seeds
1.5ml/¹/₄ tsp cumin seeds
4–6 curry leaves
pinch each of asafoetida and ground turmeric

1 In a heatproof serving dish, mix together the yogurt, fennel seeds, salt and sugar. Cover and chill until you are nearly ready to serve.

2 Heat the oil in a frying pan and fry the dried chilli, mustard and cumin seeds, curry leaves, asafoetida and turmeric. When the chilli turns dark, pour the oil and spices over the yogurt. Fold the yogurt together with the spices at the table when serving.

NUTRITIONAL NOTES	
Per 25g/1oz Portion	
Energy	36Kcals/149KJ
Fat	2.6g
Saturated Fat	0.4g
Carbohydrate	1.8g
Fibre	0g

_____ COOK'S TIP _____

Asafoetida is quite bitter. Leave it out if you prefer.

Raita

Raitas are served to cool the effect of hot curries. Cucumber and mint raita is the best known combination. This is a refreshing fruit and nut version, which is particularly good with beef curries.

INGREDIENTS

Serves 4

350ml/12fl oz/1½ cups natural (plain) yogurt
75g/3oz seedless grapes
50g/2oz/½ cup shelled walnuts
2 firm bananas
5ml/1 tsp granulated sugar
salt, to taste
5ml/1 tsp freshly ground cumin seeds
1.5ml/¼ tsp freshly roasted cumin seeds, chilli powder or paprika, to garnish

1 Place the yogurt in a chilled bowl and add the grapes and walnuts. Slice the bananas directly into the bowl and fold in gently before the bananas turn brown.

2 Add the sugar, salt and ground cumin, and gently mix together. Chill, and just before serving, sprinkle on the cumin seeds, chilli powder or paprika.

_____ VARIATIONS _____

Instead of grapes, try kiwi fruit, peaches or nectarines. Almonds or hazelnuts can be used instead of, or as well as, the walnuts.

NUTRITIONAL NOTES	
Per Portion	
Energy	184Kcals/771KJ
Fat	9.6g
Saturated Fat	1.2g
Carbohydrate	19.2g
Fibre	1g

Sweet and Sour Raita

This raita teams honey with mint sauce, chilli and fresh coriander to make a soothing mixture with underlying warmth. It goes well with biryanis.

INGREDIENTS

Serves 4

475ml/16fl oz/2 cups natural (plain) low fat yogurt
5ml/1 tsp salt
5ml/1 tsp granulated sugar
30ml/2 tbsp clear honey
7.5ml/1½ tsp mint sauce
30ml/2 tbsp roughly chopped fresh coriander (cilantro)
1 fresh green chilli, seeded and finely chopped
1 medium onion, diced
50ml/2fl oz/¼ cup water

1 Pour the yogurt into a bowl and whisk it well. Add the salt, sugar, honey and mint sauce.

3 Reserve a little chopped coriander for the garnish and add the rest to the yogurt mixture, with the chilli, onion and water.

4 Whisk once again and pour into a serving bowl. Garnish with the reserved coriander and place in the refrigerator until ready to serve.

2 Taste to check the sweetness and add more honey, if desired.

NUTRITIONAL NOTES	
Per Portion	
Energy	128Kcals/541KJ
Fat	1.18g
Saturated Fat	0.64g
Carbohydrate	24.40g
Fibre	0.53g

____ COOK'S TIP ____

A 5–10cm/2–4in piece of peeled, seeded and grated cucumber can also be added to raita. Drain the cucumber in a colander, pressing it against the sides to extract excess liquid, which would dilute the raita.

Fried Sesame Seed Chutney

This versatile chutney doubles as a dip, and also a sandwich filling with thin slices of cucumber.

INGREDIENTS

Serves 4

175g/6oz/³/₄ cup sesame seeds
5ml/1 tsp salt
120–150ml/4–5fl oz/¹/₂–²/₃ cup water
2 fresh green chillies, seeded and diced
60ml/4 tbsp chopped fresh
    coriander (cilantro)
15ml/1 tbsp chopped fresh mint
15ml/1 tbsp tamarind paste
30ml/2 tbsp granulated sugar
5ml/1 tsp oil
1.5ml/¹/₄ tsp onion seeds
4 curry leaves
onion rings, sliced chillies and
    fresh coriander (cilantro) leaves,
    to garnish

1 Dry-roast the sesame seeds and leave to cool. Grind them in a coffee grinder to a grainy powder.

NUTRITIONAL NOTES	
Per Portion	
Energy	347Kcals/1438KJ
Fat	28.31g
Saturated Fat	4.03g
Carbohydrate	25.31g
Fibre	3.63g

2 Transfer the sesame powder to a bowl. Add the salt, water, diced chillies, coriander, mint, tamarind paste and sugar, and use a fork to mix everything together. Taste and adjust the seasoning if necessary; the mixture should have a sweet-and-sour flavour.

3 Heat the oil in a heavy pan and fry the onion seeds and curry leaves. Tip the sesame seed paste into the pan and stir-fry for about 45 seconds. Transfer the chutney to a serving dish and leave to cool.

4 Garnish with onion rings, sliced green and red chillies and fresh coriander leaves and serve with your chosen curry.

Fresh Tomato and Onion Chutney

Chutneys are served with most
meat dishes in Indian cuisine.

INGREDIENTS

Serves 4

8 tomatoes
1 medium onion, chopped
45ml/3 tbsp brown sugar
5ml/1 tsp garam masala
5ml/1 tsp ground ginger
175ml/6fl oz/³⁄₄ cup malt vinegar
5ml/1 tsp salt
15ml/1 tbsp clear honey
natural (plain) yogurt, sliced green chilli
and fresh mint leaves, to garnish

_____ COOK'S TIP _____

This chutney will keep for about 2 weeks
in a covered jar in the refrigerator.

1 Wash the tomatoes and cut them
into quarters.

NUTRITIONAL NOTES	
Per Portion	
Energy	118Kcals/503KJ
Fat	0.66g
Saturated Fat	0.18g
Carbohydrate	43.90g
Fibre	2.34g

2 Place them with the onion in a
heavy pan.

3 Add the sugar, garam masala,
ginger, vinegar, salt and honey,
half-cover the pan with a lid and cook
over a low heat for about 20 minutes.

4 Mash the tomatoes with a fork to
break them up, then continue to
cook on a slightly higher heat until the
chutney thickens.

5 Spoon the chutney into a bowl
and leave to cool, then cover and
place in the refrigerator until needed.
Serve chilled, garnished with yogurt,
sliced chilli and mint leaves.

Sweet and Sour Tomato and Onion Relish

This delicious relish can be served with any savoury meal.

INGREDIENTS

Serves 4

2 medium firm tomatoes
1 medium onion
1 fresh green chilli
15ml/1 tbsp fresh mint leaves
15ml/1 tbsp fresh coriander leaves
2.5ml/½ tsp Tabasco sauce
15ml/1 tbsp clear honey
2.5ml/½ tsp salt
30ml/2 tbsp lime juice
15ml/1 tbsp natural (plain) low
    fat yogurt

1 Place the tomatoes in hot water for a few seconds. Lift each tomato out in turn, using a slotted spoon. The skins should have split, making it easy to remove them. Peel off carefully. Cut the tomatoes in half, and squeeze out the seeds. Chop them roughly. Set aside.

2 Using a sharp knife, roughly chop the onion, green chilli, mint and fresh coriander.

3 Place the herb mixture in a food processor with the Tabasco sauce, honey, salt and lime juice. Add the tomatoes to this and grind everything together for a few seconds.

_____ COOK'S TIP _____

This relish will keep for up to 1 week in the refrigerator: prepare up to the end of step 3 but do not add the yogurt until just before you want to serve it.

4 Pour into a small serving bowl. Stir in the yogurt just before you serve the relish.

NUTRITIONAL NOTES	
Per Portion	
Energy	43Kcals/180KJ
Fat	0.29g
Saturated Fat	0.06g
Carbohydrate	9.43g
Fibre	0.96g

Spicy Tomato Chutney

This delicious relish is especially suited to lentil dishes. If kept in a covered bowl in the refrigerator, it will keep for a week.

INGREDIENTS

Makes 450–500g/16–18oz/2–2¼ cups
90ml/6 tbsp vegetable oil
5cm/2in piece cinnamon stick
4 cloves
5ml/1 tsp freshly roasted cumin seeds
5ml/1 tsp nigella seeds
4 bay leaves
5ml/1 tsp mustard seeds, crushed
800g/1¾lb canned, chopped tomatoes
4 garlic cloves, crushed
5cm/2in piece fresh root
  ginger, crushed
5ml/1 tsp chilli powder
5ml/1 tsp ground turmeric
60ml/4 tbsp brown sugar

1 Pour the oil into a frying pan, karahi or wok and place over a medium heat. When the oil is hot, fry the cinnamon, cloves, cumin and nigella seeds, bay leaves and mustard seeds for about 5 minutes.

2 Crush the garlic cloves and add them to the spice mixture. Fry until golden. Meanwhile, drain the tomatoes, reserving the juices.

3 Add the ginger, chilli powder, turmeric, sugar and the reserved tomato juices. Simmer until reduced, add the tomatoes and cook for 15–20 minutes. Cool and serve.

NUTRITIONAL NOTES
Per 25g/1oz Portion

Energy	53Kcals/224KJ
Fat	3.8g
Saturated Fat	0.5g
Carbohydrate	4.8g
Fibre	0.4g

Mango Chutney

Chutneys are usually served as an accompaniment to curry but this one is particularly nice served in a cheese sandwich or as a dip with poppadums.

INGREDIENTS

Makes 450g/1lb/2 cups
60ml/4 tbsp malt vinegar
2.5ml/½ tsp crushed dried chillies
6 cloves
6 peppercorns
5ml/1 tsp roasted cumin seeds
2.5ml/½ tsp onion seeds
salt, to taste
175g/6oz/¾ cup granulated sugar
450g/1lb green (unripe) mangoes, peeled and cubed
5cm/2in piece fresh root ginger, thinly sliced
2 garlic cloves, crushed
thin peel of 1 orange or lemon, optional

1 Pour the vinegar into a pan, and add the chillies, cloves, peppercorns, cumin and onion seeds, salt and sugar. Place over a low heat and simmer until the spices infuse the vinegar – about 15 minutes.

2 Add the mango, ginger, garlic and peel, if using. Simmer until the mango is mushy and most of the vinegar has evaporated. When cool, pour into sterilized bottles. Cover and leave for a few days before serving.

COOK'S TIP

Ginger freezes very well, which can be handy if you find it difficult to get fresh ginger locally. It can be sliced or grated straight from the freezer and will thaw on contact with hot food.

NUTRITIONAL NOTES
Per 25g/1oz Portion

Energy	52Kcals/224KJ
Fat	0g
Saturated Fat	0g
Carbohydrate	13.7g
Fibre	0.7g

Tomato Relish

This is a simple relish served with most meals. It provides a contrast to hot curries, with its crunchy texture and refreshing ingredients.

INGREDIENTS

Serves 4–6
2 small fresh green chillies
2 limes
2.5ml/½ tsp granulated sugar
2 onions, finely chopped
4 firm tomatoes, finely chopped
½ cucumber, finely chopped
few fresh coriander (cilantro)
   leaves, chopped
salt and black pepper
few fresh mint leaves, to garnish

1 Using a sharp knife, cut both chillies in half. Scrape out the seeds, then chop the chillies finely and place them in a small bowl.

COOK'S TIP

For a milder flavour, use just one chilli, or dispense with the chilli altogether and substitute with a green (bell) pepper.

2 Squeeze the limes. Pour the juice into a glass bowl and add the sugar, with salt and pepper to taste. Set the bowl aside until the sugar and salt have dissolved, stirring the mixture occasionally.

3 Add the chopped chillies to the bowl, with the chopped onions, tomatoes, cucumber, chilli and fresh coriander leaves. Mix well.

4 Cover the bowl with clear film (plastic wrap) and place in the refrigerator for at least 3 hours, so that the flavours blend. Just before serving, taste the relish and add more salt, pepper or sugar if needed. Garnish with mint and serve.

NUTRITIONAL NOTES	
Per Portion	
Energy	47Kcals/198KJ
Fat	0.5g
Saturated Fat	0.1g
Carbohydrate	9.4g
Fibre	2.3g

Fresh Coriander Relish

Delicious as an accompaniment to kebabs, samosas and bhajias, this relish can also be used as a spread for cucumber or tomato sandwiches.

INGREDIENTS

Makes about 450g/1lb/2 cups

30ml/2 tbsp vegetable oil
1 dried red chilli
1.5ml/¼ tsp each, cumin, fennel and onion seeds
1.5ml/¼ tsp asafoetida
4 curry leaves
115g/4oz/1⅓ cups desiccated (dry unsweetened shredded) coconut
10ml/2 tsp granulated sugar
salt, to taste
3 fresh green chillies, chopped
175–225g/6–8oz fresh coriander (cilantro), chopped
60ml/4 tbsp mint sauce
juice of 3 lemons

NUTRITIONAL NOTES	
Per 25g/1oz Portion	
Energy	51Kcals/211KJ
Fat	5.2g
Saturated Fat	3.5g
Carbohydrate	0.8g
Fibre	0.9g

_____ COOK'S TIP _____

This may seem like a lot of coriander, but it is compacted when ground with the spices.

1 Heat the oil in a frying pan and add the dried chilli, the cumin, fennel and onion seeds, the asafoetida, curry leaves, desiccated coconut, sugar and salt. Fry, stirring often, until the coconut turns golden brown. Tip into a bowl and leave to cool.

2 Grind the spice mixture with the green chillies, fresh coriander (cilantro) and mint sauce. Moisten with lemon juice. Scrape into a bowl and chill before serving.

Red Onion, Garlic and Lemon Relish

This powerful relish is flavoured with spices and punchy preserved lemons. It reached India by way of Spain, being introduced by Jewish refugees forced to leave that country in the 15th century.

INGREDIENTS

Serves 6

45ml/3 tbsp olive oil
3 large red onions, sliced
2 heads of garlic, separated into cloves and peeled
10ml/2 tsp coriander seeds, crushed but not finely ground
10ml/2 tsp light muscovado sugar, plus a little extra
pinch of saffron threads
5cm/2in piece cinnamon stick
2–3 small whole dried red chillies, optional
2 fresh bay leaves
30–45ml/2–3 tbsp sherry vinegar
juice of ½ small orange
30ml/2 tbsp chopped preserved lemon
salt and black pepper

1 Heat the oil in a heavy pan. Add the onions and stir, then cover and reduce the heat to the lowest setting. Cook for 10–15 minutes, stirring occasionally, until the onions are soft and pale gold in colour.

2 Add the whole peeled garlic cloves and the crushed coriander seeds. Cover and cook for 5–8 minutes until the garlic is soft.

3 Add a pinch of salt, lots of pepper and the sugar. Stir, then cook, uncovered, for 5 minutes. Soak the saffron in about 45ml/3 tbsp warm water for 5 minutes, then add to the onions, with the soaking water.

4 Add the cinnamon stick, dried chillies, if using, and bay leaves. Stir in 30ml/2 tbsp of the sherry vinegar and the orange juice.

5 Cook over a low heat, uncovered, until the onions are very soft and most of the liquid has evaporated. Stir in the preserved lemon and cook gently for a further 5 minutes. Taste and adjust the seasoning, adding more salt, sugar and/or vinegar to taste.

6 Serve warm or cold, but not hot or chilled. The relish tastes best if it is left to stand for 24 hours.

NUTRITIONAL NOTES	
Per Portion	
Energy	107Kcals/442KJ
Fat	5.8g
Saturated Fat	0.8g
Carbohydrate	12g
Fibre	2.2g

English Pickled Onions

The English love of pickled onions is famous, and at the time of the Raj the popular pickle was introduced into India. They should be stored for at least 6 weeks before being eaten.

INGREDIENTS

Makes 3–4 450g/1lb jars
1kg/2¼lb pickling onions
115g/4oz/½ cup salt
750ml/1¼ pints/3 cups malt vinegar
15ml/1 tbsp granulated sugar
2–3 dried red chillies
5ml/1 tsp brown mustard seeds
15ml/1 tbsp coriander seeds
5ml/1 tsp allspice berries
5ml/1 tsp black peppercorns
5cm/2in piece fresh root ginger, sliced
2–3 blades of mace
2–3 fresh bay leaves

1 Trim off the root end of each onion, but leave the onion layers attached. Cut a thin slice off the top (neck) end of each onion. Place the onions in a bowl, then cover with boiling water. Leave to stand for about 4 minutes, then drain. Peel off the skin from each onion with a small, sharp knife.

2 Place the peeled onions in a bowl and cover with cold water, then drain the water off and pour it into a large pan. Add the salt and heat slightly to dissolve it, then cool before pouring the brine over the onions.

3 Cover the bowl with a plate and weigh it down slightly so that all the onions are submerged in the brine. Leave the onions to stand in the salted water for 24 hours.

4 Pour the vinegar into a large pan. Wrap all the remaining ingredients, except the bay leaves, in a piece of muslin or sew them into a coffee filter paper and add to the vinegar with the bay leaves. Bring to the boil, simmer for 5 minutes, then remove from the heat. Set aside to cool and infuse overnight.

5 Drain the onions, rinse and pat dry. Pack them into sterilized jars. Add some or all of the spice from the vinegar, but not the ginger slices. The pickle will get hotter if you add the chillies. Pour the vinegar over the onions to cover and add the bay leaves. Cover the jars with non-metallic lids and store in a cool dark place for at least 6 weeks before eating.

VARIATION

To make sweet pickled onions, follow the same method, but add 50g/2oz/4 tbsp light muscovado sugar to the vinegar. A couple of pieces of cinnamon stick and 5ml/1 tsp cloves are good additions to this version.

COOK'S TIP

For sterilizing, stand clean, rinsed jars upside down on a rack on a baking sheet and place in the oven at 180°C/350°F/Gas 4 for 20 minutes.

NUTRITIONAL NOTES	
Per Portion	
Energy	120Kcals/500KJ
Fat	0.7g
Saturated Fat	0g
Carbohydrate	26.3g
Fibre	4.7g

Fresh Coconut Chutney with Onion and Chilli

Serve a bowl of this tasty fresh chutney as an accompaniment for any Indian-style main course.

INGREDIENTS

Serves 4–6

200g/7oz fresh coconut, grated
3–4 fresh green chillies, seeded
   and chopped
20g/¾oz fresh coriander (cilantro),
   chopped, plus 2–3 sprigs to garnish
30ml/2 tbsp chopped fresh mint
30–45ml/2–3 tbsp lime juice
about 2.5ml/½ tsp salt
about 2.5ml/½ tsp caster (superfine) sugar
15–30ml/1–2 tbsp coconut milk, optional
30ml/2 tbsp groundnut (peanut) oil
5ml/1 tsp nigella seeds
1 small onion, very finely chopped

1 Place the coconut, chillies, coriander and mint in a food processor. Add 30ml/2 tbsp of the lime juice, then process until thoroughly chopped.

2 Scrape the mixture into a bowl and add more lime juice to taste. Add salt and sugar to taste. If the mixture is dry, stir in 15–30ml/1–2 tbsp coconut milk.

3 Heat the oil in a small pan and fry the nigella seeds until they begin to pop, then reduce the heat and add the onion. Fry, stirring frequently, for 4–5 minutes, until the onion is soft.

4 Stir the onion mixture into the coconut mixture and leave to cool. Garnish with coriander before serving.

NUTRITIONAL NOTES	
Per Portion	
Energy	168Kcals/693KJ
Fat	17.2g
Saturated Fat	11.1g
Carbohydrate	2.4g
Fibre	2.8g

Onion, Mango and Peanut Chaat

Chaats are spiced relishes of vegetables and nuts, delicious with many savoury Indian dishes.

INGREDIENTS

Serves 4

90g/3½oz/scant 1 cup unsalted peanuts
15ml/1 tbsp peanut oil
1 onion, chopped
½ cucumber, seeded and diced
1 mango, peeled, stoned and diced
1 fresh green chilli, seeded and chopped
30ml/2 tbsp chopped fresh
   coriander (cilantro)
15ml/1 tbsp chopped fresh mint
15ml/1 tbsp lime juice
pinch of light muscovado sugar

For the chaat masala

10ml/2 tsp ground toasted cumin seeds
2.5ml/½ tsp cayenne pepper
5ml/1 tsp mango powder (amchur)
2.5ml/½ tsp garam masala
pinch ground asafoetida
salt and black pepper

1 To make the chaat masala, grind all the spices together, then season with 2.5ml/½ tsp each of salt and pepper.

2 Fry the peanuts in the oil until lightly browned, then drain on kitchen paper until cool.

3 Mix the onion, cucumber, mango, chilli, fresh coriander and mint in a bowl. Sprinkle in 5ml/1 tsp of the chaat masala. Stir in the peanuts and then add lime juice and/or sugar to taste. Set the mixture aside for 20–30 minutes for the flavours to mature.

4 Spoon the mixture into a serving bowl, sprinkle another 5ml/1 tsp of the chaat masala over and serve.

_____ COOK'S TIP _____

Any remaining chaat masala will keep in a sealed jar for 4–6 weeks.

NUTRITIONAL NOTES	
Per Portion	
Energy	187Kcals/776KJ
Fat	13.3g
Saturated Fat	2.5g
Carbohydrate	11.1g
Fibre	2.9g

Apricot Chutney

Chutneys can add zest to most meals, and in India you will usually find a selection of different kinds served in tiny bowls for people to choose from. Dried apricots are readily available from supermarkets or health food shops.

INGREDIENTS

Makes about 450g/1lb/2 cups

450g/1lb/3 cups dried apricots, finely diced
5ml/1 tsp garam masala
275g/10oz/1¼ cups soft light brown sugar
450ml/¾ pint/scant 2 cups malt vinegar
5ml/1 tsp grated fresh root ginger
5ml/1 tsp salt
75g/3oz/½ cup sultanas (golden raisins)
450ml/¾ pint/scant 2 cups water

1 Put all the ingredients into a medium pan and mix thoroughly with a spoon.

2 Bring to the boil, then reduce the heat and simmer for 30–35 minutes, stirring occasionally.

3 When the chutney has thickened to a fairly stiff consistency, spoon it into 2–3 clean jam jars and leave to cool. This chutney should be stored in the refrigerator.

NUTRITIONAL NOTES	
Per 25g/1oz Portion	
Energy	118Kcals/506KJ
Fat	0.2g
Saturated Fat	0g
Carbohydrate	29.7g
Fibre	2.0g

Tasty Toasts

These crunchy toasts make an ideal snack or part of a brunch. They are especially delicious served with grilled tomatoes and baked beans.

INGREDIENTS

Makes 4

4 eggs
300ml/½ pint/1¼ cups milk
2 fresh green chillies, finely chopped
2 tbsp chopped fresh coriander (cilantro)
75g/3oz/¾ cup Cheddar or mozzarella cheese, grated
2.5ml/½ tsp salt
1.5ml/¼ tsp freshly ground black pepper
4 slices bread
corn oil for frying

1 Break the eggs into a medium bowl and whisk together. Slowly add the milk and whisk again. Add the chillies, coriander, cheese, salt and pepper, and mix well.

2 Cut the bread slices in half diagonally, and soak them, one at a time, in the egg mixture.

3 Heat the oil in a medium frying pan and fry the bread slices over a medium heat, turning them once or twice, until they are golden brown.

4 Drain off any excess oil as you remove the toasts from the pan and serve immediately.

NUTRITIONAL NOTES	
Per Portion	
Energy	267Kcals/1118KJ
Fat	14.5g
Saturated Fat	6.9g
Carbohydrate	17.8g
Fibre	0.9g

Hot Lime Pickle

A good lime pickle is not only delicious served with any meal, but it increases the appetite and aids digestion.

INGREDIENTS

Makes 450g/1lb/2 cups
25 limes
225g/8oz/1 cup salt
50g/2oz/½ cup fenugreek powder
50g/2oz/½ cup mustard powder
150g/5oz/⅔ cup chilli powder
15g/½oz/2 tbsp ground turmeric
600ml/1 pint/2½ cups mustard oil
5ml/1 tsp asafoetida
30ml/2 tbsp yellow mustard
 seeds, crushed

1 Cut each lime into 8 pieces and remove the seeds, if you like. Put the limes in a large sterilized jar or glass bowl. Add the salt and toss with the limes. Cover and leave in a warm place for 1–2 weeks, until they become soft and dull brown in colour.

2 Mix together the fenugreek, mustard powder, chilli powder and turmeric and add to the limes.

3 Cover and leave to rest in a warm place for a further 2 or 3 days.

4 Heat the mustard oil in a frying pan and fry the asafoetida and mustard seeds. When the oil reaches smoking point, pour it over the limes. Mix well, cover with a clean cloth and leave in a warm place for about 1 week before serving.

NUTRITIONAL NOTES	
Per 10g/¼oz Portion	
Energy	82Kcals/336KJ
Fat	8.9g
Saturated Fat	1.1g
Carbohydrate	0g
Fibre	0g

Green Chilli Pickle

Southern India is the source of some of the hottest curries and pickles. You might imagine that eating them would be a case of going for the burn, but they actually cool the body.

INGREDIENTS

Makes 450–550g/1–1¼lb/2–2½ cups
50g/2oz/4 tbsp yellow mustard
 seeds, crushed
50g/2oz/4 tbsp freshly ground
 cumin seeds
25g/1oz/¼ cup ground turmeric
50g/2oz garlic cloves, crushed, plus
 20 small garlic cloves, peeled but
 left whole
150ml/¼ pint/⅔ cup white vinegar
75g/3oz/⅓ cup granulated sugar
10ml/2 tsp salt
150ml/¼ pint/⅔ cup mustard oil
450g/1lb small fresh green
 chillies, halved

1 Mix the mustard and cumin seeds, the turmeric, crushed garlic, vinegar, sugar and salt together in a sterilized glass bowl. Cover with a cloth and leave to rest for 24 hours. This enables the spices to infuse and the sugar and salt to melt.

2 Heat the mustard oil in a frying pan and gently fry the spice mixture for about 5 minutes. (Keep a window open while cooking with mustard oil as it is pungent and the smoke may irritate the eyes.) Add the garlic cloves and fry for a further 5 minutes.

3 Add the chillies and cook gently until tender but still green in colour. This will take about 30 minutes on a low heat.

4 Cool thoroughly, then pour into sterilized bottles, ensuring the oil is evenly distributed if you are using more than one bottle. Leave to rest for a week before serving.

NUTRITIONAL NOTES	
Per 25g/1oz Portion	
Energy	54Kcals/226KJ
Fat	5.7g
Saturated Fat	0.6g
Carbohydrate	0.1g
Fibre	0g

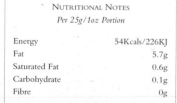

Bombay Duck Pickle

Boil is the name of a fish that is found off the west coast of India during the monsoon season. It is salted and dried in the sun and is characterized by a strong smell and distinctive piquancy. How this fish acquired the name Bombay duck in the Western world is still unknown. Bombay duck can be served hot or cold, and is usually eaten with Indian breads as an accompaniment to vegetable dishes.

INGREDIENTS

Serves 4–6

6–8 pieces boil (Bombay duck), soaked in water for 5 minutes
60ml/4 tbsp vegetable oil
2 fresh red chillies, chopped
15ml/1 tbsp granulated sugar
450g/1lb cherry tomatoes, halved
115g/4oz deep-fried onions
red onion rings, to garnish (optional)

—————— COOK'S TIP ——————

As an alternative to boil, try using skinned mackerel fillets, but don't fry them. You will only need 30ml/2 tbsp vegetable oil to make the sauce.

1 Pat the fish dry with kitchen paper. Heat the oil in a frying pan and fry the fish pieces for about 30–45 seconds on both sides until crisp. Be careful not to burn them or they will taste bitter. Drain well. When cool, break into small pieces.

2 Cook the remaining ingredients until the tomatoes become pulpy and the onions are blended into a sauce. Fold in the Bombay duck and mix well. Leave to cool, then garnish and serve, or ladle into a hot sterilized jar, cover and leave to cool.

NUTRITIONAL NOTES	
Per Portion	
Energy	233Kcals/973KJ
Fat	15.3g
Saturated Fat	1.8g
Carbohydrate	11.5g
Fibre	2g

Sweet-and-Sour Pineapple

This may sound like a Chinese recipe, but it is a traditional Bengali dish known as *tok*. The predominant flavour is ginger, and the pieces of golden pineapple, dotted with plump, juicy raisins, have plenty of visual appeal with taste to match. It is equally delicious if made with mangoes instead of the pineapple.

INGREDIENTS

Serves 4

800g/1¾lb canned pineapple rings or
   chunks in natural juice
15ml/1 tbsp vegetable oil
2.5ml/½ tsp black mustard seeds
2.5ml/½ tsp cumin seeds
2.5ml/½ tsp onion seeds
10ml/2 tsp grated fresh root ginger
5ml/1 tsp crushed dried chillies
50g/2oz/⅓ cup seedless raisins
115g/4oz/½ cup granulated sugar
7.5ml/1½ tsp salt

1 Drain the pineapple in a colander and reserve the juice. Chop the pineapple rings or chunks finely (you should have approximately 500g/1¼lb).

NUTRITIONAL NOTES	
Per Portion	
Energy	264Kcals/1124KJ
Fat	3.2g
Saturated Fat	0.3g
Carbohydrate	61.5g
Fibre	2.7g

2 Heat the vegetable oil in a karahi, wok or large pan over a medium heat and immediately add the mustard seeds. As soon as they pop, add the cumin seeds, then the onion seeds. Add the ginger and chillies and stir-fry the spices briskly for 30 seconds until they release their flavours.

3 Add the pineapple, raisins, sugar and salt. Add 300ml/½ pint/ 1¼ cups of the juice (made up with cold water if necessary) and stir into the pineapple mixture.

4 Bring the mixture to the boil, reduce the heat to medium and cook, uncovered, for 20–25 minutes.

Indian Breads

NO INDIAN meal would be complete without some form of bread. Flat and crisp or soft and puffy, they seem to be the perfect compliment to spicy food, and are ideal for mopping up the juices of a particularly sumptuous curry.

Most Indian breads are cooked on a griddle, which gives them their characteristically dimpled appearance. Naan is traditionally baked in the tandoor, the clay oven also employed for cooking meat and fish, but excellent results can be obtained using a combination of a conventional oven and a grill or broiler. Wholemeal flour is a popular choice for making the dough, although in southern India, lentils and rice are ground to make the popular pancakes known as *dosas*. Gram flour or *besan* is made from chickpeas and is used in the making of Missi Rotis. Although many Indian breads are now on sale in the supermarket, it is great fun – and also rather impressive – to have a go at making your own.

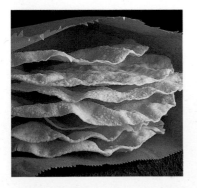

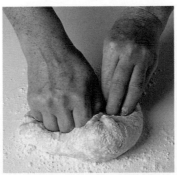

Chapatis

A chapati is an unleavened bread made from chapati flour, a ground wholemeal flour known as *atta*, which is finer than the Western equivalent. An equal quantity of standard wholemeal flour and plain flour will also produce satisfactory results, although chapati flour is available from Indian grocers. This is the everyday bread of the Indian home.

INGREDIENTS

Makes 8–10
225g/8oz/2 cups chapati flour
  or ground wholemeal
  (whole-wheat) flour
2.5ml/½ tsp salt
175ml/6fl oz/¾ cup water

1 Place the flour and salt in a mixing bowl. Make a well in the middle and gradually stir in the water, mixing well with your fingers. Form a supple dough and knead for 7–10 minutes. Ideally, cover with clear film (plastic wrap) and leave on one side for 15–20 minutes to rest.

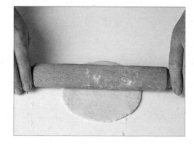

2 Divide the dough into 8–10 equal portions. Roll out each piece to a circle on a well-floured surface.

3 Place a tava (chapati griddle) or heavy frying pan over a high heat. When steam rises from it, lower the heat to medium and add the first chapati to the pan.

4 When the chapati begins to bubble, turn it over. Press down with a clean dishtowel or a flat spoon and turn once again. Remove the cooked chapati from the pan and keep warm in a piece of foil lined with kitchen paper while you cook the other chapatis. Repeat the process until all the breads are cooked. Serve hot.

NUTRITIONAL NOTES	
Per Portion	
Energy	96Kcals/408KJ
Fat	0.4g
Saturated Fat	0.1g
Carbohydrate	21.9g
Fibre	0.9g

Naan

This bread was introduced to India by the Moguls who originally came from Persia via Afghanistan. In Persian, the word *naan* means bread. Traditionally, naan is not rolled, but patted and stretched until the teardrop shape is achieved. You can, of course, roll it out to a circle, then gently pull the lower end, which will give you the traditional shape.

INGREDIENTS

Makes about 3

225g/8oz/2 cups unbleached white bread flour
2.5ml/½ tsp salt
15g/½oz fresh yeast
60ml/4 tbsp lukewarm milk
15ml/1 tbsp vegetable oil
30ml/2 tbsp natural (plain) yogurt
1 egg
30–45ml/2–3 tbsp melted ghee or butter, for brushing

1 Sift the flour and salt together into a large bowl. In a smaller bowl, cream the yeast with the milk. Set aside for 15 minutes.

2 Add the yeast and milk mixture, vegetable oil, yogurt and egg to the flour. Combine the mixture using your hands until it forms a soft dough. Add a little more of the lukewarm water if the dough is too dry.

3 Turn the dough out on to a lightly floured surface and knead for about 10 minutes, or until it feels smooth. Return the dough to the bowl, cover and leave in a warm place for about 1 hour, or until it has doubled in size. Preheat the oven to its highest setting – it should not be any lower than 230°C/450°F/Gas 8.

4 Turn out the dough back on to the floured surface and knead for a further 2 minutes.

5 Divide into three equal pieces, shape into balls and roll out into teardrop shapes 25cm/10in long, 13cm/5in wide and 5mm–8mm/¼–⅓in thick.

6 Preheat the grill (broiler) to its highest setting. Meanwhile, place the naan on preheated baking sheets and bake for 3–4 minutes, or until puffed up.

7 Remove from the oven and place under the hot grill for a few seconds until the tops brown slightly. Brush with ghee or butter and serve warm.

NUTRITIONAL NOTES	
Per Portion	
Energy	197Kcals/830KJ
Fat	8.2g
Saturated Fat	5g
Carbohydrate	29.2g
Fibre	1.2g

Garlic and Coriander Naan

From the Caucasus through the Punjab region of northwest India and beyond, these leavened breads are served. Traditionally cooked in a very hot clay oven known as a tandoor, naan are usually eaten with dry meat or vegetable dishes.

INGREDIENTS

Makes 3 naan

280g/10oz/2½ cups unbleached white
   bread flour
5ml/1 tsp salt
5ml/1 tsp dried yeast
60ml/4 tbsp natural (plain) yogurt
15ml/1 tbsp melted butter or ghee
1 garlic clove, finely chopped
5ml/1 tsp black onion seeds
15ml/1 tbsp fresh coriander (cilantro)
10ml/2 tsp clear honey
30–45ml/2–3 tbsp melted ghee or
   butter, for brushing

VARIATIONS

You can flavour naan in numerous ways:
• To make poppy seed naan, brush the rolled-out naan with a little ghee and sprinkle with poppy seeds.
• To make onion-flavoured naan, add 1 small finely chopped or coarsely grated onion to the dough in step 2. You may need to reduce the amount of egg if the onion is very moist to prevent making the dough too soft.
• To make Peshwari naan, roll out each ball of dough and sprinkle with flaked (sliced) almonds and sultanas (golden raisins). Fold over and roll to the teardrop shape.

COOK'S TIP

To help the dough to puff up and brown, place the baking sheets in an oven pre-heated to the maximum temperature for at least 10 minutes before baking. Preheat the grill (broiler) while the naan are baking.

1 Sift the flour and salt together into a large bowl. In a smaller bowl, cream the yeast with the natural yogurt. Set aside for 15 minutes.

2 Add the yeast mixture to the flour with the melted butter or ghee, and add the chopped garlic, black onion seeds and chopped coriander, mixing to a soft dough.

3 Tip out the dough on to a lightly floured surface and knead for about 10 minutes until smooth and elastic. Place in a lightly oiled bowl, cover with lightly oiled clear film (plastic wrap) and leave to rise, in a warm place, for 45 minutes, or until the dough has doubled in bulk.

4 Preheat the oven to its highest setting, at least 230°C/450°F/ Gas 8. Place 3 heavy baking sheets in the oven to heat.

5 Turn the dough out on to a lightly floured surface and knock back. Divide into 3 equal pieces and shape each into a ball.

6 Cover two of the balls of dough with oiled clear film and roll out the third into a teardrop shape about 25cm/10in long, 13cm/5in wide and about 5mm–8mm/¼–⅓in thick.

7 Preheat the grill (broiler) to its highest setting. Meanwhile, place the naan on the hot baking sheets and bake for 3–4 minutes, or until puffy.

8 Remove the naan from the oven and place under the hot grill for a few seconds, or until the top of each naan browns slightly. Wrap the cooked naan in a dishtowel to keep hot while you roll out and cook the remaining naan. Brush with melted ghee or butter and serve warm.

NUTRITIONAL NOTES	
Per Portion	
Energy	326Kcals/1378KJ
Fat	6.8g
Saturated Fat	1.3g
Carbohydrate	59.7g
Fibre	2.3g

Spiced Naan

Another excellent recipe for naan bread, this time with fennel seeds, onion seeds and cumin seeds.

INGREDIENTS

Makes 6

450g/1lb/4 cups plain
   (all-purpose) flour
5ml/1 tsp baking powder
2.5ml/½ tsp salt
1 sachet easy-blend (rapid-rise)
   dried yeast
5ml/1 tsp caster (superfine) sugar
5ml/1 tsp fennel seeds
10ml/2 tsp onion seeds
5ml/1 tsp cumin seeds
150ml/¼ pint/⅔ cup hand-hot milk
30ml/2 tbsp oil, plus extra for brushing
150ml/¼ pint/⅔ cup natural
   (plain) yogurt
1 egg, beaten

1 Sift the flour, baking powder and salt into a mixing bowl. Stir in the yeast, sugar, fennel seeds, onion seeds and cumin seeds. Make a well in the centre. Stir the hand-hot milk into the flour mixture, then add the oil, yogurt and beaten egg. Mix to form a ball of dough.

2 Tip the dough out on to a lightly floured surface and knead it for 10 minutes until smooth. Return to the clean, lightly oiled bowl and roll the dough to coat it with oil. Cover the bowl with clear film (plastic wrap) and set aside in a warm place until the dough has doubled in bulk.

3 Put a heavy baking sheet in the oven and preheat the oven to 240°C/475°F/Gas 9. Also preheat the grill (broiler). Knead the dough again lightly and divide it into six pieces. Keep five pieces covered while working with the sixth. Quickly roll the piece of dough out to a teardrop shape, brush lightly with oil and slap the naan on to the hot baking sheet. Repeat with the remaining dough.

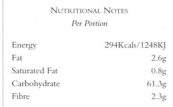

NUTRITIONAL NOTES	
Per Portion	
Energy	294Kcals/1248KJ
Fat	2.6g
Saturated Fat	0.8g
Carbohydrate	61.3g
Fibre	2.3g

4 Bake the naan in the oven for 3 minutes until puffed up, then place the baking sheet under the grill (broil) for about 30 seconds or until the naan are lightly browned. Serve hot or warm as an accompaniment to an Indian curry.

Sugar Bread Rolls

These delicious sweet rolls make an unusual end to a meal.

INGREDIENTS

Makes 10

350g/12oz/3 cups strong white
    bread flour
5ml/1 tsp salt
15ml/1 tbsp caster (superfine) sugar
5ml/1 tsp dried yeast
150ml/¼ pint/⅔ cup hand-hot water
3 egg yolks
50g/2oz/¼ cup unsalted (sweet) butter,
    softened, plus 25g/1oz/2 tbsp extra
75g/3oz Cheddar cheese or Monterey
    Jack, grated
50g/2oz/¼ cup granulated sugar

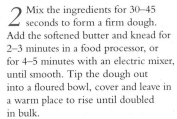

1 Sift the flour, salt and caster sugar into a food processor fitted with a dough blade or the bowl of an electric mixer fitted with a dough hook. Make a well in the centre. Dissolve the yeast in the hand-hot water and pour into the well. Add the egg yolks and leave for a few minutes until bubbles appear on the surface of the liquid.

2 Mix the ingredients for 30–45 seconds to form a firm dough. Add the softened butter and knead for 2–3 minutes in a food processor, or for 4–5 minutes with an electric mixer, until smooth. Tip the dough out into a floured bowl, cover and leave in a warm place to rise until doubled in bulk.

3 Transfer the dough to a lightly floured surface and divide it into 10 pieces. Spread the grated cheese over the surface. Roll each of the dough pieces into 12.5cm/5in lengths, incorporating the cheese as you do so. Coil into snail shapes and place on a lightly greased high-sided tray measuring 30 x 20cm/12 x 8in.

4 Cover the tray with a loose-fitting plastic bag and leave in a warm place for 45 minutes or until the dough has doubled in bulk.

5 Preheat the oven to 190°C/375°F/ Gas 5 and then bake the rolls for 20–25 minutes. Melt the remaining butter, brush it over the rolls, sprinkle with the sugar and allow to cool. Separate the rolls before serving.

NUTRITIONAL NOTES	
Per Portion	
Energy	235Kcals/986KJ
Fat	9.5g
Saturated Fat	5.9g
Carbohydrate	33.7g
Fibre	1.1g

Red Lentil Pancakes

This is a type of *dosa*, which is essentially a pancake from southern India, but used in the similar fashion to north Indian bread. North Indian breads are made of wholemeal or refined flour; in the south they are made of ground lentils and rice.

INGREDIENTS

Makes 6 pancakes
150g/5oz/¾ cup long grain rice
50g/2oz/¼ cup red lentils
250ml/8fl oz/1 cup warm water
5ml/1 tsp salt
2.5ml/½ tsp ground turmeric
2.5ml/½ tsp ground black pepper
30ml/2 tbsp chopped fresh
  coriander (cilantro)
oil, for frying and drizzling

1 Place the long grain rice and lentils in a large mixing bowl, cover with the warm water, cover and soak for at least 8 hours or overnight.

2 Drain off the water and reserve. Place the rice and lentils in a food processor and blend until smooth. Blend in the reserved water. Scrape into a bowl, cover with clear film (plastic wrap) and leave in a warm place to ferment for about 24 hours.

_____ VARIATION _____

Add 60ml/4 tbsp grated coconut to the batter just before cooking.

3 Stir in the salt, turmeric, pepper and coriander. Heat a heavy frying pan over a medium heat for a few minutes until hot. Smear with oil and add about 30–45ml/2–3 tbsp batter.

4 Using the rounded base of a soup spoon, gently spread the batter out, using a circular motion, to make a pancake that is 15cm/6in in diameter.

5 Cook in the pan for 1½–2 minutes, or until set. Drizzle a little oil over the pancake and around the edges. Turn over and cook for about 1 minute, or until golden brown. Keep the cooked pancakes warm in a low oven or on a heatproof plate over simmering water while cooking the remaining pancakes. Serve warm.

NUTRITIONAL NOTES	
Per Portion	
Energy	190Kcals/798KJ
Fat	8.5g
Saturated Fat	1.1g
Carbohydrate	26.1g
Fibre	0.5g

Parathas

Making a paratha is somewhat similar to the technique used when making flaky pastry. The difference lies in the handling of the dough; this can be handled freely, unlike that for a flaky pastry.

INGREDIENTS

Makes 12–15

350g/12oz/3 cups chapati flour or
  wholemeal (whole-wheat) flour,
  plus 50g/2oz/½ cup for dusting
50g/2oz/½ cup plain (all-purpose) flour
5ml/1 tsp salt
40g/1½oz/3 tbsp ghee or unsalted
  (sweet) butter, melted
water, to mix

1 Sift the flours and salt into a bowl. Make a well in the centre and add 10ml/2 tsp of unmelted ghee. Fold it into the flour to make a crumbly texture. Gradually add water to make a soft, pliable dough. Knead until smooth. Cover and leave to rest for 30 minutes.

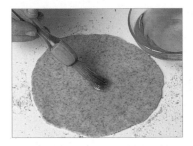

2 Divide the dough into 12–15 equal portions and keep covered. Take one portion at a time and roll out on a lightly floured surface to about 10cm/4in in diameter. Brush the dough with a little of the melted ghee or sweet butter and sprinkle with chapati flour.

3 With a sharp knife, make a straight cut from the centre to the edge of the dough, then lift a cut edge and roll the dough into a cone shape. Lift it and flatten it again into a ball. Roll the dough again on a lightly floured surface until it is 18cm/7in wide.

--- COOK'S TIP ---

If you cannot find chapati flour, known as atta, substitute an equal quantity of wholemeal (whole-wheat) flour and plain (all-purpose) flour.

4 Heat a griddle and cook one paratha at a time, placing a little of the remaining ghee along the edges. Cook on each side until golden brown. Serve hot.

NUTRITIONAL NOTES	
Per Portion	
Energy	123Kcals/521KJ
Fat	2.8g
Saturated Fat	1.4g
Carbohydrate	21.9g
Fibre	2.8g

Missi Rotis

These unleavened breads are a speciality from Punjab. Gram flour, known as *besan*, is made from chickpeas and is combined here with the more traditional wheat flour. In Punjab, missi rotis are very popular with a glass of lassi, a refreshing yogurt drink.

INGREDIENTS

Makes 4

115g/4oz/1 cup gram flour (besan)
115g/4oz/1 cup wholemeal (whole-wheat) flour
1 fresh green chilli, seeded and chopped
½ onion, finely chopped
15ml/1 tbsp chopped fresh coriander (cilantro)
2.5ml/½ tsp ground turmeric
2.5ml/½ tsp salt
15ml/1 tbsp vegetable oil
120–150ml/4–5fl oz/½–⅔ cup lukewarm water
30–45ml/2–3 tbsp melted unsalted (sweet) butter or ghee

1 Mix the two types of flour, chilli, onion, coriander, turmeric and salt together in a large bowl. Stir in the 15ml/1 tbsp oil.

2 Mix in sufficient water to make a pliable soft dough. Tip out the dough on to a lightly floured surface and knead until smooth.

3 Place the dough in a lightly oiled bowl, cover with lightly oiled clear film (plastic wrap) and leave to rest for 30 minutes.

4 Place the dough on to a lightly floured surface. Divide into four equal pieces and shape into balls in the palms of your hands. Roll out each ball into a thick round about 15–18cm/ 6–7in in diameter.

5 Heat a griddle or heavy frying pan over a medium heat for a few minutes until hot.

6 Brush both sides of one roti with some melted butter or ghee. Add it to the griddle or frying pan and cook for about 2 minutes, turning after 1 minute. Brush the cooked roti lightly with melted butter or ghee again, slide it on to a plate and keep warm in a low oven while cooking the remaining rotis in the same way. Serve the rotis warm.

NUTRITIONAL NOTES	
Per Portion	
Energy	226Kcals/958KJ
Fat	3.5g
Saturated Fat	0.5g
Carbohydrate	45.9g
Fibre	2g

Tandoori Rotis

Roti means bread and is the most common food eaten in central and northern India. Tandoori roti is traditionally baked in a tandoor, or clay oven, but it can also be made successfully in an electric or gas oven at the highest setting.

INGREDIENTS

Makes 6

350g/12oz/3 cups chapati flour
   or ground wholemeal
   (whole-wheat) flour
5ml/1 tsp salt
250ml/8fl oz/1 cup water
30–45ml/2–3 tbsp melted ghee or
   unsalted (sweet) butter, for brushing

1 Sift the flour and salt into a large mixing bowl. Add the water and mix to a soft, pliable dough.

2 Knead on a lightly floured surface for 3–4 minutes until smooth. Place the dough in a lightly oiled bowl, cover with lightly oiled clear film (plastic wrap) and leave to rest for about 1 hour.

NUTRITIONAL NOTES	
Per Portion	
Energy	181Kcals/769KJ
Fat	1.3g
Saturated Fat	0.2g
Carbohydrate	37.3g
Fibre	5.3g

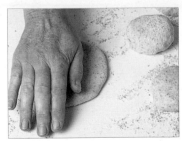

3 Tip out the dough on to a lightly floured surface. Divide the dough into six pieces and shape each into a ball. Press out into a larger round with the palm of your hand, cover with lightly oiled clear film and leave to rest for about 10 minutes.

4 Meanwhile, preheat the oven to 230°C/450°F/Gas 8. Place three baking sheets in the oven to heat. Roll the rotis into 15cm/6in rounds, place two on each baking sheet and bake for 8–10 minutes. Brush with melted ghee or butter and serve warm.

Pooris

These delicious little deep-fried breads, shaped into discs, make it temptingly easy to overindulge. In most areas, they are made of wholemeal flour, but in the east and north-east of India, they are made from plain refined flour, and are known as *loochis*.

INGREDIENTS

Makes 12
115g/4oz/1 cup unbleached plain (all-purpose) flour
115g/4oz/1 cup wholemeal (whole-wheat) flour
2.5ml/½ tsp salt
2.5ml/½ tsp chilli powder
30ml/2 tbsp vegetable oil
100–120ml/3½–4fl oz/7–8 tbsp water
oil, for frying

1 Sift the flours, salt and chilli powder, if using, into a large mixing bowl. Add the vegetable oil then add sufficient water to mix to a dough.

2 Tip the dough out on to a lightly floured surface and knead for 8–10 minutes until smooth.

3 Place in an oiled bowl and cover with oiled clear film (plastic wrap). Leave for 30 minutes.

4 Place the dough on the floured surface. Divide into 12 equal pieces. Keeping the rest of the dough covered, roll one piece into a 13cm/5in round. Repeat with the remaining dough. Stack the pooris, layered between clear film, to keep them moist.

NUTRITIONAL NOTES	
Per Portion	
Energy	79Kcals/333KJ
Fat	2.2g
Saturated Fat	0.3g
Carbohydrate	13.6g
Fibre	1.2g

5 Pour the oil for frying to a depth of 2.5cm/1in in a deep frying pan and heat it to 180°C/350°F. Using a metal fish slice (spatula), lift one poori and gently slide it into the oil; it will sink but will then return to the surface and begin to sizzle. Gently press the poori into the oil. It will puff up. Turn the poori over after a few seconds and allow it to cook for a further 20–30 seconds.

6 Remove the poori from the pan and pat dry with kitchen paper. Place the cooked poori on a large baking tray and keep warm in a low oven while you cook the remaining pooris. Serve warm.

COOK'S TIP

For spinach-flavoured pooris, thaw 50g/2oz frozen spinach, tip it into a strainer or colander and press it against the sides to extract as much liquid as possible. Add the spinach to the dough with a little grated fresh root ginger and 2.5ml/½ tsp ground cumin.

Bhaturas

These leavened and deep-fried breads are from Punjab, where the local people enjoy them with a bowl of spicy chickpea curry. The combination has become a classic over the years and is known as *choley bhature*. Bhaturas must be eaten hot and cannot be reheated.

INGREDIENTS

Makes 10 bhaturas

15g/½oz fresh yeast
5ml/1 tsp granulated sugar
120ml/4fl oz/½ cup lukewarm water
200g/7oz/1¾ cups plain
　(all-purpose) flour
50g/2oz/½ cup semolina
2.5ml/½ tsp salt
15g/½oz/1 tbsp ghee or butter
30ml/2 tbsp natural (plain) yogurt
oil, for frying

1 Mix the yeast with the sugar and water in a jug (pitcher). Sift the flour into a large bowl and stir in the semolina and salt. Rub in the butter or ghee.

2 Add the yeast mixture and yogurt and mix to a dough. Turn out on to a lightly floured surface and knead for 10 minutes until smooth and elastic.

3 Place the dough in an oiled bowl, cover with oiled clear film (plastic wrap) and leave to rise, in a warm place, for about 1 hour, or until doubled in bulk.

4 Tip out on to a lightly floured surface and knock back (punch down). Divide into ten equal pieces and shape each into a ball. Flatten into discs with the palm of your hand. Roll out on a lightly floured surface into 13cm/5in rounds.

5 Heat oil to a depth of 1cm/½in in a deep frying pan and slide one bhatura into the oil. Fry for about 1 minute, turning over after 30 seconds, then drain well on kitchen paper. Keep each bhatura warm in a low oven while frying the remaining bhaturas. Serve immediately, while hot.

NUTRITIONAL NOTES	
Per Portion	
Energy	144Kcals/605KJ
Fat	6.6g
Saturated Fat	1.4g
Carbohydrate	19.7g
Fibre	0.7g

Desserts
and Drinks

ONE OF the finest ways to end an Indian meal is with a selection of fresh fruit, especially if slightly tart. Pineapple fits the bill perfectly, but mangoes are just as refreshing. Mango flesh can be used in a range of imaginative desserts: pulped for inclusion in a stunning sorbet or stir-fried with pieces of coconut.

Indeed, coconut is used to great effect in a number of Indian-style desserts. Sweetened, it makes a crunchy filling for pancakes, while the milk is the basis of a glorious custard. In fact, Indians love milky puddings. Another favourite is ground rice and rose water, while fine vermicelli is used for a milk pudding flavoured with nuts, dates and sultanas. Kulfi, India's famous ice cream, is easy to make and tastes superb. Finally, there are the gloriously sticky sweet treats, like Toffee Apples and Sesame Fried Fruits. After such indulgence, a glass of homemade Tea and Fruit Punch, or Pistachio Lassi, will cleanse the palate.

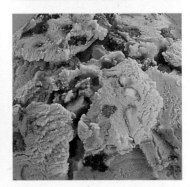

Ground Rice Pudding

This delicious and light ground rice pudding is the perfect end to a spicy meal. It can be served either hot or cold.

INGREDIENTS

Serves 4–6

50g/2oz/½ cup coarsely ground rice
4 green cardamom pods, crushed
900ml/1½ pints/3¾ cups semi-
 skimmed (low-fat) milk
90ml/6 tbsp granulated sugar
15ml/1 tbsp rose water
15ml/1 tbsp crushed pistachio nuts,
 to garnish

1 Place the ground rice in a pan with the cardamoms. Add 600ml/1 pint/2½ cups of the milk and bring to the boil over a medium heat, stirring occasionally.

2 Add the remaining milk and stir over a medium heat for about 10 minutes or until the rice mixture thickens to the consistency of a creamy chicken soup.

3 Stir in the sugar and rose water and continue to cook for a further 2 minutes. Serve garnished with the pistachio nuts.

COOK'S TIP

Rose water is a distillation of scented rose petals which has the intense fragrance and flavour of roses. It is a popular flavouring in Indian cooking. Use it cautiously, adding just enough to suit your taste.

NUTRITIONAL NOTES
Per Portion

Energy	260Kcals/1102KJ
Fat	5.80g
Saturated Fat	2.53g
Carbohydrate	46.00g
Fibre	0.30g

Traditional Indian Vermicelli

Indian vermicelli, made from wheat, is much finer than Italian vermicelli and is readily available from Asian stores.

INGREDIENTS

Serves 4

115g/4oz/1 cup vermicelli
1.2 litres/2 pints/5 cups water
2.5ml/½ tsp saffron threads
15ml/1 tbsp granulated sugar
60ml/4 tbsp low fat fromage frais or Greek (US strained plain) yogurt, to serve

To decorate

15ml/1 tbsp shredded fresh or desiccated (dry unsweetened shredded) coconut
15ml/1 tbsp flaked (sliced) almonds
15ml/1 tbsp chopped pistachio nuts
15ml/1 tbsp granulated sugar

1 Crush the vermicelli in your hands and place it in a pan. Pour in the water, add the saffron and bring to the boil. Boil for about 5 minutes.

2 Stir in the sugar and continue cooking until the water has evaporated. Strain through a sieve, if necessary, to remove any excess liquid.

3 Place the vermicelli in a serving dish and decorate with the coconut, almonds, pistachio nuts and sugar. Serve with fromage frais or yogurt.

NUTRITIONAL NOTES	
Per Portion	
Energy	196Kcals/822KJ
Fat	6.60g
Saturated Fat	2.27g
Carbohydrate	31.80g
Fibre	0.80g

_____ COOK'S TIP _____

You can use a variety of fruits instead of nuts to garnish this dessert. Try a few soft fruits such as blackberries, raspberries or strawberries, or add some chopped dried apricots or sultanas.

Kheer

Both Muslim and Hindu communities prepare Kheer, which is traditionally served at mosques and temples.

INGREDIENTS

Serves 4-6

15g/½oz/1 tbsp ghee
5cm/2in piece cinnamon stick
175g/6oz/¾ cup soft brown sugar
115g/4oz/1 cup coarsely ground rice
1.2 litres/2 pints/5 cups full cream (whole) milk
5ml/1 tsp ground cardamom
50g/2oz/⅓ cup sultanas (golden raisins)
25g/1oz/¼ cup flaked (sliced) almonds
2.5ml/½ tsp freshly ground nutmeg, to serve

1 In a heavy pan, melt the ghee and fry the cinnamon stick and sugar. Keep frying until the sugar begins to caramelize. Reduce the heat immediately when this happens.

2 Add the rice and half the milk. Bring to the boil, stirring constantly to avoid the milk boiling over. Reduce the heat and simmer until the rice is cooked, stirring regularly.

3 Stir in the remaining milk, with the cardamom, sultanas and almonds. Leave to simmer until the mixture thickens, stirring constantly to prevent the kheer from sticking to the base of the pan.

4 When the mixture is thick and creamy, spoon it into a serving dish or individual dishes. Serve hot or cold, sprinkled with the nutmeg.

NUTRITIONAL NOTES	
Per Portion	
Energy	588Kcals/2463KJ
Fat	20.6g
Saturated Fat	11.1g
Carbohydrate	90.6g
Fibre	0.7g

Fruit Vermicelli Pudding

This tasty sweet is prepared by Muslims early in the morning of Id-ul-Fitr, the feast after the 30 days of Ramadan.

INGREDIENTS

Serves 4-6

75g/3oz/6 tbsp ghee
115g/4oz/1 cup vermicelli, coarsely broken
25g/1oz/¼ cup flaked (sliced) almonds
25g/1oz/¼ cup pistachio nuts, slivered
25g/1oz/¼ cup cuddapah nuts or almonds
50g/2oz/⅓ cup sultanas (golden raisins)
50g/2oz/⅓ cup dates, stoned (pitted) and thinly sliced
1.2 litres/2 pints/5 cups full cream (whole) milk
60ml/4 tbsp dark brown sugar
1 sachet saffron powder

1 Heat 50g/2oz/4 tbsp of the ghee in a frying pan and sauté the vermicelli until golden brown. (If you are using the Italian variety, sauté it for a little longer.) Remove and set aside.

2 Heat the remaining ghee in a separate pan and fry the nuts, sultanas and dates over a medium heat until the sultanas swell. Add to the vermicelli and mix gently.

3 Heat the milk in a large heavy pan and add the sugar. Bring to the boil, add the vermicelli mixture and let the liquid return to the boil, stirring constantly.

4 Reduce the heat and simmer until the vermicelli is soft and you have a fairly thick pudding. Stir in the saffron powder and cook for 1 minute more. Serve hot or cold.

NUTRITIONAL NOTES	
Per Portion	
Energy	732Kcals/3043KJ
Fat	44.6g
Saturated Fat	23.6g
Carbohydrate	68.3g
Fibre	1.7g

Black Rice Pudding

This unusual rice pudding, flavoured with root ginger, is quite delicious. When cooked, black rice still retains its husk and has a nutty texture. Serve in small bowls, with a little coconut cream poured over each helping.

INGREDIENTS

Serves 6

115g/4oz/generous ½ cup black glutinous rice
475ml/16fl oz/2 cups water
1cm/½ in fresh root ginger, peeled and bruised
50g/2oz/⅓ cup dark brown sugar
50g/2oz/¼ cup granulated sugar
300ml/½ pint/1¼ cups coconut milk or cream, to serve

1 Put the rice in a sieve and rinse well under cold running water. Drain and put in a large pan, with the water. Bring to the boil and stir to prevent the rice from settling on the base of the pan. Cover and cook for about 30 minutes.

2 Add the ginger and both the brown and white sugar. Cook for a further 15 minutes, adding a little more water if necessary, until the rice is cooked and porridge-like. Remove the ginger and serve warm, in bowls, topped with coconut milk or cream.

NUTRITIONAL NOTES	
Per Portion	
Energy	146Kcals/616KJ
Fat	0.5g
Saturated Fat	0.1g
Carbohydrate	34.2g
Fibre	0g

Deep-fried Bananas

Fry these bananas at the last minute, so that the outer crust of batter is crisp in texture and the banana is soft and warm inside.

INGREDIENTS

Serves 8

115g/4oz/1 cup self-raising (self-rising) flour
40g/1½oz/⅓ cup rice flour
2.5ml/½ tsp salt
200ml/7fl oz /scant 1 cup water
finely grated lime rind
8 small bananas
oil for deep-frying
caster (superfine) sugar and 1 lime, cut in wedges, to serve

1 Sift the self-raising flour, the rice flour and the salt together into a bowl. Add just enough of the water to make a smooth, coating batter. Mix well, then stir in the lime rind.

2 Heat the oil to 190°C/375°F or until a cube of day-old bread dropped into the oil browns in 30 seconds.

3 Peel the bananas and dip them into the batter two or three times. Deep-fry the battered bananas in the hot oil until crisp and golden. Drain and serve hot, dredged with sugar. Offer the lime wedges to squeeze over the bananas.

NUTRITIONAL NOTES	
Per Portion	
Energy	201Kcals/840KJ
Fat	10g
Saturated Fat	1.3g
Carbohydrate	27.1g
Fibre	1.2g

Tapioca Pudding

This pudding, made from large pearl tapioca and coconut milk and served warm, is much lighter than the Western-style version. You can adjust the sweetness to your taste. Serve with lychees or the smaller, similar-tasting logans.

INGREDIENTS

Serves 4

115g/4oz/⅔ cup tapioca
475ml/16fl oz/2 cups water
175g/6oz/¾ cup granulated sugar
pinch of salt
250ml/8fl oz/1 cup coconut milk
250g/9oz prepared tropical fruits
finely shredded rind of 1 lime,
    to decorate

1 Soak the tapioca in warm water for 1 hour so the grains swell. Drain.

2 Put the measured water in a pan and bring to the boil. Stir in the sugar and salt.

3 Add the tapioca and coconut milk and simmer for 10 minutes or until the tapioca turns transparent.

4 Serve warm with some tropical fruits and decorate with the finely shredded lime rind.

NUTRITIONAL NOTES	
Per Portion	
Energy	327Kcals/1388KJ
Fat	0.6g
Saturated Fat	0.2g
Carbohydrate	80.6g
Fibre	2.2g

Sesame Fried Fruits

These delicious treats are a favourite among children and adults alike. Use any firm fruit in season. Bananas are a firm favourite, but the batter also works well with pineapple and apple.

INGREDIENTS

Serves 4

115g/4oz/1 cup plain
    (all-purpose) flour
2.5ml/½ tsp bicarbonate of soda
    (baking soda)
30ml/2 tbsp sugar
1 egg
90ml/6 tbsp water
15ml/1tbsp sesame seeds or
    30ml/2 tbsp shredded (dry
    unsweetened shredded) coconut
4 firm bananas
oil for deep frying
salt
30ml/2 tbsp clear honey, to serve
mint sprigs and lychees, to decorate

1 Sift the flour, bicarbonate of soda and a pinch of salt into a bowl. Stir in the sugar.

2 Whisk in the egg and just enough water to make a thin batter. Then whisk in the sesame seeds or the shredded coconut.

3 Peel the bananas. Carefully cut each one in half lengthways, then cut in half crossways.

4 Heat the oil in a preheated wok. Dip the bananas in the batter, then gently drop a few pieces at a time into the hot oil. Fry until golden brown.

5 Remove the bananas from the oil and drain on kitchen paper. Serve immediately with clear honey, and decorate with mint sprigs and lychees.

NUTRITIONAL NOTES	
Per Portion	
Energy	384Kcals/1607KJ
Fat	20.7g
Saturated Fat	6.3g
Carbohydrate	46g
Fibre	3g

Indian Ice Cream

Kulfi-wallahs (ice cream vendors) have always made kulfi, and continue to this day, without using modern freezers. Kulfi is packed into metal cones sealed with dough and then churned in clay pots until set. Try this method – it works extremely well in an ordinary freezer.

INGREDIENTS

Serves 4–6

3 × 400ml/14fl oz cans evaporated milk
3 egg whites
350g/12oz/3 cups icing
   (confectioners') sugar
5ml/1 tsp ground cardamom
15ml/1 tbsp rose water
175g/6oz/1½ cups pistachio
   nuts, chopped
75g/3oz/½ cup sultanas (golden raisins)
75g/3oz/¾ cup flaked (sliced) almonds
25g/1oz/3 tbsp glacé (candied)
   cherries, halved

3 Gently fold in the remaining ingredients, cover the bowl with cling film (plastic wrap) and place in the freezer for 1 hour.

4 Remove the ice cream from the freezer and mix well with a fork. Transfer to a serving container and return to the freezer for a final setting. Remove from the freezer 10 minutes before serving.

NUTRITIONAL NOTES	
Per Portion	
Energy	1123Kcals/4722KJ
Fat	47.3g
Saturated Fat	10.3g
Carbohydrate	144.2g
Fibre	5.1g

COOK'S TIP
Don't leave the cans of evaporated milk unattended. Top up the water if necessary; the cans must never boil dry.

1 Remove the labels from the cans of evaporated milk and lay the cans down in a pan with a tight-fitting cover. Fill the pan with water to reach three-quarters up the cans. Bring to the boil, cover and simmer for 20 minutes. When cool, remove the cans and chill in the refrigerator for 24 hours. Chill a large bowl too.

2 Whisk the egg whites in a large bowl until peaks form. Open the cans and empty the milk into the chilled bowl. Whisk until doubled in quantity, then fold in the whisked egg whites and icing sugar.

Mango Sorbet with Sauce

After a heavy meal, this makes a very refreshing dessert. Mango is said to be one of the oldest fruits cultivated in India, having been brought by Lord Shiva for his beautiful wife, Parvathi.

INGREDIENTS

Serves 4–6
900g/2lb mango pulp
2.5ml/½ tsp lemon juice
grated rind of 1 orange and 1 lemon
4 egg whites
50g/2oz/¼ cup caster (superfine) sugar
120ml/4fl oz/½ cup double (heavy) cream
50g/2oz/½ cup icing (confectioners') sugar

3 Remove from the freezer and beat again. Transfer to an ice cream container, and freeze until fully set.

4 In a bowl, whip the double cream with the icing sugar and the remaining mango pulp. Cover and chill the sauce for 24 hours.

5 Remove the sorbet (sherbet) 10 minutes before serving. Scoop out individual servings and cover with a generous helping of mango sauce. Serve immediately.

NUTRITIONAL NOTES	
Per Portion	
Energy	387Kcals/1631KJ
Fat	16.6g
Saturated Fat	10.3g
Carbohydrate	58.4g
Fibre	5.9g

1 In a large, chilled bowl, mix half of the mango pulp with the lemon juice and the grated rind.

2 Whisk the egg whites until peaks form, then gently fold them into the mango mixture, with the caster sugar. Cover with clear film (plastic wrap) and place in the freezer for at least 1 hour.

Pancakes Filled with Sweet Coconut

Traditionally, the pale green colour in the pancake batter was obtained from the juice squeezed from fresh pandanus leaves. Green food colouring can be used instead.

INGREDIENTS

Makes 12–15 pancakes

175g/6oz/1 cup dark brown sugar
450ml/15fl oz/scant 2 cups water
1 pandanus leaf, stripped through with a fork and tied into a knot
175g/6oz/2 cups desiccated (dry unsweetened shredded) coconut
oil, for frying
salt

For the pancake batter

225g/8oz/2 cups plain (all-purpose) flour, sifted
2 eggs, beaten
2 drops of edible green food colouring
few drops of vanilla essence (extract)
450ml/15fl oz/scant 2 cups water
45ml/3 tbsp groundnut (peanut) oil

1 Dissolve the sugar in the water with the pandanus leaf, in a pan over gentle heat, stirring all the time. Increase the heat and allow to boil gently for 3–4 minutes, until the mixture just becomes syrupy. Do not let it caramelize.

2 Put the coconut in a karahi or wok with a pinch of salt. Pour over the prepared sugar syrup and cook over a very gentle heat, stirring from time to time, until the mixture becomes almost dry; this will take 5–10 minutes. Set aside until required.

NUTRITIONAL NOTES	
Per Portion	
Energy	191Kcals/798KJ
Fat	13.1g
Saturated Fat	8.5g
Carbohydrate	15.5g
Fibre	2.6g

3 To make the batter, blend together the flour, eggs, food colouring, vanilla essence, water and oil either by hand or in a food processor.

4 Brush an 18cm/7in frying pan with oil and cook 12–15 pancakes. Keep the pancakes warm. Fill each pancake with a generous spoonful of the sweet coconut mixture, roll up and serve immediately.

Steamed Coconut Custard

This popular dessert migrated to India from South-east Asia. Coconut milk makes marvellous custard. Here it is cooked with cellophane noodles and chopped bananas, a combination that works very well.

INGREDIENTS

Serves 8

25g/1oz cellophane noodles
3 eggs
400ml/14fl oz can coconut milk
75ml/5 tbsp water
25g/1oz/2 tbsp granulated sugar
4 ripe bananass, peeled and cut in
 small pieces
salt
vanilla ice cream, to serve (optional)

1 Soak the cellophane noodles in a bowl of warm water for 5 minutes.

2 Beat the eggs in a bowl until pale. Whisk in the coconut milk, water and sugar.

3 Strain into a 1.75 litre/3 pint/ 7½ cup heatproof soufflé dish.

NUTRITIONAL NOTES	
Per Portion	
Energy	115Kcals/486KJ
Fat	2.8g
Saturated Fat	0.9g
Carbohydrate	19.9g
Fibre	0.6g

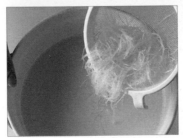

4 Drain the noodles well and cut them into small pieces with scissors. Stir the noodles into the coconut milk mixture, together with the chopped bananas. Add a pinch of salt and mix well.

5 Cover the dish with foil and place in a steamer for about 1 hour, or until set. A skewer inserted in the centre should come out clean. Serve hot or cold, on its own or topped with vanilla ice cream.

Toffee Apples

A wickedly sweet way to end a meal, this dessert evokes memories of childhood.

INGREDIENTS

Serves 4

4 firm eating apples
115g/4oz/1 cup plain (all-purpose) flour
about 120ml/4fl oz/½ cup water
1 egg, beaten
vegetable oil, for deep frying, plus
   30ml/2 tbsp for the toffee
115g/4oz/½ cup granulated sugar

1 Peel and core each apple and cut into eight pieces. Dust each piece of apple with a little of the flour.

2 Sift the remaining flour into a mixing bowl, then slowly add the cold water and stir well to make a smooth batter. Add the beaten egg and blend well.

VARIATION

Try this with bananas or pineapple pieces for a delicious change.

NUTRITIONAL NOTES
Per Portion

Energy	410Kcals/1723KJ
Fat	18.5g
Saturated Fat	2.5g
Carbohydrate	60g
Fibre	2g

3 Heat the oil for deep frying in a karahi, wok or deep pan. It will be ready when a cube of day-old bread browns in 45 seconds. Dip the apple pieces in the batter and deep fry for about 3 minutes or until golden. Remove and drain on kitchen paper. Drain off the oil from the pan.

4 Heat the remaining oil in the pan, add the sugar and stir constantly until the sugar has caramelized. Quickly add the apple pieces and blend well so that each piece of apple is thoroughly coated with the toffee. Dip the apple pieces in cold water to harden before serving.

Spiced Fruit Salad

Exotic fruits are becoming commonplace in supermarkets these days and it is fun to experiment with the different varieties. Look out in particular for physalis, star fruit, papaya and passion fruit.

INGREDIENTS

Serves 4–6
75g/3oz/6 tbsp granulated sugar
300ml/½ pint/1¼ cups water
30ml/2 tbsp syrup from a jar of stem (preserved) ginger
2 pieces star anise
2.5cm/1in cinnamon stick
1 clove
juice of ½ lemon
2 fresh mint sprigs
1 mango
2 bananas, sliced
8 fresh or drained canned lychees
225g/8oz/2 cups strawberries, hulled and halved
2 pieces stem (preserved) ginger, cut into sticks
1 medium pineapple

1 Put the sugar, water, ginger syrup, star anise, cinnamon, clove, lemon juice and mint into a pan. Bring to the boil, then simmer for 3 minutes. Strain into a bowl and set aside to cool.

2 Remove the top and bottom from the mango and cut off the outer skin. Stand the mango on one end and remove the flesh in two pieces either side of the flat stone. Slice evenly.

3 Add the mango slices to the syrup with the bananas, lychees, strawberries and stem ginger. Mix in well, making sure the fruits are well coated in the sugary liquid.

4 Cut the pineapple in half by slicing down the centre, using a very sharp knife. Loosen the flesh with a smaller, serrated knife, and remove the flesh by cutting around the rim and scooping it out. The pineapple halves will resemble two boat shapes. Do not discard the pineapple flesh, but cut into chunks and add to the fruity syrup.

5 Spoon some of the fruit salad into the pineapple halves and serve on a large dish. There will be sufficient fruit salad in the bowl to refill the pineapple halves at least once.

NUTRITIONAL NOTES *Per Portion*	
Energy	110Kcals/2009KJ
Fat	0.3g
Saturated Fat	0.1g
Carbohydrate	27.1g
Fibre	2.4g

Melon and Strawberry Salad

A beautiful and colourful fruit salad, this is suitable to serve as a refreshing appetizer or to round off a spicy meal. Don't be tempted to chill the salad; it tastes best at room temperature.

INGREDIENTS

Serves 4

1 galia or Ogen melon
1 honeydew melon or other melon of
  own choice (see Cook's Tip)
½ watermelon
225g/8oz/2 cups strawberries
15ml/1 tbsp lemon juice
15ml/1 tbsp clear honey
15ml/1 tbsp chopped fresh mint

1 Prepare the melons by cutting them in half and discarding the seeds. Use a melon ball to scoop out the flesh into balls or a knife to cut it into cubes. Place these in a fruit bowl.

2 Rinse and take the stems off the strawberries, cut the fruit in half and add them to the bowl.

3 Mix together the lemon juice and honey and add 15ml/1 tbsp water to make this easier to pour over the fruit. Mix into the fruit gently.

4 Sprinkle the chopped mint over the top of the fruit and serve.

NUTRITIONAL NOTES	
Per Portion	
Energy	114Kcals/482KJ
Fat	0.70g
Saturated Fat	0.00g
Carbohydrate	26.50g
Fibre	1.60g

—— COOK'S TIP ——

Use whichever melons are available: replace galia or Ogen with cantaloupe or watermelon with charentais, for example. Try to choose three melons with a variation in colour for an attractive effect.

Caramel Custard with Fresh Fruit

A creamy caramel dessert is a wonderful way to end a meal. It is light and delicious, and this recipe is very simple.

INGREDIENTS

Serves 6
For the caramel
30ml/2 tbsp granulated sugar
30ml/2 tbsp water

For the custard
6 eggs
4 drops vanilla essence (extract)
115g/4oz/½ cup granulated sugar
750ml/1¼ pints/3 cups semi-skimmed (low-fat) milk
fresh fruit, such as strawberries, blueberries, orange and banana slices and raspberries, to serve

1 To make the caramel, place the sugar and water in a heavy pan and heat until the sugar has dissolved and the mixture is bubbling and pale gold in colour. Pour carefully into a 1.2 litre/2 pint/5 cup soufflé dish. Leave to cool.

2 Preheat the oven to 180°C/350°F/ Gas 4. To make the custard, break the eggs into a medium mixing bowl and whisk until frothy.

COOK'S TIP

Use pure vanilla essence, not synthetic vanilla flavouring for this custard as the flavour is much better; remember essence is very strong and you only need a few drops.

3 Stir in the vanilla essence and gradually add the sugar, then the milk, whisking constantly.

4 Pour the custard over the top of the caramel.

5 Cook the custard in the oven for 35–40 minutes. Remove from the oven and leave to cool for 30 minutes or until the mixture is set.

6 Loosen the custard from the sides of the dish with a knife. Place a serving dish upside-down on top of the soufflé dish and invert, giving a gentle shake if necessary to turn out the custard on the serving dish.

7 Arrange any fresh fruit of your choice around the custard on the serving dish and serve immediately.

NUTRITIONAL NOTES	
Per Portion	
Energy	194Kcals/823KJ
Fat	4.70g
Saturated Fat	2.01g
Carbohydrate	32.90g
Fibre	0.00g

Kulfi with Cardamom

Making kulfi is easy if you use yogurt pots or dariole moulds.

INGREDIENTS

Serves 6

2 litres/3½ pints/8 cups creamy milk
12 cardamoms
175g/6oz/¾ cup caster
   (superfine) sugar
25g/1oz/¼ cup blanched
   almonds, chopped
toasted flaked almonds and cardamoms,
   to decorate

NUTRITIONAL NOTES	
Per Portion	
Energy	401Kcals/1686KJ
Fat	19.3g
Saturated Fat	11.2g
Carbohydrate	46.8g
Fibre	0.3g

1 Place the milk and cardamoms in a large heavy pan. Bring to the boil then simmer vigorously until reduced by one-third. Strain the milk into a bowl, discarding the cardamoms, then stir in the sugar and almonds until the sugar is dissolved. Cool.

_____ COOK'S TIP _____

Use a large pan for reducing the milk as there needs to be plenty of room for it to bubble up.

2 Pour the mixture into a freezerproof container, cover and freeze until almost firm, stirring every 30 minutes.

3 When almost solid, pack the ice cream into six clean yogurt pots. Return to the freezer until required, removing the pots about 10 minutes before serving and turning the individual ices out.

4 Decorate with toasted almonds and cardamoms before serving.

Pears in Spiced Wine

Familiar Indian spices, infused in a red wine syrup, give pears a lovely warm flavour. The colour is beautiful, too.

INGREDIENTS

Serves 4

1 bottle full-bodied red wine
1 cinnamon stick
4 cloves
2.5ml/½ tsp grated nutmeg
2.5ml/½ tsp ground ginger
8 peppercorns
175g/6oz/¾ cup caster
   (superfine) sugar
thinly pared rind of ½ orange
thinly pared rind of ½ lemon
8 firm ripe pears

1 Pour the wine into a heavy pan into which the pears will fit snugly when standing upright. Stir the cinnamon stick, cloves, nutmeg, ginger, peppercorns, caster sugar and citrus rinds into the wine.

2 Peel the pears, leaving the stalks intact, and stand them in the pan. The wine should only just cover the pears. Bring the liquid to the boil, lower the heat, cover and simmer very gently for 30 minutes or until the pears are tender. Using a slotted spoon, transfer the pears to a bowl.

3 Boil the poaching liquid until it has reduced by half and is syrupy. Strain the syrup over and around the pears and serve hot or cold.

_____ COOK'S TIP _____

Serve the pears with a mascarpone cream, made by combining equal quantities of mascarpone cheese and double (heavy) cream, and adding a little vanilla essence (extract) for flavour. They also taste good with yogurt or ice cream.

NUTRITIONAL NOTES	
Per Portion	
Energy	191Kcals/806KJ
Fat	0.3g
Saturated Fat	0g
Carbohydrate	43.1g
Fibre	6.6g

Mango and Coconut Stir Fry

Choose a ripe mango for this recipe. If you buy one that is a little under-ripe, leave it in a warm place for a day or two before using.

INGREDIENTS

Serves 4
¼ coconut
1 large, ripe mango
finely grated rind and juice of
    2 limes
15ml/1 tbsp sunflower oil
15g/½oz/1 tbsp butter
30ml/2 tbsp clear honey
crème fraîche or ice cream, to serve

1 Prepare the coconut if necessary. Drain the milk and remove the flesh. Peel with a vegetable peeler so that it forms flakes.

VARIATION

Nectarine or peach slices can be used instead of the mango.

NUTRITIONAL NOTES
Per Portion

Energy	357Kcals/1478KJ
Fat	32.7g
Saturated Fat	24.1g
Carbohydrate	13.8g
Fibre	7g

2 Peel the mango. Cut the stone out of the middle of the fruit. Cut each half of the mango into slices.

3 Place the mango slices in a bowl and pour over the lime juice and rind. Set aside.

4 Meanwhile heat a karahi or wok, then add 10ml/2 tsp of the oil. When the oil is hot, add the butter. Once the butter has melted, stir in the coconut flakes and stir-fry for 1–2 minutes until the coconut is golden brown. Remove and drain on kitchen paper. Wipe out the pan. Strain the mango slices, reserving the juice.

5 Heat the pan again and add the remaining oil. When the oil is hot, add the mango and stir-fry for 1–2 minutes, then add the juice and leave to bubble and reduce for 1 minute.

6 Stir in the honey. When it has dissolved, spoon the mango and coconut dessert into one large serving bowl or individual dishes. Sprinkle on the coconut flakes and serve with crème fraîche or ice cream.

COOK'S TIP

You can sometimes buy "fresh" coconut that has already been cracked open and is sold in pieces ready for use from supermarkets, but buying the whole nut ensures greater freshness. Choose one that is heavy for its size and shake it so that you can hear the milk sloshing about. A "dry" coconut will almost certainly have rancid flesh. You can simply crack the shell with a hammer, preferably with the nut inside a plastic bag, but it may be better to pierce the two ends with a sharp nail or skewer first in order to collect and save the coconut milk. An alternative method is to drain the milk first and then heat the nut briefly in the oven until it cracks. Whichever method you choose, it is then fairly easy to extract the flesh and chop or shave it.

Tea and Fruit Punch

This delicious punch can be served hot or cold. White wine or brandy may be added to taste.

INGREDIENTS

Serves 4

600ml/1 pint/2½ cups water
1 cinnamon stick
4 cloves
12ml/2½ tsp Earl Grey tea leaves
175g/6oz/¾ cup granulated sugar
450ml/¾ pint/1½ cups tropical soft
    drink concentrate
1 lemon, sliced
1 small orange, sliced
½ cucumber, sliced

1 Bring the water to the boil in a pan with the cinnamon stick and cloves. Remove from the heat and add the tea leaves. Leave to brew for about 5 minutes. Stir and strain into a large bowl and chill in the refrigerator for 2–3 hours.

NUTRITIONAL NOTES	
Per Portion	
Energy	1108Kcals/4737KJ
Fat	0g
Saturated Fat	0g
Carbohydrate	294.5g
Fibre	0g

2 Add the sugar and the soft drink concentrate and allow to rest until the sugar has dissolved and the mixture cooled. Place the fruit and cucumber in a chilled punch bowl and pour over the tea mix. Chill for a further 24 hours before serving.

Spiced Lassi

Lassi or buttermilk is prepared by churning yogurt with water and then removing the fat. To make this refreshing drink without churning, use low-fat natural yogurt.

INGREDIENTS

Serves 4

450ml/¾ pint/scant 2 cups natural
    (plain) yogurt
300ml/½ pint/1¼ cups water
2.5cm/1in piece fresh root ginger,
    finely crushed
2 fresh green chillies, finely chopped
2.5ml/½ tsp ground cumin
salt and black pepper, to taste
few fresh coriander (cilantro) leaves,
    chopped, to garnish

1 In a bowl, whisk the yogurt and water until well blended. The consistency should be that of full cream (whole) milk. Adjust by adding more water if necessary.

2 Add the ginger, chillies and ground cumin, season with the salt and black pepper and mix well. Pour into 4 serving glasses and chill. Garnish with chopped coriander before serving.

VARIATION
For a sweet version of this refreshing drink, omit the spices and add sugar to taste. A little rose water or orange flower water can also be added.

NUTRITIONAL NOTES	
Per Portion	
Energy	63Kcals/266KJ
Fat	1.1g
Saturated Fat	0.6g
Carbohydrate	8.5g
Fibre	0g

Pistachio Lassi

In India, lassi is not only made at home, but is also sold at roadside cafés, restaurants and hotels. There is no substitute for this drink, especially on a hot day. It is particularly good served with curries and similar hot dishes as it helps the body to digest spicy food.

INGREDIENTS

Serves 4

300ml/½ pint/1¼ cups natural (plain) low fat yogurt
5ml/1 tsp granulated sugar, or to taste
300ml/½ pint/1¼ cups water
30ml/2 tbsp puréed fruit, optional
15ml/1 tbsp crushed pistachio nuts, to decorate

1 Place the yogurt in a jug (pitcher); whisk until frothy. Add the sugar.

2 Pour in the water and the puréed fruit, if using, and continue to whisk for 2 minutes. Pour the lassi into serving glasses and serve chilled, decorated with crushed pistachio nuts.

NUTRITIONAL NOTES	
Per Portion	
Energy	70Kcals/296KJ
Fat	2.60g
Saturated Fat	0.63g
Carbohydrate	7.50g
Fibre	0g

_____ VARIATION _____

To make a simple savoury lassi, omit the sugar and fruit and add lemon juice, ground cumin and salt. Garnish with mint.

Almond Sherbet

Traditionally, this drink was always made in the month of Ramadan to break the fast. It should be served chilled.

INGREDIENTS

Serves 4

50g/2oz/½ cup ground almonds
600ml/1 pint/2½ cups semi-skimmed (low-fat) milk
10ml/2 tsp granulated sugar, or to taste

NUTRITIONAL NOTES	
Per Portion	
Energy	155Kcals/651KJ
Fat	9.40g
Saturated Fat	2.04g
Carbohydrate	11.00g
Fibre	0.90g

1 Put the ground almonds into a serving jug (pitcher).

_____ COOK'S TIP _____

Refreshing, cooling drinks are the perfect accompaniment to spicy Indian dishes. Similar drinks are made with fruit juices flavoured with chopped fresh mint.

2 Pour in the semi-skimmed milk and add the sugar; stir to mix. Taste for sweetness and serve very cold in long glasses. Chilling the glasses first helps to keep the drink cold and adds a sense of occasion.

Glossary

Almonds Available whole, flaked (sliced) and ground, these sweet nuts impart a sumptuous richness to curries. They are considered a great delicacy in Pakistan and India, where they are extremely expensive and are generally only used for special occasion dishes.

Asafoetida A resin added to dishes as an anti-flatulent. It has an acrid, bitter taste and only a tiny amount should be used.

Aubergines Numerous aubergine (eggplant) varieties exist in Asia, where the vegetable has been grown for more than two thousand years. Aubergine absorbs the flavours of other ingredients like a sponge, and therefore benefits from being cooked with strongly flavoured foods and seasonings.

Banana Leaves Traditionally used in Indian and Asian cooking as containers to steam foods, banana leaves are sold in Indian and Asian food stores. If unavailable, squares of lightly oiled kitchen foil or buttered baking parchment can be used instead.

Basil One of the oldest herbs known to man, basil is thought to have originated in India, although it is much more widely used in South-east Asia. Add basil to curries and salads as an ingredient and as a garnish. Avoid chopping the leaves, but tear them into pieces or add them to the dish whole.

Basmati rice A slender, long grain rice grown in northern India, in the Punjab, Pakistan and in the foothills of the Himalayas, basmati is famous for its distinctive and beautiful fragrance. It is widely used in Indian cooking, particularly in pulaos and biryanis; it has a cooling effect when eaten with hot, spicy curry dishes.

Bay leaves The large dried leaves of the bay laurel tree are one of the oldest herbs used in India. Bay leaves are used for the distinctive flavour they add to a dish.

Beancurd Fresh beancurd is commonly known in the West by its Japanese name, tofu. Made from soya beans, it is a rich source of protein in vegetarian dishes and is a popular ingredient in India and South-east Asia. Beancurd is sold in supermarkets and health food stores as silken or soft tofu, and also in a firmer form. Yellow beancurd is usually only available from Asian food stores, where it is sold cubed, ready to be deep-fried. Despite the bland taste of beancurd, the porous texture will absorb the flavour of the ingredients with which it is cooked.

Bengal gram One of the many pulses that are widely used in Indian cooking, this is related to the chickpea. It is often used whole in curries.

Bitter gourds One of the many very bitter vegetables often used in Indian cooking, this long, knobbly green vegetable has a strong, distinct taste. To prepare a gourd, just wash it, slice it in half lengthways, remove and discard the seeds, then cut into slices.

Bottle gourds As the name suggests, these gourds have a distinctive shape. Young gourds can be eaten, but taste extremely bitter, so are generally reserved for highly spiced dishes, such as curries.

Cardamom pods This spice is native to India, where it is almost as highly prized as saffron. The pale green and beige pods have a finer flavour than the coarse brown or black ones. The pods can be used whole or husked to remove the seeds. They have a slightly pungent, very aromatic taste.

Chapati flour A type of wholemeal (wholewheat flour), often sold under its Indian name, atta, in Indian food stores. It is used to make chapatis and other breads. Well-sifted wholemeal flour is an acceptable substitute.

Chillies All chilli varieties are native to tropical America and were introduced to Asia by European traders after Christopher Columbus took them home to Spain. They quickly became an integral part of Asian cuisine. Fresh and dried chillies are used in India to add heat and flavour to sauces, sambals and salads, and to cooked dishes, such as stocks, soups, curries, stir-fries and braised dishes.

Coconut milk An essential ingredient in south and east Indian and South-east Asian cooking. Coconut milk can be made at home from desiccated (dry unsweetened shredded) coconut, but is also available in cans. If the milk is left to stand, coconut cream will rise to the surface as a separate layer.

Coriander Fresh coriander (cilantro) is a favourite ingredient in all Asian countries, and its unique delicate flavour and bright green colour make it a popular garnish for curries. Coriander seeds are also available, and are used whole, or ground.

Creamed coconut or coconut cream is sold in solid blocks, created when the cream is left to solidify. In India, it is used to enrich spicy and sweet dishes. A small quantity can be cut off the block and stirred into a dish just before serving, or it can be diluted with boiling water to produce coconut milk, with the proportion of creamed coconut to water being altered according to required thickness.

Cuddapah nuts Known locally as chirongi nuts, these come from a tree that grows in the more arid regions of India. They are used as a substitute for almonds.

Cumin Cumin seeds are oval, ridged and, although described as white, are greenish brown in colour. They have a strong aroma and flavour and can be used whole or freshly ground. Black cumin seeds are not as easy to find as the paler variety. They are dark and aromatic and are used to flavour curries and rice dishes. If you buy ground cumin, as with any other ground spice, keep it in a dry, cool place and use as soon as possible, as the flavour will deteriorate rapidly.

Curry leaves Fragrant, glossy green leaves that are produced by a hardwood tree indigenous to southern India. Curry leaves are used in curries and rice dishes all over Asia, but especially in India. The leaves are sold fresh or dried in Indian food stores.

Curry paste A wet blend of spices, herbs and chillies that is used as the basis of a curry. The blending of the various components is an art; each curry paste designed to produce a flavour that will harmonise with the main ingredients. As they contain fresh ingredients, curry pastes must be stored in the refrigerator.

Curry powder A dry blend of spices and dried chillies. The spices chosen and the way in which they are roasted determine the flavour and strength.

Dhal See *Pulses*

Fenugreek Sold in bunches, this fresh herb has very small leaves and is used to flavour both meat and vegetable dishes. Always discard the stalks, which will make the dish taste bitter. Flat fenugreek seeds are pungent and slightly bitter. They are widely used in curries and rice dishes.

Garam masala A mild, sweet seasoning from north India, and a very popular curry powder. Recipes for garam masala vary, but all will contain cardamom, cinnamon, cloves, coriander and black peppercorns. What distinguishes garam masala from other curry powders is that is often added towards the end of cooking, rather than at the start.

Garlic Prized for its pungent warmth, garlic is used whole, chopped or crushed in curries.

Ghee The traditional Indian cooking fat, ghee is clarified butter that can be heated to higher temperatures than other oils without burning. Pure ghee is made from dairy milk, but vegetable ghee is also produced, and nowadays this is often used in place of dairy ghee because of its lower fat content. Many modern Indian households prefer to use vegetable oil as their chosen cooking fat.

Ginger Fresh root ginger is a basic ingredient in Indian cooking. Choose plump roots whose skin looks shiny and bright, not dry. When cut, the flesh should look moist and creamy. Ground ginger is seldom used.

Gram flour More commonly known as besan, this is used to flavour and thicken Indian curries and other spicy dishes.

Gram flour is also used as a stabilizer: when added to yogurt it helps to prevent it from curdling in hot food.

Mango powder Sold as amchur, this is made from unripe green mangoes that have been sun-dried and then finely ground. The flavour is tart and the powder is used to add a tangy flavour to curries and other dishes.

Mangosteen A fragrant fruit that looks rather like a lychee, although they are not related. Mangosteens are dried, rather like mangoes, to produce a powder called kokum, which is used as a souring agent in India.

Mustard seeds Round in shape, with a sharp flavour, mustard seeds are most often used in Indian cooking to flavour curries and pickles.

Mustard oil Made from mustard seeds, this oil has a pungent taste when raw, but becomes sweeter when heated. It is widely used in India, especially in eastern regions, where mustard crops are grown.

Nigella seeds These come from a herbaceous annual. The bulk of the crop is grown in India and the seeds have a peppery, herb-like taste. They are used in spice mixes, in dhal and vegetable dishes, pickles and chutneys. Nigella seeds are often scattered on naan and other Indian breads. They are sometimes called wild onion seeds or kalonji.

Okra Also known as ladies' fingers, this is one of the most popular Indian vegetables. The small green five-sided pods have a distinctive flavour and a sticky, pulpy texture when cooked.

Onion seeds Black in colour and triangular in shape, these seeds are used in pickles and to flavour vegetable curries.

Pandanus leaves Sometimes known as screwpine or bandan leaves, these are used in sweet and savoury dishes. A green colouring obtained from the leaves is traditionally used to tint desserts, although today, edible food colouring is often preferred for convenience.

Paneer A white, smooth-textured cheese from northern India, paneer is excellent with meat or fish, or on its own in vegetable dishes.

Pomegranate seeds Dried seeds from sour pomegranates are used in a number of Indian dishes to impart a tart flavour. Look for them in Indian food stores. They are often sold as anardana.

Pulses Hundreds of different pulses are used in India. Dried beans, peas and lentils are nutritious, easy to cook and very versatile, making them ideal ingredients for vegetarian dishes. Those featured in this book include black-eyed beans (peas); chickpeas; chana dhal, a yellow lentil for which yellow split peas can be substituted, although these two are not the same; mung beans, which can be eaten whole or split, mung dhal and masoor dhal, which is a split red-orange lentil. Tuvar dhal is a split bean that is commercially oiled and urad dhal is a black lentil with a dry texture when cooked.

Red gram Also known as pigeon peas, arhar or tur, this pulse is widely grown in India.

Saffron The world's most expensive spice is produced from the dried stigmas of the saffron crocus. Only a tiny amount of saffron is needed to flavour or colour a dish, whether sweet or savoury. Saffron is sold as threads and in powder form.

Tamarind The dried black pods of the tamarind plant are sour in taste and very sticky. Tamarind is used for its flavour, which is refreshingly tart, without being bitter. Lemon juice can be used instead, but will not have the intensity of flavour.

Turmeric This bright yellow, bitter-tasting spice is sold ground and fresh, with fresh turmeric being peeled and then grated or sliced in the same way as fresh root ginger. Turmeric is often used as a rather cheaper alternative to saffron, but the two do not compare in terms of flavour. Turmeric gives a more vibrant colour. The aroma is harsher, being peppery and musky. Ground turmeric is often used in curry powders and it is this spice that is responsible for the characteristic yellow colour.

Index

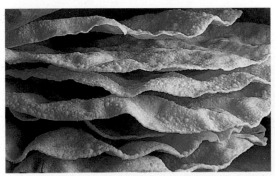

Stockists and Suppliers

The following is intended as a useful list of online outlets and information sites to help the reader source Indian groceries and cooking equipment. Their inclusion in this book does not necessarily warrant an endorsement by the publishers.

USA

www.indiavilas.com
An information site detailing products and resources available throughout the USA. Includes a comprehensive, nationwide list of grocers and restaurants, which visitors can search according to state.

www.mahabazaar.com
Online bazaar of Indian products, including dried fruits and nuts, oils, spice mixes, pastes and marinades, plus a range of herbal and beauty products.

www.namaste.com
One of the largest retailers and brands of Indian products in the USA. Online store sells a range of groceries, books and gifts, plus health, Ayurveda and beauty products.

store.indianfoodsco.com
A selection of mainstays, accompaniments, snack foods, beverages and basics, plus a guide to Indian pantry essentials and meal ideas for barbecues, street food and dinners.

www.tastybite.com
A US-sponsored retailer stocking Indian-made foods, with specific lines in vegetarian, meat and bread products. Provides information on vegan, kosher and gluten-free products for customers.

UNITED KINGDOM

www.aaindiangrocery.com
Information on sweets, savouries, pastes and powders, plus toys and gifts, with national and international delivery options.

www.netasia.co.uk/food&drink/foodhome.htm
Information and shopping outlet for the UK market selling Indian groceries and cooking ware. Also contains advice on cooking procedures and restaurant reviews.

www.spicebox.co.uk
Online information about Rafi Fernandez's two UK spice outlets, Rafi's Spicebox, based in Sudbury, Suffolk, and York. Also includes recipe ideas, books and special offers.

www.theindiangrocerystore.com
Offers a range of authentic Indian grocery products, plus a home delivery service covering Nottingham and the Midlands.

www.thespiceshop.co.uk
Information about the range of freshly ground, hand-mixed and additive-free spices sold at this West London outlet, which is based near Portobello Road in Notting Hill.

WORLDWIDE

www.ethnicgrocer.com
A world market covering various cuisines, which invites visitors to shop for products by country. The Indian category includes a wide range of cooking oils and vinegars, plus kitchenware, spices, sauces, confections and baking products.

www.getspice.com
Specialist online culinary store featuring Indian spices, teas and kitchenware. Includes a selection of rare and organic spices.

www.indiamart.com
India-based stockists of spices and condiments, which aims to export packed goods to businesses across the globe.

www.indiandownunder.com.au
Lists up to 60 Indian grocers trading throughout Australia, with the opportunity to search for outlets according to state. Also lists a selection of Indian restaurants.

www.natco-online.com
Extensive online store with perhaps the widest range of specialist Indian cooking ingredients available on the web. Up to 800 authentic foods available for purchase.

www.valueindia.com
Online outlet with specific sites set up for customers in India, USA/Canada, UK and Australia/New Zealand. Enables visitors to browse for a wide range of authentic groceries and condiments.

This edition is published by Southwater, an imprint of Anness Publishing Ltd, Blaby Road, Wigston, Leicestershire LE18 4SE

Email: info@anness.com

Web: www.southwaterbooks.com; www.annesspublishing.com

If you like the images in this book and would like to investigate using them for publishing, promotions or advertising, please visit our website www.practicalpictures.com for more information.

Publisher:.Joanna Lorenz
Editorial Director: Helen Sudell
Project Editors: Ruth Baldwin, Lindsay Porter, Judith Simons and Catherine Stuart
Book Design: Sarah Kidd
Additional Design: Diane Pullen and Public Impact
Text Editor: Jenni Fleetwood
Recipes: Mridula Baljekar, Linda Doeser, Rafi Fernandez, Jenni Fleetwood, Brian Glover, Shehzad Husain, Christine Ingram, Manisha Kanani, Lesley Mackley, Sallie Morris, Jennie Shapter, Ysanne Spevak, Steven Wheeler and Jenny White
Photography: Edward Allwright, David Armstrong, Nicki Dowey, Amanda Heywood, Ferguson Hill, Janine Hosegood, David Jordon, David King, Patrick McLeavey and Sam Stowell
Nutritional Data: Claire Brain and Wendy Doyle

ETHICAL TRADING POLICY

At Anness Publishing we believe that business should be conducted in an ethical and ecologically sustainable way, with respect for the environment and a proper regard to the replacement of the natural resources we employ.
As a publisher, we use a lot of wood pulp in high-quality paper for printing, and that wood commonly comes from spruce trees. We are therefore currently growing more than 750,000 trees in three Scottish forest plantations: Berrymoss (130 hectares/320 acres), West Touxhill (125 hectares/ 305 acres) and Deveron Forest (75 hectares/185 acres). The forests we manage contain more than 3.5 times the number of trees employed each year in making paper for the books we manufacture. Because of this ongoing ecological investment programme, you, as our customer, can have the pleasure and reassurance of knowing that a tree is being cultivated on your behalf to naturally replace the materials used to make the book you are holding.
For further information about this scheme, go to www.annesspublishing.com/trees

Previously published as *Best Ever Indian Cookbook*

NOTES

Bracketed terms are intended for American readers.
For all recipes, quantities are given in both metric and imperial measures and, where appropriate, in standard cups and spoons. Follow one set, but not a mixture, because they are not interchangeable. Standard spoon and cup measures are level. 1 tsp = 5ml, 1 tbsp = 15ml, 1 cup = 250ml/8fl oz. Australian standard tablespoons are 20ml. Australian readers should use 3 tsp in place of 1 tbsp for measuring small quantities.
American pints are 16fl oz/2 cups. American readers should use 20fl oz/2.5 cups in place of 1 pint when measuring liquids.
Electric oven temperatures in this book are for conventional ovens. When using a fan oven, the temperature will probably need to be reduced by about 10–20°C/20–40°F. Since ovens vary, you should check with your manufacturer's instruction book for guidance.
The nutritional analysis given for each recipe is calculated per portion (i.e. serving or item), unless otherwise stated. If the recipe gives a range, such as Serves 4–6, then the nutritional analysis will be for the smaller portion size, i.e. 6 servings. The analysis does not include optional ingredients, such as salt added to taste.
Medium (US large) eggs are used unless otherwise stated.
Front cover shows Masala Beans with Fenugreek – for recipe, see pages 400–1.

PUBLISHER'S NOTE

Although the advice and information in this book are believed to be accurate and true at the time of going to press, neither the authors nor the publisher can accept any legal responsibility or liability for any errors or omissions that may have been made nor for any inaccuracies nor for any loss, harm or injury that comes about from following instructions or advice in this book.